Long-run Growth, Social Institutions and Living Standards

Long-run Growth, Social Institutions and Living Standards

Edited by

Neri Salvadori

Professor of Economics, University of Pisa, Italy

Arrigo Opocher

Professor of Economics, University of Padua, Italy

Edward Elgar

Cheltenham, UK • Northampton, MA, USA

Published by
Edward Elgar Publishing Limited
The Lypiatts
15 Lansdown Road
Cheltenham
Glos GL50 2JA
UK

Edward Elgar Publishing, Inc.
William Pratt House
9 Dewey Court
Northampton
Massachusetts 01060
USA

A catalogue record for this book
is available from the British Library

Library of Congress Control Number: 2009921833

ISBN 978 1 84844 227 6

Printed and bound by MPG Books Group, UK

Contents

Contributors

Renato Balducci, *Polytechnic University of Marche, Italy*
Thomas Bassetti, *University of Pisa, Italy*
Simone Borghesi, *University of Siena, Italy*
Valentino Dardanoni, *University of Palermo, Italy*
Davide Dottori, *Polytechnic University of Marche, Italy*
Luciano Fanti, *University of Pisa, Italy*
Tamara Fioroni, *University of Pisa, Italy*
Luca Gori, *University of Pisa, Italy*
Davide Gualerzi, *University of Padua, Italy*
Bruno Jossa, *University of Naples 'Federico II', Italy*
Tommaso Luzzati, *University of Pisa, Italy*
Giuseppe Mastromatteo, *Catholic University of Milan, Italy*
Salvatore Modica, *University of Palermo, Italy*
Arrigo Opocher, *University of Padua, Italy*
Martina Pignatti Morano, *University of Pisa, Italy*
Mario Pomini, *University of Padua, Italy*
Francesco Purificato, *University of Naples 'Federico II', Italy*
Neri Salvadori, *University of Pisa, Italy*
Alessandro Vercelli, *University of Siena, Italy*

Introduction

Arrigo Opocher and Neri Salvadori

A common feature of the recent theories of economic growth is that they tend to be increasingly inclusive. Many factors which were previously considered as fixed in the background are now recognized as changing and varying across countries, requiring an explanation within the theory. Institutions, in particular, are widely studied in relation to potential growth. The quality of formal, legal institutions which, in a broad sense, define the rules of the game and the structure of economic incentives, is placed quite naturally among the fundamental factors affecting potential growth and, most importantly, among the effects of it. The many informal institutions embedded in habits and social norms, such as fertility choices, attitudes towards education and health care, and the use of leisure, are clearly recognized to interact with economic growth. Institutions and social norms are explained by means of economic categories and related mutually to growth, giving rise to a variety of self-reinforcing mechanisms. Poverty traps, increasing returns and the accumulation of human capital are among the paramount features of the modern theories of long-run growth. At the same time, and partially resulting from this growing awareness of the role of institutions, increasing stress is laid on economic growth in relation to living standards. The rate of potential growth and per capita real income are, in fact, poor indicators of the overall performance of the economic system. Broader indicators of progress in well-being, such as the quality of social relations, safety, environmental protection, life expectancy and literacy rates, are increasingly being used to characterize growth. Such indicators also interact with the strictly economic and quantitative profiles of growth and give rise to self-reinforcing mechanisms.

The fundamental breakthrough in this direction was provided in the 1980s by the theories of endogenous growth of Romer (1986) and Lucas (1988). Accumulation of physical and human capital is at the same time the proximate effect of growth, and the requisite for the continuation of growth through time. There is no natural, inevitable tendency of long-run growth rates to slow down as the economy gets bigger and bigger. This is so since all factors are accumulable and technology may exhibit increasing returns.

All this is generally considered a big leap forward starting from the traditional Solow model. Thereafter, inclusiveness in the explanation of the causes of potential growth has proceeded at an increasing pace. Technological conditions have been included in the *explanandum* list by the theories of endogenous progress of Romer (1990), Grossman and Helpman (1991) and Aghion and Howitt (1992). The process of creation of new technology, in turn, was swiftly recognized as depending on the organization of society: property regimes, product regulation, financial and labour markets, patent protection, and fiscal and education policies directly affect the creation and diffusion of new technology. But also the level of 'democracy', transparency and accountability in public governance is equally if not more important. Having recognized this, a host of other, more spontaneous, factors lent themselves as explanations of technical progress and economic growth: the degree of confidence in the stability and enforceability of the fundamental rules of society, fairness in industrial and trading relations, religion, culture, and so forth. Hence there is a variety of contributions seeking a precise, stringent relationship between some broad historical facts and economic growth. Long or very long periods have been analysed, secular time series have been reconstructed and institutional differences among countries have been analysed on a systematic and scientific basis. A valuable survey, with extensive references, of this modern institutional view of long-run growth can be found in Acemoglu, Johnson and Robinson (2005). This attempt is certainly very ambitious, because an explanation of the reasons why institutions differ across countries and evolve through time involves no less than an endogenous theory of institutions, in which the latter are determined as an equilibrium of a variety of economic, social, political and cultural factors. Moreover, so long as these theories are based on some typical economic categories, such as preferences, endowments, allocative efficiency and equilibrium, they may convey to scholars of other related fields – such as law, history, sociology, anthropology, and so on – a certain sense of economic imperialism.

The most accomplished attempt at making the many historical facts of long-run growth endogenous in a coherent model on the basis of a very few, permanent, behavioural assumptions, is the so-called Unified Growth Theory by Oded Galor. Such a theory 'is designed to capture the complexity of the process of growth and development over the entire course of human history' (Galor, 2005, p. 174). The different phases of growth and the international differences are considered as evidence of a hidden fundamental process of creation of habits, institutions, social and individual choices. Everything tends to become endogenous until a permanent structure of human rationality and choice under constraint emerges. To unveil this hidden process by means of a detailed analysis of all possible historical evidence and by means of a coherent statement of a lasting micro-foundation, is the main purpose of the Unified Growth Theory. In spite of its breathtaking ambitiousness and its profession of economic imperialism, Galor's theory had enormous success. Time was ripe, in fact, for integration between growth and development studies. The traditional distinction between a theory of economic growth in industrial societies characterized by refined market mechanisms on the one hand, and a qualitative study of the problems of institutional transition in less developed countries on the other, is increasingly found inadequate. Likewise, the related distinction between the theories of homogeneous quantitative growth and the theories of structural change can hardly any more be considered as relating to different objects of analysis. The institutional frameworks in 'advanced' countries are far from perfect: they differ from one another, which matters quite a lot in relative economic performance; moreover, they evolve and can do so in ways which may encourage or impede economic growth. In other words, growth theory needs to be connected to institutional change, and development studies need some firmer theoretical and mathematical foundations. This integration also has high potential for the many practical policy issues concerning long-run growth. Although it may be questioned whether a magnificent painting on a very big canvas such as the Unified Growth Theory is really needed, the latter is now the main point of reference for a great variety of specific studies in the fields of human capital, social capital, health, education and fertility – all in relation to growth.

***

One may reasonably wonder to what extent all this is really new. In an imaginary diagram with time on the horizontal axis and 'inclusiveness' in the explanations of growth on the vertical, are we not on the rising branch of a U-shaped curve? Are we not reverting to conceptions of growth which were common before a certain process of specialization had taken place? Adam Smith, J.S. Mill, A. Marshall and some representative development theorists (such as Myrdal, Rostow, Nurkse and Rosenstein-Rodan) are sometimes mentioned as precursors of this new approach to growth. There is more than that, however. At the end of the 18th century and first half of the 19th, it was apparent to all social philosophers and economists that economic growth, institutional and social change and living standard improvements belonged to one and the same process which required a single, coherent explanation. It is well known that Malthus's *Essay on Population* was originally meant to rebut a widespread view of an indefinite improvability in human condition in the new economic regime. Such a view was typical of French Enlightenment authors such as Condorcet and his English followers such as Godwin. Malthus himself in subsequent editions reverted to less pessimistic views, and the possibility that economic growth could foster virtuous changes in social habits, and above all fertility rates, and in legal and administrative institutions, featured prominently in his change in judgement. The Neo-Malthusian theories around the middle of the 19th century went straight along these lines. Nor was institutional change less important. The reformation of the Poor Laws and the Corn Laws, the establishment of new factory laws, the definition of new property regimes and institution of a new educational system lay at the heart of the conceptualization of economic growth by English authors during the 19th century. Mill's *The Claims of Labour* (1845) and the famous chapter of his *Principles* on 'The probable futurity of the labouring classes' are notable examples. After J.S. Mill, Arnold Toynbee's *Lectures on the Industrial Revolution of the 18th Century in England* were representative of a certain optimistic view of a positive mutual relationship between economic growth and socio-institutional change. The main idea was that 'better lives' of the population at large were at the same time a potential effect of growth and the main cause of it. Better lives, in turn, required appropriate institutions, like sound factory legislation or an efficient system of education, and the establishment of virtuous social habits. A detailed account of the progress made in this direction in England in the period 1832–1867 can be found in a very interesting 1867 book by J.M. Ludlow and L. Jones (a lawyer and a former worker, respectively), which escaped oblivion thanks to Marshall. Marshall's economic theory, in turn, is full of self-reinforcing mechanisms involving what we now call human capital: basically, industrial growth called for (and made possible) a higher fraction of skilled labour, which raised overall productivity; since competition forced employers to pay the full 'net product' of labour, wages and leisure would increase thus determining – via a better intellectual and moral cultivation – a further rise in skills and productivity.

Needless to say, the 19th century analyses of the economic progress lacked the statistical power and the mathematical refinement of the modern theories. Even though from the 1830s, in England, detailed statistical evidence of the various aspects of economic and social progress was available on a systematic basis, as shown by Porter's famous book (Porter, 1836) and the *Journal of the Royal Statistical Society*, the economic analyses typically involved a few broad statistical data and a great many qualitative, illustrative facts. Moreover, even though the crucial role of the economic inducements was fully recognized (for example in the debate on the Poor Laws), the strictly economic argument was, so to speak, on the same foot as other social, ethical, legal and broad historical arguments. Yet it can hardly be denied that they are still very helpful for a clear understanding of what the two 19th century industrial revolutions meant for the history of civilization.

The modern theories adopt the same 'secular' perspective and pay special attention to the transition from what Galor calls the Post-Malthusian Regime to the Sustained Growth Regime. It is doubtful, however, to say the least, whether that age is better analyzed by modern theories than it was by its contemporaries; and the fact that the former have been presented as a radical re-think, does not help to that effect.

***

The chapters presented in this book, which is an outcome of a wider research group on the institutional and social dynamics of economic growth, are all based on the premise that any explanation of the differences in long-run growth rates (across countries, and in the course of time) requires detailed analysis of the many mutual relationships between growth, social institutions and living standards. In a sense, this premise captures what is common to the 19th century concerns about long-run growth and the modern theories of endogenous growth. They are, however, uncommitted to a specific overall economic theory. Rather, they contribute rather freely to the understanding of specific aspects concerning labour market and participatory institutions, health, education, learning in consumption and environmental policies.

In Chapter 1, Opocher considers in a historical perspective the major question of the goals towards which society tends with its industrial and institutional progress and discusses some elements of continuity and of originality in the works of J.S. Mill, Marshall and J.M. Keynes. These authors belonged to three successive English generations whose lifetimes spanned over a century or so which was crucial for economic, social and institutional evolution. They shared the fundamental idea that a 'good life' for people at large was at the same time the possible outcome of progress and its main lasting source. They differed, however, on the relative emphasis laid on the various practical aspects of goodness in their times: broadly speaking, Mill emphasized fertility, Marshall emphasized skills, and Keynes emphasized wisdom in leisure and economic abundance.

School, factory and informal education featured prominently in Mill's and Marshall's arguments and was the subject of lively debates in England. These debates and the specific economic arguments used in them, are critically presented in Chapter 2 by Pomini. This chapter particularly deals with the establishment of a system of compulsory education and its financing. The chapter first outlines the evolution of schooling in England during the first half of the 1800s, up to the Education Act of 1870 and then considers the theories of Smith, McCulloch, J.S. Mill, Nassau Senior and Marshall. State intervention was increasingly felt as necessary in order to correct the limits of market mechanisms due to what we now call positive externalities and short-sightedness of economic agents.

Mastromatteo, in Chapter 3, offers an interpretation of the role of public institutions in Minsky's works. Starting from an attempt to identify a unifying analytical element in his treatment, attention is drawn to the originality of his thought on this subject, which distinguishes him both from the recent literature of neo-liberal orientation, and also from the tradition of post-Keynesian thought that shows the greatest affinity with his approach. Minsky's favourable assessment of policies beneficial to the lower income bands and to social consumption is linked not only to the enhanced possibility of economic growth and stabilization associated with such policies, but also to the need to achieve fairer and more satisfactory social living conditions.

In Chapter 4, Gualerzi presents a survey of the theories of consumption in which growth and development processes are the key explanatory element. The analyses of consumption which can be found in some works of Lancaster, Steedman, Pasinetti, Sen and Levine share an interest in the question 'what shall I *do*' rather than the question 'what shall I *buy*' and naturally offer the basis for a theory of consumption based on growth trajectories and evolving living standards. In the approach taken, consumption evolution is systematically linked to the growth process and rests on the existence of a positive feedback between growth and consumption, which might lead to a shift in the consumption–growth frontier.

After these four chapters, which deal with some relevant historical issues, six chapters concern education and health in relation to long-run growth. In Chapter 5, Dardanoni and Modica present an analysis of the informative value of school grades as signals of cognitive competence, and as a message for potential employers and universities. Based on evidence from Italy and international comparisons, they report some aspects of grading practices in schools and universities, and note that there are distortions which reduce the informative value of grades as market signals. Hence, it is arguable that it would be appropriate to search for some common standards to which the separate decision centres may adhere.

In Chapter 6, Pomini considers the evolution of the connection between education spending and economic growth in the passage from the exogenous growth models of the 1960s to the current endogenous growth models based on the accumulation of human capital. It is argued that increasing emphasis has been placed on the incompleteness and imperfection of markets and on the income-inequality in access to education as factors which affect the overall accumulation of human capital and the growth rate. Such emphasis has produced theories which offer an analytical justification for entrusting education to the state and not to the market.

In Chapter 7, Bassetti studies the effect of education on economic growth from other points of view. He considers the way in which education may generate the observed non-linearities in the process of economic growth and presents a model in which the assumption of a non-constant human capital obsolescence rate causes non-constant returns to education in the production of human capital. This allows us to identify the conditions under which a poverty trap may arise in a Solow growth model. Sufficient investment in education may help poor countries to escape from this trap. Some econometric analyses prove that, at the aggregate level, such theoretical conclusions are confirmed by evidence.

Chapter 8, by Fioroni, considers the effect of child mortality and fertility reduction on economic growth. It develops a two-period overlapping generations model where altruistic agents differ in their human capital endowment. Parents care about the number of their surviving children and the future level of human capital of each of them. Children's probability of surviving to adult age is an increasing concave function of parents' human capital. This framework generates Galor's 'demographic transition' and has the effect of creating multiple development regimes (such as 'Malthusian stagnation' or 'sustained growth') in which the growth rate of the economy depends on initial human capital endowments.

In Chapter 9, by means of an overlapping generations model, Dottori compares in terms of economic growth rates and income distribution two health funding regimes: private and public. Health is not only a component of human capital but it also yields direct utility and – by extending lifespans – it reduces future discounting thus affecting the propensity to invest in human capital accumulation. In the private system, health expenditure is chosen in a decentralized way, whereas in the public regime it is provided by government and funded through an income tax, with agents voting over the tax rate. Endogenous poverty and low development traps may arise. Inequality turns out to decline faster under a public regime, whereas in a private one it may be non-decreasing. A private system generally brings about higher growth rates, but when income distribution is sufficiently uneven, a public system may feature higher growth rates.

In Chapter 10, Balducci examines the effects on growth of both private and public investment in health, schooling and culture: in short, education. It is argued that the investment in education increases labour and capital stock productivity through a positive externality, and modifies saving and investment decisions through the substitutability between education and private consumption. The different effects on economic growth of publicly financed education and private investment in education are also investigated. The optimal growth rate depends on households' preferences for education, and there will be an optimal tax rate that produces the same rate of growth in alternative regimes of education financing. Universal public education exerts a strong positive externality on economic efficiency and growth, but – unlike private investments – it does not create sufficient incentives through income differentials to change consumer preferences for education.

The next pair of chapters concern labour market institutions. Chapter 11, by Jossa, considers labour-managed firms. This particular institution, together with profit sharing, was strongly supported by J.S. Mill and (albeit more mildly) by Marshall, as argued in Chapter 1, on the grounds that it would encourage efforts, skills and consciousness of workers and thereby would foster the better sides of long-run growth. Jossa argues that a necessary premise of such an argument is to show that a system of labour-managed firms is actually in a position to provide jobs to all those seeking employment more effectively than a capitalistic-firm system can do. The chapter argues that in effect labour-managed firms have many potential advantages in respect to the different kinds of unemployment.

In Chapter 12, Fanti and Gori show – contrary to prevailing common wisdom in the literature – that the introduction of minimum wages may generate production as well as welfare gains in the long run. From a policy point of view, motivated by a recent debate, the aim of this chapter is to investigate, for the Italian economy, whether the introduction of both minimum wages and unemployment benefits may eventually enhance long-run lifetime welfare if the increase in the tax burden on capital income is used for preserving the balanced budget instead of financing other public expenditures.

Environmental sustainability of long-run growth and the need for public policies is the subject of next two chapters. In Chapter 13 Borghesi and Vercelli discuss the recent trends in energy consumption and their compatibility with the requirements of sustainable long-run growth. To this purpose, they first critically discuss the conventional position on the market's capacity to resolve spontaneously the problems of energy scarcity and pollution, pointing out some important shortcomings that cast doubts on this optimistic approach. Then, starting from a simple identity applied to the energy sector, they derive a few analytic requirements for the long-term sustainability of energy trends and examine whether they are satisfied on the basis of the currently available data.

Luzzati, in Chapter 14, illustrates Karl William Kapp's major contributions concerning public policy for environment protection and more generally the satisfaction of human needs. It is argued that Kapp combined the notion of cumulative causation processes *à la* Myrdal with the view of the economy as an open system, a system embedded not only within society but also within nature. This framework implies, as a logical consequence, that ungoverned economic processes may not be able to deliver economic, social and environmental sustainability. Kapp goes beyond this and shows that governance is indeed a must due to the very nature of the economic competitive process and the high social costs it generates.

The last two chapters are devoted to public or spontaneous participatory rules in the shaping of public policies in support to economic growth. Pignatti Morano, in Chapter 15, attempts an evaluation of the trajectories followed during the 20th century by economic policy and economic thought regarding participatory approaches to economic allocation of resources, with specific focus on economic planning in developing countries. Despite the generally negative evaluation given by conventional economic theory on the pursuit of public participation in development processes, recent economic analysis of social capital and social preferences highlights the feasibility and desirability of participatory mechanisms of economic governance in a wide variety of situations. It is argued, in particular, that groups of people tend to switch from individual to collective rationality if institutions and incentives are properly set.

Purificato, in Chapter 16, provides a model to capture how economic interests linked to the distribution between profits and wages can influence political decisions and how in turn such decisions can influence the economy. The model seeks to mix ingredients from different perspectives: the *influence function approach* (Becker), which concerns behaviour of interest groups, and the *interest function approach* (van Winden), which concerns political decisions, describe capitalists' and workers' interest in the policymakers' decisional process whereas a neo-Kaleckian approach describes the operation of the economy. The analysis shows that fiscal policy has to take proper account of both the capitalists' interest and the workers' interest if it aims to favour a balanced change over time of the demand level and of productive capacity. Thus, policymakers have to solve the conflict between the capitalists' interests and workers' interests by avoiding polarization of fiscal policy.

Arrigo Opocher
Neri Salvadori

REFERENCES

Acemoglu, D., S. Johnson and J.A. Robinson (2005), 'Institutions as a Fundamental Cause of Long-Run Growth', in P. Aghion and S.N. Durlauf (eds), *Handbook of Economic Growth*, Amsterdam: Elsevier North Holland, ch. 6, pp. 385–472.

Aghion, P. and P.W. Howitt (1992), 'A Model of Growth Through Creative Destruction', *Econometrica*, **60**(2), 323–51.

Galor, O. (2005), 'From Stagnation to Growth: Unified Growth Theory', in P. Aghion and S.N. Durlauf (eds), *Handbook of Economic Growth*, Amsterdam: Elsevier North Holland, ch. 4, pp. 171–293.

Grossman, G.M. and E. Helpman (1991), *Innovation and Growth in the Global Economy*, Cambridge, MA: MIT Press.

Lucas, R.E. (1988), 'On the Mechanics of Economic Development', *Journal of Monetary Economics*, **22**(1), 3–42.

Ludlow, J.M. and L. Jones (1973) [1867], *Progress of the Working Class. 1832–1867*, New York: Augustus M. Kelley Publishers.

Porter, G.R. (1836), *The Progress of the Nation*, London: John Murray.

Romer, P.M. (1986), 'Increasing Returns and Long-Run Growth', *Journal of Political Economy*, **94**(5), 1002–37.

Romer, P.M. (1990), 'Endogenous Technical Change', *Journal of Political Economy*, **98**(5), 71–102.

1. Does economic growth ultimately lead to a 'noble life'? A comparative analysis of the predictions of Mill, Marshall and Keynes

Arrigo Opocher

> But in contemplating any progressive movement, not in its nature unlimited, the mind is not satisfied with merely tracing the laws of the movement; it cannot but ask the further question, to what goal? Towards what ultimate point is society tending by its industrial progress? (J.S. Mill, *Principles of Political Economy*).

> Wealth is evidently not the good we are seeking; for it is merely useful and for the sake of something else (Aristotle, *Nicomachean Ethics*).

1.1. INTRODUCTION

In recent literature there has been renewed interest in economic growth, not as a goal in itself, but as a means of fulfilling goals of a higher order. The so-called 'paradox of happiness' in advanced countries, and the related literature (for example Bruni and Porta, 2005 and references contained therein), are a notable example, like the notion of 'human development'[1] in less developed countries. Also the exponential growth in the studies on human capital, the economics of education and health care can be ascribed to rising interest in living conditions in relation to growth.

This point of view is certainly not new. Public happiness was, of course, a major concern of social philosophy in the Age of Enlightenment. Thereafter, the Classical economists quite naturally considered the change in standards of life, especially for the working classes, as the most important property of economic growth. In this respect, A. Smith and D. Ricardo were second to none. It was J.S. Mill, however, who first perceived the possibility that industrial growth could offer a permanent material basis for a good and happy life of the working classes.[2] He posed the question of the 'goal' towards which society was driven by industrial progress very explicitly, doing so in terms of the lifestyle of the members of society and expressing it in terms of objective standards of comfort and intellectual and moral cultivation. In his eyes, the change in these standards, rather than the increase in production and consumption *per se*, determines, for good or bad, the performance of a capitalistic economy. After Mill, and partly under his influence, A. Marshall considered standards of life and the social goals of economic growth as 'the more important side' (Marshall, 1920, p. 1) of Political Economy (the other side being 'the study of wealth').[3] At various times in his long career as an economist, he expanded some of Mill's arguments and reduced or dropped others, but never lost sight of the fact that the increase in material output was merely a means for making the life of the population fuller and nobler.

It will therefore be of some interest to analyse in detail and to compare the precise arguments put forward by Mill and by Marshall. Not only, in fact, do they offer (or should offer) a lively source of inspiration for current concerns; they also raise some interesting historical questions, which still await a comprehensive answer. In particular, how could Mill predict the coming of a Millennium of society, so different from the 'stationary state' of Smith and Ricardo, while their theories of value and distribution had so many elements in common? Conversely, how could Marshall share many of Mill's views on 'the probable futurity of the labouring classes', and yet develop a completely different theory of wages?

Dealing with these questions will lead us quite naturally to briefly reconsider also Keynes's famous one-century-ahead 1930 prophecy (Keynes, 1931a[1930]): as we shall argue, Keynes's piece, albeit essentially 'Millian' in spirit, also presents some clear Marshallian elements. When confronted with what the three of them considered the fundamental goal of economic growth – to prepare the material conditions for a new, nobler phase in human civilisation – a common milieu emerged.

Section 1.2 illustrates Mill's conception of the 'stationary state' and how it will (or can) be reached. His predictions will be discussed under three headings: his theory of population and wages, his conception of a declining importance of production and the key role he attached to education and social institutions. We shall argue that the current representations of Mill's 'stationary state' (see Schwartz, 1972, Ch. 8; Hollander, 1984a, 1984b and 1985, especially pp. 881–8) do not pay due attention to Mill's distinction between wages and standards of life and between economic growth and social progress. We shall see, in Section 1.3, that Marshall agreed with most of Mill's conclusions on issues concerning standard of life and progress. He did so, however, following a different path, in which a 'nobler life' becomes the cause no less than the effect of economic progress. This change involved a new theory of wages, based on productivity rather than population, and the abandonment of Mill's conception of the stationary state. Keynes's own predictions are briefly discussed in Section 1.4, and compared with Mill's and Marshall's. Section 1.5 concludes.

1.2. THE ULTIMATE GOAL OF ECONOMIC PROGRESS: MILL'S STATIONARY STATE

The Ricardian stationary state[4] was characterised by very low, almost vanishing profits, low wages, which were merely sufficient for subsistence and reproduction, and high rents: such was the effect of past capital accumulation and population growth on the use of limited, privately owned natural resources. From the point of view of human progress, it was therefore a rather miserable state. It is true that, according to Ricardo, technological improvements and opening up to free international trade tended to postpone the limit of accumulation and growth, but the ultimate effect of such a postponement would be that of making the world even more densely populated and natural resources even more intensively used. All the strength and the social value of a capitalistic market economy therefore was in the process of growth in itself, and *not* in the point towards which it drove society. During the process of growth, the living conditions of the working classes could improve well above subsistence (cf. Ricardo, 1951, pp. 94–5), without provoking any dramatic fall in profits, and capital accumulation allowed for a higher and more efficient production. Alas, this process was not unlimited, and when the limit had been reached, the only goal fulfilled would be that the planet's natural resources and capital stock could feed a much larger population; there would be no benefits for the individual workers of future generations, nor would there be any further substantial technological improvement, since profits have fallen to zero and capital accumulation has stopped.

J.S. Mill could not conceive of such a prospect, so discouraging for human civilisation. As we know, he had a very broad, passionate view of history and institutions: the setting of society in a certain country at a certain time was but a phase in the historical evolution of mankind and its institutions were transitory. The history of mankind ought to be (and in part was), according to Mill, a process bringing 'human nature to its greatest perfection' (Mill, 1929[1871], preface to the third edition, p. xxx), both from an intellectual and a moral point of view. These broad views were very similar to, and probably assimilated from Enlightenment thinkers, like Condorcet, whom he valued very highly and considered 'one of the wisest and noblest of men' (1989[1873], p. 99). Like his predecessors, he thought that the attainment of a stationary state was unavoidable, due to limited natural resources, but he argued that it could be a happy, not a miserable, state of society. Nineteenth-century technical progress and the accumulation of capital offered an unprecedented opportunity. Not surprisingly, then, his 'stationary state' was characterised by

> a well-paid and affluent body of labourers; no enormous fortunes (…) but a much larger body of persons than at present, not only exempt from the coarser toils, but with sufficient leisure, both physical and mental, from mechanical details, to cultivate freely the graces of life (Mill, 1929[1871], p. 780).

Conversely, the process of economic growth, driven by 'the struggle for riches', by 'trampling, crushing, elbowing, and treading each other's heels' (Mill, 1929[1871], p. 748), was altogether disagreeable, and was a deplorable 'false ideal of human society' (ibid., p. 752). It was a necessary phase, though: 'while minds are coarse they require coarse stimuli, and let them have them' (ibid., p. 749).

Mill's stationary state is therefore the precise opposite to Ricardo's (and for that matter also Smith's), the former representing the fulfilment of the fundamental goal in historical evolution, necessarily passing through several imperfect stages, and the latter representing the halting of a phase of progress and prosperity.

The interpretation of Mill's 'stationary state' as a special case of a wider Classical model of economic growth tended to obscure some differences in emphasis and judgement, which are relevant in the explanation of his results (Samuelson, 1978; and Hollander, 1984a and 1984b). For our purposes, they can be discussed under three headings: his interpretation of Malthus's theory of population, the diminishing importance he attached to production and his trust in the role of education and other social institutions.

1.2.1. Mill and Malthus's Principle of Population

Although Mill's stationary state, like Ricardo's, is based on Malthus's principle of population, he interpreted that principle quite differently (thus reaching opposite conclusions). In short, Mill stressed the practical possibility of a 'moral restraint' among the working classes much more than Ricardo (and Malthus himself)[5] and his original contribution consisted in working out theoretically their precise consequences for conditions of life and economic progress.

His prediction was based on some examples which could reasonably be considered as representative of probable future developments – a procedure he reiterated over and over in matters concerning evolution. On the one hand, he considered some countries, like Norway and Switzerland (Mill, 1929, p. 160), which were 'honourably distinguished' in this respect even in Malthus's time.[6] On the other, he considered the social classes, and their habits, which within a country exercised this 'prudence' more effectively. With specific reference to England, the role of the advance guard was played by many people among the middle classes and the skilled artisans: not only did they manage to transmit their own standards of life to their children by avoiding over-multiplication, but also made 'an additional restraint exercised from the desire of doing more than maintaining their circumstances – of improving them' (ibid.; see also p. 353). As far as the working classes were concerned, Mill was convinced that 'a well educated labouring class could, and we believe would keep up its condition to a high standard of comfort, or at least at a great distance from physical destitution, by the exercise of the same degree of habitual prudence *practiced by the middle class*' (Mill, 1967[1845], p. 379; emphasis added). On the other hand, he recognised that, in England, among the common agricultural workers, 'the checks to population may almost be considered as non-existent' (Mill, 1929[1871], p. 357). Such a lack of individual prudence, however, can and should be filled by legal interventions or, to the same effect, by customs equivalent to it. Once again, Mill presented a series of examples and in particular, various sorts of legal and practical obstacles to improvident or premature marriages, taken mainly from the experience of the German states, as well as, once again, Norway and Switzerland.

The precise mechanism via which 'prudence' sets a beneficial limit to population growth and may contribute to permanent improvements in the workers' conditions of life involved theoretical considerations. Mill assumed, like Ricardo, a minimum 'habitual standard of comfortable living' (Mill, 1929[1871], p. 161) below which population stops rising. This minimum (not fixed, of course) concerned the lower ranks of society. A rising fraction of the population, and prospectively all the labouring population, however, were above the minimum and had the dignity and self-respect to make fertility a matter of choice. Mill's specific contribution consists therefore in his analysis of the complex relationships between the variations in the standard of comfort and the variations in fertility.

1.2.2. Comfort, Wages and Fertility Habits

A certain lifestyle – defined by objective properties like the quantity and quality of education, the quality of social life, leisure time and, of course, physical comforts – becomes a 'habitual standard' if it is very common among a certain social class and, most importantly, if it can be passed on to future generations. Now Mill stressed an inverse relationship between comfort and fertility: the higher the number of children, the lower the standard that can be passed on to them and conversely.[7] It follows that, at a given wage, there is a critical habit in respect to population which permits a labourer to pass on to his family a constant habit in respect to comfort (Mill, 1929[1871], p. 159).

The actual standard of individual families can be improved by additional restraint, as noted above, and it may happen to spread through the same social group, as in the above-mentioned case of the skilled artisans, thus becoming permanent and establishing a new habitual standard.[8] This potential (and to some extent, actual) improvement is central in Mill's argument: if it was true, in the Ricardian world, that any excess of comfort over subsistence tended to be reversed by higher fertility, then it was no less true that the conditions of the labouring population could be permanently improved 'through a voluntary restriction of the increase of their numbers' (1989[1873], p. 94). Moreover it should be borne in mind that Mill advocated systems of birth control whilst Malthus abhorred them. With all this in mind, it is clear in what sense he says in his autobiography that 'Malthus's population principle we [he and his Benthamite colleagues] took up with ardent zeal in the *contrary sense*' (ibid.; emphasis added).

The above argument assumed given wages. If real wages change, the trade-off improves or worsens, as the case may be, and there can be, according to Mill, different combined responses in the habits concerning comfort and in those concerning fertility. He distinguished sharply here between social groups: the best educated people, those belonging to the middle classes and the unionised labourers, tended to transfer any rise in the real wage into higher comfort, keeping fertility constant or even reducing it, whereas they compensated any fall in the real wage with a reduction in fertility, thus preventing their habitual standard of comfort from falling. On the contrary, less educated and poorer people tended to take advantage of a wage rise to increase fertility, and compensate a wage fall with a contraction of comfort, down to the limit of mere subsistence, where Malthus's positive check was effective. As we have seen, Mill believed that the former behaviour was to dominate in a not too distant future. Wages, however, were not independent, in the long run, of fertility choices, but crucially depended on them, according to the wages fund doctrine.[9]

There was therefore an intimate connection between comfort and fertility habits on the one hand and real wages on the other; and between all of them and the attainment of a 'happy' stationary state. If all social classes conformed to the kind of behaviour then observed among the 'skilled artisans', not only would the working classes transmit a higher standard of comfort to their (fewer) children at the then ruling wage rates but also wages themselves would rise, in the long run, as an effect of the check in population. At this point, the economy takes a step towards the stationary state: higher wages would involve lower profits and a lower rate of capital accumulation (cf. Mill, 1929[1871], pp. 418–21). Interestingly, in Mill's path to the stationary state, wages can never fall: they can only rise.[10] This conformed to the empirical evidence of Great Britain: According to Giffen (1886), in the fifty years between the early 1830s and the early 1880s real wages rose by 50–100 per cent; according to Ludlow and Jones (1973[1867], p. 102) between 1844 and 1860 they rose by 10–20 per cent.

1.2.3. The Diminishing Importance of Production

Mill's stationary state, as compared with Ricardo's, is characterised by a smaller population and a higher standard of comfort. It may seem, then, that production might be the same, and diminishing returns in agriculture could operate in a like way. This does not occur, and here we find a second fundamental ingredient of Mill's stationary state. Mill's habitual standard is not entirely based on material prosperity, nor does an increase of it involve, from a certain level, an increase in the production of material goods. Education and health care, leisure time, enjoyment of the arts, short working hours, the opportunity of having social relations, etc. contributed to the habitual standard, and were the distinctive components of what made the 'graces of life' (Mill, 1929[1871], p. 750) enjoyable. They could be expanded indefinitely by a constant population without encountering a limit in natural resources. The consumption of material goods, by contrast, concerned the physical rather than the moral sphere of human life and had a limit beyond which society should not go. 'Only in the backward countries of the world' (Mill, 1929[1871], p. 749) was the mere increase in production and accumulation 'an important object'; he complained about the 'inordinate importance' (ibid., p. 752) that was attached to them in more developed countries. If society was to tend to Mill's stationary state, the rise in labour productivity should gradually allow for shorter working hours, rather than for increased production:

> Labour is unquestionably more productive on the system of large industrial enterprises; the produce, if not greater absolutely, is greater in proportion to the labour employed: the same number of persons can be supported equally well with less toil and greater leisure (Mill, 1929[1871], p. 762).

Thus Mill's stationary state can be attained *before* excessive pressure is to be exerted on natural resources,[11] and thereafter, the population being constant, any improvement should be primarily directed to moral and social progress; also improvements in the 'industrial arts', so widespread and important in the progressive phase, are still possible in a stationary state, and they, too, rather than serving the purpose of increasing material wealth, 'would produce their legitimate effect, that of abridging labour' (Mill, 1929[1871], p. 751).

1.2.4. Education

Attainment of the stationary state required adequate social institutions. Mill's plea for a reform of the property system and for redistributive policies, his passionate support for profit sharing and the co-operative movement, his intellectual and political efforts against the privileges and the arbitrary exercise of power and in favour of the legal protection and enforcement of the rights of powerless people are all so widely known as to require no further discussion here (see, in particular, Schwartz, 1972 and Ekelund and Tollison, 1976). Rather, we must briefly consider the fundamental social goal to be pursued via those institutions: the mental and moral cultivation of all people at large. No voluntary restraint in population growth, nor any interest in anything but material comfort and the 'coarser pleasures' would be possible without a sound education, primarily directed at the working people. Education is therefore a third indispensable ingredient of Mill's stationary state, without which the former two would remain abstract normative prescriptions.

At Mill's time, the 'race between Education and Population [was] far from being a neck-and-neck one' (Ludlow and Jones, 1973[1867], p. 148), and the need for a national system of children and adult education had been long debated until the 1870 Education Act.[12] A slow but continued extension of education to the labouring classes had been enthusiastically advocated by Malthus who thought that 'we may rest assured that the degree of proper pride and spirit of independence almost *invariably connected with education and a certain rank in life*, will secure the operation of the preventive check to a considerable extent' (Malthus, 1992[1803], p. 274; emphasis added).

Half a century later, Mill still considered education as a fundamental means for transmitting to the labouring classes the self-respect and habits of fertility which were usual among the middle classes, but a social reformer like him believed that this process could be quicker (or much quicker) than expected by Malthus:

> there is reason to hope that great improvements both in the quality and in the quantity of school education will be effected by the exertions either of government or of individuals, and that the progress of the mass of the people in mental cultivation, and in the virtues which are dependent on it, will take place more rapidly, and with fewer intermittences and aberrations, than if left to itself (Mill, 1929[1871], p. 758).

Mill also relied very much on what he called 'spontaneous education' (Mill, 1929[1871], p. 757), resulting from the possibility of social relations and from their quality: a necessary premise was that workers were free from the coarser toils and had sufficient leisure. Also labour-managed co-operatives played an important role in self-respect. Such spontaneous education 'may be greatly accelerated and improved by artificial aids' (ibid., p. 757) like the newspapers and cheap literature, public libraries, literary and musical entertainments for workers, lectures and discussions, industrial exhibitions, and all rational forms of recreation. Also collective deliberations on questions of common interest, trade societies and even political agitations contributed, in this wider conception, to spontaneous education.

1.3. CONDITIONS OF WORK AND A 'NOBLER LIFE': MARSHALL'S FANCIED SOCIETY

Marshall's famous speech on 'The future of the working classes', read at the Cambridge Reform Club on 25 November 1873, summarised the subject-matter of his *Lectures to Women*, delivered a few months earlier.[13] It is certainly no mere coincidence that in the same year in which Mill died (on 8 May) and his *Autobiography* was published posthumously, Marshall agreed to speak on the topic of Mill's celebrated chapter 'On the Probable Futurity of the Labouring Classes'. Mill's *Principles* had in fact an 'enormous influence' (Groenewegen, 1995, p. 145) on Marshall's economic apprenticeship and he borrowed from him, and thereafter held, a conception of economics as a science whose main practical aim was to contribute to an amelioration in the conditions of life of the working classes and of mankind in general.[14] Hence, at the very beginning of his talk, Marshall mentions Mill's *Autobiography* and the relevant chapter of his *Principles*, and very explicitly states that 'The course of inquiry which I propose for to-night will never lie far apart from that pursued by Mr and Mrs Mill, but it seldom exactly coincides with it' (Marshall, 1925[1873], pp. 101–2; as Marshall remarked, Harriet Taylor Mill informally contributed to Mill's *Principles* and to the above-mentioned chapter in particular).

Marshall's *Principles*, almost twenty years later, included a chapter – actually the last chapter of Book VI, concerning distribution (indeed the last chapter of the whole volume) – on 'Progress in relation to standards of life', which covers similar topics. Of course, Marshall's *Principles* are devoid of 'the over-sanguine temperament of youth', as he called it, whose marks were admittedly borne by the earlier paper, and present much more moderate views, which clash with Mill's radicalism. Nevertheless, the general inspiration remained the same and it is of some interest to ask what arguments have been eliminated or contracted, and what others have been expanded or newly added in the chapter (and more generally in the *Principles*), as compared both to Mill and to the 1873 conference paper.

1.3.1. The Demise of the Classical Stationary State

The most obvious change consists in the fact that the classical notion of an unavoidable stationary state plays no significant role in Marshall. As we have seen, Mill's interpretation of Malthus's population law 'in the opposite sense' radically changed that notion. With that in mind, the check on population growth, being voluntary, was no longer the necessary outcome of economic growth. Marshall's insistence on the need for a check on population growth was always along these lines (e.g. Marshall, 1920, p. 691; 1925[1873], p. 114) and had no special bearing on his theory of wages. He argued that 'wages in Britain are now but very little affected by the rate of growth of population and the pressure on the means of subsistence' (Marshall, 1925, p. 326). Wages were higher in England than in continental Europe, because productivity was higher, and trade unions had been successful in obtaining improvements. Besides, Mill's recantation of the wages fund doctrine, in 1869, concerned precisely the ability of unionised workers to secure permanent improvements. It should also be remarked that wages in America became even higher than in England and this prompted in the second half of the century a swollen tide of emigration (see Ludlow and Jones, 1973[1867], p. 233). There was therefore no need for the typical ingredients of the Classical theory of the stationary state.[15] The Classical 'stationary state' was so irrelevant for him that he felt free to adopt the same phrase in a completely new meaning (Marshall, 1920, p. 366).

In spite of this major change, however, Marshall plainly accepted, and expanded, Mill's fundamental prediction about the 'probable futurity of the labouring classes'. In the conference paper, he presented most of his argument in terms of a 'fancied country', in which 'everyone who is not a gentleman will have himself alone to blame for it' (Marshall, 1925[1873], pp. 110–11); in the *Lectures to Women* the same concept had been expressed by the rhetorical question: 'Why should you not make every man a gentleman? Every woman a lady?' (Raffaelli et al., 1995, p. 141). Later, in the *Principles*, he no longer referred to a 'fancied country', but kept the question of 'whether it is necessary that there should be any so-called 'lower classes' at all' (Marshall, 1920, p. 3) practically unchanged, like his answer. The fact that his argument was in terms of slow but steady progress, rather than in terms of a 'final' stage of society, is therefore of secondary importance, as compared with the common vision of society in the 'next' stage of human civilisation.

Mill defined the ultimate aims of economic activity in terms of 'mental and moral cultivation', 'intellect and virtue', 'higher aspirations', enjoyment of the 'graces of life', 'heroic virtues', 'greatest perfection of human nature' or, more simply, 'happiness'. Even though such attributes were broadly agreed by Marshall, in the conference paper he preferred to consider an existing 'type', the gentleman of the Victorian age, whose characteristics were obvious and naturally appreciated by his audience. Later he chose the more neutral phrase 'full citizens'[16] (e.g. Marshall, 1920, p. 720); but the kind of life he had in mind, remained the same. The goals at which, according to both Mill and Marshall, economic progress should aim were therefore intellectual and moral, and should concern the generality of the population. The problem posed by Marshall both in the conference paper and in the *Principles* was whether the failure of much of the population to cultivate the above aims was an economic necessity (cf. Marshall, 1920, p. 3 and pp. 713–14; 1925[1873], p. 102), and argued that it was not. He thought that, in his time, material wealth was growing sufficiently for the standard of life of people belonging to *all social classes* to be potentially consistent with such 'cultivation'. The problem was how these material means were to be used.

1.3.2. Standards of Comfort, Standards of Life, Education and the Aims of Economic Progress

Marshall favoured a redistributive policy much more mildly than Mill, as we know, even though he did consider redistribution an important aspect of social progress.[17] But redistribution is only one aspect, perhaps not the most important in Marshall's eyes. A sufficient income was of course a precondition, but much more important than real wages, output and consumption were activities, as pointed out by Parsons (1931), or how workers were to spend their lives. The conditions of work, the use of leisure, youth and 'after life' education, and social intercourse were the main elements shaping people's characters. The systematic report given by Ludlow and Jones (1963[1867]) on the progress made by the working classes from 1832 through 1867 abounds in details concerning the spread of more refined modes of life through the operation of legislative and institutional improvements. The strictly economic improvements are mentioned only cursorily and always in relation to what the working classes were able to do with their higher wages. Marshall was reported to be enthusiastic with this report, which he valued very highly (Groenewegen, 1995, p. 246). Expenditure and consumption were very poor indicators of being or not being a 'gentleman'. Quite the contrary, excessive liking of material comforts, both by the rich and the relatively poor, was detrimental to the formation of a 'deep full character' (Marshall, 1925[1907], p. 345) and to a man's 'inner life':

> There still remains a vast expenditure which contributes very little towards social progress, and which does not confer any large and solid benefits on the spenders beyond the honour, the position, and the influence which it buys for them in society (Marshall, 1925[1907], p. 325).

> Perhaps £100,000,000 annually are spent even by the working classes, and 400,000,000 by the rest of the population in England, in ways that do little or nothing towards making life nobler and truly happier (Marshall, 1920, p. 720).

Marshall thus had to distinguish very carefully what he called the 'standard of comfort' from the 'standard of life'. The former consists in material goods and must be kept within limits, the latter consists in human activities and can be boundlessly expanded. There is in this respect, once again, a clear similarity with Mill. Marshall's 'standard of life' is comparable to Mill's 'habitual standard of comfortable living', insofar as both of them involve a wide range of human activities, while Marshall's 'standard of comfort' broadly corresponds to Mill's 'real wages'. This distinction is greatly stressed by Marshall, and we can quote at length:

> A rise in the standard of life implies an increase of intelligence and energy and self-respect; leading to more care and judgment in expenditure, and to an avoidance of food and drink that gratify the appetite but afford no strength, and of ways of living that are unwholesome physically and morally. (…) It is true that every broad improvement in the standard of comfort is likely to bring with it a better manner of living, and to open the way to new and higher activities (…). But the only direct effect of an increase of wants is to make people more miserable than before (Marshall, 1920, pp. 689–90; a similar contrast is very vivid on p. 700).

'Careful and long continued education' (Marshall, 1925[1873], p. 104) was a substantial part of an improved standard of life. The educational effects on population growth played no significant role in Marshall, because population growth was no longer a major concern. Rather, the formation of skilled labour and the general improvement of intelligence and character became the main problem. In the conference he went so far as to predict the end of unskilled labour:

> knowledge is power; and man would have knowledge. Inventions would increase, and they would be readily applied. All labour would be skilled, and there would be no premium on setting men to tasks that required no skill (Marshall, 1925[1873], p. 112).

This prediction parallels Mill's more 'political' prediction concerning the end of hired labour.

In the *Principles*, as usual, his opinions are expressed in a more balanced way. The precise distinction between skilled and unskilled labour is acknowledged to depend on historical circumstances, and he does not venture to say that unskilled labour, in some sense, will ever disappear. Nonetheless, the importance of a material inter-generational movement from unskilled to skilled labour is still greatly emphasised:

> The children of unskilled workers need to be made capable of earning the wages of skilled work: and the children of skilled workers need by similar means be made capable of doing still more responsible work (Marshall, 1920, p. 718).

Marshall's estimate of the share of unskilled labour at the end of the 19th century was one quarter of the population (Marshall, 1920, p. 716), with a diminishing trend. Half a century before, Mill had estimated that the 'common labourers' were about one half of the population (Mill, 1929, p. 353). Marshall estimated that one century backwards, 'more than a half would have been found unfit for any skilled labour at all'. These estimates conform fairly well to the figures presented by Giffen (1886, p. 36) with reference to Great Britain.

The chief role of school education was to provide the additional supply of skilled labour, by diminishing, so to speak, the number of potential unskilled workers. In so doing, the overall productivity of the economic system would increase, and 'the share of it got by each unskilled labourer may rise faster still' (Marshall, 1920, p. 717). The general conditions of life of the lower classes may thus improve, thereby enabling the next generation to be trained better than their parents.

It should be stressed that Marshall, like Mill, had a very broad view of education. The aim of school education was not only the transfer of knowledge, but also, and more importantly, the education of character, faculties and activities (e.g. Marshall, 1920, p. 718), without which a worker would be unfit for intelligent and responsible work. By the same token, a variety of non-school institutions were relevant to education. Working class associations, and trade unions in particular, had a very important role for Marshall, like the quality of factory life, which may 'stimulate mental activity in and out of working hours' (Marshall, 1920, p. 263).

This 'education' had for Marshall more than what we now call 'positive externalities'. Its social benefits had a higher order of magnitude as compared to strictly private benefits:

> It is a vast and wholly unmixed gain when the children of any class press with the relatively small charmed circle of those who create new ideas, and who embody those new ideas in solid constructions. Their profits are sometimes large: but taking one with another they have probably earned for the world *a hundred times*

> or more as much as they have earned for themselves (Marshall, 1920, p. 719; emphasis added).

Another fundamental, and complementary, aspect of improved standards of life concerned the reduction of working hours and the expansion of leisure and adult education. In the conference paper, Marshall characterised his 'fancied country' by short hours of manual work: 'No one is to do in the day so much manual work as will leave him little time or little aptitude for intellectual and artistic enjoyment in the evening'. He thought that 'in our new society (…) a man would not in general perform manual work for more than six hours a day. (…) In heavy work three sets of men might each work a shift of four hours' (Marshall, 1925[1873], p. 113). Since, according to Webb and Webb, 'the nine hours movement (…) [was not] fully successful until 1871' (1965[1897], p. 352, n. 1), Marshall's prescription would have implied, more or less, halving the daily hours of unskilled labour. Like education, and partially by means of education, more leisure, more intellectual and moral cultivation, better social intercourse would be an independent source of productivity increase, so that the reduction of working hours (at constant wages) need not reduce output.

Once again, the bold opinions expressed in the conference paper are much moderated in the *Principles*. He still insisted that shorter hours of labour would increase efficiency and would *not*, except temporarily, reduce output (cf. Book VI, Ch. XIII, § 3 and § 4), but in the *Principles* the possibility of 'halving' them is no longer mentioned, nor are shifts of six or four hours: Marshall now advocates a '*moderate* diminution of the hours of labour' (1920, p. 694; emphasis added), which would generally exert a positive effect on the efficiency of workers. The argument is now much more balanced. The effect on efficiency mainly refers to the case of expensive, complex machinery which called for shifts.[18] By contrast, in more mature sectors, like mining, there was not much gain in efficiency from a reduction in working hours and in this case shorter hours (at the same wage) would imply some losses (cf. Marshall, 1920, p. 696) in terms of output and profits.[19] The relationship between working hours and efficiency is presented in the *Principles*, not surprisingly, as complex and multifaceted, and a quantitative evaluation is considered very difficult. On the whole, however, his judgement about the positive qualitative effect of short hours on efficiency and wages (per unit of time) remained the same.

1.3.3. Standard of Life, Wages and Economic Growth

In spite of his endless balancing of arguments, Marshall always held that a higher life standard makes for higher efficiency and wages no less so than the other way round. A better, fuller, nobler life was at the same time the cause and effect of economic progress, according to Marshall, and therefore there was a double-sided relationship between the manner of living and wages; the concluding chapter of the *Principles* is built precisely around the question of 'how far is either to be regarded as the cause of the other, and how far as the effect' (Marshall, 1920, p. 689).

Mill's conclusion was very similar, but his argument was different. As we have seen above, Mill thought that a higher habitual standard of comfort would lead to a check on population growth, and thereby to a rise in wages. Marshall was careful to stress the differences with Mill. Only when 'the wheat-fields of the world are worked at their full power' does it follow that 'a rise in the standard of *comfort* may raise wages merely by stinting the growth of numbers' (Marshall, 1920, p. 692; emphasis added). This was not the relevant case, however, as we have seen. In fact, 'while the present good fortune of abundant imported food attends on the English people, a rise in their standard of comfort could not increase their wages, merely by its action on their numbers' (Marshall, 1920, p. 692; see also pp. 691 and 697). Population was no longer the relevant aspect; nor was comfort as such relevant: what mainly mattered for wages was efficiency, and efficiency depended on the standard of life; material comfort mattered only insofar as it affected the 'manner of living' in a virtuous sense.

Having dismissed the Ricardian and Millian idea that wages were kept down by the increasing difficulty of obtaining food, Marshall could concentrate on the new idea that, by competition, wages depended on the 'net product' (Marshall's marginal product) of labour:

> When the net product due to the labour of additional workers was largely in excess of the wages that were being paid to them, a pushing employer would brave the indignation of his peers, and attract workers to him by the offer of higher wages: and (…) in progressive industrial districts this competition was sufficient to secure that no considerable body of workers should remain for long with wages much below the equivalent of their net product (Marshall, 1920, p. 705).

The quoted passage explicitly refers to the progressiveness of industrial districts as the main 'independent' source of wage rises; in this case, a better manner of living will be the effect of a wage rise, rather than the other way round. We need not, of course, insist on this effect. There are however some further, subtler effects of technical progress, which did not pass unnoticed by Marshall, and which should be mentioned here. In fact, complex machinery not only tends to reduce the need for unskilled labour, it also 'increases the demand for judgement and general intelligence' (Marshall, 1920, p. 257) and therefore 'takes over sooner or later all monotonous work in manufacture' (p. 262). This had an effect on the life standard of factory workers which was quite independent of wages. At this point, when considering technological innovations and industrial relations from the point of view of the life standard of workers, there is a gradual shift towards a consideration of the life standard itself as a cause of higher wages.

Therefore, education, a good use of leisure, a stimulating 'factory life', prompted higher living standards and thereby efficiency and wages. A special aspect of this complex relation may be briefly singled out, concerning the trade unions. Also in this case Marshall had carefully balanced opinions. On the one hand, especially at an early stage, trade unions were acknowledged to have rendered a valuable service in broadening the workers' horizons and raising their standard of social duty. This helped workers to 'obtain conditions of life consistent with true self-respect and broad social interests' (Marshall, 1920, p. 703) and was conducive to higher efficiency. Likewise, he welcomed the 'true standardisation of work and wages' (ibid., p. 706), such as a sound application of the so-called 'Common rule', for its positive effects on the general conditions of life; and on this account a rise in wages is consistent with an output growth. On the other hand, however, he feared that the Common Rule may lead to 'false standardisation' 'which tend[s] to force employers to put relatively inefficient workers in the same class of payment as more efficient workers; or which prevent[s] anyone from doing work for which he is capable, on the ground that it does not technically belong to him' (ibid., pp. 706–7). By so doing, 'obstacles were put in the way of the use of improved methods and machinery' (ibid., p. 707). Marshall severely criticised trade unions when they promoted such 'false standardisation' and praised them when they condemned it:[20] such behaviour was considered 'anti-social', because it raised wages, so to speak, artificially, without any increase in efficiency. On the contrary, by reducing efficiency, and depressing profits and capital accumulation, they tended to reduce output: the increased standard of comfort that workers may obtain in such a way had indeed, for Marshall, a very high social cost and should by all means be avoided.

1.4. BEYOND THE 'MONEY-MOTIVE': KEYNES'S GRANDCHILDREN

Mill's and Marshall's writings on the future of the working classes naturally lead us to the short conference paper that Keynes wrote on the same topic 40 years after the first edition of Marshall's *Principles*. Not only did Keynes adopt the same 'prophetic' style as his predecessors but also, in his 'Economic Possibilities for our Grandchildren',[21] he built his argument on similar ethical premises.

Keynes's paper is too widely known to require a detailed account here. It will suffice to remind the reader that he looked into the economic conditions 'one hundred years hence' (Keynes, 1931a, pp. 364 and 365) – about one generation ahead now – and in particular at the standard of life permitted by economic conditions in progressive countries at that time, assuming continuing technical progress and capital accumulation and assuming 'no important wars and no important increase in population' (Keynes, 1931a, pp. 365–6).[22] His basic prediction was that 'in the long run (…) *mankind is solving its economic problem*' (ibid., p. 364; emphasis added). There is here a fundamental common ground with Mill. Keynes's age of material abundance, in which 'the accumulation of wealth is no longer of high social importance' (ibid., p. 369) corresponds to Mill's stationary state, in which people can 'cultivate freely the graces of life'.

Keynes's piece clearly shares with Mill also a secular view of the progress in civilisation, and especially a sequence of 'ages', characterised by qualitatively different economic conditions, political and social institutions, and different codes of private and public morals:

> The modern age opened, I think, with the accumulation of capital, which began in the sixteenth century (…). From that time until to-day the power of accumulation by compound interest, which seems to have been sleeping for many generations, was re-born and renewed its strength (…). From the sixteenth century, with a cumulative crescendo after the eighteenth, the great age of science and technical innovation began, which since the beginning of the nineteenth century has been in full flood (Keynes, 1931a, pp. 361–5).

An even more specific similarity with Mill is Keynes's assessment of the historical role of the 'money-motive' in the current age of market economies. Both of them had mixed opinions. One the one hand, in fact, the 'money-makers' rendered an invaluable service to society, insofar as they speeded up the rate of material production. As we have seen, Mill thought that in the (then) current stage of civilisation, 'while minds are coarse they require coarse stimuli, and let them have them'; likewise Keynes recognised that

> The strenuous purposeful money-makers may carry all of us along with them into the lap of economic abundance (Keynes, 1931a, p. 368).

Along similar lines, in his 'The end of laissez-faire', Keynes recognised that

> the dependence upon an intense appeal to the money-making and money-loving instincts of individuals as the main motive force of the economic machine [was] the essential characteristic of Capitalism (Keynes, 1931b, p. 319).

On the other hand, they recognised the moral drawbacks of the money motive, which were to become more transparent as soon as the 'economic problem' was on the way to being solved. Even more emphatically than Mill,[23] Keynes asserted that

> The love of money as a possession – as distinguished from the love of money as a means to the enjoyments and realities of life – will be recognised for what it is, a somewhat disgusting morbidity, one of those semi-criminal, semi-pathological propensities which one hands over with a shudder to the specialists in mental disease (Keynes, 1931a, p. 369).

In this respect, capitalism is

> extremely objectionable. Our problem is to work out a social organisation which shall be as efficient as possible without offending our notions of a satisfactory way of life (Keynes, 1931b, p. 319).

The money motive was therefore a force to be welcomed only conditionally and temporarily, until the time was ripe for man to attend to his real permanent problem:

> How to use his freedom from pressing economic cares, how to occupy the leisure, which science and compound interest will have won for him, to live wisely and agreeably and well (Keynes, 1931a, p. 367).

At that time,

> It will be those peoples, who can keep alive, and cultivate into a fuller perfection, the art of life itself and do not sell themselves for the means of life, who will be able to enjoy the abundance when it comes (Keynes, 1931a, p. 368).

Keynes's wise 'peoples' are Mill's 'better minds' who are not involved in the struggle for riches and will gradually 'succeed in educating the others into better things' (Mill, 1929[1871], p. 749).

These broad and generous views of Keynes on the final goals of economic activity may have been to some extent conditioned by the occasion and the audience for which they were written. Nevertheless, it would be a serious mistake to consider them as an aside. As Harrod remarks, 'that vision of the good life (...) animated his endeavours, of which his readers catch glimpses all through his works' (Harrod, 1951, p. 186).

In Keynes's piece there are also some themes which are perhaps more Marshallian than Millian. A common passionate assessment and enthusiastic predictions of the effect of the advances in science and technology on economic growth are very clear. Symmetrically, both of them cast some doubts on the capacity of man to take due advantage of his economic possibilities and of leisure:

> To judge from the behaviour and the achievements of the wealthy classes to-day in any quarter of the world, the outlook is very depressing! For these are, so to speak, our advance guard – those who are spying out the promised land for the rest of us and pitching their camp there. For they have most of them failed disastrously, so it seems to me – those who have an independent income but no associations or duties or ties – to solve the problem which has been set them (Keynes, 1931a, p. 368).

A similar assessment of the life of the rich, with special reference to expenditure, had been made by Marshall in his 1907 article on the 'Social Possibilities of Economic Chivalry', where he complained that 'much expenditure has no touch of nobility' (Marshall, 1925[1907], p. 342) and that the 'well-to-do classes expend vast sums on things that add little to their happiness and very little to their well-being, but which they regard as necessary for their social position' (ibid., p. 324).

The situation was not very different, for the opposite reasons, in the (present) 'lower classes', who did not have the opportunity of learning to use leisure well. It may not be coincidental that Keynes considers by way of illustration the epitaph written for herself by the old charwoman, whose heaven was 'to do nothing for ever and ever', and which distinctly parallels Marshall's 'sad old picture of the needle-woman' (Marshall, 1925[1873], p. 108).

1.5. CONCLUDING REMARKS

The writings of Mill, Marshall and Keynes reviewed in this chapter share the same conception of output growth in relation to goals of a higher order: as time goes on, and capital and technical knowledge accumulate, material production has a diminishing importance, whereas the conditions of work, the use of leisure, in short, living standards, tend to become the relevant aspect for potentially all members of society.

These common aspects are still (or should be) an inspiration for the current studies on 'quality of life' issues, which are attracting increasing interest. Nonetheless, there are also differences and their precise assessment helps to clarify the specific contribution of each author. If our analysis is correct, Mill's 'stationary state' of society should be contrasted more with Ricardo's and less with Marshall's early 'fancied country', and even with Marshall's *Principles*, than currently perceived.

Although Mill's analysis of wages in relation to growth adopted the same logical scheme as Ricardo, Mill was open to the opposite conclusions, due to different assumptions concerning population, according to the post-1830 phase of progress of the working classes which Mill, but not Ricardo, observed.

We have argued that for both Mill and Marshall, wages were less important than conditions of life, and output growth was less important than 'mental and moral cultivation'. Wages and production were, so to speak, the means, while conditions of life and cultivation were the ends. The former were therefore no more than particular aspects of a wider and very complex – and indeed fundamental – relation between conditions of life and the economy. It is from this point of view, we argued, that Mill anticipated many Marshallian (and for that matter, Keynesian) themes and departed sharply from Ricardo and Malthus. Both Mill and Marshall emphasised the economic importance of self-dependence, self-respect and intelligence. Mill thought that self-dependence would lead to a voluntary check of population growth and thereby to better conditions of life and high wages in the following generation; Marshall thought that this effect could be immediately obtained by means of higher productivity. It is true that the Millian 'stationary state' is replaced by a Marshallian slow, steady progress, and that a low rate of population growth, albeit remaining an important condition, played no decisive role in Marshall, but the important question for both of them was whether sound conditions for all members of society were attainable at some stage of the process: whether, afterwards, capital would continue to be accumulated and population would continue to (moderately) grow, was secondary.

This interpretation is somehow reinforced by the synthesis of Millian and Marshallian themes which can be found in Keynes's 'Economic Possibilities'. Indeed, Keynes's sketch of a probable future of the advanced economies borrowed from Mill a secular vision of successive economic and social 'ages', in which the age of output growth, dominated by the money motive, was disagreeable yet necessary, and the next age could witness a full development of the mental and moral attitudes of mankind. This optimism concerning the potential of a market economy can also be found in Marshall of course, but a more specific Marshallian theme was a negative evaluation of the way in which the then rich, that advance guard of the society to come, made use of their income and their leisure.

NOTES

1. For example, Nussbaum and Sen (1993). The Human Development Report issued annually by a United Nations agency is of course an important practical example.
2. We are referring here to Mill (1929[1871], and especially Book IV; 1967[1845] and 1967[1869]).
3. We are referring here to Marshall (1920, especially Book VI, chapter XIII; 1925[1873] and 1925[1907].
4. Among the many formal expositions we should mention Pasinetti (1960), Samuelson (1978) and Hollander (1984a).
5. It should be remarked that Mill's predictions were soon to be confirmed by historical evolution. According to Galor (2005), the 'demographic transition [which] swept the world in the course of last century' (p. 198) had started in Europe and the US in the last decades of the 19th century.

6. With reference to Norway, Malthus argued that 'this degree of happiness, superior to what could be expected from the soil and climate, arises almost exclusively from the degree in which the preventive check to population operates' (Malthus, 1992[1803], p. 270).
7. To be sure, this was not ignored by Ricardo: 'The friends of humanity cannot but wish that in all countries the labouring classes should have a taste for comforts and enjoyments, and that they should be stimulated by all legal means in their exertions to procure them. There cannot be a better security against a superabundant population' (Ricardo, 1951, p. 100). He did not, however, draw substantial conclusions from this. In fact, he added that 'although this might be the consequence of high wages, yet so great are the delights of domestic society, that in practice it is invariably found that an increase of population follows the amended condition of the labourer (ibid., p. 407).
8. This fundamental aspect of Mill's argument is recognised, albeit mildly, by Hollander: 'Limitation of family size to the end of actually raising living standards is conceded [by Mill] amongst members of the middle class' (1984b, p. 252). Hollander's formal account of Mill's stationary state, however, is mainly based on the very different idea that 'prudence' is aimed at preventing wages from falling. This is a rather weak point, because it involves a logical error (lack of incentives) which is usually ascribed only to Malthus. See Rashid (1999, p. 322).
9. He formally abandoned that doctrine in his review of Thornton's book on labour (Mill, 1869), in which he admitted that trade unions may force capitalists to devote more capital 'in the direct purchase of labour', thus making room for permanent wage increases. Nevertheless, he never cast any doubt on the fact that a check on population growth was beneficial to wages. The precise object of Mill's recantation is still controversial: see Ekelund (1976), West and Hafer (1978), Ekelund and Kordsmeier (1981).
10. A mathematical formulation of this path is proposed by this author in Opocher (forthcoming).
11. According to Mill, there was not 'much satisfaction in contemplating the world with nothing left to the spontaneous activity of nature; with every rood of land brought into cultivation, which is capable of growing food for human beings' (Mill, 1929, p. 750) .
12. For a historical reconstruction of the long debate eventually leading to the Education Act, see Chapter 2 of this volume.
13. The *Lectures to Women* were recently published with an extensive commentary in Raffaelli et al. (1995).
14. According to Groenewegen, 'The problem which guided Marshall's work throughout the whole of his life [was that of] raising the standards of life of the working class until they had reached those of 'gentlemen' (Groenewegen, 1994, p. 278). Along similar lines is the interpretation of Himmelfarb (1991, pp. 285–300) and the seminal contribution of Parsons (1931, p. 132). As Coats noted, for Marshall 'ethics was both the 'sister' of economics and 'the good Abigail', the 'mistress' of economics' (Coats, 1990, p. 155). A fond interest in the standard of life of the working class was very common among late Victorian intellectuals, as the beautiful study of Himmelfarb (1991) shows. For a valuable survey of the Anglican ethics in Marshall's times, see Biagini (1995).
15. Marshall did not pay tribute to the Classical tradition, nor did he set himself to explain (contrary to Mill) why his predictions were so different from those of Smith or Ricardo or Malthus.
16. According to Biagini, Marshall's concept of citizenship 'was a further manifestation of the 'Anglican ethic' which inspired him. In this connection the affinities between Marshall and Arnold Toynbee (...) are worth noting. They shared a missionary approach to the problems of modern industrial society, within the framework of a civically-minded social Christianity' (Biagini, 1995, p. 34).

17. 'The inequalities of wealth (...) are a serious flaw in our economic organisation. Any diminution of them which can be attained by means that would not sap the springs of free initiative and strength of character (...) would seem to be a clear social gain. Though arithmetic warns us that it is impossible to raise all earnings beyond the level already reached by specially well-to-do artisan families, it is certainly desirable that those who are below that level should be raised, *even at the expense of lowering in some degree those who are above it*' (Marshall, 1920, p. 714; emphasis added).
18. 'Anglo-Saxon artisans, unsurpassed in accuracy of touch, and surpassing all in sustained energy, would more than any others increase their net produce if they would keep their machinery going at its full speed for sixteen hours a day, even though they themselves worked only eight' (Marshall, 1920, p. 694).
19. Marshall also stressed that a reduction of working hours was 'specially suitable to industries in which piece-work prevails' (Marshall, 1920, p. 693).
20. 'The service which the leading trade unionists rendered to the country by condemning anti-social conduct are never to be forgotten' (Marshall, 1920, p. 707).
21. Keynes (1931a[1930]). The paper, based on lectures given in Madrid in the summer 1930, first appeared in literary form in *The Nation* and *Athenaeum* of 11th and 18th October of the same year. That topic had been the subject of a lecture given to Winchester schoolboys in March 1928; see Harrod (1951, p. 394).
22. Actually, a very 'important' war was round the corner; but population was not to increase very much in progressive countries, nor was the pace of technological progress and accumulation to be reduced on average.
23. Keynes's passage quoted below may be paralleled with this of Mill: 'The idea is essentially *repulsive* of a society only held together by the relations and feelings arising out of pecuniary interest' (Mill, 1929[1871], p. 754).

REFERENCES

Biagini, E. (1995), 'The Anglican Ethic and the Spirit of Citizenship: the Political and Social Context', in T. Raffaelli, E. Biagini and R. McWilliams Tullberg (eds), *Alfred Marshall's Lectures to Women* (foreword by Giacomo Beccattini), Aldershot: Edward Elgar, pp. 24–46.

Bruni, L. and P.L. Porta (eds) (2005), *Economics and Happiness. Framing the Analysis*, Oxford: Oxford University Press.

Coats, A.M. (1990), 'Marshall on Ethics', in R. McWilliams Tullberg (ed.), *Alfred Marshall in Retrospect*, Aldershot: Edward Elgar, pp. 153–77.

Ekelund, R.B. (1976), 'A Short-Run Classical Model of Capital and Wages: Mill's Recantation of the Wages Fund', *Oxford Economic Papers*, **28**(1), 22–37.

Ekelund, R.B. Jr and W.F. Kordsmeier (1981), 'J.S. Mill, Unions, and the Wages Fund Recantation: A Reinterpretation – Comment', *The Quarterly Journal of Economics*, **96**(3), 531–41.

Ekelund, R.B. Jr and R.D. Tollison (1976), 'The New Political Economy of J.S. Mill: The Means to Social Justice', *The Canadian Journal of Economics*, **9**(2), 213–31.

Galor, O. (2005), 'From Stagnation to Growth: Unified Growth Theory', in P. Aghion and S.N. Durlauf (eds), *Handbook of Economic Growth*, Amsterdam: Elsevier, Vol. 1A.

Giffen, R. (1886), 'Further Notes on the Progress of the Working Classes in the Last Half Century', *Journal of the Statistical Society of London*, **49**(1), 28–100.

Groenewegen, P. (1994), 'Alfred Marshall and the Labour Commission 1891–1894', *The European Journal for the History of Economic Thought*, **1**(2), 273–95.

Groenewegen, P. (1995), *A Soaring Eagle: Alfred Marshall 1842–1924*, Aldershot, UK and Brookfield, US: Edward Elgar.

Harrod, R.F. (1951), *The Life of John Maynard Keynes*, London: Macmillan.

Himmelfarb, G. (1991), *Poverty and Compassion. The Moral Imagination of the Late Victorians*, New York: Vintage Books.

Hollander, S. (1984a), 'The Wage Path in Classical Growth Models: Ricardo, Malthus and Mill', *Oxford Economic Papers*, **36**(2), 200–212.

Hollander, S. (1984b), ' "Dynamic Equilibrium" with Constant Wages: J.S. Mill's Malthusian Analysis of the Secular Wage Path', *Kyklos*, **37**(2), 247–65.

Hollander, S. (1985), *The Economics of John Stuart Mill*, Oxford: Blackwell.

Keynes, J.M. (1931a[1930]), 'Economic Possibilities for our Grandchildren', in *Essays in Persuasion*, London: Macmillan.

Keynes, J.M. (1931b[1930]), 'The End of Laissez-Faire', in *Essays in Persuasion*, London: Macmillan.

Ludlow, J.M. and L. Jones (1973[1867]), *Progress of the Working Class. 1832–1867*, New York: Augustus M. Kelley Publishers.

Malthus, T.R. (1992[1803]), *An Essay on the Principle of Population*, Cambridge: Cambridge University Press

Marshall A. (1920), *Principles of Economics*, London: Macmillan, 8th edition.

Marshall, A. (1925[1873]), 'The Future of the Working Classes', in A.C. Pigou (ed.), *Memorials of Alfred Marshall*, Reprints of Economics Classics, New York: Kelley, pp. 101–18.

Marshall, A. (1925[1907]), 'Social Possibilities of Chivalry', in A.C. Pigou (ed.), *Memorials of Alfred Marshall*, Reprints of Economics Classics, New York: Kelley, pp. 323–46.

Mill, J.S. (1967[1845]), 'The Claims of Labour', in J.M. Robson (ed.), *Collected Works of John Stuart Mill*, Toronto: University of Toronto Press, Vol. IV, pp. 631–68.

Mill, J.S. (1967[1869]), 'Thornton on Labour and Its Claims', in J.M. Robson (ed.), *Collected Works of John Stuart Mill*, Toronto: University of Toronto Press, Vol. V, pp. 365–89.

Mill, J. S. (1929[1871]), *Principles of Political Economy*, edited with an introduction by Sir W.J. Ashley, London: Longmans, 7th edition.

Mill, J.S. (1989[1873]), *Autobiography*, edited with an introduction by J.M. Robson, London: Penguin books.

Nussbaum, M. and A. Sen (eds) (1993), *The Quality of Life*, Oxford: Clarendon Press.

Opocher, A. (forthcoming), 'Does Economic Growth Ultimately Lead to a Nobler Life? A Mathematical Formulation of Mill's Stationary State', in *Essays in Honour of Ian Steedman*, London: Routledge.

Parsons, T. (1931), 'Wants and Activities in Marshall', *The Quarterly Journal of Economics*, **46**(1), 101–40.

Pasinetti, L.L. (1960), 'A Mathematical Formulation of the Ricardian System', *The Review of Economic Studies*, **27**(2), 78–98.

Raffaelli T., E. Biagini and R. McWilliams Tullberg (eds) (1995), *Alfred Marshall's Lectures to Women* (foreword by Giacomo Beccattini), Aldershot: Edward Elgar.

Rashid, S. (1999), 'Review Essay. Hollander on Malthus', *Journal of the History of Economic Thought*, **21**(3), 315–24.

Ricardo, D. (1951), *Principles of Political Economy*, in P. Sraffa (ed.), *Works and Correspondence of David Ricardo*, I, Cambridge: Cambridge University Press.

Samuelson, P.A. (1978), 'The Canonical Classical Model of Political Economy', *Journal of Economic Literature*, **16**(4), 1415–34.

Schwartz P. (1972), *The New Political Economy of J.S. Mill*, London: Weidenfeld and Nicolson.

Webb, S. and B. Webb (1965[1897]), *Industrial Democracy*, Reprints of Economics Classics, New York: Kelley.

West, E.G. and R.W. Hafer (1978), 'J.S. Mill, Unions, and the Wages Fund Recantation: A Reinterpretation', *The Quarterly Journal of Economics*, **92**(4), 603–19.

2. The debate on education financing in the classical perspective

Mario Pomini

2.1. INTRODUCTION

Reflection on the relationship between education policies and the conditions to promote economic progress and welfare is not new in the history of economic thought: it was a matter of considerable interest to the classical economists[1] and in general to economists actively interested in social issues. The classical economists analysed education to some extent, and in some cases conducted in-depth treatment of the topic, while others considered aspects of economic reality of their time (Miller, 1966). The only notable exception was Ricardo, who neglected education entirely, even in his detailed treatment of work and wages (Blaug, 1975).

Analysis of education, and of the various economic problems connected with it, by the economists considered herein largely developed within the general framework established by Adam Smith in the *Wealth of Nations* (1952[1776]), and it was distinguished by two main features. First, education was always regarded as the responsibility of the Sovereign, which reflected the importance of the role of the state in this sphere of social life. Indeed, it is a general characteristic of the nineteenth century that even the supporters of *laissez-faire* and the superiority of private enterprise realized that education had distinctive features which ill-suited it to the operation of market mechanisms. They were well aware that education was an economic good which by its very nature fell outside the pure individualistic logic of demand and supply. Secondly, the classical economists made only vague reference to the notion of human capital – which would instead become central to the modern economic analysis of education. They focused not so much on the connection between education and labour productivity as on the positive and beneficial effects of the schooling process on society as a whole. This is not to say that the notion of human capital did not exist; but it was considered of secondary importance, though constituting a significant element in wage differentiation (Bowman, 1990).

Besides Smith, the economists who made an original contribution in this field were J.S. Mill, to a lesser extent N. Senior and J. McCulloch (Tu, 1969). McCulloch, a pupil of Ricardo's, also dealt widely with education in pedagogical terms, and was the first to put forward the radical proposal that primary education should be made compulsory. Although this proposal was again advanced in 1825, it was only many decades later in England that it gave rise to the Educational Act of 1870, which founded the national system of education. Mill, for his part, subsequently developed Smith's reflections on market failure in the educational sector by introducing a perspective which came close to that of transaction costs analysis. Within the first generation of neoclassical economists, the topic of education was developed mainly by H. Sidgwick (1883) and A. Marshall (1964[1890]). Whilst Sidgwick merely reiterated the theses of Mill, it was Marshall who thoroughly developed this theme, on the one hand, bringing the classical tradition to completion, and on the other, introducing new directions of inquiry.

This chapter will deal with a particular, though probably not secondary, aspect of education, namely its financing; and it will concentrate on compulsory education. This is not to imply that the classical economists did not concern themselves with the other levels of education as well, particularly higher, but it was the utility of compulsory schooling and its forms of financing that received their closest attention (West, 1964). The chapter is organized as follows. Section 2.2 outlines the evolution of schooling in England during the first half of the 1800s. Section 2.3 considers the theories of Smith, while Section 2.4 examines the different position taken by McCulloch. Section 2.5 is devoted to the synthesis performed by Mill, while Section 2.6 examines the contribution of Nassau Senior. The final section discusses the resumption of these themes during the Marshallian period and makes some concluding remarks.

2.2. THE SITUATION OF PRIMARY-LEVEL EDUCATION IN ENGLAND IN THE FIRST HALF OF THE 1800s

The nineteenth century was a period of key importance from the point of view of education policies, in that it saw the birth and consolidation of the national education systems. Indeed, by the second half of the century all European countries had introduced some sort of compulsory schooling, albeit to very limited extents. The first state to take decisive action in this regard – an example frequently cited by the classical economists – was Prussia, which in 1773 enacted a law that introduced compulsory primary schooling. The General Civil Code of 1794 established the *Volkschule*, state elementary schools, as institutions of the state, financed mostly by local taxes. In France, the centralized education system created by Napoleon in the early nineteenth century survived the Restoration and was subsequently reinforced. The Ferry law of 1882 made primary education free, universal, and compulsory, further increasing the proportion of students enrolled in state schools. In Italy, primary education (two years) was made compulsory in the Kingdom of Piedmont with the Casati Law of 1859, and was then extended throughout the new Kingdom of Italy. In England, it was not until the 1870 Education Act that primary education was made compulsory, although not yet free.

What were the conditions of school attendance, and in general of literacy, in the central period of the Industrial Revolution in England, conditions that would serve as the background for the reflections of the classical economists? Quantitative analysis of the English situation in the first half of the 1800s is very difficult, for various reasons ranging from a lack of data to their scant homogeneity. However, some recent studies provide a fairly complete picture as regards both the demand and the supply sides (Stephens, 1998). The earliest available statistics, which refer to 1818, indicate that the proportion of children regularly attending primary school was just 10 per cent in Scotland, 5 per cent in Wales, and 6.6 per cent in England (Stephens, 1998, p. 22). During the advent of the Industrial Revolution, the data show that school attendance improved since some worker families were now able to afford school fees (West, 1978). In 1851 primary school attendance rose to 10.8 per cent in Scotland, 7 per cent in Wales, and 10 per cent in England (Stephens, 1998, p. 22). Hence, primary education had progressed substantially in only one generation, although it was still a good available only to the affluent (West, 1970, p. 89).

On the supply side, the primary education situation was highly diversified. Various types of schools existed: some were entirely private, others connected to the parishes; and then there were state schools (that is, open to all, but upon payment), and finally grammar schools.[2] None of these was free, and attendance fees could be very expensive. The fact that primary education was only available upon payment explains why it was accessed by only a small fraction of the population. The government, for its part, only started to provide public funding for education with the Factory Act of 1883.

The fact that the great majority of children did not regularly attend primary school does not mean that they were entirely deprived of an education. The lower classes were taught to read and write outside the school system by philanthropic or religious initiatives epitomized by the Charity Schools and the Sunday Schools. The former were run mainly by the Church of England and taught highly varied curricula to children aged seven and over: some did no more than impart the basic skills, while others offered a wide range of subjects and could also prepare for university entrance. The

Charity Schools movement reached its apogee towards the end of the 1700s, but thereafter declined because of the rise of the Sunday Schools (Dogliani, 2003). The main purpose of the latter was to instruct lower-class children in the aim of moralizing the burgeoning working class. Young people attended Sunday School for four to six hours, on average for four years, and they learned to read and do sums, but not necessarily to write. Given their characteristics, the Sunday Schools were not restricted to school-age children alone but were also open to adults. In 1851, before entering their decline, they were attended by around two million students. The Sunday Schools therefore performed a role of enormous importance in the social process of giving literacy to the lower classes before the advent of compulsory education.

In substance, therefore, the first half of the 1800s saw a constant increase in school attendance due mainly to demographic growth, urbanization and industrial transformation. The phenomenon was especially marked in urban areas, where increases in wages fuelled increasing demand for education. However, despite this progress, primary education and, to a greater extent, secondary and higher education, remained a privilege restricted to affluent families. As West has stressed: 'on our evidence the mass of people in the 1830's already did appreciate the advantages of education; it was mainly lack of income which prevented their having more; with the passage of time increasing incomes were generally leading to increased private demand for schooling' (West, 1970, p. 89). Not surprisingly, therefore, one of the main worries of the classical economists was that the education level of workers might be entirely inadequate to meet the needs of production. And alongside the problem of access, there was also the problem of the quality of education, which in many cases was modest, if not poor.

2.3. EDUCATION IN A. SMITH BETWEEN STATE AND MARKET

This section considers Smith's view on education, which he put forward on various occasions in the *Wealth of Nations*. Those who seek to show that Smith anticipated the notion of human capital (Bowman, 1990) cite a passage in Book I where he states that in every occupation the pay must be such that it also defrays the expenses sustained by the worker to acquire an education and skills. But Smith considered education as not so much a form of individual investment which increased the worker's productivity as, from a general point of view, an important social institution. And this was his point of view in the general treatment of education to be found in Book V, which examines the duties of the sovereign. In fact, the functions of the state are already outlined at the end of Book IV, in a paragraph that serves as an introduction to the next book. These duties of the sovereign are defence, the administration of justice and

> Thirdly, the duty of erecting and maintaining certain public works and certain public institutions which it can never be for the interest of any individual, or small number of individuals, to erect and maintain; because the profit could never repay the expense to any individuals, thought it may frequently do much more repay it to a great society (Smith, 1952[1776], p. 300).

Among the institutions that contribute to the general well-being but cannot be sustained by individual advantage, Smith includes those that have the duty of providing education, both to children and to adults. In the part devoted to education, Smith's treatment is particularly long-winded, touching upon numerous arguments with ample historical digressions. He begins with highly critical comments on the English university system compared with Scotland's, differences which Smith attributes to the different ways in which the two systems were financed. He then extols the superiority of higher education in antiquity. A long section is devoted to the education of adults, which for Smith consists essentially in religious education. The central part of the section entitled *Of the Expense of the Institutions for the Education of Youth* addresses the issue of interest to us here by asking the question:

> Ought the public, therefore, to give no attention, it may be asked, to the education of the people? Or if it ought to give any, what are the different parts of education which it ought to attend to in the different orders of the people? And in what manner ought it to attend to them? (Smith, 1952[1776], p. 340).

Smith's answer is that education is a good that cannot be entrusted to the market, by virtue of the superiority of the collective advantage over that of the individual (Freeman, 1969). On the one hand, the return to private education is very low and is unable to sustain adequate demand by families. Contributing to this are numerous factors: the poor quality of teachers, the scant utility of the subjects taught, the difficulty of finding employment, also the uncertainty of the conditions of life, and the fact that truly useful preparation can be acquired through practical apprenticeship. On the other hand, the social return is very high, for two reasons on which Smith dwells at length. Firstly, the education of the people must be undertaken by the state to prevent a loss of 'intellectual, social and martial qualities' due to the division of labour. Reduced to a monotonous and repetitive daily occupation, the worker:

> whose whole life is spent in performing a few simple operations, of which the effects are perhaps always the same, or very nearly the same, has no occasion to exert his understanding or to exercise his invention in finding out expedients for removing difficulties which never occur. He naturally loses, therefore, the habit of

> such exertion, and generally becomes as stupid and ignorant as it is possible for a human creature to become. The torpor of his mind renders him not only incapable of relishing or bearing a part in any rational conversation, but of conceiving any generous, noble, or tender sentiment, and consequently of forming any just judgment concerning many even of the ordinary duties of private life. Of the great and extensive interests of his country he is altogether incapable of judging, and unless very particular pains have been taken to render him otherwise, he is equally incapable of defending his country in war. The uniformity of his stationary life naturally corrupts the courage of his mind [...]. His dexterity at his own particular trade seems, in this manner, to be acquired at the expense of his intellectual, social, and marital virtues. But in every improved and civilised society this is the state into which the labouring poor, that is, the great body of the people, must necessarily fall, unless government takes some pains to prevent it (Smith, 1952 [1776], p. 341).

Faced with this desolating picture of the worker's degradation brought about by the division of labour, the state cannot be indifferent and must intervene. This is a moral argument stemming from the Enlightenment. Smith's proposal to limit this damage is to make primary education compulsory through the creation in every parish of a primary school to teach children to read, write and do sums. This minimal form of education could also be compulsory if an examination were made obligatory for entry into a corporation or the practice of a trade. On the example of the system in Scotland, the state should not pay teachers entirely, for this would induce them to neglect their work; their salary should be integrated with a modest remuneration which even a common worker could afford. Therefore, also in the case of the financing of compulsory education, Smith adheres to his scheme of reference based on the strength of individual incentive.

Smith also provides a second reason justifying intervention by the state: the fact that general education ensures greater social cohesion and stability. The section on the *Expense of the Institutions for the Education of Youth* closes with the following considerations:

> Though the state was to derive no advantage from the instruction of the inferior ranks of people, it would still deserve its attention that they should not be altogether uninstructed. The state, however, derives no inconsiderable advantage from their instruction. The more they are instructed, the less liable they are to the delusions of enthusiasm and superstition, which, among ignorant nations, frequently occasion the most dreadful disorder. An instructed and intelligent people, besides, are always more decent and orderly than an ignorant and stupid one. [...]. They are more disposed to examine, and more capable of seeing through, the interested complaints of faction and sedition, and, they are, upon that account, less apt to be misled into any wanton or unnecessary opposition to the measures of government (Smith, 1952[1776], p. 343).

Smith's argument – which we could call one of social control – that education contributes decisively to ensuring social stability was taken up by all subsequent authors and constituted a key reference for discussion of the topic by the classical economists. Almost the same words are used, for example, by Malthus in Chapter 10 of his *Essay on Population*, where he writes that 'on this subject [education] I agree most cordially with A. Smith in thinking, that an instructed and well informed people would be much less likely to be led away by inflammatory writings, and much better able to detect the false declamation of interested and ambitious demagogues, than an ignorant people' (Malthus, 1986[1826], p. 527). Not only was Malthus in complete agreement with Smith's proposal of a system of parish education, but he went further by proposing that school syllabuses should include notions of political economy, so that pupils could reflect on the true causes of their economic circumstances.

The *Wealth of Nations* described education as an activity which is necessary but nonetheless extraneous to the economic order dominated by market forces. Industrial development, for good or ill, created the premises for a new analysis of what the duties of the state should be. Universal education was an investment for the whole of society, rather than for the individual. Smith's position on compulsory education, however, was somewhat ambiguous. On the one hand, according to a thesis taken up by all subsequent authors, he maintained that there are institutions, among them the education system, which cannot be left to the market and which are notable exceptions to the principle of the invisible hand. On the other, Smith did not take the argument to its theoretical conclusion; instead, with an attitude marked by great pragmatism (Viner, 1927), he merely proposed that the organizational model should be that of the Scottish schools, where the landowners paid for the construction of school buildings and their maintenance, while the students contributed to the costs of the teaching staff. Free tuition, he said, would deprive teachers, parents and children of incentives, whereas an educational market would provide competition amongst suppliers of education and reduce costs in schools. But as the subsequent literature pointed out, this position was entirely in the minority: instead, further arguments were advanced for the direct management of compulsory education, arguments based both on externalities and on the ignorance of parents concerning the positive effects of education.

2.4. McCULLOCH AND THE SOCIAL FUNCTION OF EDUCATION

McCulloch (1789–1864) was the classical economist who dealt most extensively with problems connected with education, and with schooling in general (O'Brien, 1970). He wrote on both economic theory and pedagogy, criticizing in numerous writings – many of them published in the *Quarterly Journal on Education* – the excessive severity of the teaching methods of the time. His approach to education was influenced more by Malthus that by Smith, in that it placed greater importance on education as a means to achieve moral improvement and economic progress than on its nature as a public good.

The distinctive feature of McCulloch's thought is that it concentrated almost exclusively on the importance of education's social function, and in particular as a means to alleviate the conditions of the poor. As a consequence, his theory was analytically weak and did not achieve the profundity of Smith's. McCulloch initially agreed with Malthus that education was an important cultural device with which to solve the problem of demographic growth. Secondly, suitable schooling would contribute to the maintenance of social order and would prevent social turmoil. In an age when cities and towns were undergoing rapid growth, the security of property was essential for the economic development that would ensue from appropriate levels of literacy. McCulloch then adopted a more interventionist stance based on his conviction that a national education system, supported and managed by the state mainly to fight poverty, was necessary. Education thus became the crucial factor in the battle to improve the conditions of the working class.

McCulloch's *Principles of Political Economy* (1965[1849]) deals with education after a long section devoted to detailed analysis of legislation on the poor which, by that time in England, was almost three hundred years old. McCulloch's opinion is clear:

> Of the various means for providing for the permanent improvement of the poor, few, if any, promise to be so effectual as the establishment of a really useful system of public education. Poverty is, probably, the principal source of misery and crime; and ignorance, or a want of the knowledge of the laws of circumstances that determine the condition of the great bulk of mankind in society, is, indirectly at least, an efficient source of poverty, and, therefore, of crime. It is now, indeed, very generally acknowledged, that the providing of elementary instruction for all classes of its subjects is one of the most pressing duties of government; and during the half-century, and especially since the termination of the late French war, some of the principal Continental states have taken every means in their power to ensure the efficient discharge of this important duty (McCulloch, 1965[1849], p. 396).

Following Smith, McCulloch argues that the social advantages of education lie in its contribution to the civic formation of people, and therefore also lie outside the economic sphere. Both in Smith and McCulloch, schooling exerts a beneficial effect by improving the character and heightening the capacity for conceptual elaboration. He accordingly proposed the creation of a national education system, limited to elementary schools, which would eliminate the costs associated with ignorance, and lead to greater social justice. He was a firm believer in the necessity of universal education and he was strongly of the opinion that this should be provided by the state rather than by the market. A state system would not degrade the pupils and would be uniform in quality and quantity. He stated explicitly that the *laissez-faire* principle cannot be applied to education: for under the system of supply and demand the poor would be too little educated and the charitable institutions would be unable to provide the level of education that they lacked. He observes further: 'We fear, however, that these, and other advantages of sound education, can never be fully realised so long as we are left, without any adequate public provision, to depend principally on the effort of individuals and associations' (McCulloch, 1965[1849], p. 399). Like other economists of his time, his mistrust of private schools was total, because he believed that they were run by irresponsible administrators and often staffed by poorly-trained teachers. Moreover, like Malthus, he wanted schools not only to teach humanities but also to impart basic notions of political economy, with particular reference to population theory and the theory of income distribution.

McCulloch was aware of the difficulties implicit in this ambitious project of compulsory primary education. There were not only economic difficulties connected with its financing, but also various other practical difficulties concerning the organizational and political complexity of education, the preparation of textbooks, and the selection of subjects to be included in the curriculum. He wrote:

> At the same time it must be admitted, that it is an exceedingly difficult matter to suggest any plan for a national system of education against which many very weighty objections may not be fairly urged. Suppose it were enacted, that a school for the elementary branches of instruction should be founded and endowed by government in every parish, or other convenient district: the knotty questions would immediately occur – Whether shall any, and, if any, what system of religious instruction be introduced into these schools? – To whom shall the drawing up, or choice, of class-books be instructed? Shall the same class-books, and the same plan of instruction, be adopted in all the schools, or if not, to what extent, and under what circumstances, shall it be varied? – Shall it to be compulsory, as in Prussia, on parents to send their children to school, or shall it be optional? […]. But so many and such formidable objections, originating partly in the difficulties inherent in the subject, and partly and principally in the discordant

> views and prejudices of the different religious sects and political parties among us, might be, and no doubt would be, made to every proposal for a national system of education, that, however beneficial, there are certainly but slender grounds on which to hope for its establishment (McCulloch, 1965[1849], p. 399).

McCulloch did not subject the issue of education to the mere analysis of market failure, as in Smith; rather, he treated it in all its complexity as a fundamental component of the new social order. Moreover, he showed no trace of Smith's optimism. Industrialization had created a mass of poor, disinherited individuals whose protests might endanger the whole of society. McCulloch's pessimism on the possibility of achieving compulsory primary education was well justified. As Green (1990) has pointed out, his proposal aroused the hostility of both conservatives and progressives. The former were opposed to the extension of schooling because they feared that it would upset existing social equilibria. The latter feared that greater education of the masses in traditionalist subjects would further increase their subjugation. Indeed, McCulloch's proposal was only approved in 1870, when elementary education became compulsory, even if it was not made completely free until the end of the century.

2.5. J.S. MILL AND THE RELEVANCE OF 'TRANSACTION COSTS'

With J.S. Mill the classical school's reflections on education are at their most mature and accomplished. As previously in Smith, Mill makes some mention of education in Book Two of the *Principles of Political Education*, where he discusses wage differences. But he conducts his general treatment in the book's final chapter (XI) on *Grounds and Limits of the Laisser-faire or Non-Interference Principle*. This is an important chapter, also theoretically, in which Mill sets out the liberal principle according to which the activity of the public powers must be restricted in consideration of the fact that individuals are the best judges of their own interests (Hollander, 1985). Immediately after this general assertion, he observes that there are nevertheless many cases in which government interference is justifiable, and one of them is the supply of education. Mill contends, on the basis of the Smithian argument of positive externalities, that there are some works of public utility which should never be realized with a view to individual profit. 'At some times and places, there will be no roads, docks, harbours, canals, works of irrigation, hospitals, schools, colleges, printing-presses, unless the government establishes them' (Mill, 1965[1848], p. 949). This happens because private individuals do not have the necessary resources; or because the organizational costs are too high in comparison to the anticipated profit.

This traditional line of reasoning – which Mill considered to be obvious and therefore outlined only briefly – was not followed by the customary reference to the beneficial effects of education in terms of greater social and cultural progress. In keeping with his liberal and Benthamist beliefs, Mill followed an entirely different route, which highlighted further aspects of the complexity of education as an economic good. He wrote:

> Now, the proposition that the consumer is a competent judge of the commodity, can be admitted only with numerous abatements and exceptions. He is generally the best judge of the material objects produced for his use. [...] But there are other things, of the worth of which the demand of the market is by no means a test; things of which the utility does not consist in ministering some inclinations, nor in serving the daily uses of life, and the want of which is least felt where the need is greatest. This is peculiarly true of those things which are chiefly useful as tending to raise the character of human beings. The uncultivated cannot be competent judges of cultivation. Those who most need to made wiser and better, usually desire it least, and if they desire it, would be incapable of finding the way to it by their own lights (Mill, 1965[1848], p. 947).

The new circumstance which Mill brings to the reader's attention in this passage is that the choice of the optimal quantity of education entails costs additional to those required for ordinary goods exchanged on the market, and which derive from the fact that the consumer is unable to know with precision the characteristics of the good in question. The resources spent in the bargaining phase to determine the quality and characteristics of the good are nothing other, to use modern terminology, than 'transaction costs'. Although the market is an extremely efficient allocation mechanism when the transaction costs due to uncertainty and incomplete information are negligible, it tends to lose this efficiency as the latter increase. When transaction costs are high, transactions tend to move outside the market and are regulated through administrative activity, thereby coming under the competence of the state. Education is one of the cases in which the presence of these costs is substantial because, according to Mill, parents are unable to appraise the importance of education for their children, and if they were able to do so, they would probably not have the means to afford it. The conclusion is that, in the educational field, broad public intervention is necessary.

> Education, therefore, is one of those things which it is admissible in principle that a government should provide for the people. The case is one to which the reasons of the non-interference principle do not necessary or universally extend (Mill, 1965[1848], p. 949).

If this holds for education in general, in the case of elementary education one must go further, for those who will benefit are children, who will bear the consequences of their parents' choices for the rest of their lives. In this case, government action is twofold. On the one hand, legislative intervention is desirable to force parents to provide for the education of their children. On the other, the state must furnish the financial means which enable all parents to fulfil their legal obligation. Mill describes the English situation, which he regarded as largely unsatisfactory, thus:

> In England, and most European countries, elementary instruction cannot be paid for, at its full cost, from the common wages of unskilled labour, and would not if it could. The alternative, therefore, is not between government and private speculation, but between a government provision and voluntary charity: between interference by government, and interference by associations of individuals, subscribing their own money for the purpose, like the two great School Societies (Mill, 1965[1848], p. 949).

Faced with this alternative, Mill decisively opts for government intervention. Referring to various reports on education, and in particular to that of 1831, he argues that education based on the voluntary principle, and therefore on private charity for the needy, is insufficient in quantity, and poor in quality. In conclusion, for Mill it is necessary to move to an educational system accessible to all:

> The education provided in this country on the voluntary principle has of late been so much discussed, that it is needless in this place to criticise it minutely, and I shall merely express my conviction, that even in quantity it is, and is likely to remain, altogether insufficient, while in quality, though with some slight tendency to improvement, it is never good except by some rare accident, and generally so bad as to be little more than nominal. I hold it therefore the duty of the government to supply the defect, by giving pecuniary support to elementary schools, such as to render them accessible to all the children of the poor, either freely, or for a payment too inconsiderable to be sensibly felt (Mill, 1965[1848], p. 950).

Further and definitive reflection on the role of the state in education and its financing is conducted in Mill's essay of 1859, *On Liberty*. In chapter V, devoted to the application of his principle of liberty as with interference by others, Mill returns to the theme of education, and above all its financing. His reasoning develops in two stages. He first reiterates the need for legislative intervention by the state in educational affairs because parents often underestimate the importance of education for their children. But he then goes further by observing that:

> Were the duty of enforcing universal education once admitted, there would be an end to the difficulties about what the State should teach, and how it should teach, which now convert the subject into a mere battle-field for sects and parties, causing the time and labour which should have been spent in educating, to be wasted in quarrelling about education. If the government would make up its minds

> to *require* for every child a good education, it might save itself the trouble of *providing* one. It might leave to parents to obtain the education where and how they pleased, and content itself with helping to pay the school fees of the poorer class of children, and defraying the entire school expenses of those who have no one else to pay for them (Mill, 1989[1859], p. 106).

Here Mill introduces the distinction between the public financing of education and its management, which can instead be both public and private, a distinction which would subsequently become a core contention of liberal ideology (Friedman, 1962). Accordingly, the state makes economic resources available to families, above all needy ones, and then leaves space for free competition to take place among schools. This idea of Mill's recalls Smith's proposal that schools should be wholly or partly financed with the fees paid by families. But, unlike the latter, the reasoning is not economic but philosophical. Mill is worried that public education may annul individual liberty and favour despotism. He then postpones fulfilment of this principle of the liberty of educational choice to a future in which society has moved beyond the current phase of economic backwardness and can therefore have 'a sufficient number of persons qualified to provide education under government auspices' (Mill, 1989[1859], p. 106).

Mill thus went beyond, and completed, Smith's analysis of education. The education market is a particular kind of market in which demand is, as a rule, socially insufficient, not only because of the presence of general benefits for society, but also because of the existence of additional costs which reduce the intensity of transactions. Since the damage deriving to society from a low level of schooling would be severe, Mill also opted for abandonment of the *laissez-faire* principle and for legitimation of direct intervention by the state. The possibility alluded to of a direct contribution to families to help them meet the costs of their children's education, leaving them free to choose among schools, had no practical outcome either in the 1800s or in the next century.

2.6. NASSAU SENIOR AND THE REPORT ON POPULAR EDUCATION (1861)

Of all the classical economists, Nassau Senior probably showed the greatest interest in the details of education reform. The significance of Senior's view on education was enhanced because he represented a type which became more common after his time: that of the economist who takes an important advisory part in the affairs of the government (Bowley, 1967). Among other government services, he was probably more responsible than many others for the Reform of the Poor Law in 1834. He was co-author of the Report of the

Royal Commission on Education, 1857–61. Because of his rather extensive service in the government, much of what he has to say about education appears more empirically grounded than the arguments of other economists of his time.

The contribution of Nassau W. Senior to the economics of education is not contained in *An Outline of the Science of Political Economy* (1838), which in fact makes no mention of this topic, but mainly in his *Suggestions on Popular Education* (1861), which sets out the findings of the Royal Commission on Popular Education created in 1858 to examine the condition of elementary education in England. Although the work of the Commission did not yield any innovative theoretical insights, it nevertheless provided an accurate description of the education of the popular classes and made recommendations for educational policies that were subsequently taken up in the 1870 Educational Act.

The report provided a detailed account of the situation of basic schooling in Great Britain. It showed that the process of elementary schooling was by now complete, with 95 per cent of children attending some kind of school. Moreover, this process, contrary to what happened in the other European countries, was mainly driven by the growth of private schools, which had been considerable in recent decades. The report also highlighted the state's greater financial commitment. The annual state contribution to education introduced in 1833 had increased exponentially from £20,000 in the first year to £666,435 in 1858. For our purposes here it is sufficient to conduct a brief examination of the suggestions to improve the state of primary education in England set out at the beginning of the report. The principal points are the following:

Resolutions proposed on the 9th of February

1. That the object of society is to protect individuals from wrong.
2. That those who cannot protect themselves are as much entitled to protection as adults.
3. That children are as much entitled to protection as adults.
4. The education is as much necessary to a child as food is.
5. That it is as much the duty of a parent to educate his child, as it is to feed it
6. That a child is as much wronged by being left uneducated, as it is being left unfed.
7. That it is as much the duty of the community to see that the child is educated as it is to see that it is fed.
8. That unless the community can and will compel the parent to feed the child, or to educate the child, the community must do so.
9. That the elementary education of a child costs no less than 30s a year.
10. That there is no reason to believe that now, or at any time that can be defined, that sum is or will be obtainable from the parent.

11. That it is the duty of the State to aid private benevolence in supplying the sum that is not obtainable from the parent.
12. That we ought to recommend a system of State assistance for that purpose.

(Senior, 1861, p. 1)

It is evident from these recommendations that the Commission adopted J.S. Mill's paternalistic position that the state had the duty to protect individuals against wrong choices. In this perspective, education was a fundamental good for children which must be provided in the first place by their parents. Only if families were negligent did the obligation revert to the state. The points on which Senior concentrates in his comment are mainly 10) and 12). Senior argued, especially against those who wanted to reduce the state's already modest contribution to elementary education, that in the current situation no worker family was able to afford the costs of education. This was due not only to the presence of direct expenses but also, and especially, to the opportunity cost represented by the forgone wage. If the state eliminated the public contribution, the consequences would be extremely serious, in both economic and social terms.

> The Report may then give an outline of the probable results of the withdrawal of Government interference: the desertion of the training colleges, the cessation of the supply of trained masters and mistresses, the closing of a large portion of the existing schools, the absence of view ones, and the general deterioration, moral and intellectual, of the laboring population (Senior, 1861, p. 6).

Both for Mill and for Senior, this public contribution should not be definitive. Rather, it should be provisional until the economic conditions of workers had improved to such an extent that they could meet their education expenses themselves. But until that time – which for Senior was still rather remote – intervention by the state was necessary, in regard not only to access to education but also to its quality. The report is also harshly critical of the quality of the education provided by private schools. The following extract is eloquent:

> Among the results of our inquiry, I know no one proved by such satisfactory, such over flowing evidence as the inferiority of private to public schools. The atmosphere of the private schools is described by our assistant Commissioners as pestilential, the discipline as inefficient, the instructor as still more so, and the masters and mistresses as persons who, having failed in other trades, have taken up this, without learning or experience. Yet to these dens of ignorance and malaria one-third of the labouring classes still send their children, and that although good and cheap public schools are at their doors (Senior, 1861, p. 29).

Hence, besides theoretical arguments, it was actual experience which, according to Senior, required the state's substantial intervention in compulsory elementary education, both to provide the poor with some form of education and to guarantee its quality, which otherwise was unsatisfactory. Also for Senior direct management by the state could be considered an intermediary phase which would not always be necessary. In his Utopia, a condition in which all citizens could enjoy the advantages of the middle class, management might not be necessary. Nevertheless it was clear that this day was still distant and intervention by the state was necessary for the time being (Senior, 1861).

2.7. THE QUESTION OF EDUCATION FINANCING IN THE MARSHALLIAN ERA

The theme of education was almost entirely neglected by the first generation of the neoclassical economists. For example, Wicksteed (1910) and Taussig (1918) dealt only marginally with education, briefly mentioning it in regard to the determination of wages and the functioning of the labour market. Pareto, despite devoting much of his *Manuale* (1906) to analysis of demographic factors, entirely neglected education, as did Walras. The only exceptions were Sidgwick, but above all Marshall, who conducted detailed analysis of these matters, drawing on the classical tradition but also making meaningful innovations, in chapter VI of Book IV of *Principles* (1964[1890]), devoted to industrial training.

The link with the Millian tradition is very strong in Sidgwick, who sought in his *Principles of Political Economy* (1883) to re-establish, but with scant success, Mill's economic theory. Not surprisingly, therefore, education as an economic good is examined in a long final part of the book devoted to cases in which government interference in economic activity can be justified. Sidgwick resumes Mill's arguments on the need for state intervention to guarantee a minimum of compulsory schooling, with the purpose of ensuring that underestimation of the value of education by parents, or their economic difficulties, do not give rise to too low a demand for education.

> The community derives an economic gain from the education of its young members – so far as they are thereby rendered more efficient labourers – which the self-interest of private employers cannot be relied upon to provide, owing to the difficulty of appropriating the advantage of the increased efficiency. Hence a national provision for education may to some extent be considered and justified as a measure for improving national production (Sidgwick, 1883, p. 464).

For Sidgwick the *laissez-faire* principle had shortcomings not only in regard to elementary education, but also in the equally important case of technical and vocational training. Although 'the community may gain an adequate return for its expenditure in the greater abundance and better quality of the skilled labor so provided' (Sidgwick, 1883, p. 465), these benefits for society may be lost because workers cannot correctly evaluate the advantages deriving from greater specialization. Therefore, Sidgwick not only reiterated Mill's theory of bounded rationality but extended it well beyond elementary schooling in order to respond to the new exigencies of the productive system. The Smithian age when an apprenticeship was enough to learn a trade had come to an end, and only formal instruction provided by the education system could guarantee possession of the necessary professional skills.

Marshall addressed the theme of education by introducing a number of significant innovations, although he still firmly adhered to the classical tradition. He dealt with such matters in the section of the *Principles* devoted to industrial training, hence vocational training in the strict sense. Education at the end of the nineteenth century was no longer a generic instrument for the moral elevation of the working class. Rather, it crucially determined the extent to which science and technique could become decisive production forces. Discoveries and inventions presupposed an activity devoted to this purpose, and therefore a solid apparatus which guaranteed the accumulation and diffusion of scientific knowledge. Education thus became a factor of prime importance in order to improve labour productivity.

After examining the forces that regulate demographic trends, and therefore the quantitative aspect, Marshall turned to the qualitative aspect, which concerned the forms of knowledge that increase the worker's productivity. He distinguished between a general ability tied to the environment and elementary education, and a specific ability that must be acquired with technical training. A general education was important because:

> a good education confers great indirect benefits even on the ordinary workman. It stimulates his mental activity; it fosters in him a habit of wise inquisitiveness; it makes him more intelligent, more ready, more trustworthy in his ordinary work; it raises the tone of his life in working hours and out of working hours; it is thus an important means towards the production of material wealth (Marshall, 1964[1890], p. 176).

One recognizes in this passage the typical Smithian argument to the effect that education leads to the moral improvement of individuals. But Marshall also highlights a second aspect which characterizes modern education systems: that they are powerful instruments of social mobility.

> We must however look in another direction for a part, perhaps the greater part, of the immediate economic gain which the nation can derive from an improvement in the general technical education of the mass of the people. We must look not so much at those who stay in the rank and file of the working classes, as at those who rise from a humble birth to join the higher ranks of skilled artisans, to become foremen or employers, to advance the boundaries of science, or possibly to add to

> the national wealth in art and literature. [...]. There is no extravagance more prejudicial to the growth of national wealth than that wasteful negligence which allows genius that happens to be born of lowly parentage to expend itself in lowly work. No change would conduce so much to a rapid increase of material wealth as an improvement in our schools (Marshall, 1964[1890], p. 176).

It is evident from this passage that Marshall recasts Smith's argument on the social advantages of education by adapting it to the new context at the turn of the century. Social stability, a theme of close concern to the classical tradition, is no longer guaranteed generically by the fact that schooling makes people more cultured, but by the specific circumstance that it allows any person, whatever their social origin, to improve their position in the social hierarchy. In the new economic system created by industrial capitalism, everyone is able to achieve higher positions regardless of their initial situation. This function of constantly rearranging the social structure, not on the basis of inherited opportunities but of individual talent, is one of the fundamental tasks assigned to the educational system. Marshall does not treat this just as a matter of social equity, although it is a theme present in his discussion, but rather of economic efficiency: education systems are important because it is their task to bring out talents and potential intellectual resources. And it is for this reason that Marshall considers education to be a national investment.

> We may then conclude that the wisdom of expending public and private funds on education is not to be measured by its direct fruits alone. It will be profitable as a mere investment, to give the masses of the people much greater opportunities than they can generally avail themselves of. And the economic value of one great industrial genius is sufficient to cover the expenses of the education of the whole town (Marshall, 1964[1890], p. 179).

That said, the question of how education should be financed is still unanswered. On this point, Marshall was an advocate of greater state aid to education mainly for the purposes of providing opportunities for those born into the working classes. He points out that 'there are few practical problems in which the economist has a more direct interest than those relating to the principles on which the expense of the education of children should be divided between the State and the parents' (Marshall, 1964[1890], p. 180). He then recalls Mill's observation that parents, especially those of the popular classes, are liable to underestimate the advantages of education for their children, considering them remote in time. Marshall notes:

> Most parents are willing enough to do for their children what their own parents did for them; and perhaps even to go a little beyond it if they find themselves among neighbours who happen to have a rather higher standard. But to do more than this requires, in addition to the moral qualities of unselfishness and a warmth of affection that are perhaps not rare, a certain habit of mind which is as yet not very

> common. It requires the habit of distinctly realizing the future, of regarding a distant event as of nearly the same importance as if it were close at hand; this habit is at once a chief product and a chief cause of civilization, and is seldom fully developed except among the middle and upper classes of the more cultivated nations (Marshall, 1964[1890], p. 217).

Going beyond concerns with economic efficiency and welfare, Marshall, like Mill before him, saw in education a means to achieve other goals of equal importance. Like Mill, he believed that the inequalities of wealth were a serious flaw in our economic organization. In education he found a basis for optimism in the evolution of society. In Marshall's account, education raised labour productivity and the national dividend out of which higher wages are paid. The process was cumulative in that higher wages led to increased investment in personal capital, which raised productivity levels and the wages of the next generations of workers. State support of education would facilitate the process.

Summarizing, Marshall pursued the classical line by reiterating the social advantages of education and adding some new considerations. Intervention by the state in education is necessary not only to correct market distortions, as in Smith and Mill; Marshall goes further by considering education as a necessary form of national investment. By guaranteeing high social mobility through the educational system, the state reduces social inequalities and promotes economic development because 'all that is spent during many years in opening the means of higher education to the masses would be well paid for if it called out one more Newton or Darwin, Shakespeare or Beethoven' (Marshall, [1890] (1964), p. 180). Other authors who touched on this theme, albeit marginally, in the Marshallian period were Pigou (1920) and Dalton (1925). The former, stressed that, for society, investment in education could be much greater than investment in physical capital, and this could justify the provision of free and universal primary education. Dalton, a pupil of Pigou's, emphasized that education, by generating greater social mobility, could lead to the more efficient use of resources.

2.8. CONCLUDING REMARKS

It can be seen from this brief excursion into the early literature that the classical economists provided, between them, a most comprehensive treatment of the economics of education. To various extents, they were preoccupied by the fact that investment in education might be socially inefficient, that is, too low to maintain the conditions for economic progress. This could happen both for objective reasons, the social positive externalities of education, and for subjective ones, the bounded rationality and short-sightedness of economic agents. State intervention was therefore necessary to correct the limits of market mechanisms. Smith's initial proposal that education should be financed with contributions by families was not taken up: indeed, from McCulloch to Marshall there were ever more reasons to support the public financing, and also the public management, of education – at least at the primary level. McCulloch, Mill and Senior denied the relevance of the principle of choice in the field of compulsory education. Although Mill did in the end come down in favour of private schooling, he did not do so because of the efficiency argument, but rather because he was afraid that the state would abuse its monopoly of education. Marshall, for his part, resumed and strengthened Mill's argument that direct intervention in education was necessary because of the ignorance of parents, applying it to the new economic context in which education, especially of a techno-scientific nature, was becoming a production factor of primary importance.

NOTES

1. The term 'classical economists' has been used here as a broad classification for pre-Keynesian economists.
2. By the late medieval period in Britain there were many schools teaching Latin grammar. In England the Tudor King Edward VI reorganized these schools or instituted new ones so that there was a national system of 'free grammar schools' that were in theory open to all and offered free tuition to those who could not afford to pay fees.

REFERENCES

Blaug, M. (1975), 'The Economics of Education in English Classical Political Economy: A Re-Examination', in A. Skinner and T. Wilson (eds), *Essays on A. Smith*, Oxford: Clarendon Press, pp. 568–99.

Bowley, M. (1967), *Nassau Senior and Classical Economics*, London: Allen & Unwin.

Bowman, R.S. (1990), 'Smith, Mill, and Marshall on Human Capital Formation', *History of Political Economy*, **22**(2), 239–59.

Dalton, H. (1925), *Some Aspects of the Inequality of Income in Modern Communities*, London: Routledge.

Dogliani, P. (2003), *L'Europa a scuola*, Rome: Carocci.

Freeman, R.D. (1969), 'Adam Smith, Education and Lassez-Faire', *History of Political Economy*, **1**(1), 173-86.

Friedman, M. (1962), *Capitalism and Freedom*, Chicago: Chicago University Press.

Green, A. (1990), *Education and State Formation*, New York. St. Martin's Press.

Hollander, S. (1985), *The Economics of J. S. Mill*, Oxford: Basil Blackwell.

Malthus, T.R. (1986[1826]), *An Essay on the Principle of Population*, London: William Pickering.

Marshall, A. (1964[1890]), *Principles of Economics*, London: Macmillan.

McCulloch, T.R. (1965[1849]). *The Principles of Political Economy*, New York: August M. Kelley.

Mill, J.S. (1965[1848]), *Principles of Political Economy*, London: Routledge & Kegan Paul.

Mill, J.S. (1989[1859]), *On Liberty*, S. Collini (ed.), Cambridge: Cambridge University Press.

Miller, W.L. (1966), 'The Economics of Education in English Classical Economics', *Southern Economic Journal*, **32**(1), 294–309.

O'Brien, D.P. (1970), *J.R. McCulloch. A Study in Classical Economics*, London: George Allen & Unwin.

Pareto, V. (1906), *Manuale di Economia Politica*, Milan: Soc. Ed. Libreria.

Pigou, A.C. (1920), *The Economics of Welfare*, London: Macmillan.

Senior, N. (1838), *An Outline of the Science of Political Economy*, London: W. Clowes and Sons.

Senior, N. (1861), *Suggestions on Popular Education*, London: John Murray.

Sidgwick, H. (1883), *The Principles of Political Economy*, London: Macmillan.

Smith, A. (1952[1776]), *An Inquiry into the Nature and Causes of the Wealth of Nations*, Chicago: Encyclopaedia Britannica Inc..

Stephens, W.B. (1998), *Education in Britain 1750–1914*, London: Macmillan.

Taussig, F.W. (1918), *Principles of Economics*, New York: Macmillan.

Tu, Pierre N.V. (1969), 'The Classical Economists and Education', *Kyklos*, **22**(4), 691–717.

Viner, J. (1927), 'A. Smith and Lassez Faire', *Journal of Political Economy*, **35**(2), 192–232.

West, E.G. (1964), 'Private versus Public Education: a Classical Economic Dispute', *Journal of Political Economy*, **72**(5), 465–75.

West, E.G. (1970), 'Resource Allocation and Growth in Early Nineteenth-Century British Education', *The Economic History Review*, **23**(1), 68–95.

West, E.G. (1978), 'Literacy and Industrial Revolution', *The Economic History Review*, **31**(3), 369–83.

Wicksteed, P.H. (1910), *The Common Sense of Political Economy*, London: Routledge.

3. The role of the public sector in the thought of Hyman Minsky

Giuseppe Mastromatteo

3.1. INTRODUCTION

In considering the role of the public sector in the economy and society, economic theories have proposed a number of interpretations rooted in divergent and alternative approaches. In particular, Keynesian and post-Keynesian theories have emphasized the decisive function of public sector intervention, although such theories have been compelled to assess the non-trivial problem of the institutional, financial and opportunity constraints involved.

Among economists, Minsky was one of the scholars who most successfully provided insight into the role and limits of the State. Yet despite the relevance of his analysis of the public sector, his thought has been largely neglected and the Minskian contribution has mainly been seen as linked to the operation of the private sector, with focus on analysis of the macroeconomic effects of investment decisions.[1] Only recently have some important studies begun to reflect on specific aspects of Minsky's position, such as fiscal policy as a tool of macroeconomic intervention (Arestis and De Antoni, 2007), the financial fragility of the State and the issue of open economies integrated at the international level (Wray, 2006, 2007a), employment policy and the war on poverty as a means to achieve a fair society (Bell and Wray, 2004; Wray, 2007b).

The aim of this chapter is to offer an interpretation of the role of the public sector in Minsky's works. Starting from an attempt to identify a unifying analytical element in his treatment, attention is drawn to the originality of his thought on this subject, which distinguishes him both from the literature most widely accepted today (see Barro and Sala-i-Martin, 1995), and also from the tradition of post-Keynesian thought that shows the greatest affinity with his approach.

The unifying element is found to reside in Minsky's analytical method, which describes individual and collective decisions as influenced by the cash flow problems the economic units find themselves facing. This analytical method, introduced at first for private sector decisions, is then extended to public sector decisions. The method makes it clear that interventions in this sector generate real effects describable as complex, that is to say, mediated through financial effects which influence the budgets of the individual economic units by modifying surpluses and cash deficits, and which also influence portfolio choices by the issue of old and new financial tools designed to meet public administration liquidity requirements. These effects, whose repercussions have a bearing on the overall trends of the economy and society and on the potential for income growth and stabilization, were particularly noticeable and effective in the decades immediately following the 1929 crisis, which witnessed an increase in size of the public sector.

In Minsky's view, the presence of the public sector has an impact on the stability of financial institutions, in various ways. This may come about through the creation of the second line reserves that financial institutions utilize to increase their liquidity, or by acting on the composition of financial organizations. In the latter case, such action may take the form of modification in the tools available to such organizations, or it may result from the formation of markets that tend to adapt to the needs of such a large operator as the public administration. Minsky places particular emphasis on the peculiar position of the public sector in these markets, which allows stabilization of the debt/GDP ratio towards positive values. He even goes as far as to argue for the possibility of an enduring speculative position on the part of the State, although he never loses sight of the importance of having a public sector with a solid and solvent financial position.

In this context, it is interesting to note that the Minskian perspective bears certain characteristics that distinguish it from the Neoclassical approach.[2] His analysis does not imply balancing the State budget. However, he does not fail to address the need to guarantee conditions of financial sustainability, asserting the importance of future budget surpluses as a guarantee of the credibility of the institutions governing public finance.

Minsky's method enables him to obtain a periodization of the modern history of the USA economy and of the role ascribable to the public sector in the different eras.

Finally, the same analytical method allows Minsky to justify some economic and social policy options he proposes for the most recent period of the economic history of the USA, namely the period of global financial integration. Minsky's favourable assessment of policies beneficial to the lower income bands and to social consumption is linked not only to the enhanced possibility of economic growth and stabilization associated with such policies, by virtue of the cash flow stabilization of the economic units, but also to the need to achieve fairer and more satisfactory social living conditions.

This chapter is organized as follows. The second section dwells on the evolution of Minsky's thought on the public sector, leading up to his analysis of Big Government, which also indicates the limits of State intervention with regard to assuring stability and growth. In the third section, a link is forged between an understanding of the historical and institutional aspects of changes in the public sector and the balance/imbalance of the financial positions of the major economic subjects (households, firms, public administration), highlighting the related effects on production (formation and growth of profit, composition of financial demand) and finance. The fourth section focuses on the policies viewed as most suited to consolidating the perspective of lasting growth and a fair society. Such a perspective, in Minsky's eyes, is best guaranteed by reinforcement of the financial coverage of the economic units through stable full employment and balanced income distribution. The conclusions underline the points of major interest and the limits of an 'open' theoretical construct, as conceived by Minsky, in offering interpretations and indications of use to the most recent evolution of contemporary economics in the developed countries.

3.2. THE CASH FLOW METHOD APPLIED TO THE STATE IN THE EVOLUTION OF MINSKY'S THOUGHT

3.2.1. Fundamental Evolutionary Stages of Minskian Thought

As early as the draft of his doctoral dissertation (see Minsky, [1954]2004), one of the key aspects of the American economist's inquiry concerned the analysis of the financial positions of individual units. This method, introduced in order to analyze private sector decisions, was then extended to public sector choices and their effects.

Despite the fact that throughout the 1960s and '70s Minsky's inquiry directed attention to the public sector, a complete systematic account of his method of analysis with regard to study of this sector did not come until the collection *Can 'It' Happen Again?* dating from 1982 and the publication of *Stabilizing an Unstable Economy* in 1986. The temporal gap between his application of the method to the private economy in the 1960s and its full-blown application to the State in the 1980s can be attributed to the author's intellectual itinerary, his decisions concerning in-depth analytical analysis being influenced by the importance he ascribed to the predominant policy problems.

His research interests developed in the following manner. During the first phase of his academic career, Minsky shared the line of thought proposed by Lerner (see Wray, 2007a, p. 4). Analyzing the Minskian manuscripts drafted in the early 1960s (Adelman and Minsky, 1960), it can be noted that the author perceived no problems whatsoever for the sustainability of the public debt issued in sovereign currency and for the chronic fiscal problems of the main OECD economies. In a closed economy, state debt represented net financial wealth for the private sector, and a significant percentage of public debt in private portfolios contributed to rendering their assets and liabilities more secure. He therefore argued that such a situation normally stimulated expenditure by the private sector, and in an economy enjoying stable growth, as in the case of the United States in the 1960s, the public deficit made it possible to maintain full employment.[3] However, it was underlined as early as 1963, in a work reprinted in *Can 'It' Happen Again?* (see Minsky, [1963a]1982, pp. 31–3), that the positive evolution of the positions of the individual economic units (households and firms) in critical macroeconomic contexts could be explained by the increased weight of public intervention, highlighting the less dramatic consequences of the 1962 financial crisis as compared to that of 1929. The problems of financial instability of the private sector in contrast to the positive effects of public intervention were addressed in Minsky (1963b), where he argued that an expansion guided by private investment tended to increase indebtedness and financial fragility, while development sustained by public investment could reinforce macroeconomic stability with the supply of more secure assets (government bonds issued to address the deficit).

An essay published in 1964 (see Minsky, 1964) likewise contained the germs of ideas later treated more systematically in *Can 'It' Happen Again?* (Minsky, 1982b), suggesting that analysis both of the cash flows of individual operators and also of the evolution of their complex debts and credits system was crucial for his interpretation of the stability and growth of the economic system.

Between the mid 1960s and the first half of the 1970s, his attention concerning the debate on the relation between the private economy and the public system was absorbed by the question of growth stabilization in conditions approaching full employment (see Minsky, 1968). This phase of Minsky's thought culminated in his alternative interpretation of Keynes (Minsky, 1975a) and of the events resulting from the economic strategy of the Kennedy–Johnson era that was based on high investment, elevated profits and massive military expenditure.

During this phase Minsky gained a clear awareness of the 'pluses' and 'minuses' of the public policies enacted at that time. Since the Great Depression of 1929, the function of anticyclical stabilization had traditionally been given concrete form through policies of Big Government, by means of the public deficit and debt creation. Big Government had gained strength and become consolidated over time, especially during the late postwar period, and Minsky realized that the policy of expansion of public expenditure had revived global demand and had prevented the recurrence of profound depressions, but without devising a solution to the intrinsic instability of the economic system. This policy would inevitably lead to inflation and continual threats of financial crises unless adequate controls over the mechanisms of investment financing were set up and unless a policy of high consumption and low private investment were assured (see Minsky, 1975a, p. 167).

From the mid 1970s onwards, the perspective of Minsky's theoretical analysis underwent a significant change. This was a period marked by the important transition consisting of abandonment of the *dollar-exchange standard* and the *Bretton Woods System*, as well as by the changes, in the contemporary open economies, deriving from the fluctuations in the exchange systems among the main currencies, where the notion of limits on government budgets increasingly constituted a constraint that had to be respected. Such changes rendered the position of the State more fragile, leading to the need for more careful assessment of the position of the public sector on the financial markets. With growing concern, Minsky pointed out the risk, especially in a flexible exchange system, arising from the phenomenon whereby

> the structure of the balance of payments of the banking center of the Bretton Woods system, the United States, became that of an impoverished economy...; with this impoverishment, demand liabilities denominated in dollars lost some of their attractiveness (Minsky, 1979, p. 103).

And, specifying that 'standard economic theory (which is used by the advisers to U.S. policymakers) ignores the financial aspect of their economies' (Minsky, 1979, p. 104), he pointed out that

> the technique of managing the net foreign acquisition of international money by influencing private investment abroad requires that the basic balance – the sum of Tier I (current imports and exports of goods and services, including remittances and other invisibles) and Tier II (receipts and expenditures due to income from capital assets owned abroad) be in surplus (Minsky, 1979, p. 117; on his definitions of Tier 1 and Tier 2, p. 111).[4]

Consequently,

> for the international banks that acquired dollar-denominated assets as they emitted dollar-denominated liabilities, a run on the dollar means that they cannot sell new dollar liabilities as such liabilities mature (Minsky, 1979, pp. 117–18).

Therefore, even an economy 'whose currency is functioning as a key or reserve currency in international monetary relations' (Minsky, 1979, p. 119), like the USA, would be strongly influenced by the deficitary international financial position (at least on the level of the above mentioned basic balance), with the risk of seriously compromising even the position of 'loan seekers', *in primis* the State, as the latter would be obliged to refinance its loans under more stringent conditions and would face a weakening of its stabilizing capacity in the presence of recessive trends.

During the 1980s, after considering the impact of *supply side economics* based on tax cuts and an increase in military expenditure, Minsky turned his attention to the problems of the financial sustainability of the State. He thus gave a more complete picture of his hypothesis of financial instability in *Can 'It' Happen Again?*[5] (Minsky, 1982b) and put forward his own sharp criticism of *Big Government* in *Stabilizing an Unstable Economy* (Minsky, 1986). These works are among Minsky's fundamental theoretical contributions, in which he emphasizes the need to build up a 'robust' system of institutions and policy measures to counter the endogenous instability of the system, containing the effects resulting from the propagation of financial collapses, with their aftermath of recessive and deflationary pressures, while at the same time avoiding the introduction of measures that could engender a process of chronic inflation.

3.2.2. The Role of the Public Sector in the Financial Instability Hypothesis

Minsky is best known for his *Financial Instability Hypothesis*, which implies an indissoluble relation between the real and the financial dimension of modern capitalist systems. He endorses the idea that the existence of uncertainty, which leads to an intrinsic instability of expectations, lies at the root of cyclical fluctuations, also highlighting the evolutionary nature, dependent on the historical background, of all institutions.

In the introduction to *Can 'It' Happen Again?* (Minsky, 1982b) and in chapters V, VI and X,[6] Minsky integrates into his framework the crucial but not necessarily positive role (inasmuch as it is potentially destabilizing) of the State. In this analysis, as is known, examination of cash flows resulting from the relation between credits and debits can place each economic unit in a 'covered' financial position, i.e. with an expectation of revenue greater than payment commitments at all periods of future time, or else in a 'speculative' financial position, i.e. having periods of time – generally of short duration – in which payment commitments exceed revenue, or finally, in an 'ultraspeculative' (or Ponzi) position when the expectation is that in many future periods debt servicing will exceed the net revenue of the economic unit and it will therefore be necessary to embark on new debts and/or proceed to selling assets.

By virtue of the relation between contractual commitments of liability payments and incoming flows, households, firms and public sector units may be positioned in any of the three financial positions described (Minsky, 1982b, pp. 22–23). Transition from one to another of such positions affects the evolution of credit relations as well as financial structures, thus influencing the dynamics of the entire economic system.

The fragility of the economic system, which is defined by the likelihood of a sudden inversion of the economic cycle due to a pessimistically oriented revision of previously positive, if not even euphoric, expectations, and also by the severity of the effects triggered by such an inversion, depends on the relative presence of speculative and/or ultraspeculative positions, as compared to covered positions. The greater the relative weight of units operating in a 'speculative' or 'ultraspeculative' position, the greater the fragility of the system, i.e. the higher the risk of instability.

In the Minskian interpretation, the State is by its very nature in a non-covered financial position, but its management of this position must be directed towards assuring the financial conditions necessary in order to continue to be a protagonist, both in supporting private capital in an anticyclical function, and also in adopting measures that will be of aid not only on the social level but also for employment.

Minsky's approach makes it clear that the role of public intervention is eminently dynamic, in the sense that its action is essential for containment of the instability and fragility that springs from a growth process pulled by the evolution of investments. The latter, in turn, are rooted in the complex interaction between expectations and pressure of financial constraints, i.e. in the relation between the expectation of profit and the situation of liquidity (Minsky, 1986, p. 197). Additionally, his approach sheds light on the mechanisms that determine the financial position of the public sector and the problems that limit its potential for intervention and effectiveness.

The Minskian causal chain starts out from an increase in investments which, according to the author, increases national income and profit.

The analysis of the cyclical trend begins conventionally from the end of a recession that can be seen from a twofold perspective. On the one hand, the recession has led the system to experience a contraction of production, with the ensuing increase in unemployment and in unused production capacity, drop in incomes, expenditure and savings; on the other, it has implied a decrease in fragility (and thus, basically, a stabilization of expectations),[7] due to the failure and consequent general disappearance of ultraspeculative and speculative units. In this context, an increase in potential demand translates into an increase in effective demand, without producing inflationary tensions: thus expectations are fulfilled and may even be surpassed by the results. This sparks a general orientation towards an upwards revision of expectations on future returns and profits; furthermore, financial institutions' perception of the risk of failure is lowered, with the effect of decreasing the spread applied as a means of allowing for financial risk. The profits achieved make it possible to increase the resources available to firms and thus drive new investments that are planned on the basis of a yield – and, obviously, risk – profile either in line with the past or more probably increasing. The combination of a more optimistic assessment of future expected margins and a common attenuated perception of risk, likewise due to upwards revision of expectations, leads to increased debt levels and promotes financial investments that are less liquid, thereby provoking the reappearance of speculative or ultra-speculative positions.

In this perspective the link between effective demand and profitability takes on a crucial role. Here Minsky adopts Kalecki's approach:

> Profits are not the result of the technical productivity of capital but are due to the types and sources of financed demand.
> The great insight into the determination of profits in our economy that is associated with Kalecki- is that profits arise out of the impact of the accumulation process on prices (Minsky, 1982b, *Introduction,* p. xix).

Minsky follows Kalecki's approach and argues that *the public sector demand for goods and services* (Minsky, 1986, pp.144–70) *plays a positive role in determining profit levels.* Once again, Minsky's treatment does not overlook an evaluation of the historical-institutional context:

> Whereas in the small government economy of the 1920s profits were well nigh exclusively dependent on the pace of investment, the increase in direct and indirect state employment along with the explosion of transfer payments since World War II means that the dependence of profits on investment has been greatly reduced. With the rise of big government, the reaction of tax receipts and transfer payments to income changes implies that any decline in income will lead to an explosion of the government deficit. Since it can be shown that profits are equal to investment plus the government's deficit, profit flows are sustained whenever a fall in investment leads to a rise in the government's deficit. A cumulative debt deflation process that depends on a fall of profits for its realization is quickly halted when government is so big that the deficit explodes when income falls (Minsky, 1982b, *Introduction*, pp. xix–xx).

Therefore, in Minsky's approach an analysis of the evolution of the financial positions of the individual economic units cannot be divorced from examination of 'any given regime of financial institutions and government interventions' (Minsky, 1982b, p. 22), especially given the existence of a public sector the impact and extent of which has a profound influence over the organization of the financial markets and the tools utilized in such markets. On the other hand, even in the presence of public intervention 'the performance of the economy depends upon the satisfaction of financial as well as income production criteria' (Minsky, 1982b, p. 22), which implies that the financial dimension is not only affected by the State, but also acts upon the latter. An alternative account of the causal chain in Minsky's theory can be put forward in the following manner: the long-term growth rate is determined by sales and profits, whose fluctuations are in turn linked to oscillations in investments which, together with public expenditure, determine income level, income and wealth distribution, and the evolution of the economy. By interacting with investment decisions and influencing government spending policies, credit and finance become the drivers of development. The propulsive thrust of the economy derives from expectations concerning profits, which translate into concrete investment projects. Should the propulsive thrust show signs of slowing down, a tool is available in the form of monetary policy (Minsky, 1986, pp. 303–4), which influences the income and employment trend by acting both on the value of assets and also on the financial aspects (solvency of firms, households and financial institutions). However, the effectiveness of monetary policy is limited, in that if current and expected profits are contained, monetary policy cannot stimulate investments, unlike fiscal policy, which directly sustains the level of demand, incomes and profits. Refinancing through action by the lender of last resort becomes effective only if it is combined with the stabilizing effect on profit exerted by public sector deficits.

Finally, the public sector's financing needs end up influencing the tools and organization of the financial markets, generating a new operative context that has to be taken into account by any economic unit facing major decisions. It follows that public intervention affects the trend of the economy, partly because policy measures sustain demand, for example by redistributing income in favour of less well-off classes, and also because they transform the financial structure. However, while the effect of the public deficit on income, which operates through the demand for goods and services, has been analyzed in the literature, the financial effects pointed out by Minsky (1986, pp. 26–33) have often been neglected. These effects are felt in terms of their influence – through the generation of surpluses and cash deficits – on the budgets of the individual economic units; in addition, they affect not only individual portfolio decisions but also the financial organizations, which depend on the issue of old and new tools to satisfy public sector requirements.

Examining the case of the 1975 recession in the USA, Minsky (1986, p. 35) points out that public deficit financing took place through the purchase of debt securities by the financial institutions, but the deficit was offset by the liabilities of these institutions in terms of savings deposits and other technical forms in the field of householders' insurance and retirement savings. It is thus clearly underlined that in the United States, in recessive contexts, the substantial purchase of public debt securities by banks and finance institutions allowed the creation of second line reserves that enabled such organizations to reduce their risk exposure towards the private economy and to improve the financial structure of their budget, with the result that

> the huge acquisition of government debt by commercial banks and other financial organizations thus financed the government debt, and in the process, the balance sheets of acquiring organizations were markedly changed. Government debt is free of default risk: whatever the government debt contract says will be forthcoming will, in fact, be forthcoming (Minsky, 1986, p. 35).

The dimension of debt also affects the evolution of financial markets, which become more liquid and more extensive, tending to adapt to the needs of a large operator like the public.

Minsky argued that the State is certainly in a better position than other units to issue debt on account of the existence in the markets of a hierarchy (or a pyramid of operators) with different revenue and financial disbursement potential or tools. In the case of the public sector, the reliability and credibility of the institutions that manage economic policy guarantees the sustainability of the debt: 'government debt is marketable, and its marketability is ultimately guaranteed by the Federal Reserve System' (Minsky, 1986, p. 35). Furthermore, the public sector can reschedule its debt repayments, if necessary adapting the repayment structure to the private sector's need to invest in low-risk long-term activities. In this regard, Minsky observes that the public debt also fulfils the function of financial stabilizer – a 'storehouse of financial power', as it were – to which resources with a predefined yield can be destined, temporarily if so desired, while awaiting the rise of scenarios more favourable to private investment (Minsky, 1986, p. 37).

The stabilization effects of Big Government during recessive phases, due to the fact that financial institutions and private concerns can acquire safe assets through the purchase of public debt securities, is linked to an improvement in the liquidity of financial portfolios (Minsky, 1986, pp. 36–7), even though aggregate income and employment are declining.

In Minsky's eyes, the effects whereby profits, portfolios and financial organizations are stabilized represent crucial results of the formation of Big Government, yet this has also generated the premises for new forms of instability of the economic system. In *Stabilizing an Unstable Economy,* Minsky explains why the US economy was more unstable in the 1970s and 1980s than had been the case in the previous thirty-year period, and why this instability nevertheless did not lead to a depression analogous to that of 1929.

The reasons, according to Minsky, are to be found in the synergic role of Big Government and the Federal Reserve System. Analysis of the 1975 and 1982 crises and of the difficulties that arose, albeit to a lesser extent, in 1966, 1970 and 1979 clearly shows the positive impact of coordination between the action of fiscal support by Big Government and that of prompt intervention assured by the lender-of-last-resort (or guarantor of the solvency of monetary and financial markets) for prevention of depressions and to buttress stabilization.

> Big Government stabilizes not only employment and income but also business cash flows (profits) and as a result asset values; the Federal Reserve System, in cooperation with other government agencies and private financial institutions, acts as a lender of last resort. It will be argued that the combined behavior of the government and of the central bank, in the face of financial disarray and declining income, not only prevents deep depressions but also sets the stage for a serious and accelerating inflation to follow. The institutions and usages that currently rule have not prevented disequilibrating forces from operating. What has happened is that the shape of the business cycle has been changed: inflation has replaced the deep and wide trough of depressions (Minsky, 1986, pp. 14–15).

Thus Big Government (Minsky, 1986, p. 19) has played a crucial role in the contemporary economy, with both positive but also deleterious effects. According to Minsky (1986, pp. 13–37), the experience of history shows the overall ability of the public deficit spending system to counteract the recession, while at the same time also revealing the presence of adverse side effects generated by public intervention. The most prominent adverse effect is inflation, which leads to inefficiency as regards investment decisions and constitutes an unjust tax, if implemented in non-recessive phases (Minsky, 1986, pp. 283–4).

Touching again on public transfer/payment schemes, which in his view 'have become so large a part of government since World War II that the cyclical impact of government spending is now largely determined by their impact' (Minsky, 1986, p. 19), Minsky indicates another adverse effect of public intervention: such schemes represent a reference for minimal monetary salaries, and therefore they potentially affect the conditions under which the workers are willing to accept a job offer. Thus they can imply a decrease in participation in the labour market and a decline in the production capacity of the economy (Minsky, 1986, p. 26).

What worried Minsky is that state intervention could be rendered ineffective in its role of macroeconomic stabilization if it is guided towards fiscal crisis scenarios by imprudent policies (Minsky, 1982a, 1996). That is to say, while the financial stability of the public sector, as a structural balance between incomings and outgoings (in terms of cash flow), takes into account the hierarchy among the financial market operators, it cannot, as pointed out earlier, disregard the same principles that affect the other economic units and which evolve over time in relation to historical and institutional transformations.

The deterioration of the financial balance of the State takes effect both in the case of debt issued in currency and held abroad, because this leads inevitably to a devaluation of the exchange rate, and also in the case of domestic debt, which triggers inflation and an increasingly heavy burden of interest payment, as expressed in *Stabilizing an Unstable Economy:*

> A government can run a deficit during a recession without suffering a deterioration of its creditworthiness if there is a tax and spending regime in place that would yield a favorable cash flow (a surplus) under reasonable and attainable circumstances.
> There is nothing special about government debt, and a flight from government debt can occur. For a foreign-held debt such a flight will lead to a deterioration of currency on the exchanges; for a domestic debt the flight can lead to inflation and a need to pay ever higher interest rates to have the debt held (Minsky, 1986, p. 302).

Further, Minsky repeatedly emphasizes the importance of having a public sector endowed with a solid and solvent financial structure, with a fiscal system that is effective in generating surplus in the future in order to avert deterioration of debt quality:

> Incidentally, if the central bank – the Federal Reserve – monetizes government debts in order to maintain its nominal price in the face of a deteriorating willingness to hold such debt, there can be a run from the Federal Reserve as well as from commercial bank liabilities. Just as private debts have to be validated by profits, as bank liabilities by receipts from assets, as a foreign debt by an export surplus, so government debt has to be validated by an excess of tax receipts over current expenditures. These validating cash flows need to be forthcoming at every moment of time; it is sufficient that reasonable circumstances exist in which a positive cash flow is generated (Minsky, 1986, p. 302).

Examining this point in greater detail, Minsky reproposes the theme of the credibility of the institutions that govern public finance. Credibility is to be concretely achieved in the commitment to marketability of the debt,[8] as guaranteed in the USA by the Fed. He also underlines the need that there should at least be a concrete promise of positive primary surpluses of the public budget:

> Any organization with large debts outstanding cannot deviate by very much or for very long from *at least the promise* of a cash flow surplus without having the quality of the debt deteriorate. Any deviation from a government budget that is balanced or in surplus must be understood as transitory – the war will be over, the resource-development program will be finished, or income will be at the full-employment level (Minsky, 1986, pp. 302–3, emphasis added).

An effective fiscal system is a fundamental condition for maintaining the quality of the debt, partly because when macroeconomic conditions are satisfactory from the point of view or income and employment, it can curb the risk of an inflationary impact:

> from a theoretical analysis, it is evident that policy should aim at achieving and sustaining a robust financial structure. A key element in the robustness is the quality of the best available short-term asset – short-term government debt. An in-place tax structure that yields a surplus when the economy either does well on the income and employment front or poorly on the inflation front is a necessary condition for maintaining the quality of government debt (Minsky, 1986, p. 305).

A robust financial structure is necessary for the public administration as well, although this does not imply the requirement of having constantly positive cash flows. Rather, it means that each economic unit should have a financial position that is sustainable over time. With specific reference to the public budget, Minsky notes:

> Debts embody payment commitments, promises to make payments. For these promises to have value any debtor *has to be able* to generate a positive cash flow in its favor. It achieves this by operating in the various markets where it buys and sells so as to achieve a cash flow net of operating costs that exceeds the commitments to pay on account of debt. 'Has to be able' does not means does. A unit may have negative cash flows for a considerable period and its liabilities would still be of value because it is accepted that the negative cash flows are *transitory*. The unit will have a positive cash flow in circumstances that it is reasonable to expect will occur (Minsky, 1986, p. 302, italic added).

On this point, in the case of the US structural deficit resulting from Reagan's fiscal policy and expenditure on weapons, Minsky recalls the negative consequences for the exchange rate or inflation:

> there will either be a run from the dollar or a substantial debt repudiation through inflation. Either way, interest rates will rise to new highs as markets react and as the Federal Reserve either moves to protect the dollar or stop inflation (Minsky, 1986, p. 303).

The consequences for the financial structure (both in terms of cash flow and of assets/liabilities of the economic units) of the public sector constitute a decisive element in influencing the evolution of the relation between the typology and characteristics of state intervention and the development of the economy.

Minsky's attention to the relation between development and the sustainability of the public debt/deficit appears to be in line, on the one hand, with the new growth theories, and, on the other, with modern theories of international trade, which underline that dynamic comparative advantages (technological development, investment in human capital, scientific research and infrastructure) and 'systemic' competition among regions and nations, as well as among individual firms, constitute important aspects underpinning economic development. Since the market tends to invest less than would be socially optimal in these essentially public goods, modern theory implicitly underlines the importance of state intervention both as a means of directly producing these factors that are crucial for development, and also in terms of the stimulus and coordination it can offer to the private sector in this direction (Barro and Sala-i-Martin, 1995). Building on the tripartite division of the functions of the State proposed by Musgrave (1959) (macroeconomic stabilization, wealth redistribution and resource allocation), Minsky develops a particularly broad concept of public goods: in his theoretical vision, the role exerted by the State with regard to macroeconomic stabilization and wealth redistribution, through creation of job opportunities providing an adequate income to the poorer components of society, also becomes a tool for efficient allocation of resources.[9]

At the same time, Minsky's criticism of Big Government incorporates the observations of the Public Choice school (Buchanan, 1986 and Buchanan and Wagner, 1977), indirectly endorsing the idea that the 'failure of the market' to produce the optimum level of public goods is associated with the failure of the political system, which is inefficient in sustaining or guaranteeing private investments and generates an accumulation of public debt well beyond the social optimum.[10] This critical approach is set in a historical and evolutionary perspective, and it in no way implies a weakening of Minsky's conviction of the need for an effective Government capable of focusing on specific objectives of pronounced social interest, as he demonstrates through his reading of the role of the State in the different phases of US capitalism.

3.3. MINSKY'S READING OF THE ROLE OF THE STATE IN THE HISTORICAL PERIODIZATION OF THE AMERICAN ECONOMY

With the aid of the cash flow method Minsky formulates a periodization of the different historical stages of US capitalism (see Whalen, 1999 and 2001), enabling him to delineate the way the State has influenced (and at the same time is influenced by) the institutional evolution of the American economy. He identifies five stages of American capitalist development: (i) merchant or commercial capitalism (1607–1813); (ii) industrial capitalism (1813–1890); (iii) banking or financial capitalism (1890–1933); (iv) managerial capitalism (from the New Deal to the beginning of the 1980s, with the second oil crisis and the free-trade era of the Reagan Administration); (v) capitalism guided by institutional investors (from the 1980s to the present day).

The role of the public sector expanded after the 1929 crisis (Minsky, 1982b, p. 42). In Minsky's view, the 1929 depression highlighted the need for public intervention to stabilize economic activity and protect it against severe crises. The reactions of the individual economic units to economic downturns (lending reductions, price decreases, shrinking production and employment) led to adverse consequences, on the aggregate level, that were even more disastrous for the economic situation. But, he argues, F.D. Roosevelt's New Deal provided the appropriate answer, paving the way to this new phase of capitalism (Minsky, 1986, p. 121; 1996, p. 361, par. 4). As a result of public intervention to support profits, the individual economic units were able to avoid the risk, inherent in conditions of recession, of a shift towards non-covered (speculative or ultraspeculative) positions: public expenditure generated additional demand, contributing to an improvement in expectations and a reduction in the spreads deriving from evaluation of risk, which was perceived as more contained. The conditions were created for the activation of new investment programmes and the system tended to move cumulatively upwards. The extension of the public sector and of the corresponding deficit had the effect of stabilizing the economy, given that the consolidation of profit flows allowed expectations to be confirmed.

This notwithstanding, in general the mechanisms that lead to stabilization and economic growth also create – and this is typically an original result of Minsky's analytical approach (1982b, pp. 65–6) – the premises for a subsequent crisis phase: if the downwards instability of profits decreases due to the effects of intervention by a broad public sector, debt financing is thereby encouraged and the private economy, on different grounds as compared to the reasons leading up to the 1929 crisis, becomes more fragile. Non-covered positions become predominant, as perception of the risk inherent in new investment programmes is diminished and the economic system remains by its very nature intrinsically unstable (Minsky, 1986, p. 143). In his 1986 work, Minsky notes that this phase of 'managerial capitalism' was characterized by a marked involvement of public action in the sphere of monetary and banking policy. The introduction of the Emergency Banking Act aimed to propose an accommodating monetary policy, reorganization of the banks, and institutional reforms that included deposit guarantee systems and the specialization of financial institutions (separation of investment banks from commercial banks, prohibition on the development of banking organizations operative in more than one state). This complex action of public legislation was combined with anticyclical fiscal policies, manoeuvres in support of agriculture and regulation of the labour market, thereby helping the economy to embark on a route of stability and growth that was achieved in the period following the end of the second world war and which contributed to reinforcing the financial positions of the major economic units.

Public intervention, which was massively directed to sustaining investments, was developed in the postwar context in a situation characterized by oligopolistic markets, fairly insignificant foreign competition and macroeconomic control by the state authorities. The managers of American companies enjoyed a marked degree of independence from pressure exerted by the banks and shareholders, and in the long run this resulted in firms' progressive adaptation to the economic climate that had arisen. This made the managerial context more sluggish and less prepared to face inflation deriving from the oil crisis. Furthermore, economic prosperity and the guarantee offered by the monetary intervention of the Fed. as a lender of last resort encouraged reduction of credit security margins, more widespread confidence in debt repayment capacity and a growing orientation towards short-term financing. In a 1992 work, *The Capital Development of the Economy and the Structure of Financial Institutions*, Minsky notes that from the 1970s, with the abandonment of the economic and financial balance fixed by the Bretton Woods Accord and with the inflationary impact deriving from increased energy prices, and up to the turbulent 1980s, the cash flow and the financial positions of firms and households worsened:

> The financial structure is significantly more fragile now, in early 1992, than was earlier in the post world war II epoch. The leveraged buy out movement of the 1980's led to the growth in highly leverages firms. The growth in the money market mutuals in the 1980's led to a large demand for short term marketable corporate liabilities. The combined effect of these two developments was the growth in speculative financing. Leverage buy outs often included 'payment in kind' bonds, i.e. the capitalization of interest (Ponzi finance) (Minsky, 1992, p. 19).

The effects of this evolution, as regards the private economy, led to an expansion of non-banking financial institutions, with a strong drive to innovations such as the securitization of loans and the use of off-balance sheet guarantees and commitments. As far as households were concerned, the need to optimize the relation between risk and yield prompted a shift of individual savings from banks to professionalized management, so that individual wealth progressively took on the form of ownership of investment funds rather than of the liabilities of individual firms (Minsky, [1990]1993a, pp. 110–11).

Another important field of development of financial innovation was linked to the increasing role of institutional investors, such as treasury management organizations, pension funds, trustee funds, and so forth. These financial enterprises drew their source of demand and profits not so much from the public sector as from the progressive and massive increase in financial transactions, which mainly resulted from the processes of international liberalization.

The 1980s saw the rise of a process of international integration of trade, but above all of finance, which generated a stable and growing source of demand for financial services. At the same time a process of transformation of the role of the State was set in motion. The transition to capitalism guided by institutional investors (Minsky and Whalen, 1996–97, pp. 158–9) marked the opening of a neoliberal era, which led to an attenuation of the functions of the State.

Starting from the facts as outlined above, Minsky showed notable awareness that Big Government in a non-covered financial position could lead to a growing risk under market integration conditions. Some of his writings indicate that elevated deficits and rising public sector debt could have adverse consequences on the effectiveness of support for the private economy during a recession, underlining the difficulty of utilizing this lever in deficit circumstances:

> The United States economy is burdened by a deadweight government debt (deadweight government debt is debt that is not the result of government resource creating activity) accumulated as a result of the dreadful abuse of the government budget during the 1980's, an abuse which is continuing today. These conditions mean that a recovery from the current recession will not be accompanied by buoyant private demand. A deliberate move of the government towards a significantly larger deficit at the current level of income and structure of spending and taxes is not available (Minsky, 1992, p. 20).

Minsky realized that in the above conditions it could be reasonable to put forward the suggestion of reducing the extent of public intervention (such requests and proposals had, in his view, failed during the Reagan era), although he was concerned that this could 'make our economy more susceptible to downside instability' (Minsky, 1986, p. 22). At the same time, he underlined the lack of equivalence between a decrease in taxation and an increase in public expenditure, arguing that the tool of tax reduction was in actual fact a hindrance to policy implementation (Minsky, 1992, p. 20).

He likewise pointed out that no decrease in the extent of public intervention was genuinely occurring. Rather, what was being set in motion was a process of redistribution of the benefits of public intervention, from the weaker social groups to those better able to exert pressure on the political institutions (without solution of continuity with respect to Minsky, 1986, p. 318).[11]

In the context of this process, public expenditure was directed more substantially towards specific objectives of national defence and security, and to a lesser degree towards social expenditure (Minsky, 1986, p. 305).

From Minsky's viewpoint, this new scenario represented a possible alternative, but not the only feasible route. He perceived its dangers and expressed his concerns by pointing out that a decrease in social expenditure implied the loss of an extensive and stable source of demand, with adverse consequences not only for the cash flow of the individual economic units but also for entire economies (Minsky, [1990]1993a, pp. 112–13 and Minsky, 1996, section 6).

In the private economy, institutional investors were by now managing a significant share of national savings and had extended their influence not merely over the financial markets and activities of firms, but also over the criteria for judging the success of an investment. As a result, their aims were increasingly linked to maximization of yield and investment value. Corporate administrators became more sensitive to short-term profit objectives and to capitalization of firms on the stock markets. Managers were often granted stock options as a reward for achieving their targets, and were thus encouraged to seek innovative solutions in the sphere of production and finance in order to reduce costs and increase returns. Numerous opportunities arose for the creation of innovative financial tools in response to the increasing demand by institutional investors for risk diversification and allocation of new savings. The ensuing array of new solutions acted as the constant driver of special financing operations such as mergers, acquisitions, break-ups, leveraged buy-outs, capital management (asset-backed securitization transactions, subordinated notes and mezzanine finance etc.), shareholder buybacks. Fund managers, as Minsky pointed out in 1996, (p. 361, section 4) thus had a strong interest in supporting the various proposals which allow them to increase the value of portfolio investments and, at the same time, to supply the financial resources required to ensure the success of special operations for taking control of enterprises (by means of private equity or venture capital funds), as their remuneration is linked to the performance of the companies involved.

While this phase had not entered into a profound crisis, it did display notable limits of economic and financial sustainability over time, and in particular it was resulting in increasingly significant effects on the social plane, with negative medium/long-term repercussions on consumption and aggravation of the potential risks affecting retirement savings funds as well as the prospects for stabilization of economic growth.

As Minsky (1995) noted, a transition to a new era was about to be ushered in, with a gradual shift from the search for profit characterizing money manager capitalism towards a global financial integration capable of inducing progressive reduction in the potential range of State intervention. The new era would thus move in the opposite direction compared to the protection offered by Government to combat crises. In this context, Minsky was increasingly concerned as to how the financial and fiscal control and the institutional support so far provided by national governments could handle the consequences of the growing global financial fragility in international situations of deflation and debt crisis (Minsky, 1995, p. 93), a fragility that may affect integrated economic areas just as much as individual States.

Central to Minsky's considerations was his claim that it is vital to gain insight into how the requirement of the profitability of entrepreneurial activity can be made compatible over time with the need for security and stability that is strongly felt by households, while at the same time safeguarding the need for the development of investments and capital which is one of the pillars of economic growth.

Minsky argues that the global financial system should be structured in such a manner as to sustain growth and contain instability but without compromising or disabling the only tool that has proved to be effective in an anticyclical function, namely the action of the public administration in providing support for demand.

The current relevance of his contribution is particularly significant in a context of the increased financial fragility of the American economy of today (elevated public debt and government deficit, commercial deficit and weakness of the dollar). Compared to Minsky's fundamental 1986 analysis of Big Government, the institutional set-up of the USA has undergone a profound change over the last twenty years. The decades after 1986 saw the accumulation of an unprecedented trade deficit and capital-account surplus, creating a pronounced asymmetry in the global economic structure, and generated a growing demand for dollars. This hegemony, which featured the transition from a regime with an undervalued dollar in the 1970s to the 'high dollar' regime (see Dymski, 2002, p. 8) during and after the 1980s, was ascribable to the power structure of the United States, more specifically its supremacy in the economic (predominance of Wall Street), industrial and military field, which made it a source of attraction for worldwide wealth in the quest for elevated productivity and elevated profitability (see Dymski, 2002, pp. 6–7).

The disappearance of one or more favourable conditions highlights the weaknesses and concerns over a downside instability that led Minsky to seek different and alternative policies, that would on a case-by-case basis be more conducive to relative stability and growth in a system that is by its very nature unstable. For a more detailed treatment see Wray (2006, pp. 18–19).

3.4. POLICY ALTERNATIVES AND A NEW ROLE OF THE STATE

In Minsky's interpretation the instability of the economic system was a phenomenon whose negative effects on the social plane were likely to be all the more devastating in a context characterized by a declining capacity of the State to intervene effectively in order to address critical situations with appropriate macroeconomic stabilization policies. The US experience of policies designed to contain public intervention in the social sphere, enacted from the 1980s onwards, made the overall economic system more fragile: the cash flows of the middle class and of the poorer households tended to shrink and become unstable and the gap between the increasingly smaller number of very rich individuals and the overwhelming majority of the population widened. However, the overall extent of public expenditure was not substantially reduced: rather, it was channelled towards transfers to politically influential sectors and pressure groups.[12] There were no significant benefits for the cash flows of households and firms, or for the public sector. Minsky's word of warning about the need for solidity of the State budget thus adds force to the concepts he had always championed, namely his focus on interventions that would lessen the financial fragility of economic subjects (households and firms), yet without negative effects on profits, and which would, with the aid of public intervention, guide the economy towards full employment and more balanced income distribution. This, he believed, was a precondition for lasting growth and the battle against instability.

Once again, the role of the State is stressed, despite the severe criticism frequently levelled against the public function by the most commonly accepted versions of economic theory, which contend that it is disproportionately large and inefficiently managed. Sharing the thought of Henry Simons (1948), Minsky maintains that economic efficiency is not the only objective of public action: rather, policies should aim to assure the civil standards that are characteristic of a democratic and open society (Minsky and Whalen, 1996–97, p. 162).

By declining to acknowledge the evidence of the failure of the State in fulfilling goals of economic efficiency that can better be achieved by the private sector, Minsky effectively placed a limit on his theory. But it was a limit that sprang from his awareness that the lack of adequate tools to counter market failures could jeopardize the stability and development of the economy.

Since he believed that the development and growth of the economy is driven by endogenous and historically determined mechanisms, Minsky tended to adopt a pragmatic viewpoint. He thus brushed aside the limits of his analysis by pointing out that there exists no policy tool capable of offering effective solutions in every case and in every context (Minsky, 1986, p. 333). Policies which in the past were found to function successfully may later prove to be inadequate as a result of innovations arising from the financial sector or from entrepreneurial activities, or due to the onset of new problems (ibid., p. 293). For instance, as early as the 1970s he foresaw that the economy could pass through successive phases linked to cyclical changes and social change, so that different strategies would have to be activated at the various stages. For instance, periods of elevated investment and high profits could be followed by a period in which more elevated levels of consumption and more egalitarian income distribution could turn out to be more appropriate as a means of providing continuity and new growth opportunities (Minsky, 1975a, p. 168). He suggested adopting a strategy for reducing the degree to which economic systems depend on private investment, that is to say, an alteration of income distribution as a means of increasing the average propensity to consume, through consumption programmes and social investment. However, it should be underlined that Minsky's aim was not that of a simplistic increase in effective demand through an increase in consumption: rather, what he had in mind was the implementation of a well-thought-out economic policy capable of reducing income disparities, limiting household debt levels, reining in oligopolistic and monopolistic powers and stimulating individual skills acquisition and entrepreneurship (Minsky, 1971a and 1975a, p. 167; 1981).

First and foremost, Minsky hoped to eliminate unemployment-related poverty. A programme of this kind had as its characteristic that it 'takes the unemployed as they are and tailor-makes jobs to their skills' (Minsky, 1972d, p. 6). Secondarily, he believed that an increase in the number of individuals hired on the labour market would contribute to increasing the number of persons in a family holding a job, and this, in turn, would decrease the number of those living in poverty or on the breadline. Thirdly, the expansion of employment would raise the salaries of low-wage workers more rapidly than those of medium-high income earners, with significant redistributive effects (Minsky, 1972d, made reference to the analysis by Anderson (1964) which underlined the more contained wage differentials in periods of a more robust labour market). Moreover, Minsky believed it was indeed possible to 'decrease (labor-profit) inequality by decreasing capital's share of income' (Minsky, 1973, p. 94).

In order to bring about stable and full employment without inflationary effects on prices and wages, Minsky (1972d, p. 5; 1986, pp. 141–70) awarded a prominent place to price limitations on the goods and services of enterprises with the highest wage levels. This was designed to compensate increases in low-wage workers' remuneration when such increments exceeded productivity (Minsky, 1965, p. 183).[13]

Analogously, in the 1980s and 1990s, in an endeavour to combine the intuitions of Schumpeter and Keynes (Minsky [1990]1993a, pp. 106–7), he defined a developmental path guided by an approach that provided an alternative to free trade theories, while at the same time taking into account the evolution of the institutional structure of the economic system. Thus in order for economic policies to sustain stability and economic development over time, tools (both active fiscal policies and institutional regulation mechanisms) were needed that would have some degree of control over profits, although the latter remained the fundamental element driving growth.

In this phase, the adverse social consequences of the policies implemented in the USA, which had led to an increasing concentration of wealth, led Minsky to sharpen his critique of the predominant orientations (Minsky, 1986, pp. 287–333). He contended it was necessary to invert the substantially pre-Keynesian approach based on reinforcement of supply, suggesting that priority should always be awarded to the goal of full employment over that of accelerated growth. He thus raised the issue of the structure and limits that should be set in place in order to ensure the establishment of a Government that would be effective and could foster development under conditions of full employment, and profit and price stability.

He warned the advocates of neo-free trade policies not to overlook that 'Big Government is the most important reason why today's capitalism is better than the capitalism which gave us the Great Depression' (Minsky, 1986, p. 296). This notwithstanding, Minsky did not neglect the limits of Government, which he delineated both in quantitative and qualitative terms. On the quantitative plane, i.e. in the sense that 'size matters', Minsky (1986, pp. 297–99) maintained that the optimal size of government spending should be that whereby public expenditure can balance the oscillations of private investment by means of deficit interventions, thus maintaining profit stability.

On the qualitative plane, in Minsky's view profound reforms were required to achieve effective Government. Such reforms should consist in substituting public spending on a multitude of transfers and subsidies by objectives focusing on programmes of allowances/indemnities to assure a minimum wage and above all to help young people to avoid the poverty trap which, in the case of large families, derives from the impossibility of meeting necessary household expenses despite holding a regular job (Minsky, 1986, p. 301). The revision of the system of public transfers should be designed to avert any obstacles that might hinder young people's entry into the labour market and should avoid favouring income protection measures – such as subsidies to agriculture – which, in the past, were granted in the form of support for prices that were inevitably destined to fall as a result of the continuous increase in productivity of the sector (Minsky, 1986, pp. 299–302).

The orientation of economic policy towards the aim of full and consolidated employment (Minsky, 1996, p. 368) was concretely expressed in his proposal that 'the government become an employer of last resort', reviving suggestions he had formulated in earlier years (Minsky, 1968, p. 338).

The concrete possibility of balancing the improvement in the cash flows of households and firms represents an objective that constantly appears in an overall interpretation of the policies championed by Minsky. Such an interpretation is reinforced in the above-mentioned argument in favour of the need to substantially reform the transfer-based Big Government approach. There remain some doubts, which one may share with Wray (2006, p. 26), with respect to this objective insofar as foreign deficit problems are concerned.[14]

Aware of these objections, in the 1990s Minsky developed the concept of shared prosperity (Minsky and Whalen, 1996–97, pp. 166–67). The need to take social and collective needs into consideration was underpinned by his attention to public investment in human capital and in technological, scientific and material infrastructures. The complementarity between public and private investment should aim to (i) encourage individual and collective productivity as a response to the mounting awareness of the inadequacy of social capital in the American economy, (ii) harness and build on the assets of the nation [*rise of 'brain-power' industries – industries such as microelectronics and biotechnology that can be located wherever the necessary talents are coordinated* (Minsky and Whalen, 1996–97, p. 164)], and (iii) improve employability among the general population.

These new policies require additional institutional elements over and above traditional development policies. Such elements include reinforcement of the lowest wage bands, and greater involvement of trade unions and workers' associations in economic policy choices, provision of benefits for employment in a manner that is more responsive to the needs of households, as well as other proposals to safeguard against the widespread insecurity that is a feature of the contemporary evolution of the family.

As early as the 1960s (Minsky, 1963b, pp. 401–12), Minsky had looked unfavourably on excessive labour market flexibility. Now, in the 1990s, his criticism was heightened: attention should, he felt, be directed towards opposing the generalized effects of the increasing lack of job security and the destructuring of the welfare policies that had in the past enabled households to cope with unexpected or natural events (accidents, illness, old age). He also noted the rising tide of indebtedness, above all among households,[15] resulting partly from expansionary monetary policies,[16] partly from the growing presence of new consumption models, and also from gradual reduction in the opportunities for individual accumulation.[17]

It was thus becoming important to counter the tendency towards a worsening of financial positions, by engaging in action designed to support households in the field of education and training[18] as well as social welfare and healthcare,[19] and as an effective antirecessive remedy. This would also contribute to improving the quality of the economic system and would reinforce productivity and competitiveness. Overall,

> federal, state, and local officials could easily design programs that would enable unemployed citizens to support themselves by making useful contributions to their communities' (Minsky and Whalen, 1996–97, pp. 163).

Significantly, Minsky and Whalen (1996–97, p. 161) conclude with the hope that citizenship rights can be translated into opportunities to utilize and develop individuals' talents and thus to usher in the prospect of an improved standard of living for workers and their households.

The marked upsurge of needs that require complex and costly programmes to support social welfare and boost the war on poverty calls for a revision of the macroeconomic strategies of Big Government. In the new vision, such strategies should instead be anchored to a public spending programme oriented towards fostering employment and compatible with sustainability of the deficit and the State debt.

Action taken in an endeavour to stabilize and improve the financial positions of the economic units should be carefully targeted, and should be capable of directing support to the components of society that are most fragile and exposed to the risk of negative cash flows. Programmes should aim to ensure that the deterioration of the State's financial position does not diminish the effectiveness of policies addressed to the sectors of society that are most in need, especially in moments of weakness of the economy on the national and international level.

Minsky continued to maintain that prompt anticyclical fiscal policies can prevent severe crises (Minsky, 1982b, p. 56). He firmly believed that anticyclical fiscal policies contribute to sustaining the profits of firms, and kindle the revitalization of investments. Equally important, in his view, is the above-mentioned role of monetary policy, with its action in fixing reference rates and introducing measures to counter negative situations within the cycle, as well as in supplying liquidity to avert systemic crises, according to the typical function of the lender of last resort generally performed by Central Banks.

3.5. CONCLUDING REMARKS: ORIGINALITY AND LIMITS OF MINSKY'S THOUGHT

Minsky's thought on the role of the State offers a solid reference approach in a macroeconomic perspective, and provides insight into the way individual choices contribute to modelling behaviour on the aggregate level. The interpretation of Minsky put forward here helps to show that on the question of stabilization and economic growth the effectiveness of the public sector (although this sector has its own exclusive characteristics in terms of the hierarchy of solvency) is subject to the same conditions as those that determine investment and development decisions in all economic units, as they are constrained by the need to procure funds.

Minsky's attention to the cash flow of the economic units leads to recognition of the need for a 'mixed economy', in which public intervention has a twofold function: it allows consolidation of the set-up of the contemporary economy (Wray, 2007a), and makes it possible to establish a robust economic and financial basis for households and firms, in contexts that tend towards increasing fragility and instability.

The role of the public sector is analyzed by Minsky against the backcloth of the historical development of the contemporary economy. He examines its impact on corporate profits, enquiring into the rise of the financial sector, whose overall trends have an increasing influence on policy choices. In Minsky's view, since the great 1929 crisis the State has had a decisive function with regard to macroeconomic stabilization, and has been instrumental in preventing situations of financial fragility from triggering profound crises. His claim is that the cash flow method has been crucial in shaping the behavioural choices of the economic units (State, firms, banks and households); accordingly, the State should devote particular attention to such issues, as it is entrusted with the delicate task of stabilizing the cash flows of private actors in order to absorb situations of economic fragility and avert systemic crises. Maintenance of a robust financial structure is, he believes, a necessary condition for the State and its macroeconomic stabilization function, to be achieved through absorption of inflation and excessively high incomes with budget surpluses and through deficit financing of recession and underemployment phases. The financial solidity of the State is likewise necessary for an effective role of redistribution and the war on poverty, as well as to help break down barriers that impede entry into the labour market and improve the employability of the general population.

The reading of Minsky's thought proposed here has sought to highlight his rich and multifaceted vision of the State as a tool offering balanced guidance towards a 'new age of shared prosperity'.[20] The limits of his theoretical and methodological approach pointed out in some contributions in the literature are, however, not disregarded. Such limits can be ascribed to a basic presupposition of his analysis: his intellectual affinity with a post-Keynesian and evolutionary stream of economic analysis according to which a robust and active role by the State is always a fundamental prerequisite for economic and social stability and development (see Burlamaqui, 1998). On the other hand, the Minskian approach remains in line with an analytical framework that pays due attention to Wagner's law, and to Kalecki's indications on the anticyclical function of public spending. Moreover, it has the distinctive feature of not shying from a critical assessment of a Keynesian tradition as to the relations between demand for government transfers and supply capacity. In his assessment, this tradition was incapable of fully appraising the negative effects of excessive public intervention due to transfers that aim to support investments and consumption.

The proposals for a far-reaching re-organization of public intervention he formulated in the 1980s highlight the modernity of his thought, aware as he was of the need to consolidate over time the effectiveness of the primary function of the State: only thus would it be possible to strengthen public initiative directed towards socially relevant ends and objectives. By emphasizing the effects of the public finances on the cash flow of firms and households, and by stressing the importance of the financial solidity of the public operator, his theory, as it gradually evolved over time, opened up debate centring on the 'full balance-sheet approach'. This new conception broadens the perspective to encompass policies which provide an incentive to innovate and boost productivity by building on human capital.

The modernity and current relevance of Minsky's contribution is all the more significant in that it makes no separation between analysis of growth and stabilization and analysis of income distribution. His work underscores the technical, institutional and political implications that need to be taken into account in concretely designing policies whose aim is to achieve, at one and the same time, economic efficiency, social justice and individual freedom.

NOTES

1. For the methodological analysis of the microeconomic bases of Minsky's thought, see Toporowski (2006); for the analysis concerning the *Financial Instability Hypothesis,* see Lavoie (1986 and 1997), Wray (1992), Lavoie and Seccarecia (2001), Vercelli (2001), De Antoni (2007); for models of the Minskian system, see Nasica and Raybaut (2005), Tymoigne (2006a, 2006b, 2006c),.
2. An in-depth examination of the problems of the financial sustainability of the economic units is undertaken in Bagliano and Bertola (1999) and in Afonso and Rault (2007).

3. These interesting references are taken from a manuscript by Adelman and Minsky (1960).
4. According to Minsky (1979, p. 110), this implies that 'the financial environment hospitable to operations designed to resist efforts to switch is one that makes the reserve currency scarcer, and thus more valuable, whenever switches are attempted'.
5. It is worth recalling that *Can 'It' Happen Again?* is the outcome of a collection of revised and reworked versions of a number of studies Minsky undertook between the mid 1950s and the early 1980s.
6. The chapters mentioned are re-elaborations of earlier works. Specifically: Chapter V 'The Financial Instability Hypothesis: A Restatement', in *Thames Paper in Political Economy*, 1978; Chapter VI 'Financial Instability Revisited: The Economics of Disaster' – a reduction of the original version that was written in 1966, revised in January 1970, then published in Minsky (1972b); Chapter X 'An Exposition of a Keynesian Theory of Investment' (Minsky, 1972a).
7. The reasons underlying the existence of a limit to the fall of the system represent one of the most controversial points in the interpretation of Minsky's contribution. The reader is referred to such works as Dymski and Pollin (1992 and 1994).
8. As already pointed out earlier, Minsky (1986, p. 35) underlines that 'its marketability is ultimately guaranteed by the Federal Reserve System, a guarantee that does not necessarily extend to other debt'.
9. As early as Minsky (1965, p. 200; 1975a, p. 166), levers for income redistribution, through creation of job opportunities and stabilization policies, are identified as constituting the bases for efficient resource allocation. In particular, Minsky (1975a, p. 166) points out that 'Taxes and a distribution of the benefits of government intervention that are deemed to be fair or equitable are necessary for any economy, but especially for a controlled economy, to be robust. In a sense, the measures undertaken to prevent unemployment and sustain output 'fix' the game that is economic life; if such a system is to survive, there must be a consensus that the game has not been unfairly fixed'. Likewise in Minsky (1986, p. 296), it is stated that 'a system that promotes allocational efficiency may be stability inefficient'.
10. A re-reading of the last chapter of *Stabilizing an Unstable Economy*, which Minsky entitled *An Agenda for Reform* (Minsky, 1986, pp. 294–333) clarifies the essential points of his interpretation of the cases of failure of the State and the market: 'because of limitations of the capacity of government to administer, decentralized markets are a preferred mechanism for coordination and control' (p. 296). However, he observes that 'The market is an adequate regulator of products and processes except when market power or externalities exist' (p. 329), adding that 'in a world where profits are cyclically unstable, market power can arise from the banker's requirement that unfavorable outcomes must be constrained before capital-intensive production techniques are financed' (p. 329) ... 'Once Big Government stabilizes aggregate profits, the banker's reasons for market power loses its force' (p. 330). And on the subject of externalities he recalls the case of the railroads and nuclear power: 'Both are industries combining capital intensity with enormous externalities. Although even the suggestion raises difficult political questions, public ownership should be tried; where these industries work well in other advanced economies they are almost always publicly owned' (p. 331).
11. Minsky (1986, p. 318), points out that 'Big or giant organizations carry an implied public guarantee (i.e., contingent liability) on their debts. This introduces a financial bias favoring giant corporations and giant banks, for the implicit public liability leads to preferred market treatment. Government intervention to validate the cash flow commitments takes place even if investment are inept.'
12. Scathing criticism is advanced by Minsky and Whalen (1996–97, p. 165) against public spending policies in the United States: according to the two authors, what is adopted is 'an

approach to budgeting that treats biotechnology research no differently from a White House dinner party'.

13. In this regard he suggested trade union agreements so that in high wage enterprises, remunerations would be increased less than their workers' productivity increases. Furthermore, to avoid inflationary tendencies on profits deriving from oligopolistic sectors or from sectors less exposed to competition, he advised direct action so that the benefits resulting from a decrease in unit costs could be transferred to the consumer (Minsky, 1965, p. 183).
14. As pointed out by Wray (2006, p. 26): 'Minsky's call for a budget that can balance at high employment must be modified. To allow the private sector to strengthen its balances, the budget should be biased to run deficits somewhat larger than the trade deficit at full employment'.
15. Attention is also drawn to the difficulties involved in the supply of financial services to some more vulnerable groups of consumers (low income citizens, ethnic minorities, entrepreneurs with a low range of business), small businesses and business start-ups considered unsuitable for attracting the interest of commercial and investment banks. In this regard, Minsky, together with other economists of the The Levy Economics Institute of Bard College, developed a detailed project of banks for the development of local communities, with the mission of supplying credit, financial services and payment services to social groups not adequately supported by the financial system (Minsky, 1993b, pp. 33–41 and Minsky et al., 1993).
16. This is a policy that had been strongly advocated by Minsky since as early as the 1970s: 'A correct policy posture in the current situation will not encourage private debt finance spending. Thus rather than increasing the investment tax credit, it should be repealed. The Federal Reserve should once again be authorized to institute down payment and term to maturity regulations on mortgages and consumer credit, with the objective of cutting household debts. If aggregate income is sustained the above policies in time will directly generate the need improved in corporate and household balance sheets and indirectly improve the balance sheets of banks and other financial institutions. The basic weapon to sustain income and employment should be a reinstituted and modernized W.P.A., C.C.C. and N.Y.A. (In order to ease the inflationary burden of social security upon the economy, an older worker's employment arm should be developed as a part of this effort.)' (Minsky, 1975b, pp. 40–41; on pp. 350–51, in the Compendium for the Committee).
17. 'With the end of the managerial financial era, stability in U.S. industrial relations has also ended. Workers at nearly all levels are insecure, as entire divisions are bought and sold and as a corporate boards exhibit a chronic need to downsize overheads and to seek out the least expensive set of variable inputs ... Many families cannot distinguish recession from recovery ... income stagnation for many but also longer employment searches, increased family dependence on multiple job holdings, and an explosive growth in part-time and contingent work' (Minsky and Whalen, 1996–97, pp. 159–60).
18. The system of financial incentives should, according to Minsky and Whalen, be oriented towards inducing firms to share with their workers the gains obtained in terms of productivity and profitability, and should provide for more extensive participation of worker representatives on Boards of Directors.
19. With reference to the case of the USA, Minsky and Whalen highlight the need for a health care system that will assure care and basic treatment for all citizens.
20. In Minsky and Whalen (1996–97, p. 162), it is pointed out that 'as Henry Simons suggested long ago, economic efficiency – even when considered from a dynamic perspective – should not be the sole aim of economic policy. Rather, policy should strive to assure the civilized standards of an open and democratic society. A humane society should not be sacrificed on

the altar of narrow efficiency (Simons, 1948)'. And in the conclusion of the reflections on the fiftieth anniversary of Truman's *Employment Act*, the final remarks of Minsky and Whalen's text (1996–97, p. 168) provide a strikingly effective posthumous overview (Hyman Minsky died on 24 October 1996) of the economist's dedicated commitment to his work, which produced a rich and fertile heritage of analyses and proposals for stable and full employment: 'The goals of the Employment Act are best honored by working to achieve a new age of shared prosperity'.

REFERENCES

Adelman, I. and H. Minsky (1960), *On the National Debt and Economic Growth*, Manuscript in the Minsky Archives at The Levy Economics Institute.

Afonso, A. and C. Rault (2007), 'What Do we Really Know About Fiscal Sustainability in the EU? A Panel Data Diagnostic', *European Central Bank Working Paper*, no. 820, October.

Anderson, W.H.L. (1964), 'Trickling Down: The Relationship between Economic Growth and the Extent of Poverty among American Families', *Quarterly Journal of Economics*, **78**(4), 511–24.

Arestis, P. and E. De Antoni (2007), 'Rediscovering Fiscal Policy Through Minskian Eyes', *Department of Economics Working Papers*, no. 0731, Department of Economics, University of Trento.

Bagliano, F.C. and G. Bertola (1999), *Metodi dinamici e fenomeni macroeconomici*, Bologna: Il Mulino.

Barro, R.J. and X. Sala-i-Martin (1995), *Economic Growth*, New York: McGraw Hill.

Bell, S. and L.R. Wray (2004), 'The War on Poverty after 40 Years. A Minskian Assessment', *Economics Public Policy Brief Archive*, no. 78.

Buchanan, J.M. (1986), *Liberty, Market and State: Political Economy in the 1980s*, New York: New York University Press.

Buchanan, J.M. and R.E. Wagner (1977), *Democracy in Deficit: the Political Legacy of Lord Keynes*, New York: Academic Press.

Burlamaqui, L. (1998), 'Evolutionary Economics, State and Democracy: Some Critical Issues for a 21st Century Agenda', Paper prepared for the Anpocs Conference – Coxambù, October 1998.

De Antoni, E. (2007), 'Minsky on Investments and Business Cycles: Some Comments', in G. Zezza and P. Arestis (eds), *Advances in Monetary Policy and Macroeconomics*, Basingstoke, NY: Palgrave Macmillan. Paper presented at the Cassino International Conference on *The Keynesian Legacy in Macroeconomic Modeling*, 15 September 2005.

Dymski, G. (2002), 'Post-Hegemonic U.S. Economic Hegemony: Minskian and Kaleckian Dynamics in the Neoliberal Era', *Journal of the Japanese Society for Political Economy*, April.

Dymski, G. and R. Pollin (1992), 'Hyman Minsky as Hedgehog: The Power of the Wall Street Paradigm', in S. Fazzari and D.B. Papadimitriou (eds), *Financial Conditions and Macroeconomic Performance*, Armonk, NY: M.E. Sharpe, pp. 27–61.

Dymski, G. and R. Pollin (1994), 'The Costs and Benefits of Financial Instability: Big Government Capitalism and the Minsky Paradox', in G. Dymski and R. Pollin (eds), *New Perspectives in Monetary Macroeconomics*, University of Michigan Press, pp. 369–401.

Lavoie, M. (1986), 'Minsky's Law or the Theorem of Systematic Financial Fragility', *Studi Economici*, **41**(29), 3–28.

Lavoie, M. (1997), 'Loanable Funds, Endogenous Money, and Minsky's Financial Fragility Hypothesis', in A.J. Cohen, H. Hagemann and J. Smithin (eds), *Money, Financial Institutions and Macroeconomics*, Boston: Kluwer Nijhoff, pp. 67–82.

Lavoie, M. and M. Seccarecia (2001), 'Minsky's Financial Fragility Hypothesis: A Missing Macroeconomic Link?', in R. Bellofiore and P. Ferri (eds), *Financial Fragility and Investment in the Capitalist Economy*, Vol. 2, Cheltenham, UK and Northampton, MA, USA: Edward Elgar, pp. 76–96.

Minsky, H.P. ([1954]2004), 'Induced Investment and Business Cycles', in D.B. Papadimitriou (ed.), *Induced Investment and Business Cycles*, Cheltenham, UK and Northampton, MA, USA: Edward Elgar.

Minsky, H.P. ([1963a]1982), 'Can "It" Happen Again?' in D. Carson (ed.), *Banking and Monetary Studies*, Homewood, IL: R.D. Irwin, republished in Minsky (1982b).

Minsky, H.P. (1963b), 'Financial Institutions and Monetary Policy. Discussion', *American Economic Review*, **53**(2), 401–12.

Minsky, H.P. (1964), 'Financial Crisis, Financial System and the Performance of the Economy', in Commission on Money and Credit (ed.), *Private Capital Markets*, Englewood Cliffs: Prentice-Hall, pp. 326–70.

Minsky, H.P. (1965), 'The Role of Employment Policy', in M.S. Gordon (ed.), *Poverty in America*, San Francisco: Chandler Publishing Company.

Minsky, H.P. (1968), 'Effects of Shifts of Aggregate Demand upon Income Distribution?', *American Journal of Agricultural Economics*, **50**(2), 328–39.

Minsky, H.P. (1971a), *Where Did the American Economy – and Economists – go Wrong?*, unpublished manuscript, noted and commented upon in S.A. Bell and L.R. Wray, 'The War on Poverty after 40 Years. A Minskian Assessment', *Economics Public Policy Brief Archive*, no. 78/2004, Levy Economics Institute of Bard College.

Minsky, H.P. (1972a), 'An Exposition of a Keynesian Theory of Investment', in G.P. Szegö and S. Shell (eds), *Mathematical Methods in Investment and Finance*, Amsterdam: North-Holland, reproduced in Minsky (1982b).

Minsky, H.P. (1972b), 'Financial Instability Revisited: The Economics of Disaster', in Board of Governors of The Federal Reserve System (ed.), *Reappraisal of The Federal Reserve Discount Mechanism*, Washington, DC: Board of Governors, volume 3; abbreviated in Minsky (1982b).

Minsky, H.P. (1972d), *Economic Issues in 1972: A Perspective*, Note from a presentation to a symposium on the economics of the candidates sponsored by the Department of Economics at Washington University, St. Louis, October 6.

Minsky H.P. (1973), 'The Strategy of Economic Policy and Income Distribution', *The Annals of the American Academy of Political and Social Science*, **409**(September), 92–101.

Minsky, H.P. (1975a), *John Maynard Keynes*, New York: Columbia University Press.

Minsky, H.P. (1975b), 'Financial Instability, the Current Dilemma, and the Structure of Banking and Finance', in *Compendium of Major Issues in Bank Regulation*, Washington, DC: U.S. Government Printing Office.

Minsky, H.P. (1978), 'The Financial Instability Hypothesis: A Restatement', in *Thames Papers in Political Economy*, Autumn, 1978. Now in P. Arestis and T. Skouras (eds), *Post Keynesian Economic Theory*, New York: M.E. Sharpe.

Minsky, H.P. (1979), 'Financial Interrelation and the Balance of Payments, and the Dollar Crisis', in J.D. Aronson (ed.), *Debt and the Less Developed Countries*, Boulder: Westview Press.

Minsky, H.P. (1981), 'Financial Markets and Economic Instability, 1965–1980', *Nebraska Journal of Economics and Business*, **20**(4), 5–17.

Minsky, H.P. (1982a), 'The Financial Instability Hypothesis: Capitalist Process and the Behavior of the Economy', in C.P. Kindleberger and J.P. Lafargue (eds), *Financial Crises*, New York: Cambridge University Press.

Minsky, H.P. (1982b), *Can 'It' Happen Again? Essays on Instability and Finance*, New York: M.E. Sharpe.

Minsky, H.P. (1986), *Stabilizing an Unstable Economy*, New Haven, CT: Yale University Press.

Minsky, H.P. (1992), 'The Capital Development of the Economy and the Structure of Financial Institutions', *Levy Economics Institute Working Paper 72*.

Minsky, H.P. ([1990]1993a), *Schumpeter and Finance*, in S. Biasco, A. Roncaglia and M. Salvati (eds), *Market and Institutions in Economic Development*, London: Macmillan, pp. 103–15; English version of the volume by S. Biasco, A. Roncaglia and M. Salvati, *Istituzioni e mercato nello sviluppo economico. Saggi in onore di Paolo Sylos Labini*, Roma-Bari: Laterza, 1990.

Minsky, H.P. (1993b), 'Community Development Banks. An Idea in Search of Substance', *Challenge*, **36**(2), 33–41.

Minsky, H.P. (1995), 'Longer Waves in financial relations: Financial Factors in the More Severe Depressions II', *Journal of Economic Issues*, **29**(March), 83–95.

Minsky, H.P. (1996), 'Uncertainty and the Institutional Structure of Capitalist Economies', *Journal of Economic Issues*, **30**(June), 357–68.

Minsky, H.P. and C.J. Whalen (1996–97), 'Economic Insecurity and the Institutional Prerequisites for Successful Capitalism', *Journal of Post Keynesian Economics*, **19**(2), 155–70.

Minsky, H.P., D.B. Papadimitriou, R.J. Phillips and L.R. Wray (1993), 'Community Development Banking. A Proposal to Establish a Nationwide System of Community Development Banks', *Economics Public Policy Brief Archive*, no. 3/1993, Levy Economics Institute of Bard College.

Musgrave, R.A. (1959), *The Theory of Public Finance: a Study in Public Economy*, New York: McGraw Hill.

Nasica, E. and A. Raybaut (2005), 'Profits, Confidence and Public Deficits: Modelling Minsky's Institutional Dynamics', *Journal of Post Keynesian Economics*, **28**(1), 135–55.

Simons, H.C. (1948), *Economic Policy for a Free Society*, Chicago: University of Chicago Press.

Toporowski, J. (2006), 'Methodology and Microeconomics in the Early Work of Hyman P. Minsky', *Levy Economics Institute Working Paper*, no. 480.

Tymoigne, E. (2006a), 'The Minskian System. Part. I: Properties of The Minskian Analysis and How to Theorize and Model a Monetary Production Economy', *Levy Economics Institute Working Paper*, no. 452.

Tymoigne, E. (2006b), 'The Minskian System, Part II: Dynamics of the Minskian Analysis and the Financial Fragility Hypothesis', *Levy Economics Institute Working Paper*, no. 453.

Tymoigne, E. (2006c), 'The Minskian System, Part III: System Dynamics Modeling of a Stock Flow–Consistent Minskian Model', *Levy Economics Institute Working Paper*, no. 455.

Vercelli, A. (2001), 'Minsky, Keynes and the Structural Instability of a Sophisticated Monetary Economy', in R. Bellofiore and P. Ferri (eds), *Financial Fragility and Investment in the Capitalist Economy: The Economic Legacy of Hyman Minsky*, Vol. II, Cheltenham, UK and Northampton, MA, USA: Edward Elgar.

Whalen, C.J. (1999), 'Hyman Minsky's Theory of Capitalism Development', *Levy Economics Institute Working Paper*, no. 277.

Whalen, C.J. (2001), 'Integrating Schumpeter and Keynes: Hyman Minsky's Theory of Capitalist Development', *Journal of Economic Issues*, **35**(4), 805–23.

Wray, L.R. (1992), 'Minsky's Financial Instability Hypothesis and the Endogeneity of Money', in S. Fazzari and D.B. Papadimitriou (eds), *Financial Conditions and Macroeconomic Performance*, Armonk, NY: M.E. Sharpe.

Wray, L.R. (2006), 'Extending Minsky's Classifications of Fragility to Government and the Open Economy', *Levy Economics Institute Working Paper*, no. 450.

Wray, L.R. (2007a), 'Demand Constraints and Big Government', *Levy Economics Institute Working Paper*, no. 488.

Wray, L.R. (2007b), 'Minsky's Approach to Employment Policy and Poverty: Employer of Last Resort and the War on Poverty', *Levy Economics Institute Working Paper*, no. 515.

4. Economic progress and the standard of life: notes on a dynamic approach to needs and consumption

Davide Gualerzi

4.1. INTRODUCTION

Economic growth is considered a goal in itself by most economists; a growth rate theory thus often exhausts the question of economic progress. Part of the same framework is the firmly established growth–consumption trade-off. Growth depends on saving and saving struggles with consumption, like two opposites. The 'golden rule of accumulation' is then spelt out as a growth equilibrium condition that maximizes consumption per capita.

This approach, however, increasingly conflicts with the criticism of the established measures of economic performance. In particular, development studies have pointed out that GDP measures only market transactions and is therefore a limited indicator. This concern lies behind the effort, pioneered by A. Sen, to establish indicators of human development and welfare that go beyond standard economic measures. More recently, the dissatisfaction with the traditional approach to economic progress has opened the way to rethink its goals completely, towards questions traditionally outside the domain of economic analysis, such as that of happiness (Bruni and Porta, 2005).

This has an interesting counterpart in the history of economic thought. An examination of the writings of fundamental figures such as J.S. Mill, Marshall and Keynes (Opocher, in this volume) suggests that they considered the goals of economic progress a very complex question, one that led them to consider an objective standard of comfort, often associated with the notion of a nobler life. Its improvement is fundamental to measure economic performance.

The main objective of the chapter is to clarify the notion of a standard of life and its improvements with respect to an evolving standard of consumption, and discuss the extent to which the latter can explain the former, thus contributing to the question of the goals of economic progress. In the approach taken here consumption evolution is systematically linked to the growth process, so that we speak of a dynamic approach to consumption. Such an approach rests on the existence of a second relationship, besides the consumption–growth trade-off: the positive feedback between growth and consumption, which might cause a shift of the frontier along which the trade-off operates. This requires transformation, which is in principle driven by the social construction of the need structure and made real by the evolution of consumption patterns (Gualerzi, 2001).

Fortunately, for the main task of the chapter, i.e. shedding light on the relationship between consumption, economic growth and the standard of life, we do not need to develop a dynamic approach to consumption, which is clearly beyond the reach of these notes (see Gualerzi, 1998, 2001). It is sufficient to indicate the theoretical framework and fundamental concepts that lead to considering the question of need and need development. It is, however, first necessary to briefly clarify how the approach relates to the debate on demand theory.

In their introduction to a supplement of *History of Political Economy* on demand theory (2006), Mirowski and Wade observe that 'the history of demand theory is a play in two (or possibly three) acts', referring to 'the ordinal revolution' that superseded the early neoclassical theory based on 'hedonistic psychology' (p. 3), the only additional development being Samuelson revealed preference theory. 'Notwithstanding technical and mathematical improvements, and various pedagogical innovations, the demand theory of the 1940s is the demand theory of today' (ibid.).

The contributions in the HOPE supplement aim to dig deeper into the problems left open by the stabilization of demand theory (act two) and its relationship to the (failures) of general equilibrium theory, offering an overview of the questions internal to the development of the theory. A good example is the examination of the contributions of Allen and Hicks by Fernandez-Grela (2006). He points out that Allen was convinced that the basic hypothesis on consumer behaviour had to find empirical confirmation first to have a sound theory. Referring to the 'escape from psychology' (p. 46) he then brings to the fore the vexed question of the relationship between observed data and the (subjective) theory of demand, an issue that runs through the entire history of demand theory.[1]

As noticed by Duesenberry (1949, pp. 18–19) economists want to speak of individuals choice and stay away from analysing their psychology. It is not clear whether that makes their theory invincible or fundamentally flawed. In fact, demand theory makes psychological assumptions, although they might not be a satisfactory description of human psychology.[2] Camerer et al. (2005) observe that behavioural economics is based precisely on a re-established relationship with psychology, beyond these assumptions. The advances of medical science, and of neuroscience in particular, can now offer a fresh view on the problem, contributing to economics 'new insights and useful perspectives on old problems' (p. 31).

Whether this solves the problems raised by demand theory has to be discussed elsewhere. For the present purpose, it is important to note the great difference between the questions addressed in the debate on demand theory and those posed in the dynamic approach outlined here. The latter is not concerned with choice and its underlying causes (explanations), but focuses instead on the process that brings into being new commodities and establishes change in consumption. It looks at consumption and its changes in the perspective of development, rather than that of choice. This is conceivably a more promising way to discuss the relationship of consumption to growth and the improvement of the standard of life.

Not surprisingly, the first step of the research agenda is still the critique of traditional consumer theory. The first section of the chapter focuses on two lines of criticism that have more direct implications for the main goal of the chapter: one is rather an attempt at improving traditional theory and concerns taking into account technical change and new products; the second focuses on a time-conscious consumer theory. The question of new products is a premise to the fuller consideration of change in consumption in section two; the question of time-uses becomes relevant when the overlapping and the difference of an evolving standard of consumption and the improvement of the standard of life are analyzed in the last section of the chapter.

In Section 4.2 Pasinetti's structural dynamics and Sen's capabilities are briefly examined to point out how they frame the question of a dynamic approach to consumption. Despite their non-negligible differences, complementarities with respect to this task are more important. They ultimately share both the critique of standard consumer theory and, more importantly, an orientation to the question of growth and development in which the evolution of consumption patterns is an aspect of the growth process itself. But it is especially the illuminating comparison of the two approaches by Walsh that permits us to define in what sense they lead to considering the question of need.

Quite conceivably, needs are not only satisfied in the static sense of being fulfilled, they are rather developed. Neither structural dynamics nor the capabilities approach discuss this aspect of the problem, which is addressed in Section 4.3. The notion of socially determined need (Levine, 1981, 1998) allows for a discussion of need development as it occurs in a market economy by means of new products and innovation in consumption (Gualerzi, 1998). In a market economy, need development is both the potential for market expansion, i.e. a growth determinant, and the basis for construction of socially determined individuality and differentiated life styles, stressing an endogenous process of preference formation.

It transpires that the focus on need development: a) takes us already considerably close to the questions raised by the notion of standard of life, pointing to the significant overlapping with the standard of consumption; b) permits a fundamental distinction to be drawn between changes in consumption that fuel market expansion, i.e. growth, from the improvements of what we more broadly regard as the standard of life that have a more tenuous link to consumption as such, or no link at all. This allows for the distinction between need development as the basis for market expansion and personality development within a system of market relations, and need development as individuals' self-fulfilment 'independent' of the market. This is the key to the relationship between a standard of consumption and a standard of life, which is discussed in the last section of the chapter.

4.2. CHANGE AND TIME IN CONSUMER THEORY

4.2.1. Consumer Theory and New Products

One of the fundamental limits of traditional consumer theory lies in the difficulty of addressing analytically the question of change in consumption. Nor has this been widely discussed in the debate on demand theory.

Consumer theory rests on a model of preference ordering and income allocation, stressing a very specific understanding of rationality and consumer sovereignty. As such it is static and has difficulties accommodating change in a broad sense, but also in the fine sense of change in the items of consumption. This should probably be thoroughly investigated with respect to the role consumption has in the main traditions of economic analysis.[3] It can be argued that consumer theory is largely defined by the overall goal of Neoclassical theory to determine prices according to supply and demand.[4] Nevertheless, the problem of change in consumption has not gone unnoticed and is the focus of the two attempts to improve traditional theory examined below. As we will see, this has involved reconsidering some transitions in the history of economic analysis.

An attempt at 'dynamizing' consumer theory is that of Lancaster's characteristic model (1966, 1971), which addresses the issue of new products and product differentiation. In traditional theory 'we can do only two things: (i) ignore the changes, and proceed as if the new variant is the same good as before or (ii) regard the variant as an entirely new good, throwing out any information concerning demand behavior with respect to the original variant, and start from scratch' (1971, p. 8) This follows from the fact that utility indexes are associated directly with goods, rather than with 'characteristics', i.e. properties, which make these goods the object of 'wants'. 'Any change in any property of any good implies that we have a new preference pattern for every individual' (p. 4). Lancaster's objective is to put the 'characteristics model' at the core of demand theory. Characteristics are the objective properties of a good. Therefore 'the relationship between people and things' is a 'two-stage affair'. It is composed of the relationship between things and their characteristics (objective and technical) and the relationship between characteristics and people, involving individual preferences (p. 7). He notes that his 'consumption technology approach' is found elsewhere and is the foundation of 'the diet problem'. Hicks drew explicitly the analogy with the entrepreneur choosing means to satisfy objectives, but abandoned the approach because of its 'technical difficulties'.

The revision of consumer theory suggested by Ironmonger (1972) goes in the same direction. The focus is also on the problem created for traditional consumer theory by new commodities and quality changes. The revision is centred on a consumption technology, intended to satisfy 'various separate wants', leading to the choice of an 'optimum budget ... (which) is found to be a solution of a linear programming problem'. The main conclusion is that new commodities add a dimension, independent of taste, income and prices, to consumer choice.

This follows from the fact that Ironmonger's analysis rests not on characteristics, but rather on wants separability. Wants arise from physiological and psychological needs. *They* are the object of satisfaction, rather than 'a single desire, happiness or utility'. The introduction of wants and desires into economic theory is traced back to Marshall, who acknowledged the work of earlier theorists such as Menger, Jevons and others. The point is, Ironmonger argues, that Marshall's reference to satiable wants and diminishing marginal utility resulted in a refocusing of the theory on utility maximization. The original distinction was then lost. Indeed, Lancaster also finds the roots of his approach in early Marginalists, especially Menger (1971, pp. 9 and 146).

We can conclude that it is precisely the discontinuity of separate wants of early Marginalism which is the conceptual basis for taking into account technical change in the commodities entering consumption. It has a further consequence, one of great relevance to the discussion of consumption theory in the next sections. Wants discontinuity is indispensable to consider an order in the satisfaction of needs. This is the basis of lexicographic models. More generally, it opens the way to consider the pattern of evolution of the consumption structure with respect to a hierarchical arrangement of needs, a fundamental aspect of Pasinetti's structural dynamics.

4.2.2. 'Consumption Takes Time'

Drawing attention to characteristics and new commodities departs little from the main focus on consumption bundles and optimal choice. Indeed, these are efforts at improving standard theory. It is then interesting to briefly consider a critique of consumer theory that goes in an altogether different direction. In *Consumption Takes Time*, Steedman (2001) argues that

> the received theory of consumer behavior is firmly centred on the allocation of money expenditure amongst commodities and pays only marginal, or even no, attention to the consumer's allocation of time (p. 1).

This fundamental flaw calls into question the entire analysis of the consumer and 'filling the lacuna does indeed result in making the theory significantly different' (p. 19). His time-use centred approach to consumer theory first draws the consequences of adding a time constraint to the usual budget constraint and then focuses on time use as a direct object of choice. In doing so, Steedman follows Gossen's 'brilliant but ill-fated work' of 1854 which centres on the time-allocation problem.[5] At any rate, his 'Gosseian' analysis recognizes that 'both time and money act as constraints' (p. 31).[6]

We are not concerned here with the analytical aspects and the technicalities arising from a consumer theory centred on the use of time, rather with the implications that the argument has for an analysis of the notion of standard of life beyond commodities-centered consumption. Focusing on time proves quite helpful in this respect.

Steedman makes reference to 'the time-allocation problem facing Vecchio, an elderly man convinced that he has just six months to live'. Even with no binding budget constraint 'he still has to decide what to do, how to use his time, over his remaining six months' (p. 21). Such a change in perspective is the fundamental point of the criticism of the established theory. 'To put it crudely, do we take the agent to think in terms of 'what shall I consume?' or in terms of 'what shall I do?' (p. 107). The ultimate consequence of time constraints is affecting the role of relative prices in demand analysis. Hardly a secondary effect. Indeed, time constraints must be recognized, 'if certain long-run patterns of change in capitalist market economies are to be understood' (p. 141).

The focus on the different uses of time and 'exclusively on "pure consumption time" sets this approach aside from that of Becker's [1965] household production time'.[7] Steedman quotes Winston (1982, p. 163), saying that in household-production theory 'time has been fully "reified", treated as a "thing"' (p. 5). The problem posed by Vecchio is distinctively different. The approach rests on the distinction between work, consumption and leisure time, recognizing that consumption requires time *per se*. This changes the problem of consumer choice. Interestingly for the present purposes time-uses are then associated to (rates) of consumption of commodities as well pure leisure activities, with no association at all with consumption (p. 108).

The focus on time draws attention to what has been recognized by economists, albeit often in passing: the really scarce resource. By implication time-uses stress what individuals consider really valuable in life. Steedman's argument is interspersed with numerous references to economists, and especially Marshall, as well as writers and philosophers, conveying a sense in which the focus on time is on what individuals pursue in their lives. This is quite consistent with what Steedman regards as the ultimate result of the analysis, that is, to draw a number of implications of the time-centred consumption theory for issues 'not always seen as falling within the scope of the theory of consumption' (p. 107).

Broadening the scope of the analysis leads us to consider a number of questions relevant to a discussion of the standard of life. We can single out one more directly touching on the question, although many others offer hints in the same direction. It is based on the observation that uses of time are shared uses; agents 'prefer to do together what could be done alone' (p. 135). This applies to many activities, such as taking a walk or attending a concert, that could be done by an individual alone, but are regarded as more pleasurable, or are customarily done, with other people. Other such activities, like playing a game or having a conversation, could hardly take place if not together. This is an example of the way the question of time uses and that of the standard of life intersect, with the noticeable absence, at least in principle, of commodities consumption involved. It suggests that a standard of life may depend on many aspects that are not directly linked to consumption as such, involving instead social interaction and life routines.[8]

Steedman concludes that the broader scope of the analysis of time-uses allows for a more fruitful collaboration of social scientists. This suggests that there is a common ground where the economist can join forces with other social scientists to analyze what really matters to individuals, what drives their choices over time, consumption and life 'strategy'.

4.3. CONSUMPTION PATTERNS CHANGE: A DYNAMIC APPROACH TO CONSUMPTION

4.3.1. Structural Dynamics and Consumption Theory

The attempts to insert change into consumer choice examined above begin to tackle the issue of need and new products. In particular, Ironmonger's conclusion that new commodities add a dimension to consumer choice can be further developed. Focusing on the pattern of diffusion of new commodities we can go beyond the question of change in the items of choice to that concerning the patterns of change in consumption. A broader view of consumption structure evolution, such as that underlying Pasinetti's structural dynamics, can then allow for better understanding of the role played by new commodities. In particular, in a dynamic perspective new products help to understand the process of need development that is examined below.

The analysis of consumption built into Pasinetti structural dynamics (1981, 1993) is one of the distinguishing features of his model of growth and structural change. The well-known consequence is an economic system whose structure changes both on the production and demand side. A changing consumption composition becomes a crucial aspect of the growth process. In particular, if full employment is to be maintained, either we assume that demand adjusts passively, increasing in step with productivity in each sector, or demand composition must change and spending must be redirected to new areas of consumption. This follows exclusively from the existence of technical change or, more generally, learning, independently of any institutional framework.[9]

The possibility of a meaningful investigation of change in consumption requires us to refocus away from the 'rational' consumer who is busy to determine his/her preferred basket of consumption making marginal substitutions. Indeed, need satisfaction depends not only on the amount, but also on the order in which goods are consumed. The recognition of an order in the satisfaction of needs – already suggested by wants separability – implies that a certain level of consumption for a commodity must be reached if any other commodity can bring in any utility at all. Relative prices become important only when the level of demand is approaching saturation levels. In other words, relative prices do not matter as much as the hierarchical pattern of need satisfaction. This stresses that needs satisfaction is the ultimate goal of consumption.

Structural dynamics focuses precisely on the evolution of consumption patterns as an aspect of the growth process. Focus on the needs hierarchy shifts attention away from choice of the utility-maximizing basket of consumption given income, to the idea of a (changing) pattern of consumption spending dictated by income growth. This conflicts with the assumption so often made by economists that preferences are homotetic.

Pasinetti argues that there is one thing we do know about consumption expenditure, it does not expand proportionally: actually, an empirical regularity indicates that there is a certain pattern of evolution endogenously determined by income growth. The non-proportional growth of consumption expenditure is then based on a generalization of the Engel curve, a well-known, albeit somewhat neglected, concept.

The second foundation of the dynamic theory of consumption contained in structural dynamics is consumer learning. The process of learning is prior and more fundamental to consumer choice than the notion of rational behaviour, which can guide choice only over a given set of products and at a given level of income. Mere rationality is the static counterpart of learning, as maximization of marginal utility is the static criterion of choice as opposed to the need hierarchy. Furthermore, learning is likely to become increasingly important as income increases.

In the basic scheme of structural dynamics, changes in demand composition are then determined by income growth through the endogenous law of non-proportional expansion of consumption expenditure, technical change and consumer learning. This suggests a picture of consumption whose fundamental concerns are quite distinct from those of traditional theory. In income-driven dynamics a prominent role is played by the sequential satisfaction of needs, reflecting biological, but also social priorities, and the limits sets by market saturation.

4.3.2. The Capabilities Approach

A second element of the dynamic approach to consumption pursued herein is that of capabilities. Sen's capabilities approach also rests on a criticism of traditional consumer theory, the theory of the 'rational fools' (1977). Continuity of preferences, he argues, is indispensable for the principle of substitution. However, once we abandon the example of trading apples for oranges and instead consider lifestyles, alternative systems of preferences individuals evaluate and choose from, the plausibility of the continuity assumption becomes far less obvious. Sen also observed (1985) that preferences refer not to needs, but rather to goods in the market, which are defined in a market economy by other economic agents. Moreover, needs can be satisfied by different types of goods, in different consumption forms (individual, family, social). It follows that there is a discrepancy between preferences and needs.[10]

Interestingly, also Sen's theory of human capabilities follows from a dynamic perspective, that of development, which he contributed to redefining, addressing issues of human development and social justice. If social justice is a goal of development, then the traditional distinction between positive and normative analysis breaks down, and development theory must be modified accordingly.

It can be noted that we are dealing with a concept that has distinctively broad implications beyond consumption theory. Not consumption as such, but well-being is the goal, as stressed by the criticism of rational fools. This raises a question concerning subjective evaluations, such as those involved in the pursuit of happiness, although an objective foundation remains in the notion of need. The point that concerns us here is simply to stress that goods' characteristics are one thing, but the result obtained in terms of needs satisfaction depends on capabilities. This stresses that, rather than in the sense of axiomatic maximization, rationality is redefined in more general terms of systematic exploitation of information and reasoning, but also that individuals are active in defining what can actually be the outcome of goods in satisfying a particular need.

The notion of 'subject capability' refers to what individuals can accomplish with the resources available to them, given the constraints and the causation links that affect the capabilities set.[11] This is no uncontroversial issue. A recent development of the capabilities approach (Nussbaum, 2000) proposes a definite list of capabilities. This contrasts with Sen's insistence on the fact that there can be no such list and we cannot anticipate in any meaningful way what individuals can accomplish with the goods available. The contention might be explained by the distinct goals pursued by Sen and Nussbaum.[12]

In the context of the dynamic approach to consumption discussed here capabilities have then a limited, but fundamental role to play. They allow for the full consideration of the subjective element that concurs to determine need satisfaction, hence the ultimate effects of consumption. On the other hand, it is by means of capabilities that the final specification of a product and its insertion into the structure of consumption are obtained. Until individuals discover the various ways in which a good can satisfy needs, a good is not fully established in the consumption pattern. Capabilities then account for what we can call innovation in consumption (Gualerzi, 1998).

What we are suggesting is that the development of capabilities can then be seen as part of the process by which individuals, according to social rules and socially devised practices, define the feasibility of a form of need satisfaction and contribute to establish that as a new standard for the satisfaction of a certain need.[13] The development of commodities, interacting with social practices and consumer learning, then drives changes in the way needs are satisfied and hence change in consumption patterns.

4.3.3. Structural Dynamics and Capabilities: Towards a More Cultivated Life

What of the relationship between structural dynamics and the capabilities approach. In what way does it lead us to formulate the problem of need development within a dynamic approach to consumption? This is well clarified by Walsh (2003) in an insightful comparison carried out within a larger account of the developments in Classical theory.

Walsh stresses that the question of change lies at the centre of structural dynamics. Not only does it make the assumption of a balanced path of growth driven by technical progress impossible, but it also bears all its consequences for consumption and consumption choice. If we further observe that new goods, at least some of them, are likely to diffuse and become the new basis of consumption patterns, then the question arises as to the relationship of these new goods and capabilities. Here the argument made by Walsh rests on one basic point: although there is no strict correspondence, 'there *is* … a significant relationship nonetheless' (p. 376). Structural dynamics presents a truly dynamic process by which new commodities that appear are conceivably capable of the realization of vital capabilities; but the rise of new commodities follows a sequence, dictated on the one hand, by unbalanced technical progress, on the other, by the hierarchy of human needs, which is satisfied sequentially. There is no reason to suppose a tight relationship of these two sequential processes, even less assume a tight relationship with the development of capabilities.

Nor can the problem be solved by observing that the need hierarchy can go well beyond basic needs to include the full development of human personality. Let us assume an extreme hierarchy of needs, going bottom-up, from basic needs, such as food and shelter, to 'higher' needs, well beyond those of mere survival, up to those relating to self-fulfilment: there would still be no necessary relationship, aside from the limits posed by market saturation, between the need structure and the sequential development of the material basis for the satisfaction of needs implicit in the path of structural dynamics. This conclusion is emphasized by considering capabilities. There is no guarantee that a particular amount of a particular commodity will be necessary (or sufficient) to allow the fulfillment of a particular capability. *Sometimes* it will happen' (Walsh, 2003, p. 377). Nor can the question be solved by defining a list of capabilities.[14]

This leads to full appreciation of the contribution that the capabilities approach can give to structural dynamics. Through capabilities we can take into account what can be accomplished by individuals through consumption. Although no doubt this will depend on the commodities that are brought out by technical progress – and, we might add, by investment in these commodities – it will also depend on a subjective element and on the social form in which needs are satisfied. This is why Walsh (2003) says that structural dynamics, and the evolving basket of consumption it implies, does not indicate a tight mapping to the list of capabilities, 'but surely a soil and a climate in which capabilities can flourish' (p. 377). Indeed, capabilities, while reaching beyond the traditional idea of consumption, must rest on an evolving material basis.

Although further work seems necessary to fully evaluate the relationship between structural dynamics and the capabilities approach, Walsh's insight indicates their complementarities. As suggested above, their complementarities depend on a fundamentally similar view of long-run development and ultimately of economic progress. It is not that of growth with an unchanging structure of consumption, nor of consumption reflecting only the satisfaction of basic material needs. It takes into account the full range of possibilities relating to the 'development' of the need structure and of individuals. Indeed, structural dynamics implies a consumption composition of an improved and 'more cultivated life' (p. 375). At the same time, it is precisely their complementarities that raise the question of need and need development, which appears to lie behind the problem discussed by Walsh and the missing element of a dynamic approach to consumption.

4.4. BEYOND THE NEEDS HIERARCHY: NEED DEVELOPMENT

4.4.1. Consumption and Need Structure

Before moving on, let us summarize what has been said so far and examine how it leads into discussing need and need development.

The fundamental law of motion of the consumption structure of Pasinetti's model, i.e. the dynamic theory of consumption contained in structural dynamics, makes reference to an evolving material basis aimed at satisfying needs that are arranged in a hierarchy from basic to higher level needs. Higher level needs become areas of expansion of consumption spending, such that the consumption structure evolves. In this sense we could say that income growth reveals the structure of needs. The production of the means to satisfy needs, and new commodities in particular, highlight, as pointed out by Walsh, an issue of consistency of technical change with the ascending pattern dictated by the needs hierarchy. The reference to capabilities makes that more evident.

Capabilities move us a step forward because through them we can take into account what individuals can accomplish with goods. The capabilities approach suggests that commodities are conditions, but outcomes depend on what individuals can do with them.[15] On ascending through the needs hierarchy, i.e. moving towards higher needs, needs satisfaction increasingly depends on the subject's capabilities. This only exacerbates the lack of any necessary correspondence between commodities, need and capabilities. It highlights the limits imposed on the analysis precisely by a notion of need as a given, and of the need structure as a hierarchical arrangement itself fundamentally given. We could say that in this framework needs can be satisfied, not quite developed.

This suggests that the notion of need and needs structure are not adequately investigated, precisely with respect to the very dynamic process that shapes consumption patterns. It is thus necessary to discuss explicitly the question of need development, to seek the reasons for the forms taken by the satisfaction of needs, their effects on the volume of spending and the evolving structure of demand. In other words, Walsh's remarks on the lack of correspondence can be taken to indicate a deeper question: the adequacy of the notion of a needs hierarchy and the role it plays in structuring consumption patterns. It exposes precisely the unsatisfactory conceptualization of need and need development.

If we remove the notion of a fixed needs structure, we may then look at structural dynamics and capabilities and their complementarities from a new angle, which also gives full scope to the claim that the capabilities approach can add and complete structural dynamics. A really interesting aspect is how capabilities allow us to speak of need and of need development. If we think of capabilities as part of personality development, then capabilities become part of need development driven by the individual's search for self-fulfilment. This means taking into account need development as it actually occurs, that is, by means of consumption innovation, i.e. a combination of commodities and consumption practices.

4.4.2. Need Development and Socially Determined Needs

The approach to need development presented here is based on the discussion of needs that is central to the reconsideration of the economic theory of David Levine (1981). It is not any notion of need belonging primarily to the sphere of nature, nor the general notion of human and social needs at the centre of the analysis, but rather a specific notion of 'socially determined needs'. They are not only the potential for expansion of the market, in relation to what Levine calls the structure of expansion,[16] but also the basis for the development of individual identity.[17]

The structure of expansion is responsible for determining the growth rate of aggregate circulation, i.e. the growth of the market in aggregate. It exploits what Levine calls 'the latent structure of the market', realizing its developmental potential. This in turn involves the process of determining consumption patterns. It can be illustrated as follows: in principle, market growth depends on need development. This occurs by means of the interaction of consumers with new products, which are tested and validated in the process of consumption innovation to become part of the consumption structure. Thus the drive to expansion is validated by changes in consumption patterns.[18] Indeed, in this scheme the structure of expansion cannot be sustained unless it finds its counterpart in the process of determination of consumption. The latter reflects the development of socially determined needs, which proceeds on the basis of the constitution of the individual personality within a system of persons.

As opposed to subsistence needs, 'which are imposed on the individual' (Levine, 1981, Vol. II, p. 280), socially determined needs contribute to the individual's self-seeking and personal identity. It is precisely the freedom according to which needs are developed, which makes them impossible to determine *a priori*. This is in sharp contrast with the notion of needs 'by which the species renews itself within a determinate system of natural relations' (Levine, 1981, Vol. I, p. 45). In other words, socially determined needs are not a necessity of nature, but contribute to individual identity, which is itself a dynamic concept, inherently subject to development. For the same reason there is no predetermined path to needs development, since it reflects a social process. To that extent we can say that socially determined needs are not deterministic. At the same time, the reference to the social process, and not to nature or individuals as such, indicates where their determination comes from. The development of needs, latent in the idea of their social determination, is a constant stimulus to change and the potential for the expansion of the market. To the extent in which needs are developed, new markets will emerge, affecting the structure of demand and sustaining demand growth.

Levine argues that, although insisting on the social determination of needs, Classical theory cannot articulate the notion of need that remains 'relegated to the life of the individual outside society ... since (it) entails the element of constraints and determination which is connected to a requirement of life but not to an individual whim'.[19] This raises a number of interesting questions on the notion of subsistence and the role it plays in the Classical system. Here it is sufficient to note that it effectively prevented fuller analysis of consumption that indeed plays little role in the Classical system.

The question of needs and personality development is too difficult and complex to be fully addressed here. For the present purposes it is sufficient to stress that the importance of Levine's notion of socially determined needs is that of clarifying that we are concerned with needs as requirements of social life, but also as the manifestation of the self-seeking of individuals. This in turn is shaped by their constitution as individuals in a system of persons and market relations. Levine's needy individual is not the result of biological necessity, nor the simple replication of a social uniform pattern. It is the result of socially shaped personality development within a system of market relations.

Therefore, in the approach to consumption pursued here the main purpose of the notion of socially determined needs is that of establishing the fundamental difference with a notion of needs arising from 'nature', which usually serves to displace the issue of taste formation into the domain of an extra-economic determination. In this perspective taste formation appears instead inextricably linked to the development of a socially determined identity. This stresses a particular notion of endogenous preferences.

Endogenous preferences have been associated in the literature to habit formation, preferences interdependence and adaptive behaviour. They suggest that, rather than individual choice in a narrow sense, what matters is social interaction. In the present context they attain a further connotation, since taste formation proceeds on the basis of the constitution of individuals within social life.

Precisely by insisting on the very social determination of needs, needs development does not obliterate individuality as a source of differences and change, but actually magnifies its role in determining consumption patterns. Uniformity of needs, Levine argues, would call into question the very existence of individuality, but also that of the market. Indeed, while needs development can occur only through change in the forms of their satisfaction, change is the key to the dynamism of the market economy. 'No matter how complex the structure of production and consumption, if it is unchanging, then the market is superfluous to its process of renewal. … Change ... poses the economic problem' (Levine, 1981, Vol. II, pp. 283–4). We could say that need development is therefore a defining trait of a market economy consistently operating in the 'regularly progressive mode' of the theory of Transformational Growth (Nell, 1998, p. 15).

4.4.3. An Evolving Standard of Consumption and Growth

The theory of need development based on the notion of socially determined needs completes the basic scheme of a dynamic approach to consumption grounded on structural dynamics and the capabilities approach. In this perspective an evolving standard of consumption is associated with the socially determined evolution of the material basis of individuality. The need structure is revealed by, and need development is structured around, commodities and innovation in consumption. This implies that the very notion of need can be grasped only in conjunction with the commodities that determine its social manifestation, consumption patterns.

The neediness of individuals is therefore limited by the very mechanism of expansion resting on need development. This mechanism is set in motion by the firm's effort to exploit the potential implicit in the development of need. The latter, however, depends also on the creation of 'uncommitted income'. Levine defines uncommitted income as the income that is not committed to sustain a given structure of consumption, and therefore becomes available for its development. This drives attention on the one hand to the firm's effort to develop the market and their pricing policies; on the other, to the wage level and structure, hence to the relationship between growth and distribution.

In sum: identification through a specific pattern of consumption occurs through the system of market relations, which makes change possible and sustains income creation. Consequently, what can be accomplished by individuals through innovation in consumption and variations in lifestyles must be seen within the broader process of creation and distribution of income. Need development is therefore both sustained and constrained by the logic governing Levine's 'structure of expansion'. In particular, need development is constrained by the capacity of the system to create innovation *and* uncommitted income. The latter reflects the strength and pattern of the accumulation process.

This indicates that ordering in the pattern of need development may come from the technical and social process which establishes new commodities in consumption goods markets.[20] Variability in the forms of social provision, be it private, collective, public, or otherwise, opens interesting questions for the long-term evolution of the demand structure (Nell, 2002). What matters here is to stress that in the dynamic approach outlined above the forms of need satisfaction and the standard of consumption associated with differentiated lifestyles are inextricably linked to commodities; similarly, the self-seeking of individuals is shaped and constrained by need development as it occurs through the market. This follows from the very effort to establish need development as the key to market expansion and growth.

To examine need development beyond the consumption of goods produced in the market, we need to shift our attention to need development as it may occur 'outside' the market. The standard of life includes precisely this second aspect of need development.

4.5. NEED DEVELOPMENT AND THE STANDARD OF LIFE

4.5.1. Shifting Focus

While focused on consumption and growth, the dynamic approach to consumption discussed above has a number of implications for the analysis of the standard of life. Interestingly, precisely the focus on need development helps to define overlapping and distinction of the two related concepts.

There is indeed an obvious relation between the two; an evolving standard of consumption is indispensable for an improvement in the standard of life. But then the latter seems to look beyond consumption, to consider what may be regarded as the true goals of life. The question then arises of the extent to which the laws governing an evolving material basis for need satisfaction, i.e. a standard of consumption, address this broader issue. In particular, is need development also the yardstick against which we could measure the move towards an improved standard of life?

From the reasoning in the previous sections, one thing should be clear: although the focus is not directly on the standard of life, we are taking the viewpoint, using Walsh language, of a richer and more cultivated life. This approach is certainly taking us already very close to the concerns behind the notion of a standard of life. At the same time, consumption, in whatever broad way we wish to consider it, does not necessarily answer the question exhaustively. To fully address this difference we ought to focus directly on need development as a measure of the quality of life, reflecting a more general concern for the well-being of individuals and what they regard as a better life (although probably not yet what can be called happiness).

This clarifies the fact that need development can also be an attribute of social life, social interaction and human development as such, reaching beyond the limits imposed on consumption by the expansion mechanism. We ought then to speak of need in a very broad sense indeed, not necessarily socially necessary need. But then the link to growth can no longer be the main focus, which shifts directly to the standard of life, or to what fundamental figures of the past have hinted at as a 'nobler life'.

However, even if our focus shifts to the pursuit of the true meaning of human life, this should not lead us to a sort of paradox, i.e. taking for granted the development of the material basis of an improving standard of life. In other words, we should not lose sight of the close relationship of any comfort in life with the material conditions of social reproduction and with the wage level. Otherwise the question of a wage constraint on an improving standard of life never arises. Unpleasant as it is, the reference to the subsistence of Classical Theory leaves no doubt as to the limits imposed on the standard of living of the working population. In a similar way, a consumption-based standard of living highlights the limits imposed by the logic of expansion of a market economy on the neediness of individuals.

This fundamental clarification then lays the ground for distinguishing between an evolving standard of consumption linked to long-term growth and improvements in the standard of life.

4.5.2. The Possibility of an Improving Standard of Life

This distinction emerges quite clearly on examining how the two concepts (partially) overlap with respect to key aspects of the dynamic approach to consumption.

1) *Need hierarchy and need development.* We have seen above that discussing need development we consider an *extreme* need hierarchy, of the kind one finds for instance in Maslow (1954), going from basic needs to self-fulfilment needs. We note that the growing importance of higher level needs, such as health and education, typically associated with income growth, quite clearly contributes to improvements in the standard of life. These are indeed specific aspects of the problem discussed in this volume.

Most of these needs are hardly satisfied exclusively, or not even predominantly, by commodities and market forces. This would then open the way to consider the role played by the public sector and more generally by public policy and income redistribution, but also that of social institutions, whether formal or informal, cultures and practices, that might have a positive effect on the standard of life, while having little direct relationship to the economic structure. The overlapping of an evolving standard of consumption and an improving standard of life considerably weakens and it almost dissipates when we further consider higher needs of the kind associated with individual self-fulfilment. Intellectual cultivation, leisure and aesthetic pleasure represent, no doubt, an ascent in the need structure and a fundamental aspect of need development. While that might be intertwined with the rise of new industries (from cultural tourism to continuing education), there is also another aspect, the human development they imply, which affects nothing else but the improvement in the standard of life.

2) *The subjective element.* The dynamic approach to consumption already takes into account a subjective element, that is, the agency of individuals in establishing viable new forms of need satisfaction as part of their drive to self-fulfilment. The development of personal identity contributes to shape consumption innovation and the evolving material basis for need satisfaction. The construction of socially determined individual identity and individuals' effort towards self-fulfilment are then emphasized as processes occurring through consumption. However, self-fulfilment has other dimensions, more

broadly rooted in ethical and cultural values. This forces attention to the non-economic aspect of personality development, which is not grasped by analyzing market forces, but rather as a result of inner development and social interaction.

3) *Lifestyles*. The notion of 'lifestyle' can be easily incorporated into the dynamic approach to consumption outlined above. It reflects the variability of the standard of consumption, of the forms in which needs are satisfied and developed. A lifestyle is a sort of social manifestation of a standard of consumption, introducing more variables into the analysis of consumption. It can take into account rules of behaviour and 'strategies' of consumption (Earl, 1986).

In general, need development can be articulated in differentiated lifestyles, reflecting social hierarchy, class structure and income levels. This brings us to consider social priorities and values regarded as important for the quality of life and human development. This gives full significance to social interaction as an element that is valuable *per se* in defining the standard of life. Time-uses are for instance a major aspect of an individual's life strategy. Whereas this follows from the fact that 'consumption takes time', a second aspect now comes to light. Time is indispensable for activities that are independent of consumption, but which contribute to shape lifestyles and to the improvement in the standard of life.

We can draw a general conclusion from the analysis above. Precisely due to the complexity of modern consumption and market development in advanced industrial economies, one thing is to focus on need development as an incentive to new industries and market expansion, quite another to consider it as a pure attribute of free time and relief from the pressure of work. While the former clarifies the relationship of need development with the growth potential of the market economy, the latter represents a reorientation of interest away from commodities, consumption and wealth towards what is regarded by individuals as truly important in life.

The approach to the standard of life based on need development considers aspects that have a rather tenuous link to commodities and the market, up to a point in which there is hardly any. It implies that: a) there are patterns of need development that do not depend on commodities and the market; b) there are improvements in the standard of life resting on developing subjectivity and lifestyles beyond an economic determination and the provision of goods and services.

Although concerned with an altogether different question (the effort to improve a consumer choice approach to consumption) the analysis of time constraints arising in consumption serves well to clarify this point. Time-uses are clearly part of the individual's choices and life strategy, affecting the evolution of lifestyles as well as consumption change. They force attention, in particular, on what individuals pursue and want from life, i.e. what individuals consider really valuable in life, bringing into focus what is involved in improving the standard of life, rather than consumption.

4.6. CONCLUDING REMARKS

The dynamic approach to consumption based on structural dynamics and the development of human capabilities treats the evolution of consumption patterns as part of the growth process. Its aim is an improved standard of consumption, with a systemic link to long-run development. Introducing higher level needs, human capabilities and the self-fulfilment of individuals bring us close to the question of what individuals regard as most important in life; hence the concerns behind the notion of an improving standard of life.

As shown, climbing up the need structure and need development do imply an improving standard of living and a more cultivated lifestyle. The focus on higher level needs (education, entertainment) and identity needs (informal education, arts, leisure, self-fulfilment) indicates the partial overlapping between consumption and improvement in the standard of life, at the same time suggesting that we move increasingly into an area of needs which, by their very nature, flow from and are satisfied by social interaction and individual life strategies independent of the market. The standard of life then inevitably leads us beyond the question of economic growth, to consider what can be more broadly regarded as the desirable goals of economic progress, although not necessarily a privileged topic of economic investigation.

The point is that our focus on need development clarifies a fundamental distinction between the evolution of a standard of consumption linked to the growth process and the improvement in the standard of life, which does not necessarily involve consumption but, for example, choices between time-uses. It is quite conceivable that there might be, as Marshall suggests, a positive feedback for example between the improvement in living conditions and productivity growth. The chapter does not address this aspect, confining its analysis to a better understanding of what is involved in setting the improvement in the standard of life as the ultimate goal of economic progress.

NOTES

1. In this respect one may recall Sraffa's search for an 'objectivist' foundation for economic science (cf. Kurz and Salvadori, 2005)
2. As pointed out by Panico and Rizza (2009) Myrdal argued that these assumptions, resting on Bentham's utilitarian philosophy, lack scientific foundations.
3. The Classical tradition has mainly focused on production and distribution; it did not attempt to develop a theory of consumption as such, for reasons that would require discussion of the notion of subsistence and its function in the Classical system. The Keynesian tradition mostly discussed consumption as a component of aggregate demand, consistently maintaining the focus on its contribution to spending, but did not elaborate greatly on its motivations, nor on its internal structure and evolution. Therefore the question of output composition remains mostly open in the Classical and Keynesian theory and is instead entrusted to (given) consumer preferences in mainstream theory.
4. As observed by Zamagni (1986) consumer theory has a specific analytical purpose reflecting the role of demand in the Neoclassical theory of value. The analytical apparatus is necessary to derive demand curves with the desired properties, so that they can concur with supply curves to determine equilibrium prices. It does not aim to analyze the consumer and consumption patterns as such (Gualerzi, 1998).
5. 'Gossen worked, one might say, at the "opposite pole" from the now standard analysis of consumer behavior. While the latter ignores the consumption time constraint, Gossen began by ignoring the budget constraint' (p. 21).
6. In the same vein he says: 'our proposal that consumer theory should center on the use of time carries no implication that the economist should cease to care very much about commodity use, commodity prices and consumer expenditure!' (p. 60).
7. This does not imply it is 'either unhelpful or uninteresting, it is simply different' (p. 5).
8. Steedman discusses elsewhere (1989) the question of non-autonomous preferences and beliefs, arguing that 'The individual agent, invoked (quite properly) in economic theory, is…an *intrinsically* social individual agent' (p. 212) and 'it is incoherent to treat the individual's knowledge, beliefs and preferences as fundamental data' (p. 214). In discussing the relationship between rationality and altruism in Wicksteed he points out that the latter favoured a 'consideration of the "whole" individual' (p. 194) rather than the limited motives of 'economic man' when analyzing consumption choices.
9. This is why Pasinetti speaks of a 'natural system', independent of institutions, whose analysis represents a second step in the investigation (see Pasinetti, 2007).
10. Gibbard (1986) has pointed out that Pareto ordinality focuses on satisfaction of preferences, not of needs.
11. For a stylized representation of the several dimensions affecting the capabilities set, see Robeyns (2005).
12. As noted by Robeyns (2005, pp. 103–4) 'Nussbaum enters the capability approach from a perspective of moral-legal-political philosophy … Sen's work on the capability approach is closer to economic reasoning than Nussbaum's'.
13. It is not the need for food or shelter that matters for a dynamic theory of consumption, but rather a socially accepted, although differenciated and technically feasible form of satisfaction of need. The reason why this has been difficult for traditional theory to grasp is possibly because it calls into question the traditional view of the consumer and of consumer choice (Gualerzi, 1998).
14. Walsh quotes Sen as saying '[t]here can be substantial debates on the particular functionings that should be included in the list of important achievements and the corresponding capabilities' (Sen, 1999).

15. It is a drastically different approach from that embodied in the diet problem, in which combinations of characteristics satisfy a given need in a given need structure.
16. The notion of structure of expansion combines the idea of structure with that of investment as the moving force of change. 'Investment is the activity of building the structure of expansion. But the peculiarity of capital is to be found in the fact that the building of the structure is also the purpose of the structure. It is as if the putting up of a house, rather than living in it, were the purpose of a house (which is, appropriately enough, the case so far as the contractor is concerned)' (p. 184).
17. With respect to the individual, need is 'the content of his self-determination, and the objective of his self-seeking' (Levine, 1981, vol. I, p. 45).
18. In fact, the structure of expansion, i.e. the producing and marketing structure, is such only to the extent that a particular capital succeeds in establishing its product within the structure of consumption.
19. 'Within society the individual can at best articulate a set of preferences, which as such cannot be considered to constitute any real determination. Ultimately the idea that there are needs articulated exclusively within society stands as a reproach to the whole of the history of social theory' (Levine, 1981, vol. I, p. 47).
20. In fact, it directs the attention to the relationship of consumption patterns and investment in new products and new industries, that is, the composition of the growth process (Gualerzi, 2005). The question of consumption composition and product innovation has recently resurfaced under the heading of quality improvement and variety growth. Recent developments have examined how variety sustains consumption spending (Bils and Klenow, 2001) and the reasons for consumption fluctuations (Parker and Preston, 2005).

REFERENCES

Bils, M. and P. Klenow (2001), 'The Acceleration of Variety Growth', *American Economic Review*, **91**(2), 274–80.

Becker, G. (1965), 'A Theory of the Allocation of Time', *Economic Journal*, **75**(299), 493–517.

Bruni, L. and P.L. Porta (2005), *Economic and Happiness. Framing the Analysis*, Oxford: Oxford University Press.

Camerer, C., G. Lowenstein and D. Prelec (2005), 'Neuroeconomics: How Neuroscience Can Inform Economics', *Journal of Economic Literature*, **34**(1), 9–64.

Duesenberry, J. (1949), *Income, Saving and the Theory of Consumer Behavior*, Cambridge: Harvard University Press.

Earl, P. (1986), *Lifestyle Economics*, New York: St Martin's Press.

Fernandez-Grela, M. (2006), 'Disaggregating the Components of the Hicks-Allen Composite Commodity', *History of Political Economy*, **38**(Suppl 1), 32–47.

Gibbard, A. (1986), 'Interpersonal Comparisons: Preference, Good, and the Intrinsic Reward of a Life', in J. Elster and A. Hylland (eds), *Foundations of Social Choice Theory*, Cambridge: Cambridge University Press, pp. 165–93.

Gualerzi, D. (1998), 'Change, Choice and Innovation in Consumption', in M. Bianchi (ed.), *The Active Consumer: Novelty and Surprise in Consumer Choice*, London: Routledge, pp. 46–63.

Gualerzi, D. (2001), *Consumption and Growth: Recovery and Structural Change in the U.S. Economy*, Cheltenham, UK and Northampton, MA, USA: Edward Elgar.

Gualerzi, D. (2005), 'Consumption Composition: Growth and Distribution' in R. Balducci and N. Salvadori (eds), *Innovation, Unemployment and Policy in the Theories of Growth and Distribution*, Cheltenham, UK and Northampton, MA, USA: Edward Elgar, pp. 72–105.

Ironmonger, D.S. (1972), *New Commodities and Consumer Behavior*, Cambridge: Cambridge University Press.

Kurz, H. and N. Salvadori (2005), 'Representing the Production and the Circulation of Commodities in Material Terms: On Sraffa's Objectivism', *Review of Political Economy*, **17**(3), 413–41.

Lancaster, K.J. (1966), 'A new Approach to Consumer Theory', *Journal of Political Economy*, **74**(2), 132–57.

Lancaster, K.J. (1971), *Consumer Demand: A New Approach*, New York: Columbia University Press.

Levine, D.P. (1981), *Economic Theory*, Vol. I and II, London: Routledge & Kegan Paul.

Levine, D.P. (1998), *Subjectivity in Political Economy. Essays on Wanting and Choosing*, London: Routledge & Kegan Paul.

Maslow, A. (1954), *Motivation and Personality*, New York: Harper.

Mirowski, P. and H.D. Wade (2006), 'Introduction to Agreement on Demand: Consumer Theory in the Twentieth Century', *History of Political Economy*, **38**(Suppl.), 1–6.

Nell, E. (1998), *The General Theory of Transformational Growth*, Cambridge: Cambridge University Press.

Nell, E. (2002), 'Notes on the Transformational Growth of Demand', in M. Setterfield, (ed), *The Economics of Demand-Led Growth*, Cheltenham, UK and Northampton, MA, USA: Edward Elgar.

Nussbaum, M. (2000), *Women and Human Development: The Capabilities Approach*, Cambridge: Cambridge University Press.

Opocher, A. (2008), 'Does Economic Growth Ultimately Lead to a "Nobler Life"? A Comparative Analysis of the Predictions of Mill, Marshall and Keynes'. In this volume.

Panico, C. and M.O. Rizza (2009), 'Myrdal, Growth Processes and Equilibrium Theories', in N. Salvadori, P. Commendatore and M. Tamberi (eds), *Geography, Structural Change and Economic Development: Theory and Empirics*, Cheltenham, UK and Northampton, MA, USA: Edward Elgar, pp. 181–200.

Parker, J. and B. Preston (2005), 'Precautionary Saving and Consumption Fluctuations', *American Economic Review*, **95**(4), 1119–43.

Pasinetti, L.L. (1981), *Structural Change and Economic Growth*, Cambridge: Cambridge University Press.

Pasinetti, L.L. (1993), *Structural Economic Dynamics*, Cambridge: Cambridge University Press.

Pasinetti, L.L. (2007), *Keynes and the Cambridge Keynesian*, Cambridge: Cambridge University Press.

Robeyns, I. (2005), 'The Capability Approach: a Theoretical Survey', *Journal of Human Development*, **6**(1), 93–114.

Sen, A. (1977), 'Rational Fool: A Critique of the Behavioral Foundations of Economic Theory', *Philosophy and Public Affairs*, **6**(4), 317–44.

Sen, A. (1985), *Commodities and Capabilities*, Amsterdam: North Holland.

Sen, A. (1999), *Development as Freedom*, New York: Knopf.

Steedman, I. (1989), *From Exploitation to Altruism*, Oxford: Basil Blackwell.

Steedman, I. (2001), *Consumption Takes Time*, London: Routledge.

Walsh, V. (2003), 'Sen after Putnam', *Review of Political Economy*, **15**(3), 315–94.

Winston, C. (1982), *The Timing of Economic Activity*, Cambridge: Cambridge University Press.

Zamagni, S. (1986), 'La teoria del consumatore nell'ultimo quarto di secolo: risultati, problemi, linee di tendenza', *Economia Politica*, **3**(3).

5. The need for standards in students' grading

Valentino Dardanoni and Salvatore Modica

5.1. INTRODUCTION

School grades are a signal of cognitive competence, and as a message it is received by potential employers and universities. University degree scores are signals of higher proficiency for the labour market. In addition, evaluating students' cognitive achievements is increasingly important for policy makers[1] and to assess the impact of education on economic growth.[2]

How informative are these signals? We briefly report a few empirical results which suggest that in Italy there is some room for improvement, in the direction of some form of standardization. In particular, we describe the results on school grades contained in Dardanoni et al. (2007), and report preliminary data on degree scores for some faculties at the University of Palermo.

It may be argued that the problem is alleviated by the presence of other signals, such as direct cognitive ability tests like those provided in the PISA-OECD surveys or those used for university admissions. But while this is true for school students, university scores cannot have such substitutes. And even for the case of lower education, the measurement of achievements by cognitive tests raises difficult problems, since no test is perfect, and repeated tests carry the risk that 'only what gets measured gets done'. Grades, on the other hand, are costless, abundant, frequent and population-wide; but to be useful they should accurately reflect underlying competence, since the lower their information content, the higher the signalling noise generated by the sender and the de-codification costs incurred by the receiver.

The paper by Dardanoni et al. (2007) contains international comparisons. In particular, it explores how a country's educational system affects the way grading policy varies across schools, at a given time. They first develop a theoretical model which investigates how a school's grading policy may depend on the distribution of competence of its own students, such as when teachers in weaker schools tend to grant higher grades for a given level of achievement. Their theoretical model yields four possible classes of grading policies, each corresponding to a possible institutional scenario which holds above school level (educational system). The econometric model derived from theory is then estimated for five countries, namely Australia, Germany, Italy, the Netherlands and the USA, using the OECD PISA 2003 test scores and the information reported in the students' questionnaire on school grades. Using a probit model for each country, they obtain an estimate of the relationship between the teachers' evaluation of students' competence and its level as measured by PISA test scores, and of the dependence of this relationship on the mean and variance of student competence within each school. Each country corresponds rather closely to one of the four institutional settings identified by the model. In particular, in the Australian educational system grading policies do not seem to vary significantly at the school level, while in Germany, the Netherlands and Italy there seems to be a rather substantial dependence, for a given level of student competence, between school grades and school characteristics. This dependence seems of a different kind in Germany and the Netherlands as compared to Italy: while in Germany and the Netherlands both strong and weak students coming from weaker schools achieve uniformly higher grades, in Italy the difference in grades between schools is wider for weak students. This may be partially due to the tracking system which is present in Germany and the Netherlands.

The first evidence on university degree scores comes from our own university when we begin to collect data on student scores in the different subjects in the various faculties. Albeit very preliminary, the results reveal large differences in the distribution of average scores in the different faculties. Thus for some faculties around 20 per cent of students graduate with top grades, in others more than 50 per cent.

In both cases one may argue that the signal arriving from student evaluation is far from perfect. It would then be desirable that some steps towards standardization be designed both for schools and universities. In the conclusion we advance concrete proposals as a basis for discussion.

5.2. GRADING IN SCHOOLS

Here we summarize the theory developed and the estimation results obtained in Dardanoni et al. (2007), whose aim was to study the relationship between cognitive competence and school grades, in different institutional contexts, keeping in mind that teachers' evaluations may differ across schools within each country.

The basic notation is as follows: in a given institutional context (country) $c=1,\ldots,C$ there are S_c schools, and in each school $s_c=1,\ldots,S_c$ there are

$n(s_c)$ students with competence levels $x_1,\ldots, x_{n(s_c)}$, which are independent real random variables extracted from some school-dependent cdf F_{s_c}. It is assumed that, in terms of grading policies, within each institutional context schools differ only in the distribution of student competence. Thus a school s is identified with F_s. Teachers in school s choose a (possibly s-dependent) valuation $y_i \in \mathbb{R}$ for students with competence x_i, where of course better students should get higher valuations. Thus the teachers' problem in a given school in a given country is to choose an increasing map $y=v_s(x)$ which is to be used in their school.

Given first of all that grading policies vary between schools operating in the same institutional context we omit the subscript c from s_c. To model the fact that usually the main issue in grading within schools is what to do with the weak and the strong students, the existence is assumed of external constraints which take the form of two reference competence levels $x_c^-(s)<x_c^+(s)$, a low and a high one – which may depend both on the given school and on the country where it operates – for which grades must be fixed at $y_c^-<y_c^+$:

$$v_s\left[x_c^-(s)\right]=y_c^- \ , \ v_s\left[x_c^+(s)\right]=y_c^+. \tag{5.1}$$

For example, y^- may denote the minimum valuation required for the pass grade, while y^+ may be the minimum valuation required for some higher grade. The two reference competence levels $x_c^-(s)$, $x_c^+(s)$ may be for example quantiles, or may be fixed independently of school parameters.

To account for the fact that teachers, when choosing v_s, are constrained by students' perception of unfairness on their part, it is assumed that given any two students with competence levels x and x', the difference in their valuations $v_s(x)-v_s(x')$ must be non-decreasing in $x-x'$.

Under these two assumptions it is then shown that the valuation function must be linear:

$$v_s(x)=\alpha(s)+\beta(s)x. \tag{5.2}$$

Linearity of the valuation function in student competence levels implies that, within each country, school heterogeneity affects the valuation process only through the intercept and slope parameters $\alpha(s)$ and $\beta(s)$. The latter depend on c via x_c^- and x_c^+, so the next step is to investigate how valuation depends on s in different types of institutional contexts.

Turning to the comparison of different institutional contexts, note that each is characterized by the constraints which determine the two reference points $[x_c^-(s), y_c^-]$ and $[x_c^+(s), y_c^+]$ for each school. Recall that the values y_c^- and y_c^+ were assumed to be school-independent; on the other hand, since even within the same country each school may experience quite a different distribution of student competence, $x^-(s)$ and $x^+(s)$ in principle may vary across schools. Thus, in the model there are four possibilities which describe different institutional scenarios: i) $x^-(s)$ and $x^+(s)$ are both s-independent; ii) $x^-(s)$ and $x^+(s)$ are both s-dependent; iii) $x^+(s)$ is s-dependent; iv) $x^-(s)$ is s-dependent. The four institutional settings can be described in detail as follows:

[A] *Absolute Valuation.* Grades follow common procedures at above-school level. In this case, constraints on school-level grading amount to setting a common scale, that is, $x_c^-(s)$ and $x_c^+(s)$ are fixed independently of the school, at $x_c^- < 0$ and $x_c^+ > 0$.

[R] *Relative Valuation.* The proportion of students below y^- and above y^+ – determined by probability levels p^-, p^+ respectively – is fixed above the school level. In terms of the constraints, this amounts to having $x_c^-(s)$ and $x_c^+(s)$ determined as the p^--th and p^+-th quantiles. This is equivalent to scenario A if the competence distribution is invariant across schools. If, on the other hand, school populations are heterogeneous, the weaker the school population the lower quantiles will generally be.

[AL] *Absolute Lower Bound.* In this case there is a minimum absolute acceptable level of competence required for the valuation y^-; however, the upper tail (valuations above y^+) is determined in relative terms within each school by p^+. Formal translation of this case implies that x_c^- is school-independent and $x_c^+(s)$ is the p^+-th quantile in school s.

[RL] *Relative Lower Bound.* In this case in each school s there is a maximum acceptable fraction of failed students, but the high competence level is fixed in absolute terms. This implies that $x_c^-(s)$ is the p^--th quantile in school s while x_c^+ is fixed.

Given linearity, to study how the valuation function v_s varies across schools when c belongs to one of these institutional contexts amounts to studying how, in each different setting, the intercept $\alpha(s)$ and slope $\beta(s)$ vary depending on the distribution of competence levels F_s. Concentrating on the mean μ_s and standard deviation σ_s of F_s, it is convenient to simplify our notation further: given identification of s with F_s and the latter with its first two moments (μ_s, σ_s), a school is effectively identified with a pair (μ, σ). In the sequel we shall then write $s=(\mu, \sigma)$.

Under another technical assumption, holding for example in the special case where F_s belongs to a family of location-scale distributions with μ and σ as location and scale parameters, the authors show that in the four scenarios [A], [R], [RL], [AL] the coefficients α, β in equation (5.2) satisfy:

[A] $\alpha_\mu = \beta_\mu = \alpha_\sigma = \beta_\sigma = 0$ [R] $\alpha_\mu < 0,\ \beta_\mu = 0,\ \beta_\sigma \le 0$

[AL] $\alpha_\mu < 0,\ \beta_\mu < 0,\ \alpha_\sigma \le 0,\ \beta_\sigma \le 0$ [RL] $\alpha_\mu < 0,\ \beta_\mu > 0,\ \alpha_\sigma \ge 0,\ \beta_\sigma \le 0.$

The result implies that in institutional settings where [A] holds there is a homogeneous valuation across different school types. This is the benchmark, undistorted system. Its simplest implementation is identifiable with country-level curriculum-based external exit examinations, but we shall see this is not strictly necessary for nationwide standards to emerge. In the other cases, if variation in competence across schools is non-negligible, departure from absolute valuations implies that, within the same country, both the intercept and the slope of the valuation function may become school-specific; in these cases not only may valuations in some schools be uniformly inflated (intercept effect), but also in some schools the less capable students are over-evaluated and the stronger ones penalized (slope effect). If these effects are substantial, the grading signal may become much less informative of the students' underlying ability.

The above theory provides the framework for empirical estimation, and it is applied to the 2003 OECD-PISA Survey. Taking a first order approximation of α and β with respect to school's mean and standard deviation μ_s and σ_s, and ignoring higher order moments, the valuation function is linearized in all covariates; after adding two student-specific terms regarding family background and sex the valuation is written, using subscripts for partial derivatives for α and β, as

$$v_{is} = a + bx_{is} + \alpha_\mu \mu_s + \alpha_\sigma \sigma_s + \beta_\mu \mu_s\ x_{is} + \beta_\sigma \sigma_s\ x_{is} + \gamma' z_{is} + \varepsilon_{is} \tag{5.3}$$

In practice, true evaluations of students, v_{is}, are not observed, but can be considered as a continuous latent representation of the observed binary variable p_{is}, which assumes the value 1 if the student obtains a pass grade (that is, $v_{is} > \bar{v}$, where $\bar{v}$ denotes the school-independent valuation level necessary to pass), and 0 otherwise. Under the assumption that ε_{is} has a standard normal distribution, it follows that the following probit equation holds:

$$\begin{aligned} &\Pr(p_{is} = 1 \mid x_{is},\ \mu_s,\ \sigma_s,\ z_{is}) = \\ &= \Phi(a_0 + bx_{is} + \alpha_\mu \mu_s + \alpha_\sigma \sigma_s + \beta_\mu \mu_s\ x_{is} + \beta_\sigma \sigma_s\ x_{is} + \gamma' z_{is}), \end{aligned} \tag{5.4}$$

where Φ denotes the standard normal link. In the application p denotes whether the student has obtained a pass grade in mathematics, x is the PISA measured mathematical competence score (originally scaled to an average of 500 points with 100 points standard deviation across OECD countries), μ and σ respectively measure the mean and standard deviation of PISA mathematical competence in each school, and z contains two covariates, namely student's gender and his/her socio-economic family background. With these specifications, the probit equation (5.4) is estimated for Australia, Germany, Italy, the Netherlands and the USA.

Given that the purpose of estimation is to evaluate differences in grading practices, it is important to see how different the studied countries are in the first place, in particular with regard to variability between schools. Table 5.1 contains the main characteristics.

Table 5.1. Scores

Country	Average score	Variance in % of OECD average	Between-school var.,% of total	% Students above pass
AUS	524 (2.1)	104.9	21.1	83.2 (0.7)
DEU	503 (3.3	105.1	51.7	92.3 (0.6)
ITA	466 (3.1)	108.3	52.2	62.0 (1.0)
NLD	538 (3.1)	91.9	58	72.2 (1.2)
USA	483 (2.9)	106.5	25.7	87.9 (0.6)
OECD	500 (0.6)	100		

Source: OECD (2005). Estimates are provided with the corresponding standard error in brackets. For details on score assignment see the Technical Report.

The five countries present significant differences. In terms of average competence the Netherlands and Australia rank above the others; variance is higher than the OECD average in all of them except the Netherlands. As to between-school variance – in terms of our model the variability of μ – when differences between schools are small, relative valuation is closer to absolute; and the table shows that in the five countries we are considering there are large differences, with between-school variance being around 20–25 per cent in Australia and the USA while in Germany, Italy and the Netherlands it is over 50 per cent. The whole distribution of school mean μ besides its variance reveals that there are also more subtle differences. For example, the upper and lower panels of Figure 5.1, referring to Italy and the Netherlands respectively, reveal two different pictures. The first presents a 'normal' bell-shaped distribution of μ with within-school variance increasing with school quality: there are relatively few good students in weak schools, but good and poor students alike populate the high-performing ones. By contrast, in the lower panel the bimodality of the mean distribution describes a system partitioned in two performance-based school clusters, a story reinforced by the fact that competence variability in the better schools is lower.

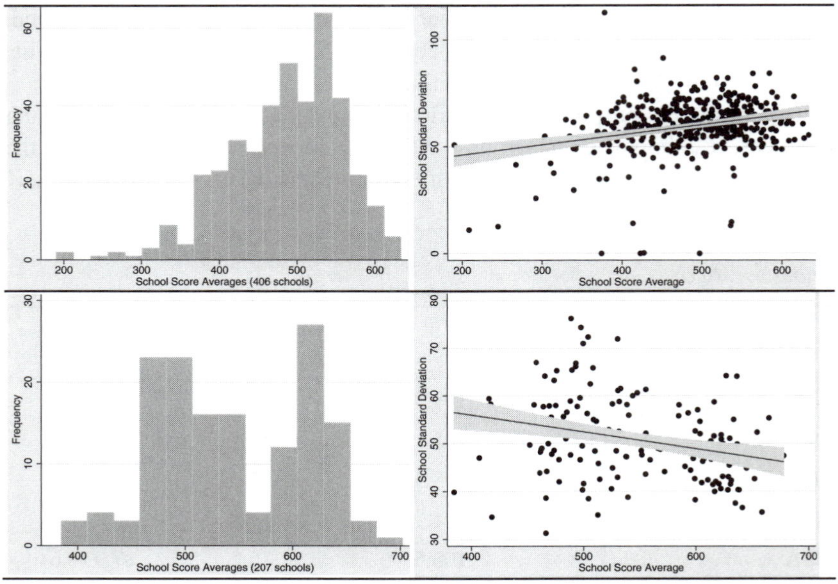

Figure 5.1. Schools means and std: Italy above, the Netherlands below

Dardanoni et al. (2007) carry out estimation of equation (4) using STATA's survey probit weighted ML routine with robust linearized SE. A Wald test was carried out, in each country, for the hypothesis that $\alpha_\mu = \beta_\mu = \alpha_\sigma = \beta_\sigma = 0$, i.e. that grading conforms to the hypothesis [A]. This hypothesis is not rejected for USA and AUS with p-values respectively equal to 0.152 and 0.195. For DEU and NLD the results suggest that in below-average-competence schools grades may be uniformly inflated. Therefore, grading practices in DEU and NLD are compatible with hypothesis [R]. On the other hand, in Italy there are strongly significant intercept and slope effects according to school competence heterogeneity, with signs (when significant) compatible with hypothesis [RL].

To evaluate the quantitative impact of these distortions, the authors compare, for each country, the difference in valuation between a good and a poor school, at a low and high level of student performance. Thus one has to identify the distribution of competence (μ and σ) in a typical strong and weak school, and two appropriate levels of competence which may be considered representative of good and poor students. Given benchmark schools chosen with μ_s and σ_s equal to their country average, strong and weak schools are taken with μ at the 75th and 25th percentiles respectively, with corresponding standard deviations adjusted along the regression line of σ on μ (see Figure 5.1). As to performance, in the six PISA levels in

Mathematics, the threshold between the first and the second level – a score of 420 – was taken as a low performance, and that between the fifth and sixth (670) as high. The question is then: given the estimated valuation of a student scoring 420 in an average school, what is the competence score of a student who receives the same valuation in a good [resp. poor] school? The same question is then repeated for the 670 score. Intuitively, if school evaluation is relative, to obtain any given valuation in a good school a student must have a higher competence level (i.e. score) than if he were in a poor school; so the good school line must lie below the other. The results are shown in Figure 5.2 (the average school lines are not shown), where the lines are drawn on the basis of the coefficients of the probit regression.

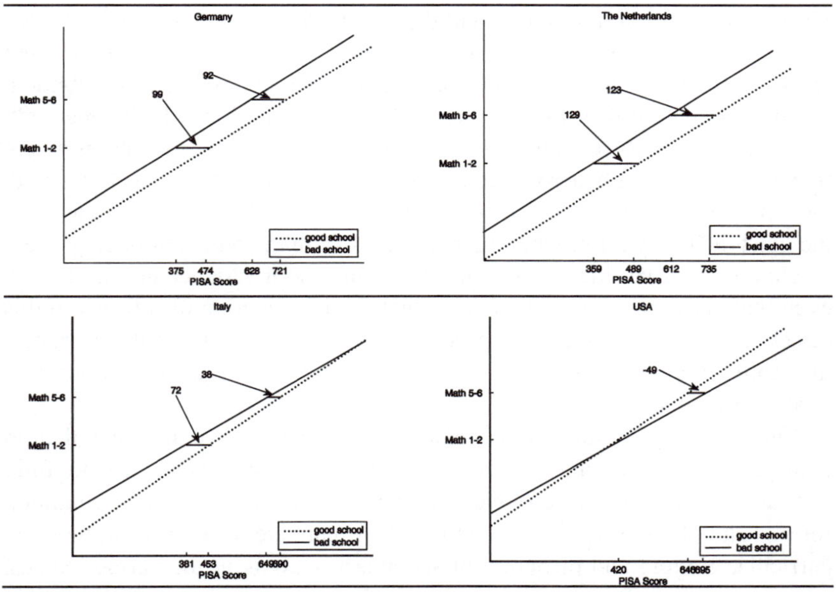

Figure 5.2. Pisa scores needed for valuation corresponding to thresholds between Mat levels 1–2 and 5–6 (420 and 670 in an average school)

A glance at Figure 5.2 reveals that in Germany and the Netherlands the difference in school grading is substantial: given the same teacher evaluation, there is a full PISA-level difference in competence between good and bad schools, both at the low and high end of the spectrum. This may be partly due to the tracking system present in these countries' educational structure. In the case of Australia (not shown) the two lines essentially coincide. In Italy, confirming the predictions of case [RL], the difference is more marked for low than for high levels, and is substantial (one PISA level) only for poorly performing students.

5.2.1. Comments on the Italian Case

We interpret the results of Dardanoni et al. (2007) concerning Italy in the light of the model predictions, which are that countries with absolute standard requirements imposed at above-school level or low variance of average competence across schools should be in class [A], while under different constraints at above-school level (like a fixed percentage of failed students in each school) the grading policy should depend on school parameters.

Italy is the only country in our sample which falls in [RL]: exams at the end of secondary schools are designed at the national level, but grading is on a local basis, so the system is effectively decentralized. Weaker schools are located especially in the South, and the 'political' need not to fail too high a fraction of students from poorer areas accounts for fixing a school-dependent $x^{-}(s)$, producing higher grades at the bottom end of the distribution. Contrasting with this is a strong national cultural tradition, which apparently induces teachers to require high standards from the best students, who are then graded uniformly across the country. The resulting picture is [RL], with the detrimental consequence that the strong students from poorer areas have the most difficulty differentiating themselves from the others through grades.

On the negative side we note that between-school variance in Italy is high even without a tracking system, such that the introduction of reforms in this direction would exacerbate the problem. Recall that the higher this variance, the more pronounced the effect of variations in grading practices in different types of schools.

Cause for optimism, on the other hand, comes from the fact that in countries where grading policies show no distortions there are no fully centralized exams in place (which, as stated above, is a sufficient condition for undistorted grading). Indeed, in the USA there are differences in funding, curricula, grading and difficulty of secondary schools in the various States, and mandatory exit exams are present only in 22 States (see Kober et al., 2006). In Australia the situation is similar to the USA, with exit exams standardized only at state level in various degrees in the nine States (see Masters et al., 2007). In the USA too there are elements of centralization, in that colleges and universities require applicants to submit scores from a Scholastic Achievement Test (SAT) established as early as 1901, where SAT scores are intended to supplement the secondary school record and help college admission officers to put local data – such as course work, grades, and class rank – in a national perspective.

The conclusion is that some elements of centralization, which in this case is synonymous with standardization, together with the low variance of school quality (variance of μ), may produce a system without school-dependent grading policy distortions.

5.3. UNIVERSITY SCORES: THE CASE OF PALERMO

We have just begun to collect data on average student scores in our university, referring to the period 1995–2005. In Italy the degree score, which ranges from 66 to 110 (with midpoint 88), is the sum of the average of the grades the candidate earns in the exams he/she passes plus a score for a final thesis. Below we discuss the average score *before* the thesis.

Of course it is arduous, and possibly inappropriate, to compare the quality of an engineer with that of an Ancient Greek scholar. It is also hard to contend that in some absolute sense Mathematics, say, is more difficult than Political Science. Thus, one should perhaps be content with comparisons among students of the same disciplinary areas. And even within this limited range, many would agree that a given mark in Mathematics at the Scuola Normale Superiore di Pisa signals a better student than the same mark earned at most other Italian universities.

On the other hand, the differences we have begun to observe in average scores in the various faculties of the University of Palermo are impressive, as a glance at Figure 5.3 reveals. For example, while Law (top left) quite closely resembles a Normal distribution centred around the range midpoint (88), Literature (bottom left) is extremely skewed to the right. Indeed, in the latter faculty more than half of the students get an average above 103, hence usually graduate with top marks; in the Faculty of Law only 10 per cent achieve this distinction. Of course students may come from different pools: Medicine is also markedly skewed to the right, with almost 30 per cent of their students graduating with top marks, but this may be partly due to better student selection (and/or self-selection). Unfortunately we do not yet possess data on Diploma scores to study such correlations.

It is clear that the informative value of these signals could be increased at no cost, and that this would be beneficial for the message receivers. In the presence of the aforementioned difficulties inherent in cross-faculty comparisons, some form of standardization might be studied within each faculty. A possibility would be for example to conform to an unwritten rule according to which in each subject, the long-term average of marks given to students should have a mean equal to the midpoint of the marks range (in Italy this would be 24, midpoint between 18 and 30). In this case the quantiles would be similar in each faculty. This would produce uniform information about relative rankings in the different faculties, but it is to be

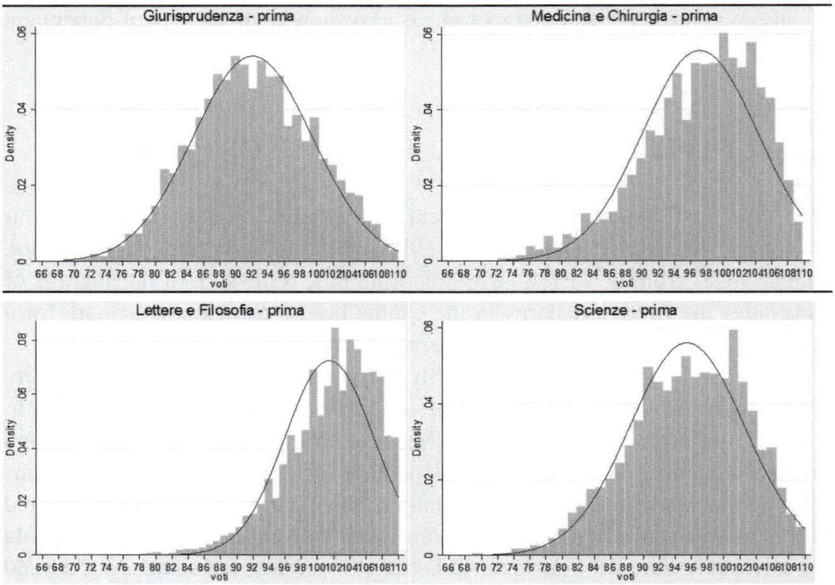

Figure 5.3. Original score distributions in Law, Medicine, Science and Literature

stressed that these are preliminary remarks, for the desirable content of the information that university grades should convey is itself a subject worth closer examination.

To get an inkling of the effect of adjusting the original scores we performed a simple experiment. Within most faculties there are 'harder' and 'easier' exams: a high average final score may be attained by getting a not-so-high mark in the few difficult exams, and scoring highly on a plethora of 'simpler' subjects. How strong is this simpler-subjects effect? To see this we computed adjusted final scores by eliminating all subjects which on average granted marks above the overall faculty average, and retaining only the remaining, 'tougher' ones. Figure 5.4 reports our results for the Faculties of Economics and Engineering. The corrected distributions are more symmetric, centred closer to the midpoint and, importantly, have markedly higher standard deviations. In the cases reported in the figure, for example, standard deviations increase from 5.88 to 7.46 for Engineering, and from 6.3 to 7.4 for Economics. Moreover, the percentage of students graduating with top marks falls from 13.8 to 5.9 for Engineering, and from 17.5 to 6.6 for Economics. Although still at an informal level, we feel such findings are indeed more informative than the original ones.

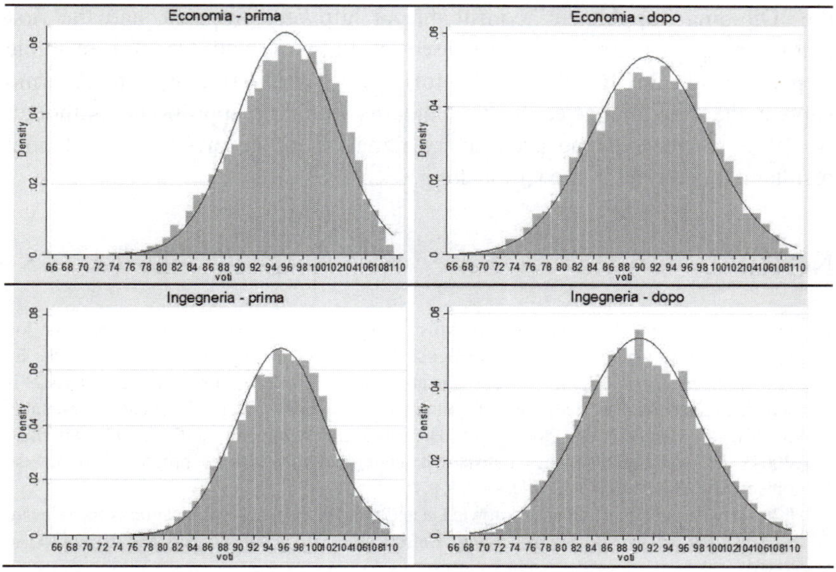

Figure 5.4. Score distributions in Economics and Engineering: original and without high-scoring subjects

5.4. CONCLUSIONS

In the previous sections we reported some aspects of grading practices in schools and universities, and remarked that in both cases there are distortions which reduce the informative value of grades as market signals. Hence, it is arguable that it would be appropriate to search for some common standards to which the separate decision-making centres may adhere.

For schools, the obvious candidate is the implementation of system-wide curriculum-based external exit examinations; the problem is that the costs associated with this course of action may be very high. Fortunately, according to empirical estimates in Dardanoni et al. (2007) it may not be necessary to go all the way in that direction. In the case of Australia for example, competence standards appear to be fixed at system (country) level, but external exams are held at sub-system (state) level. Possibly, some element of centralization associated with a moderate variability of competence between schools might considerably reduce distortions.

With regard to universities the problem is aggravated by the absence of alternative signals (such as cognitive tests), and grades are of course the last signal sent from education to the labour market. At the European level the search for standards is on the agenda, as emerges from the documentation on the 'Diploma Supplement' consultable at http://ec.europa.eu, and the first recommendations are being discussed in Italy as well (see for example http://www.crui.it/CRUI/DS/finale.htm). Our initial findings in Palermo support the view that a search for standards would be appropriate. Although we have advanced some preliminary remarks on the problem, substantial results in this direction are still lacking.

NOTES

1. Indeed, the emphasis on educational skills as signals has shifted over time, from the job market context where it was first recognized in the 1970s (e.g. in the classic works by Arrow, Spence and Stiglitz), to the education policy context, where the central issue is whether educational services are performing well and whether the producers are accountable for it (Jacobs and van der Ploeg, 2006; Hanushek and Wößmann, 2007a, 2007b; Pritchett, 2004), i.e. whether there are 'transparent, consistent measures of progress towards the objectives' (Pritchett, 2004, p. 4).
2. It has been argued that students' knowledge and not simply years of education is the relevant variable that influences growth'; see e.g. Barro (2001) and Hanushek and Wößmann (2007a, 2007b).

REFERENCES

Barro, R.J. (2001), 'Human Capital and Growth', *American Economic Review*, **91**(2), 12–17.

Dardanoni, V., S. Modica and A. Pennisi (2007), 'Grading in Heterogeneous Schools', mimeo.

Hanushek, E.A. and L. Wößmann (2007a). 'The Role of School Improvement in Economic Development', *NBER Working Paper*, no. 12832.

Hanushek, E.A. and L. Wößmann (2007b). 'The Role of Educational Quality in Economic Development', *World Bank Policy Research Working Paper*, no. 4122.

Jacobs, B. and F. van der Ploeg (2006). 'Guide to Reform of Higher Education: A European Perspective', *Economic Policy*, **21**(47), 535–92.

Kober, N., D. Zabala, N. Chudowsky, V. Chudowdsky, K. Gayler and J. McMurrer (2006), *State High School Exit Exams: A Challenging Year*, Washington, DC: Center on Education Policy.

Masters, G. and G. Matters (2007), *Year 12 Curriculum Content and Achievement Standards*, Report prepared by the Australian Council for Educational Research for the Department of Education, Science and Training, Canberra: Australian Government.

OECD (2004), *Learning for Tomorrow's World – First Results from PISA 2003*, Paris: OECD

OECD (2005), *PISA 2003 Technical Report*, Paris: OECD.

Pritchett, L. (2004), 'Towards a New Consensus for Addressing the Global Challenge of the Lack of Education', *Copenhagen Consensus 2004 Challenge Paper.*

6. Education and endogenous growth in the neoclassical tradition

Mario Pomini

6.1. INTRODUCTION

The literature of the 1960s assigned a significant role to education as a means to promote economic growth and improve the skills of the labour force. Indeed, various economists from the classical era onwards reflected on the benefits of investment in education for economic growth (Blaug, 1978), but only the economists of that period were able to bring this element into the context of a formal model of economic growth, beginning with Uzawa's contribution (1965). In recent years, the relation between education and growth has received renewed attention within the New Growth Theory (Aghion and Howitt, 1988, ch. 10). Economists have begun to study the influence of education spending on consumption-saving decisions in models that allow for the possibility of persistent growth, starting from the seminal study by Lucas (1988). To the extent that formal schooling is a significant component of human capital investment, educational institutions are important for economic growth (Glomm and Ravikumar 1992, 1997).

The aim of this chapter is to analyse the evolution of the relationship between education spending and economic growth within the neoclassical framework. In this regard we may distinguish two phases: the one that developed during the 1960s, and the current phase, which has arisen from the theory of endogenous growth. As will be seen, the novelty of the ideas advanced by endogenous growth theory (EGT) is considerably reduced when the first generation of growth models is considered. On the other hand, the fundamental difference between them consists in the fact that the recent literature considers education to be a peculiar form of human capital, namely a production factor which, like the other traditional factors, labour and capital, can be accumulated. This assumption has generated a large body of literature showing the complexity of the relationship between economic growth and the accumulation of knowledge through education. The new approach allowed theorists to tackle a new range of problems mentioned in the earlier approach, in particular that of education financing as a fundamental means to reduce inequality in the initial distribution of resources, thereby fostering economic growth. The economic policy implications of this public intervention in the field of education are important because such intervention corrects market inefficiencies, allows for greater accumulation of human capital, and promotes economic growth.

6.2. EDUCATION AND ECONOMIC GROWTH: THE FAVOURABLE CONTEXT OF THE '60s

The emergence of the economics of education as an autonomous field of study is usually associated with T. Schultz's presidential address to the annual meeting of the American Economic Association in 1960. In his address, followed later by other publications (such as *The Economic Value of Education* in 1963) he promoted the importance of the educational benefits of an economic approach to education. As a result, during the 1960s, a large amount of work was produced reflecting the conviction that expenditure on education had an important effect on the economic performance of individuals and of society as a whole. In the 1960s many factors, theoretical, institutional and political, contributed to the successful development of the economics of education as a separate field of study.

Initially, a key element was the importance of the study of economic growth following WWII. Efforts to clarify the sources of economic growth created space for focusing on the specific role of education. Of prime importance in this regard were the works of E. Denison (1966, 1967) on the accounting of growth. Denison sought to identify the contribution of different production factors to economic growth in the United States and later in other Western countries, showing that an increase in the traditional factors (capital and labour) was unable to explain the growth rate of the American economy. As the joint contribution of the two factors was 0.9 per cent, a very high residual of 2 per cent still had to be explained. Denison broke the residual down into its constituent parts, seeking to identify the specific contribution of education on the basis of the growth of wages. His calculations showed that education made a 0.8 per cent contribution to the growth of the overall economy. In conclusion, education accounted for 23 per cent of the economy's growth in the first half of the 20th century in the United States. His work suggested that the quality of the factors was more important than their quantity. The relevance of this topic was also evident in the field of development economics. The early phase of development studies gave an important role to education in promotion growth (Arndt, 1987).

Also the political context presented some features that promoted the emergence of the economics of education. The spread of Keynesian ideas opened the door to higher public expenditure, including expenditure on education: the government was expected to play a more visible role in the economic system. In the case of education, the increase in public expenditure seemed to be economically significant (Papi, 1966). On the other hand, international institutions, in particular the OECD, absorbed the idea that investment in education was a condition for economic growth. An important event in the diffusion of this approach was a study group created within the OECD that was responsible for organizing important conferences in this field (Papadopoulos, 1994). Among these conferences were ones on the financing of education (1964) and social objectives in educational planning (1965).

How can education contribute to making economic growth an endogenous process? Denison furnishes a clear answer:

> More education may contribute to growth in two distinct ways. First, it may raise the quality of the labour force, defined to include all occupations from the highest to the lowest. This may be presumed to increase labour productivity, independently of any tendency for a larger number of educated people to speed the enlargement of the society's stock of knowledge relevant to production. Second, an upgrading of the educational background of the population may accelerate the rate at which society's stock of knowledge itself advances (Denison, 1966, p. 215).

In this passage, Denison distinguishes between two aspects of the impact of education on economic growth, which his work focused on. The first aspect which he sought to measure was the increase in labour productivity consequent upon a higher level of education. In general, education increases the quality of the labour force and therefore its capacity to contribute to economic growth. There is then a second effect, which consists in the fact that a high level of education favours the assimilation of technical progress. Denison was not concerned in his calculations with this aspect, which he attributed not so much to education as to a generic advance in the stock of knowledge available to the economy (Denison, 1966, p. 259). It is significant that the formal models developed in the second half of the decade to capture the relationship between education and growth followed these two roads marked out by Denison. One strand dealt with the connection between education and labour productivity, and its main exponents were Uzawa (1965), Sheshinski (1968) and Weizsäcker (1973). The other was developed by Nelson and Phelps (Nelson 1964, Nelson and Phelps, 1966), and Shell (1969), who instead highlighted the importance of education as a factor facilitating the transmission and assimilation of technical progress.

6.3. EDUCATION AND GROWTH: THE EARLY FORMAL MODELS

The first formal model on the role of education in economic growth was advanced by Uzawa (1965). In its time, this study passed almost unnoticed, probably because of its great technicality as the first case of an optimizing model with two sectors, one producing the final good and the other producing the increase in schooling. Only in the 1980s, with the study's rediscovery by Lucas (1988), was its value fully recognized.

In Uzawa's model the assumptions underlying the Solow model are fully accepted and technical progress takes the pure labour-augmenting form. There are two special assumptions. First, labour can be divided into two types: productive L_P and educational L_E. Only L_P can be used as input in the production function. Second, the rate of increase in labour-augmenting technical progress is a concave, increasing function of teaching personnel, L_E/L. In other words, the higher the proportion of the total labour force devoted to education, the faster the increase in labour productivity, but this increase is less than the increase in the L_E/L ratio. This presumes that education benefits the whole labour force and not just those workers who receive the training. The educational function proposed by Uzawa is:

$$\dot{A} = Af\left(\frac{L_E}{L}\right) \qquad f'(\cdot)>0 \qquad f''(\cdot)<0 \tag{6.1}$$

Equation (6.1) contains one discretionary parameter: the labour allocation ratio. Uzawa uses optimal calculus to show that the unique optimal trajectory tends to the stationary state, $z^* = k^*/A^*$. This result essentially depends on the concavity of the labour efficiency accumulation function according to the number of educated workers.

Uzawa's model has been considered one of the most interesting attempts to endogenize economic growth through the introduction of education (Wan, 1971, p. 238). Nevertheless, as a model of endogenous growth it does not achieve its objective. Even if the parameter that determines labour productivity and economic growth depends on the resources allocated to education, the model's hypotheses are such that in the long period we again have the results of Solow's model: the economy reaches a stationary state in which growth is annulled.

With Sheshinski (1968), attention shifted from spending on education to the time devoted by each worker to education and vocational training. Sheshinski hypothesized that increased education augments, albeit at a decreasing rate, the productivity of workers. In equilibrium, the value of a further year devoted to education should be equal to its opportunity cost, and in this way it is possible to determine the optimal value of schooling. Weizsäcker also moved in this direction in his paper 'Notes on Endogenous Growth of Productivity' presented to the 1973 Conference of the International Economic Association dedicated to formal models of economic growth. Here, as in Sheshinski, the key variable is the number of years of education. Weizsäcker identifies two optimal investment programmes. In the first, the worker devotes resources to education solely in the first period of life, while in the second his/her accumulation of new knowledge is nil. In the second programme, the time horizon is divided into three periods in which investments in education are maximum in the first, intermediate and constant in the second, and nil in the third.

A completely different approach to analyse education's contribution to economic growth was proposed by Nelson and Phelps (1966) and by Shell (1969). Already in a long review article of 1964, Nelson had expressed doubts that the increase in productivity not attributable to capital and to a greater number of workers – Solow's famous residual – could be explained by education. Criticising Denison, Nelson observed that the fundamental problem was the strong complementarity among the production factors, which meant that their contributions could not be considered as independent of each other (1964, p. 591).

This new perspective was elaborated two years later by Nelson and Phelps. The point of departure of the two authors is different from Uzawa's:

> Most economic theorists have embraced the principle that certain kinds of education equip a man to perform certain jobs or functions, or enable a man to perform a given function more effectively. The principle seems a sound one. Underlying it, perhaps, is the theory that education enhances one's ability to receive, decode, and understand information, and that information processing and interpretation is important for performing or learning to perform many jobs (1966, p. 69).

It is clear that in this passage the role of education is conceived as being primarily that of facilitating the flow of technological information. Nelson and Phelps define education as the process of training the productive actors in the economy to receive and absorb the technological information being transmitted by other sectors in the economy. The notion of the theoretical level of technology at time t, $R(t)$, plays an important role in the model. If all best technological practices are available to all economic agents, then $R = A$. When this is not the case, $A < R$.

The educational function in this model is:

$$\dot{A} = (R - A) f(h) \tag{6.2}$$

where h is a measure of the educational level of society (with $f'(h)>0$). The rate of increase in the technology in practice is an increasing function of educational attainment and is proportional to the 'gap' $(R-A)$. Following the Schumpeterian hypothesis that invention does not depend upon other economic variables, it can be assumed that R grows at the constant rate $(\dot{R}=\rho R)$.

Nelson and Phelps show that the long-run equilibrium path of technology is given by:

$$A^* = \frac{f(h)}{f(h)+\rho} R_0 e^{\rho t} \tag{6.3}$$

such that the gap between A and R tends to a long-run constant value for constant h. In this model, not only is the technical progressiveness of the economy omitted, but even more importantly, the determination of the level of education h is taken as given.

A final relevant study is Shell's (1969), in which the author sought to unify the two previous approaches. In this model, the equation for the accumulation of labour efficiency is again described by relationship (6.2), but the general level of schooling, h, is not exogenous as in Nelson and Phelps, but instead depends on the share of workers employed in the education sector $(1-u)$,

$$\dot{h}=f[(1-u)L] \tag{6.4}$$

Because Shell assumes that equation (6.4) presents decreasing returns, the optimal choice of educational programme determines an equilibrium value for the control variable u^*. With this value known, the system reaches a position of stationary state for capital, output and consumption, as in the previous models.

6.4. ASSESSMENT OF THE EARLIER MODELS

The models considered in the previous section constituted one the strands into which endogenous growth theory divided during the 1960s (Wan, 1971, ch. 7). Arrow's (1962) approach based on accumulation through experience, and Kennedy's (1964) that introduced the technical progress frontier as a function of factor prices were two other important strands that were advanced to explain Solow's residual. Despite their notable analytical intuitions, however, neither of these approaches were able to furnish an endogenous theory of technical progress. The models of Uzawa, Sheshinski, Phelps, Shell and Weizsäcker, which sought to endogenize technical progress by introducing education, were interesting variations on Solow's model, rather than being theoretical proposals able to supersede it, as would happen with the models of the 1980s.

During the 1970s, the interest in growth theory suddenly subsided. On the one hand, theoretical difficulties arose that made it difficult to extend the results obtained in the one-sector case to the more general one with a plurality of sectors (Britto, 1974). On the other hand, the oil crisis and the consequent recession shifted attention from long-period policies to short-period ones, redirecting the interest of macroeconomists to the theory of economic fluctuations.

On the analytical level, the underlying reason for the failure of this first generation of endogenous growth models was that their point of departure was an aggregate production function in which technical progress was neutral in the Harrodian sense, with $Y=F(K,AL)$ (Solow, 1994). In this analytical scheme, the level of education was regarded as a factor that could exert its influence on parameter A, labour efficiency. However, this hypothesis did not modify the essential characteristics of the initial aggregate function, which introduced decreasing returns to scale in the sole accumulated factor, namely physical capital. In the long period the profitability of capital diminished to such extent that it annulled the accumulation process, and the economy reached a stationary state.

Why did the macroeconomists of endogenous growth of the 1960s, whatever the direction of their research, remain faithful to the analytical assumption of the neutrality of technical progress in Harrod's sense? A possible answer may be the fact that only with this functional form could the economic system reach a stationary state (Burmeister and Dobell, 1970, p. 97). If the returns to scale of the factors are decreasing, whatever the economy's initial position, due to the flexibility of technology and the perfect mobility of prices, the economic system reaches a position of static equilibrium. In a certain sense, in the wake of Solow's original approach, the 1960s macroeconomists of growth, driven by the need to solve the problem of the instability of Harrod's model, were more interested in constructing dynamic aggregate systems that guaranteed the existence of a stable stationary state than in determining the causes of long-period growth. To obtain completely different results, and therefore constant rates of growth in the long period, it would be necessary to abandon the Harrodian framework, and also the hypothesis that the returns on the accumulated factor decrease, as happened with the new theory of endogenous growth developed in the 1980s. Symmetrically, the new literature no longer posed for itself the problem of the stability of equilibrium solutions that had played such a large part in multisectoral dynamic analysis (Burmeister and Dobell, 1970).

6.5. EDUCATION AND ENDOGENOUS GROWTH: THE NEW ANALYTICAL FRAMEWORK

Also the new theory of endogenous growth viewed education spending as one of the possible mechanisms with which to sustain long-period growth (Jones and Manuelli, 1997). This body of literature is commonly held to begin with Lucas's (1988) study, which openly acknowledged that its approach can be considered a development of Uzawa's model. In effect, the two models are identical in formal terms, the only difference being that in Lucas's the accumulation of human capital comes at a constant rate, suggesting that at the aggregate level the returns on the accumulation of human capital do not decrease, but are constant. However, in Lucas's model human capital is not represented by spending on education but rather by time spent at school, as in Sheshinski and Weizsäcker.

The first contribution to the theory of endogenous growth that expressly considered the connection between education spending and human capital formation was Glomm and Ravikumar (1992), which can be regarded as the true point of departure of the subsequent literature on these topics. To understand the characteristics of the new approach to the role of education in economic growth, it is worth examining a variant of this model in which, for simplicity, the optimal choice of the time devoted to education is omitted.

Consider an economy populated with a unit measure of households, each consisting of a parent and a child, in which all decisions are made by parents who determine the amount of investment in their children's schooling. Parents invest in their children's schooling because of a bequest motive, deriving utility from consumption c_t, from the consumption in the next period c_{t+1} and from their offspring's education investment E. Assigning the same utility function to all parents, we write

$$\ln(c_t)+\ln(E)+\beta\ln(c_{t+1}) \tag{6.5}$$

This formulation abstracts from important issues regarding the relationship between school spending and the quality of schooling and from differences in children's innate abilities. Parents allocate their income between consumption, present and future, and education, reflecting the assumption that credit constraints do not allow them to borrow against their children's future income. Normalizing all prices to unity, we have the following new budget constraint:

$$c_t+s_t+E=w_t h_t$$

$$c_{t+1}\leq(1+r_{t+1})s_t \tag{6.6}$$

where s_t is the individual savings and each individual takes the wage rate, w, as given.

Members of each generation are endowed with one unit of leisure in their youth and h_t units of human capital. Human capital is accumulated according to the production function,

$$h_{t+1} = H(h,E) = h^{\gamma} E^{1-\gamma} \tag{6.7}$$

where E is public expenditure on education. In equation (6.7) human capital stock can be augmented through the resources allocated to education.

Each firm produces output y at time t according to the technology,

$$y = Ak^{\alpha}(nh)^{1-\alpha} \tag{6.8}$$

where k is the amount of capital rented by the firm, nh is the amount of skill-weighted or effective labour input. Under private schooling, utility maximization subject to constraint yields the following expression

$$s = \frac{\beta}{2+\beta} wh \tag{6.9}$$

Profit maximization by firms yields

$$w_t h_t = (1-\alpha) A k_t^{\alpha} h_t^{1-\alpha} \tag{6.10}$$

In equilibrium $k_{t+1} = s_t$,

$$k_{t+1} = \frac{\beta}{2+\beta}(1-\alpha) k^{\alpha} h^{1-\alpha} = \Theta(1-\alpha) A k^{\alpha} h^{1-\alpha} \tag{6.11}$$

The optimal amount of private education spending by parents is

$$E = \frac{1}{2+\beta}(1-\alpha) A k^{\alpha} h^{1-\alpha} \tag{6.12}$$

Inserting this last equation (6.11) in the equation expressing the accumulation of human capital, we obtain

$$h_{t+1} = \left(\frac{1-\alpha}{2+\beta}\right)^{1-\gamma} A^{1-\gamma} h^{\gamma} (k^{\alpha} h^{1-\alpha})^{1-\gamma} = \Omega h^{\gamma} (k^{\alpha} h^{1-\alpha})^{1-\gamma} \tag{6.13}$$

Thus, the ratio of human capital to physical capital evolves according to

$$\frac{h_{t+1}}{k_{t+1}} = \frac{\Omega}{\Theta} \frac{h^{1-\alpha+\alpha\gamma} k^{\alpha(1-\gamma)}}{k^{\alpha} h^{1-\alpha}} = \frac{\Omega}{\Theta}\left(\frac{h}{k}\right)^{\alpha\gamma} \tag{6.14}$$

This ratio converges monotonically to a unique steady state, z^*, given by

$$\ln z^* = \frac{1}{1-a\gamma}\frac{\Omega}{\Theta} \tag{6.15}$$

Consumption, physical capital, human capital output and public expenditure on education will grow at the same rate obtained by inserting equation (6.15) in equation (6.11). The economy does not converge to a steady state level but to a sustained growth path. The model's predictions are similar to those of the endogenous growth literature: the presence of human capital, in the form of educational expenditure, may relax the constraint of diminishing returns to capital and may give rise to long-term per capita growth in the absence of exogenous technological progress.

The simple analytical scheme considered in this section clearly illustrates how the relationship between education and economic growth has been reinterpreted within endogenous growth theory in order to overcome the difficulties encountered by the economists of the 1960s. There are two main differences with respect to the Solowian set-up: one analytical, the other interpretative. On the analytical level, the introduction of spending on education makes it possible to counterbalance the effect of decreasing returns on the accumulation of physical capital, as usually occurs in this family of models. Education is therefore one of the many mechanisms introduced to eliminate the decreasing returns of the accumulable factor. On the interpretative level, one observes that, on the basis of equation (6.14), the factor that is really accumulated is spending on education in ratio to capital, h/k, which is constant in the long period. To obtain an endogenous growth result, it is necessary that in equilibrium the two factors are perfect complements in the production function. Otherwise, the system tends to follow a path *à la* Solow, in which endogenous growth is either impossible or tends to have an explosive dynamic, as was common in the literature of the 1960s.

This brings us to a further observation. The models of endogenous growth theory liken spending on education to one of the traditional production factors. Education is no longer an element that determines the quality of the labour force, as in the models of the 1960s, but is instead an autonomous production factor that can be accumulated by devoting resources to this purpose. This theoretically radical hypothesis made it possible to supersede the traditional view of technical progress found in the Harrodian formulation.

6.6. EDUCATION, INEQUALITY AND GROWTH

We have seen that education has been introduced into models of endogenous growth according to a method common to this strand of inquiry. Since the growth rate depends on the accumulation of human capital via spending on education, scholarly attention has concentrated on the conditions that might facilitate or impede this process. The key factor in the process of human capital accumulation is inequality in the initial distribution of resources. This section will examine how the new models have revisited the links among education, inequality and economic growth.

The endogenous growth models have certainly had the merit of reviving interest in the problem of how different initial endowments of resources can condition economic growth. With reference to human capital, a series of studies (Galor and Zeira, 1993; Bénabou, 1994, 1996, 2002; and Galor, 2005) have explored the consequences of market imperfections for economic growth, these being among the essential characteristics of this form of capital. The feature shared by these studies is that, in the presence of liquidity constraints, less well-off individuals are unable to invest optimally because they find it difficult to raise the necessary funds. If income were distributed less unequally, economic agents would not be rationed and the accumulation of human capital could occur more efficiently. In the presence of externalities, affluent individuals would profit from this redistribution by forgoing initial resources to have more resources in the future. Inequality in the initial positions is a brake on growth, but nobody has an interest in eliminating it because, in the short period, the private benefit would be less than its cost. In this case a government that intervened to reduce inequality would foster economic growth – and also enhance social equity.

The same conclusions are reached when the relationship between economic growth and inequality is seen through the lens of access to educational opportunities. The point of departure was the study by Glomm and Ravikumar (1992), which demonstrated the consequences for economic growth of different systems of financing education systems. In the model each agent's stock of human capital depends on the parent's stock of human capital, time spent in school, and the quality of schools. Each parent has a bequest motive and values the quality of education passed on to their offspring. Under the public education regime, a government levies taxes on the income of the old and uses tax to provide free public education. The quality of education is an increasing function of the tax revenues. In this case the equation of human capital accumulation becomes

$$h_{t+1} = AH^{\gamma}h^{\delta} \tag{6.16}$$

where H is the aggregate stock of human capital, h the human capital of the representative household and A a parameter depending upon technology and preferences. In the private regime of education financing, the optimal evolution of human capital is the following,

$$h_{t+1} = Bh^{\gamma+\delta} \quad (6.17)$$

with $B > A$, depending upon the parameters of model. From these two laws of motion, Glomm and Ravikumar establish the condition for the existence of the endogenous growth path. The key parameter that determines growth in this model is the sum $\gamma+\delta$. For the case $\gamma+\delta<1$ the long-run growth rate is zero and endogenous growth is not possible. When $\gamma+\delta>1$ we obtain unbounded growth depending on the initial conditions. The only relevant case is $\gamma+\delta=1$ in which the accumulation function of human capital is a linear function of his stock. In this case the growth rate is constant in the long period and the magnitude of this constant depends on the parameters of the model.

Given the conditions to obtain endogenous growth, Glomm and Ravikumar distinguish two cases: the first involves a representative agent, and in the second the households have a different income distribution (heterogeneous case). In the case of the representative agent and of perfect capital markets, a school system entirely financed by households achieves a higher growth rate, because more gifted individuals devote more resources and more time to education. The situation is reversed if we instead consider an economy in which household incomes are distributed according to a log-normal distribution. In this case, the market solution is more efficient than that of public financing only if the initial inequality is modest. Otherwise, the public system is able to guarantee greater growth because the advantage accruing to society from the increased schooling of the less well-off compensates for the initial damage caused to the affluent.

Glomm and Ravikumar also endogenize the choice of educational system. If, as usually is the case, the median income is less than the average income, electors will always choose a state school system. Agents whose income is below the mean support the introduction of a state school system; in their model, a state school system increases the educational attainment of the poor more than it harms that of the rich, realizing a net efficiency gain. Thus, the greater the distance between median and average income, the greater the political support for a public education scheme.

6.7. SOME MAJOR ASPECTS OF EDUCATION FINANCING

With respect to financing, school organization involves two debates: state versus private schools and centrally versus locally financed schools. In a state system financed through general taxation all students receive identical treatment, whereas in a private system the resources available to students depend on family wealth. The second element partially overlaps the first, as long as families are territorially mobile. These two dimensions can be combined in different ways, as in fact happens.

Regarding the first issue, an interesting line of inquiry has been developed in a series of studies by Fernandez and Rogerson (1999, 2001, 2003), who analyse the consequences for economic growth deriving from the different financing systems (public versus private) of school systems. The fundamental problem is that market mechanisms are unable to generate an optimal level of investment for less well-off households that cannot access the financing necessary for the education of their children. This socially non-optimal investment is transformed at the aggregate level into lower economic growth and into scant inter-generational mobility. The negative effect of the initial inequality of the resources on economic growth can be countered by public intervention, either through direct management or through grants to families (vouchers). Given the importance of public intervention, Fernandez and Rogerson have considered in great detail the consequences deriving from three different voucher systems: lump-sum vouchers (every student gets the same voucher), means-tested vouchers (every student below a certain income gets a voucher), and power-equalizing vouchers (every student with less than a certain income gets a voucher that rises as his family's income falls). Using a calibrated model they demonstrated that the vouchers, especially the power-equalizing vouchers, generate large increases in the nation's income and well-being. The key insight is that vouchers, because they are specific to individual students, generate more optimal investment in education than any version of current school finance could generate.

A completely different approach has been developed by Epple and Romano (1998, 2003), who compare public and private financing of education on the hypothesis that educational performance, and hence the demand for education, is a function not only of household income but also of the average performance by the class to which a student belongs. In this model, the fees charged by private schools depend on both household income and the abilities of their students. Moreover, in order to attract the ablest students who do not have the requisite economic means, the private schools set up a system of scholarships. In this way, through the formation of the school's classes, the affluent families make available to their children talents that originate from lower social groups. Essentially, the higher-income families are purchasing the positive peer effect of the higher-ability types. Given this scheme, not surprisingly the most efficient solution in the Paretian sense is a complete stratification of the education system: at the top of the classification stand the most prestigious but also most expensive schools, and at the lowest level the schools with the lowest fees but also offering the least satisfactory instruction. Epple and Romano identify three possible equilibria in regard to the financing of the school system: a mixed system, one entirely private, and one entirely public. It is interesting that, even in an entirely public system, a form of social stratification comes about through the residential choices of families. The best state schools will be situated in the districts where affluent families live.

The choice between local and central financing of education implies a trade-off between the advantages of local control in achieving a better fit between preferences and spending and the advantages of centralized funding in achieving greater equality of opportunities. The most interesting contributions in this vein are those of Bénabou (1994, 1996, 2002). He compares the dynamic implications of central versus local education financing in a dynamic growth model with initial regional inequalities and production spillovers. In this case the choice is between local financing, which would increase the differences among the schools situated in various neighbourhoods, and centralized financing, which would instead give rise to a system in which all schools have the same educational characteristics. In Bénabou's (1966) model of overlapping generations, the human capital accumulation function depends on education spending and is written as follows:

$$h^i_{t+1} = (h^i_t)^a (L^i_t)^b (H_t)^\gamma \tag{6.18}$$

where h_t is the individual worker's level of human capital, H is an index for aggregate human capital, and L^i_t is a new variable representing the hypothesis about education financing. Using Bénabou's terminology, we may say that L^i_t incorporates the local connection, while H_t represents the global or aggregate connection because the input, in this case labour, is a complementary factor in the production function. Two cases can be distinguished. On the hypothesis that $L^i_t = h^i_t$ the optimum choice is for the community to divide itself into districts: this is the case of complete stratification (local financing of education); whilst if $L^i_t = H_t$ there is a single large community where the differences among individual schools are annulled, which is the case of complete integration (with centralized financing).

In the model the effects on aggregate efficiency are not univocal but depend on the time horizon. In the short period, high social stratification may exert a positive influence on growth by increasing the efficiency of accumulation. However, because technology exhibits strong complementarity, a low level of human capital accumulation would also have negative consequences for the higher-skilled, and therefore most affluent, workers. Bénabou shows that the system of local financing favours the accumulation of human capital in the short but not long period. In the short term, affluent families lose more than they gain from others, but this initial redistribution of resources enables society to overcome the limits of the credit market. The more far-sighted families are, the more they will vote for public and national financing, while the more impatient they are, the greater their propensity for a private and local system at the state level, incorporating residential choice.

Fernandez and Rogerson (1999) calibrate a political economy model of school finance using United States data to assess the dynamic effects of centralized school finance. The segregation that results from purely local financing allows households more efficiently to sort themselves into communities according to their demand for education quality, compared to a centralized regime. However, centralized school finance is more effective in reducing income inequality, which has a positive effect on long-run growth, as in Bénabou's model. Nonetheless, it is not possible to determine in general which of these effects is stronger, since the calibration indicates that the centralized system results in higher average income and greater social welfare in the long run than local financing.

To summarize: in the case in which the relationship between inequality and growth is viewed through the lens of spending on education, the general conclusions do not change. Inequality in access to education is a factor that in the long period reduces the accumulation of human capital, and therefore also economic growth. Large differences in the quality of the education system between wealthy and poorer districts undermine the principle of equal opportunity, and the inequality this situation generates has significant welfare costs for society as a whole. An intervention by the state that removes these liquidity constraints will induce greater growth of the economic system. The debate concerns the form that redistributive action by the state should take: whether it should consist in direct management, as usually happens, or whether it should be restricted to making financial resources available, leaving the selective mechanisms of the market (school choice) free to operate.

6.8. CONCLUDING REMARKS

This chapter considered the evolution of the connection between education spending and economic growth in the neoclassical models. It showed that there are significant differences, both analytical and interpretative, between the approach that developed in the first phase of growth theory during the 1960s and the current one. The recent literature has discarded the view of education as being able to increase labour efficiency, in order to emphasise its role in human capital formation through education expenditure. The traditional research sector is replaced by the notion of human capital, but, above all, the accumulation of human capital depends linearly on the expenditure that each worker dedicates to study and training or on public intervention in this field. With these modifications of interpretation and with the linear dynamic analytical structure, long-run growth rate becomes endogenous in the sense that it depends on the fundamental parameters of the economic system, such as preferences and technology. Expenditure on education becomes a new tool that combats the effect of decreasing returns to scale for the economy as a whole.

Moreover, the typical problems of this production factor have emerged, namely the incompleteness and imperfection of markets. Much of the literature has explored the relationship between education spending and economic growth in light of inequality in the distribution of resources. In general, inequality is a negative factor that slows economic growth, hence the need for public action to remove the financial constraints on less well-off families. The conclusions drawn from the literature on endogenous growth help us understand why in modern economies education is entrusted to the state and not to the market. On the other hand, this view is not new in the history of economic thought. It was also put forward by neoclassical economists like Marshall ([1890]1964), who indeed went further by considering education expenditure to be an essential national investment.

REFERENCES

Aghion, P. and P. Howitt (1998), *Endogenous Growth*, Cambridge: MIT Press.

Arndt, H. (1987), *Economic Development: The History of an Idea*, Chicago: University of Chicago Press.

Arrow, K.J. (1962), 'The Economic Implications of Learning by Doing', *Review of Economic Studies*, **29**(3), 155–73.

Bénabou, R. (1994), 'Human Capital, Inequality, and Growth: A Local Perspective', *European Economic Review*, **38**(3–4), 817–26.

Bénabou, R. (1996), 'Heterogeneity, Stratification and Growth: Macroeconomic implications of Community Structure and School Finance', *American Economic Review*, **86**(3), 584–609.

Bénabou, R. (2002), 'Tax and Education Policy in an Heterogeneous-Agent Economy: What Level of Redistribution Maximise Growth and Efficiency?', *Econometrica*, **70**(2), 481–517.

Blaug, M. (1978), *Economics of Education*, Oxford: Pergamon.

Britto, R. (1974), 'Some Recent Developments in the Theory of Economic Growth: An Interpretation', *Journal of Economic Literature*, **11**(4), 1343–67.

Burmeister, E. and A.R. Dobell (1970), *Mathematical Theories of Economic Growth*, New York: Macmillan.

Denison, E.F. (1966), 'Measuring the Contribution of Education to Economic Growth', in E. Robinson and J. Vaizey (eds), *The Economics of Education*, London: Macmillan, pp. 202–61.

Denison, E.F. (1967), *Why Growth Rates Differ: Postwar Experience in Nine West Countries*, Washington: The Brookings Institution.

Epple, D. and R. Romano (1998), 'Competition Between Private and Public Schools, Vouchers and Peer-Group Effect', *American Economic Review*, **88**(1), 33–62.

Epple, D. and R. Romano (2003), 'Neighbourhood Schools, Choice, and the Distribution of Educational Benefits', in C. Hoxby (ed.), *The Economics of School Choice*, Chicago: The University of Chicago Press.

Fernandez, R. and R. Rogerson (1999), 'Education Finance Reform and Investment in Human Capital: Lessons from California', *Journal of Public Economics*, **74**(3), 327–50.

Fernandez, R. and R. Rogerson (2001), 'The Determinants of Public Education Expenditures: Longer-Run Evidence from the States', *Journal of Education Finance*, **27**, 567–83.

Fernandez, R. and R. Rogerson (2003), 'Equity and Resources: An Analysis of Education Finance Systems', *Journal of Political Economy*, **111**(4), 858–97.

Galor, O. (2005), 'From Stagnation to Growth: Unified Growth Theory', in P. Aghion and S. Durlauf (eds), *Handbook of Economic Growth*, Amsterdam: North-Holland.

Galor, O. and J. Zeira (1993), 'Income Distribution and Macroeconomics', *Review of Economic Studies*, **60**(1), 35–52.

Glomm, G. and B. Ravikumar (1992), 'Public Versus Private Investment in Human Capital: Endogenous Growth and Income Quality', *Journal of Political Economy*, **100**, 93–128.

Glomm, G. and B. Ravikumar (1997), 'Productive Government Expenditures and Long-run Growth', *Journal of Economics Dynamics and Control*, **21**(1), 183–204.

Jones, L.E. and R.E. Manuelli (1997), 'The Sources of Growth', *Journal of Economic Dynamics and Control*, **21**(1), 75–114.

Kennedy, C. (1964), 'Induced Bias in Innovation and the Theory of Distribution', *Economic Journal*, **74**(295), 541–57.

Lucas, R.E. (1988), 'On the Mechanics of Economic Development', *Journal of Monetary Economics*, **22**(1), 3–42.

Marshall, A. [1890] (1964), *Principles of Economics*, London: Macmillan.

Nelson, R. (1964), 'Aggregate Production Functions and Medium-Range Growth Projections', *American Economic Review*, **54**(5), 575–606.

Nelson, R.R. and E. Phelps (1966), 'Investment in Humans, Technological Diffusion and Economic Growth', *American Economic Review*, **56**, 69–75.

Papadopoulos, G. (1994), *Education 1960–1990: The OECD Perspective*, Paris: OECD.

Papi, G.U. (1966), 'General Problems of the Economics of Education', in E. Robinson and J. Vaizey (eds), *The Economics of Education*, London: Macmillan, pp. 3–23.

Sheshinski, E. (1968), 'On Individual's Life Time Allocation Between Education and Work', *Metroeconomica*, **20**(1), 42–9.

Schultz, T.W. (1963), *The Economic Value of Education*, New York: Columbia University Press.

Shell, K. (1969), 'Technological Knowledge and Economic Growth', in United Nations, *Planning for Advanced Skills and Technologies, Industrial Planning and Programming Series No. 3*, New York: United Nations Industrial Development Organization, pp. 79–90.

Solow, R. (1994), 'Perspectives on Growth Theory', *Journal of Economic Perspectives*, **8**(1), 45–54.

Uzawa, I. (1965), 'Optimal Technical Change in an Aggregative Model of Economic Growth', *International Economic Review*, **6**(1), 18–31.

Wan, H.Y. (1971), *Economic Growth*, New York: Harcourt Brace Jovanovich.

Weizsäcker, C. (1973), 'Notes on Endogenous Growth of Productivity', in J. Mirrlees and N. Stern (eds), *Models of Economic Growth*, London: Macmillan.

7. Education and poverty in a Solow growth model*

Thomas Bassetti

7.1. INTRODUCTION

In macroeconomic literature, education is considered one of the most important inputs to produce human capital, which can be defined as: 'the stock of accumulated skills and experience that make workers more productive' (Stiglitz and Boadway, 1994).

A common assumption in the theory of economic growth is that human capital is produced under constant returns to scale, using education as a single input. Yet there is no compelling evidence to support this assumption. On the contrary, an increasing number of analyses show that the production of human capital exhibits increasing returns to scale for low levels of education and decreasing returns to scale for high levels of education. For instance, Krueger and Lindahl (2001) find evidence in favour of an inverted U-shaped relationship between the stock of human capital and the GDP growth rate. By comparing different regression models, they find that the best fitting of the data is provided by a regression model that considers a quadratic form for education. The inverted U pattern suggests that social returns to schooling are increasing only for countries with a low level of education (below 7.5 average years of schooling), while for countries with high levels of education (above 7.5 average years of schooling) social returns to schooling are decreasing. In analyzing the effect of human capital in an open economy, Isaksson (2002) confirms Krueger and Lindahl's result concerning the existence of a non-linear relationship between education and economic growth. By introducing a measure for trade openness, Isaksson also finds important interaction effects between education and trade openness when education enters in a non-linear fashion.

At the micro level, Trostel (2004) obtains the same results. By using an international micro-dataset to estimate an aggregate Mincerian equation (from Mincer, 1974), he shows that the production function of human capital displays increasing (private) returns at low levels of education and decreasing (private) returns at high levels of education. Since these nonlinearities occur primarily within countries, Trostel concludes that such nonlinearities could be a direct consequence of the process of human capital accumulation. In other words, he shows that the human capital production function has a cubic shape, that is, the typical production function used in microeconomics courses.

Traditionally, human capital does not play an explicit role in the exogenous growth theory, while it is central in the endogenous growth theory.[1] There are many endogenous growth models that consider human capital externalities and in which human capital drives growth. These models suggest that the individual stock of human capital may enhance the productivity of other factors such as physical capital or the human capital of others, through channels that are not internalized by households or firms. Lucas (1988) provides an endogenous growth model in which external effects arise from the aggregation process of human capital. According to Lucas, the presence of social interaction among more skilled workers increases their productivity. Nevertheless, empirical evidence for these external economies is ambiguous. That is, there is no strong evidence for positive externalities, nor is there any evidence that externalities are small or even absent.[2] Moreover, these models do not explain why in microeconometric studies, based on Mincerian equations, private returns to education are first increasing and later decreasing.

At the same time, the exogenous growth model has been recently extended to include human capital by Mankiw, Romer and Weil (hereafter MRW) (1992). By using a cross-country analysis, they show that data are fairly consistent with a Solow model augmented to take into account human capital as a factor of production. They obtain a rather satisfactory estimate of the aggregate production function. In this framework, education does not produce externalities at the aggregate level. That is, education appears as a private input, which is remunerated according to its marginal product. Barro and Sala-i-Martin (1995), through an extensive test on cross-country data, show that the MRW model can explain several empirical facts.

In this chapter, we aim to provide an exogenous growth model able to explain Krueger and Lindahl's results as well as Trostel's results. To do this, we introduce a possible mechanism to explain the non-linear relationship between education and human capital and then between education and economic growth. Here, as in standard literature, education is a fundamental input to produce human capital. Nevertheless, with respect to standard theory, we do not assume *a priori* the existence of constant returns to scale in producing human capital through education. In particular, we study the effect of a non-constant depreciation rate of human capital on GDP growth.

Following studies such as Rosen (1976), McPherson and Winston (1983) and Neumann and Weiss (1995), we assume that the depreciation rate of human capital is positively related to the level of education attained by an individual.[3] As we will see, given this hypothesis, education may generate a non-linear process of human capital accumulation. We will then use this result to show how the process of human capital accumulation may cause the existence of multiple equilibria, and consequently the existence of a poverty trap, in a Solow growth model.[4] There we will see how investing in education is a possible way out from a situation of persistent poverty.

In the second part of the chapter, we use a cross-section of 78 countries to conduct an econometric analysis. The aim of this analysis is to show that, at the aggregate level, returns to education are not constant. To see this fact, we estimate the impact of education on total factor productivity (TFP) growth. We will show that evidence is consistent with our theoretical conclusions.

The rest of the chapter is organized as follows: Section 7.2 contains our modified Solow growth model; Section 7.3 contains our econometric analysis; Section 7.4 illustrates the main conclusions of this work.

7.2. THE MODEL

In this section, we propose a growth model in which the process of human capital accumulation can explain the existence of non-linearities in the economic growth path. To do this, we divide the model into two parts. In the first part of the model, we show how, through the acquisition of formal education, individuals can accumulate human capital in a non-linear way. In the second part of the model, we put this result into a traditional Solow growth model in order to study the consequences of these non-linearities on the aggregate level of output.

7.2.1. The Process of Human Capital Accumulation

Consider a closed economy in which markets are competitive and economic activity is performed over continuous time. Time is indexed by t, and individuals live for an infinite time horizon. Let L_t be the mass of population at time t, and assume that a representative agent i exists. Let u be the constant fraction of time that each individual devotes to work, while $e_{i,t}$ denotes the amount of time that agent i has already invested in education at time t.[5] Hereafter, for the sake of simplicity, we will omit the subscript i when there is no risk of confusion.

We temporarily assume that individual i has already decided the amount of time to invest in education. That is, in this section, we do not make any particular assumption on the determinants of e_t, while in the next section we will specify a functional form for e_t.

Following the standard literature on human capital and economic growth, we consider education as the only input to produce human capital. Nevertheless, with respect to the standard theory, we do not assume *a priori* the existence of constant returns to scale in producing human capital. Therefore, using a general human capital production function for individual *i*, we have

$$h_t = h(e_t),\ h'(e_t) > 0 \tag{7.1}$$

where h_t is the individual stock of human capital at time *t*, and *h*(.) is an unknown function. Equation (7.1) states that the individual stock of human capital depends on the time already invested by an individual in education at time *t*.[6] Nevertheless, this equation does not explicitly describe the relationship between education and human capital. In order to obtain a more specific formulation for equation (7.1), we must specify the mechanism through which individuals accumulate human capital.

As in MRW (1992), human capital variation will be determined by the difference between the human capital created in a given period and the human capital destroyed in the same period. Nevertheless, with respect to MRW, we will assume that the destruction (depreciation) of human capital will depend on the quantity of human capital subject to obsolescence. In particular, we will assume that the depreciation rate of human capital increases as the stock of human capital increases.

In analyzing the effect of technological change on schooling-specific obsolescence, that is the obsolescence of skills acquired at school, various papers provide theoretical and empirical arguments in favour of this hypothesis.[7] According to this literature, technological progress increases the depreciation rate of human capital. This is due to the fact that new technologies require the acquisition of new knowledge, which replaces part of the existing knowledge. Therefore, the higher the rate of technological innovation, the higher the depreciation rate of human capital will be. In these studies, two causes may justify the assumption of an increasing depreciation rate of human capital:

1. the first cause is known as the 'vintage effect' and is well illustrated in Neumann and Weiss (1995). There, they give evidence that high skilled workers are more affected by depreciation of human capital than low skilled workers. Neumann and Weiss observe that, with respect to traditional sectors, high-tech sectors are subject to a higher rate of technological innovation. Since high-tech sectors use a highly specialized workforce – that is a workforce comprised of engineers,

computer scientists, biologists, etc. – at any given time we may reasonably expect a higher rate of obsolescence for the most specialized workers, who are typically the most educated ones. Assuming that the degree of knowledge specialization increases with the grade of education, we may conclude that: 'at the individual level, the knowledge obsolescence increases as specialization increases' (McPherson and Winston, 1983).

2. The second cause is known as 'technical depreciation' and concerns the fact that the speed of technological change has accelerated over time. As stressed in de Grip (2004), in a context in which innovation accelerates over time, we must expect also the obsolescence rate of knowledge to accelerate continuously. This view is largely supported by the experience of the past several decades, during which technological changes have produced an increasing demand of skills by firms. This happens independently of the level of education of a worker. Today an engineer, with respect to thirty years ago, experiences a higher rate of knowledge obsolescence; hence knowledge becomes obsolete more quickly in any production sector. For this reason, it is reasonable to assume that an increasing speed of innovation leads to an increasing depreciation rate of human capital.

Even if the above-mentioned causes of human capital obsolescence can operate separately, we expect to observe both phenomena simultaneously. According to Rosen (1976), these two causes of human capital depreciation are indistinguishable. However, Neumann and Weiss (1995) argue that, since the vintage effect is not the same in all sectors while technical depreciation is, it is possible to identify both causes by comparing data from low and high technology sectors. Consistent with this point of view and with our future assumption of a constant exogenous rate of technological progress, we will consider only the vintage effect.

Now, we can write our human capital accumulation function:

$$\frac{dh_t}{de_t} = Bh_t - \phi(h_t)h_t, \; \phi'(h) > 0 \tag{7.2}$$

where dh_t/de_t is the human capital variation with respect to e_t, $B>0$ is a measure of gross productivity of the education sector, $\phi(.)$ is the depreciation coefficient of human capital and $\phi'>0$ captures the vintage effect mentioned above. In equation (7.2), as in Lucas (1988), the term Bh_t represents the gross creation of human capital due to the acquisition of formal education, while the term $\phi(h_t)h_t$ represents the depreciation of human capital due to obsolescence.

Given equations (7.1) and (7.2) and assuming a linear relationship between the stock of human capital and its depreciation rate, that is $\phi(h_t)=\sigma h_t$, we have:

$$\frac{dh_t}{de_t}=Bh(e_t)-\sigma[h(e_t)]^2 \tag{7.3}$$

where σ is a positive parameter that represents the unitary variation of the depreciation coefficient of human capital. We assume that the productivity of the education sector is greater than the unitary variation of the depreciation coefficient due to the vintage effect, that is, $B>\sigma$. This hypothesis ensures that an additional investment in education will always increase the individual stock of human capital.

To study how our economic system produces human capital, we have to solve equation (7.3).[8]

By normalizing the productivity of an illiterate worker to one, i.e. $h(0) = 1$, we obtain the following solution:

$$h_t=\frac{B\exp(Be_t)}{B-\sigma+\sigma\exp(Be_t)} \tag{7.4}$$

Equation (7.4) represents our human capital production function, which depends on individual choices concerning the schooling level. In particular, here we have obtained a logistic production function of human capital. In other words, the process of human capital accumulation is non-linear. This means that the individual stock of human capital is not directly proportional to the time invested in education by agent *i*.[9] By assuming $B=1$ and taking the value of σ estimated by Arrazola et al. (2005) for Spain ($\sigma=0.017$), in Figure 7.1 we provide a graphical representation of equation (7.4).[10]

Figure 7.1 shows how returns to education in the production of human capital are increasing for low levels of education and decreasing for high levels of education. In particular, if human capital depreciation increases by about two percentage points for each additional unit of human capital, the production function of human capital starts to show decreasing returns to education after about 4.5 years of schooling.

We can also interpret Figure 7.1 in another way. The figure shows that the effort (in terms of time invested in education) required to acquire an additional unit of human capital initially decreases with the stock of human capital already accumulated by an individual and subsequently increases. This means that an additional year of schooling has different effects if it is attended by an individual with a low level of human capital or by an individual with a high level of human capital.[11]

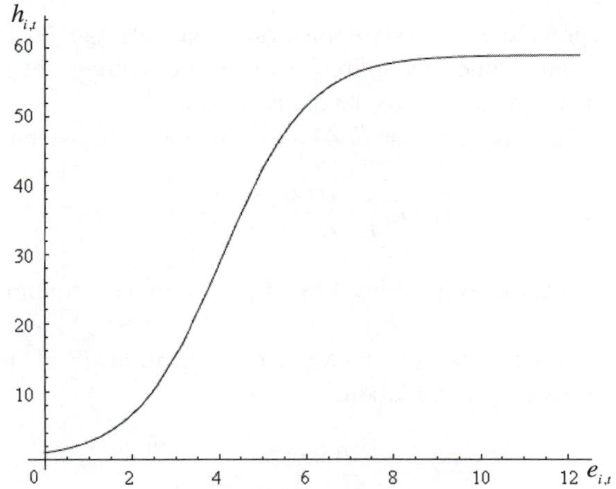

Figure 7.1. The logistic process of human capital accumulation

By using a neoclassical framework, in the next section, we study the consequences of a logistic process of human capital accumulation on output growth.

7.2.2. A Modified Solow Growth Model

7.2.2.1. Production function

Assume that output is produced by using a Cobb–Douglas production function with constant returns to scale,

$$Y_t = K_t^{\beta}(uH_tA_t)^{1-\beta},\ \beta \in [0,1] \quad (7.5)$$

where K_t is the total stock of physical capital, H_t is the total stock of human capital, and A_t is a technology parameter. In equation (7.5), human capital and technological progress enter multiplicatively. That is, technological progress is human capital-augmenting. As we will see, this hypothesis will allow us to write the production function in terms of units per effective-labour by making the analysis much simpler.

Assuming that, in contrast with Lucas (1988), there are no external effects in the aggregation of human capital and given that a representative agent exists, we can aggregate individual capacities as follows:

$$H_t = \int_0^{L_t} h_{i,t}\,di = L_t\bar{h}_t \quad (7.6)$$

where $\overline{h}_t$ is the average level of human capital at time t. Equation (7.6) states that, at the aggregate level, what matters is the average level of human capital. At the same time, according to (7.4), the average level of human capital will depend on the average level of education.

Therefore, by putting equation (7.4) into equation (7.6), we have

$$H_t = L_t \frac{B\exp(B\overline{e}_t)}{B-\sigma+\sigma\exp(B\overline{e}_t)} \tag{7.7}$$

where $\overline{e}_t$ represents the average level of education in our economic system at time t.

Finally, given equation (7.7), we write equation (7.5) in terms of quantities per unit of effective-labour,

$$y_t = k_t^{\beta}\left[\frac{B\exp(B\overline{e}_t)}{B-\sigma+\sigma\exp(B\overline{e}_t)}\right]^{1-\beta} \tag{7.8}$$

where k_t and y_t are, respectively, the amount of physical capital and output per unit of effective-labour, that is, $k_t \equiv (K_t / uL_t A_t)$ and $y_t \equiv (Y_t / uL_t A_t)$. In the production function described by (7.8), education is not a proxy variable for human capital as usual but enters as input in the production of human capital.

In the next section, we examine the dynamic behaviour of the inputs into production. Since this is a fairly standard analysis, we will especially emphasize the main differences of our model with respect to the standard version of the Solow model.

7.2.2.2. Dynamics of the inputs into production

As in the exogenous growth theory, we assume that technology and labour grow at the exogenous rates g and n, respectively.[12] Moreover, since output is divided between consumption and investment, we can write the Solowian accumulation function of physical capital as follows:

$$\dot{k}_t = sy_t - (\delta+g+n)k_t \tag{7.9}$$

where s is the exogenous saving rate and δ is the exogenous depreciation rate of physical capital.

Now we must substitute equation (7.8) into equation (7.9) in order to study the whole dynamics of our economic system

$$\dot{k}_t = s\left[k_t^{\beta} h(\overline{e}_t)^{1-\beta}\right] - (\delta+g+n)k_t. \tag{7.10}$$

Expression (7.10) is similar to the Solowian dynamic equation of capital per labour services, except for the presence of human capital. Given equation

(7.10), we can find the steady-state level of physical capital per capita (k^*) simply by setting k_t to zero and solving for k_t:

$$k^*: s\left[k_t^{\beta} h(\overline{e}_t)^{1-\beta}\right] = (\delta + g + n)k_t \tag{7.11}$$

Once we have found k^*, we can insert it into equation (7.8) in order to obtain the steady-state level of output given a certain average level of education.

7.2.2.3. The possibility of a poverty trap

Until now, in the equations of the model, physical and human capital have always been considered separately. Nevertheless, some macroeconomic studies suggest that output growth, and consequently physical capital accumulation, can influence the average level of education.

For example, Bils and Klenow (2000) find that the level of education registered in a country depends positively on its GDP growth. They investigate the presence of a reverse causality between human capital and growth. In contrast with previous studies such as Barro (1991), Benhabib and Spiegel (1994) and Barro and Sala-i-Martin (1995), they conclude that the causality direction is from economic growth to schooling and not the opposite. In a more recent work, Glewwe and Jacoby (2004) find a positive relationship between the individuals' investment in education and their levels of wealth.

Therefore, in line with these studies, we assume that, at the aggregate level, there exists a positive relationship between the physical capital per capita of a country and the average level of education of its population.[13] This assumption can be formalized as follows:

$$e_t = k_t^b,\ b > 0 \tag{7.12}$$

Equation (7.12) states that in a rich country individuals invest more time in education than those in a poor country. This means that the average stock of human capital depends positively on the stock of physical capital per unit of effective-labour and on the constant elasticity coefficient of e with respect to k, that is, b.

By combining expressions (7.4), (7.8) and (7.12) we can obtain a more specific formulation for y_t in which output depends only on physical capital. In this way, we can obtain the dynamics of y_t from the dynamics of k_t,

$$y_t = k_t^{\beta}\left[\frac{B\exp(\underline{B}bk_t)}{B - \sigma + \sigma\exp(\underline{B}bk_t)}\right]^{1-\beta} \tag{7.13}$$

where $\underline{B} \equiv B^{1/b}$. Now, the steady-state solutions of our augmented Solow model can be found as follows:

$$k^{*}: sk_t^{\beta}\left[\frac{B\exp(\underline{B}bk_t)}{B-\sigma+\sigma\exp(\underline{B}bk_t)}\right]^{1-\beta}=(\delta+g+n)k_t \tag{7.14}$$

or

$$k^{*}: F(k_t)=(\delta+g+n) \tag{7.14'}$$

where

$$F(k_t)=sk_t^{\beta-1}\left[\frac{B\exp(\underline{B}bk_t)}{B-\sigma+\sigma\exp(\underline{B}bk_t)}\right]^{1-\beta}.$$

While in the Solow growth model the function $F(k_t)$ is monotonically decreasing, here $F(k_t)$ may be a non-monotonic function.[14] This means that, as in Figure 7.2, we could observe the existence of three different stationary equilibria, two of which are stable and one unstable.[15] To be exact, the low equilibrium (k_L) and the high equilibrium (k_H) are stable, while the middle equilibrium (k_M) is unstable. The low equilibrium is also known in literature as the poverty trap, that is, an equilibrium with low levels of capital (human and physical) and income per capita.

Let us examine the dynamics of physical capital implied by Figure 7.2. Assuming an initial level of physical capital k_0 such that $0<k_0<k_L$ (or $k_M<k_0<k_H$), Figure 7.2 states that the accumulation of physical capital per unit of effective labour will exceed the depreciation of physical capital due to obsolescence, technical progress and population growth. Therefore we will observe an increase in the level of k_t. This increase in k_t will raise the level of output either directly as input for the production of y_t or indirectly causing an increase in the level of education and consequently of human capital. In this situation, k continues to rise until it reaches the value k_L (or k_H), at which level physical capital will remain constant.

On the contrary, if $k_L<k_0<k_M$ (or $k_H<k_0<+\infty$), the depreciation of physical capital due to obsolescence, technical progress and population growth will exceed the accumulation of physical capital per unit of effective labour. Therefore we will observe a decrease in the level of k_t until it reaches the value k_L (or k_H). We can conclude that the convergence of k_t towards the value k_L or the value k_H depends on the initial value of physical capital per unit of effective labour, k_0.

In the next section, we provide a numerical example in which we show that, under plausible values of parameters, the model presented in this section can explain the existence of multiple equilibria.

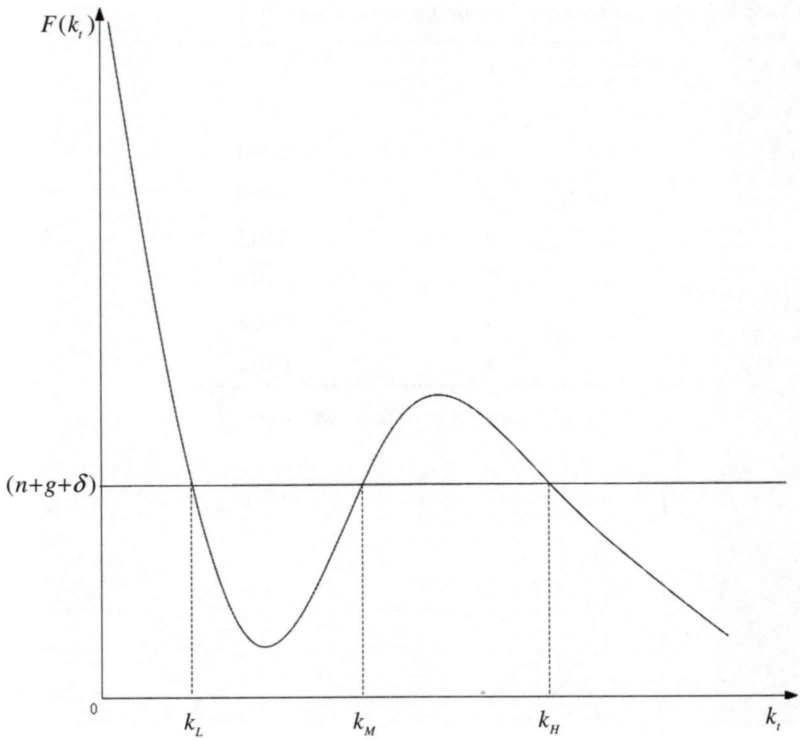

Figure 7.2. Convergence in physical capital per capita

7.2.2.4. Investing in education to escape from the trap

Here, we study the consequences of parameter changes on our theoretical model. To do this, we use a numerical analysis in which the values of exogenous parameters are those observed for the European Union (EU-15) in 2001 (Eurostat, 2004). As the depreciation coefficient of physical capital was not available for all countries, we took the depreciation coefficient observed by MRW (1992). Table 7.1 contains the parameter values used to draw Figure 7.3.

In Table 7.1, the value of σ refers to that estimated by Arrazola et al. (2005) for Spain, while parameter *b* was estimated by using our dataset and described in the next section.[16]

Figure 7.3 shows that, under plausible values of the exogenous parameters, the function $F(k_t)$ is non-monotonic. Nevertheless in Figure 7.3, since we used parameters from developed countries, $F(k_t)$ equals the

Table 7.1. Parameters used in the numerical example

B	1
s	0.127
b	0.504
β	0.250
σ^{*}	0.017
δ^{**}	0.030
g	0.028
n	0.014

Notes: * Arrazola et al. (2005); ** MRW (1992).

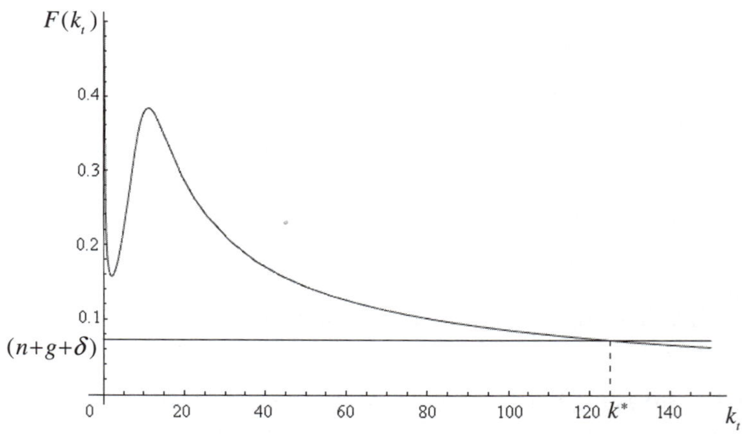

Figure 7.3. The convergence path for EU-15

constant value $n+g+\delta$ in only one point. This means that for countries of EU-15 we have a unique steady-state equilibrium (k*).

Figure 7.4 shows what happens to F when the elasticity coefficient of e with respect to k, that is b, changes. If the value of b is 0.10, the function F will match the constant value $n+g+\delta$ in three different points (k_L, k_M, k_H). These points are three different steady-state equilibria, two of which are stable (k_L, k_H). In this situation, as discussed in the previous section, countries with a stock of physical capital per capita lower than k_M will converge to the equilibrium with a low level of physical capital per capita, k_L: that is, these countries fall into a poverty trap. At the same time, countries with a stock of physical capital higher than k_M will converge to the highest equilibrium, k_H. Figure 7.4 also shows that a sufficiently large increase in b ($b=0.50$) will shift the function F up enough to eliminate the lower steady-state. This means that a highly educated society, that is a society in which individuals spend much of their time to studying, will converge to a high level of physical capital per capita. Indeed, above a certain level of b, the lower and middle equilibria disappear, and we will observe only one (high) equilibrium. This result supports the idea that policies to increase the average years of schooling in less developed countries can help these countries to escape from a poverty trap.[17]

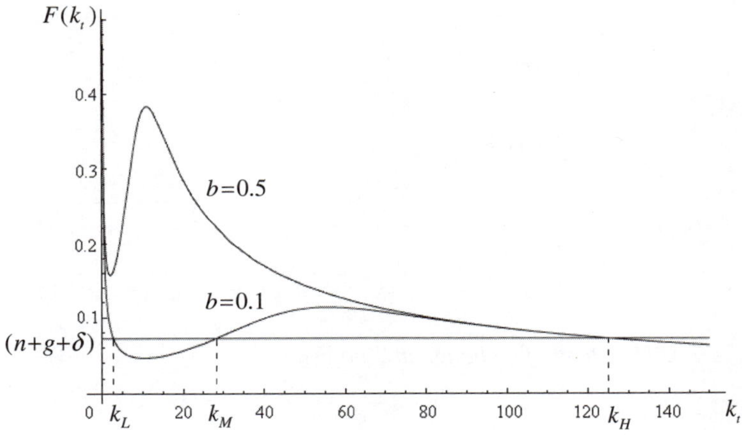

Figure 7.4. The effect of a change in b *on* F(k$_t$)

Figure 7.5 shows that if β rises our graph becomes smoother. This is due to the fact that we are keeping the hypothesis of constant returns to scale in production. That is, if β increases, the elasticity coefficient of human capital $(1-\beta)$ decreases and the non-linear effect of education becomes relatively less important. Note that when β increases multiple equilibria may appear, disappear or remain. In particular, in Figure 7.5 an increase in β implies only a higher steady-state level of *k*.

Finally, let us discuss the effect of a change in the value of σ. Figure 7.6 shows that multiple equilibria tend to disappear when the unitary depreciation of human capital due to the vintage effect rises: an increase in σ slows down the process of human capital accumulation which causes the existence of non-linear dynamics in our model. Therefore, if σ increases enough, we will observe only one equilibrium as in the traditional Solow model. However, in this situation, given the small contribution of human capital to the production of output, the unique steady-state equilibrium will be lower than the highest equilibrium observed in a situation with multiple equilibria. Symmetrically, when σ decreases, the accumulation of human capital becomes easier and non-linearities more pronounced. This means that, given the assumption of an increasing depreciation coefficient of human capital (due to the vintage effect), the dynamics of output growth tends to be non-linear, and such non-linearities are more important when σ is smaller.

In the next section, we evaluate the impact of education on TFP growth.

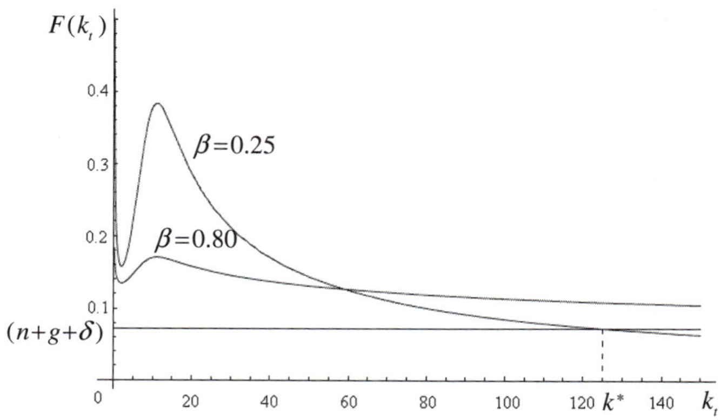

Figure 7.5. The effect of a change in β *on* F(k_t)

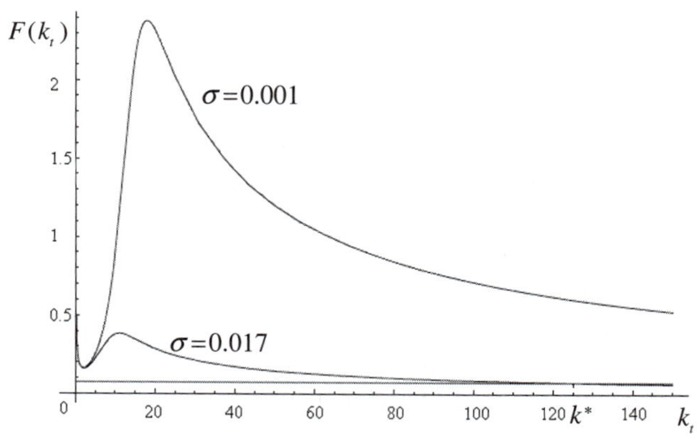

Figure 7.6. The effect of a change in σ *on* F(k_t)

7.3. EMPIRICAL ANALYSIS

In this section, we set out to test the effects of education on economic growth. By relaxing the assumption of a linear relationship between education and growth, we show that important non-linearities emerge in this relationship. In particular, as predicted by our model, we will observe an inverted U-shaped relationship between education and TFP growth.

7.3.1. Data and Variables

Data come from two different sources: average years of schooling from Barro and Lee (2001); real per capita income growth, inflation, the investment rate, financial depth, and trade variables from World Development Indicators (WDI) (2004). Our sample consists of 78 countries with data for the period 1960–2000. In order to eliminate business cycle effects, data were collected in groups of five-year averages. Therefore, in this dataset the effects of short run variations are reduced. In Appendix 7A.2 we report the country list.

De la Fuente and Doménech (2000), Cohen and Soto (2007), Krueger and Lindahl (2001) and Temple (2001) stress the importance of data quality in order to find a robust relationship between education and growth. For instance, according to De la Fuente and Doménech (2000), Barro and Lee's dataset performs poorly if the data is used in first differences. It is also true that Barro and Lee's dataset probably remains the most widely used reference for educational attainment in the economic literature. Moreover, De la Fuente and Doménech (2000) provide data only for 21 OECD countries, while Cohen and Soto (2007) take a single observation for each decade, and this notably reduces the number of observations. For all these reasons we decided to use this dataset.

Since, as stated by (7.12), investment in education may be an endogenous variable, we decided to take as dependent variable the TFP growth rate instead of the GDP growth rate. Moreover, in the endogenous growth theory, TFP is a 'black box' that needs to be filled with economic contents. TFP growth was estimated from a Cobb–Douglas production function with constant returns to scale by setting the capital share at 1/3 and the labour share at 2/3.[18] Among the explanatory variables, particular attention is paid to the effect of education (EDU) on TFP growth. Since our theoretical model explicitly considers the average level of education, here education is measured by the average years of schooling of the population aged 15 years and older. However, there are other important reasons to use average years of schooling instead of adult literacy rates or enrollment rates. Literacy is not uniquely defined across countries and thus creates biases in cross-country analyses. Furthermore, adult literacy rates omit important components of human capital such as logical and analytical reasoning and scientific and technological knowledge. That is, adult literacy rates ignore the contribution of advanced skills and knowledge to production of output. Enrollment rates are poor proxies for the present stock of human capital. Indeed, enrollment rates measure the education of students, who do not constitute the current labour force. On the contrary, average years of schooling takes into account the total amount of formal education acquired by the workforce, that is, average years of schooling proxy more accurately the existing stock of human capital in a country. For this reason, in line with the recent literature, we consider average years of schooling as one of the most reliable human capital proxies currently in use.[19]

In this chapter, we also estimate the effects of some control variables on TFP growth: investment share (INV), measured as a fixed investment share of GDP; financial depth (LLY), measured as the ratio of liquid liabilities to GDP, in order to control for the effect of financial development on growth; the trade openness ratio (TRADE), measured as the ratio of exports plus imports to GDP; the inflation rate (PI) in order to consider macro policy outcome; the population growth rate (POP); and two dummy variables (D70, D80), to control for time period effects with reference to the 1970s and 1980s. Except for the average years of schooling, all the explanatory variables are expressed in terms of growth rates. There are several reasons to control for specific time effects: the 1970s and 1980s were decades dominated by oil shocks and high inflation in many countries. In particular, oil shocks, which raised the real price of energy between 1973 and 1974, may have caused the so-called 'productivity slowdown' during the 1980s. Moreover, there are significant differences in GDP volatility between the 1970s and the 1980s (see, e.g., Easterly, 2001). All these effects seem to be exogenous and this is why the inclusion of two dummy variables for the 1970s and 1980s is quite common in growth regressions.

7.3.2. Econometric Models

As in Hall and Jones (1999) and in line with our theoretical framework, we develop the econometric analysis by starting from an aggregate production function equal to previous equation (7.5):

$$Y_t = K_t^{\alpha}(A_t H_t)^{1-\alpha} \tag{7.15}$$

where A_t represents the exogenous component of technological progress, $H_t \equiv h_t L_t$ and labour is assumed to be homogeneous within a country.[20]

Moreover, as suggested by Hall and Jones (1999) and Bils and Klenow (2000), we consider the following human capital production function:

$$h_t = \exp[f(\overline{e}_t)]. \tag{7.16}$$

According to Bils and Klenow, equation (7.16) represents the appropriate way to incorporate the average years of schooling into an aggregate production function. Here, the function $f(e_t)$ captures the efficiency of a unit of labour with e_t years of schooling, while the derivative $f'(e_t)$ captures the returns to schooling in producing human capital, that is, an additional year of schooling raises the efficiency of labour by $f'(e_t)$. Therefore, $f'(e_t)$ also represents the returns to schooling estimated in a Mincerian wage regression.[21]

In this section we seek to estimate the shape of $f(e_t)$. As suggested by Josephson (2006), the best way to do this is to take the TFP growth rate instead of the real GDP growth rate as a dependent variable.[22]

Let us write equation (7.15) in terms of output per worker

$$y_t = k_t^{\alpha}(A_t h_t)^{1-\alpha} \tag{7.17}$$

where $y_t \equiv Y_t / L_t$ and $k_t \equiv K_t / L_t$. Now, we can decompose output per worker into inputs and productivity simply by taking the logarithm of (7.17)

$$\ln y_t = \alpha \ln k_t + (1-\alpha)\ln A_t + (1-\alpha)\ln h_t \tag{7.18}$$

that is,

$$\ln TFP_t = (1-\alpha)\ln A_t + (1-\alpha) f(\overline{e}_t) \tag{7.19}$$

where $\ln TFP_t = \ln y_t - \alpha \ln k_t$. As specified in the previous section, we imposed $\alpha = 1/3$ in order to obtain the values of TFP.

Finally, we can write equation (7.19) in terms of growth rates

$$g_{TFP_t} = (1-\alpha) g_{A_t} + (1-\alpha) g_{h_t} \tag{7.20}$$

where $g_{TFP_t} = \ln TFP_{t+1} - \ln TFP_t$, $g_{A_t} = \ln A_{t+1} - \ln A_t$ and $g_{h_t} = f(\overline{e}_{t+1}) - f(\overline{e}_t)$. In line with the growth accounting literature, the term g_{A_t} can be calculated from (7.20) as residual.

We will use different specifications for the last equation in order to test different hypotheses concerning the returns to education. The first specification refers to the hypothesis that the percentage gain in human capital from each year of schooling is constant. This hypothesis can be formalized as follows:

$$g_{TFP_t} = \beta_0 + \beta_1 \overline{e}_t + \gamma X_t^T + \varepsilon_t \tag{7.21}$$

where β_0 is the intercept and represents the gain (or loss) of TFP when a country's labour force is completely illiterate, β_1 is the coefficient of e_t, γ

is a vector of coefficients, X_t is a vector of control variables expressed in terms of growth rates and ε_t is a white noise error.

To verify the hypothesis of a non-linear contribution of education to TFP growth, as suggested by our theoretical model, we must estimate alternative human capital accumulation functions. With respect to the previous specification, we now consider a model in which education enters in a quadratic form,

$$g_{TFP_t} = \beta_0 + \beta_1 \overline{e}_t + \beta_2 \overline{e}_t^2 + \gamma X_t^T + \varepsilon_t \tag{7.22}$$

Note that to observe increasing returns for low levels of education and decreasing returns for high levels of education, the coefficient β_2 should be negative. To make the regression model more sensitive to changes in educational attainment, especially for high levels of education, we also estimate a cubic specification,

$$g_{TFP_t} = \beta_0 + \beta_1 \overline{e}_t + \beta_2 \overline{e}_t^2 + \beta_3 \overline{e}_t^3 + \gamma X_t^T + \varepsilon_t \tag{7.23}$$

The introduction of a cubic term, in the case of a positive value for β_3, will make the last equation closer to a logistic specification, where the decrease in returns to schooling slows down for high levels of education. As outlined in Temple (2001), measurement errors will tend to bias regression analyses. He stresses that, over a twenty- or thirty-year sample the assumption of equal fixed effects is highly implausible. In particular, Temple shows how heteroskedasticity and outliers are important problems in the empirical growth regression literature. To avoid the problem of heteroskedasticity for cross-section data, models (7.21)–(7.23) were estimated by using a traditional GLS method.[23]

7.3.3. Estimation Results

Table 7.2 contains our estimates for equations (7.21)–(7.23). The coefficients of control variables have the expected signs in all regressions, even if not all of these coefficients are statistically significant. In particular, the intercept and the coefficients of investments, trade openness and dummy variable for the 1970s are statistically significant (at 1 per cent). A negative intercept means that in a country in which our explanatory variables are absent TFP will decrease continuously. The coefficient of the dummy variable for the 1970s is negative, evidence consistent with the period of stagflation that economists ascribe to the oil shocks observed in those years. Finally, we can see how an increase in the private investment share, as well as in the trade openness ratio, enhances TFP growth.

Table 7.2. Cross-country regressions on TFP growth rate (1960–95)

	GLS (eq. 7.21)	GLS (eq. 7.22)	GLS (eq. 7.23)
	Control Variables		
Intercept	–0.0149 (2.172)**	–0.0208 (2.8102)**	–0.0243 (3.073)**
D70	–0.0103 (3.219)**	–0.0097 (3.038)**	–0.0095 (2.955)**
D80	–0.0047 (1.494)	–0.0041 (1.361)	–0.0042 (1.336)
POP	0.2637 (1.592)	0.3068 (1.844)*	0.2710 (1.607)
INV	0.0545 (3.418)**	0.0626 (3.828)**	0.0665 (3.998)**
PI	0.0056 (0.680)	–0.0015 (0.174)	–0.0009 (0.103)
TRADE	0.0139 (3.585)**	0.0138 (3.573)**	0.0141 (3.654)**
LLY	0.0015 (0.251)	0.0004 (0.069)	0.0010 (0.171)
	Main Variables		
EDU	0.0019 (3.190)**	0.0058 (3.016)**	0.0105 (2.483)**
EDU^2		–0.0004 (2.097)**	–0.0014 (1.658)*
EDU^3			0.0001 (1.252)
Obs	540	540	540
AIC	–1952.034	–1938.822	–1920.435
BIC	–1910.679	–1893.355	–1870.86
Log-Lik	986.017	980.411	972.217

Note: t-statistics are given in parentheses: ** (1%), * (5%).

The first column of Table 7.2 shows estimates of the model represented by (7.21), where we assumed a linear contribution for education. As can be seen, at this level of the analysis, the effect of education on TFP growth is positive and statistically significant at 1 per cent. The estimate of β_1 is 0.0019, this value indicating that an additional year of schooling raises the level of TFP by 0.19 per cent. This is far from the value provided by Psacharopoulos (1994) for private return to schooling, which was 10.1 per cent for the world as a whole. Following Lange and Topel (2006), we can say that: 'the possibility that social returns are smaller than private ones typically views education as merely redistributive – able individuals use schooling to signal their ability, which may raise wages even if it has not impact on productivity'.

Column (2) of Table 7.2 reports the estimated parameters for the quadratic model represented by (7.22). The quadratic model explains data much better than the linear one. Here, the positive coefficient on the linear term (0.0058) and the negative coefficient on the squared term (–0.0003) suggest that there is an inverted U-shaped relation between education and productivity growth. Moreover, the coefficients on both the linear and squared terms are statistically significant at 1 per cent. In other words, consistent with our theoretical model, these findings suggest that education enters non-linearly into equation (7.19). In particular, returns to schooling are increasing for low levels of education and decreasing for high levels of education. However, a quadratic specification implies that after a certain level of education (7.3 years of schooling) returns to schooling become negative, that is, human capital starts to decrease. For this reason, we have included a cubic term to allow for a more sensitive analysis of non-linearities.

Column (3) of Table 7.2 reports the estimation results for equation (7.23). By looking at the log-likelihood value, we can say that this model fits data better than the linear and quadratic models. According to our findings, the magnitudes of the linear and quadratic terms are higher than in the quadratic specification and still significant at 1 per cent. The coefficient of cubic term is positive (0.0001) but not statistically significant. This means that, in line with the logistic model proposed in Section 7.2, the decrease in returns to schooling may slow down for high levels of education.

Although the cubic model yields a statistically significant third order coefficient, this appears to be driven by the highest levels of education, where the number of observations is small. On the other hand, this specification indicates that the relationship between education and TFP growth is more complex than previously thought.

By integrating the quadratic or the cubic specification and putting the result into the human capital production function, consistent with our theoretical model and also with Trostel's results, we obtain the expected logistic shape for (7.16). Moreover, our estimates confirm the previous findings of Krueger and Lindahl (2001) whereby, before 7.5 years of schooling, returns to education are increasing, and thereafter decreasing.

7.4. CONCLUSIONS

In this chapter we studied the effect of education on economic growth. In particular, we showed theoretically and empirically that education may have a non-linear effect on the process of economic growth. By assuming that higher educated workers are more affected by depreciation of human capital than lower educated workers, in Section 7.2 we provided a theoretical model, which explains why the returns to scale in producing human capital through education initially increase and later decrease.

Subsequently, we used this result to modify a Solow growth model augmented by the presence of human capital. There, we showed that a positive relationship between physical capital and education leads to a situation in which multiple equilibria may arise in the GDP growth path. Through a numerical example, we also showed that, under plausible values of the exogenous parameters, our model may generate the expected non-linearities and consequently the possibility of multiple equilibria in the economic growth path. Moreover, we studied the effects of parameter variations on these equilibria. In particular, we saw that investing in education is one way for poor countries to exit from an equilibrium with low levels of physical capital per capita.

In the last part of the chapter, we investigated the empirical relationship between education and growth. Here, we saw that for low levels of education, an increasing relationship emerges between years of schooling and TFP growth, while for high levels of education, the same relationship is decreasing.

Major criticisms were levelled at cross-country growth regressions. First, these regressions reveal the presence of a correlation among variables but not necessarily the presence of any causal link among them. Second, the assumption of exogeneity is not so plausible for some regressors. Third, some unobserved fixed effects (e.g. initial efficiency) might be correlated with some regressors. Fourth, since human capital influences other explanatory variables, the estimated impacts of human capital on growth contain indiscriminately direct and indirect effects. Finally, the already discussed issue of data quality remains a central question.

In conclusion, even if education may not be the only reason for a non-linear economic growth path, future growth regressions should account for these non-linearities. At the same time, as suggested by this chapter, theoretical studies should take into account the idea that the process of human capital accumulation may be a source of such non-linearities.

APPENDIX 7A.1 THE PRODUCTION FUNCTION OF HUMAN CAPITAL

Note that we can write equation (7.3) as follows:

$$\frac{dh}{Bh - \sigma h^2} = de.$$

Thus, by integrating both sides, we have

$$\int_{h(0)}^{h(e_t)} \frac{dh}{h - \eta h^2} = Be_t.$$

where $\eta \equiv \sigma / B$. That is,

$$\int_{h(0)}^{h(e_t)} \left(\frac{1}{h} + \frac{\eta}{1 - \eta h} \right) dh = Be_t.$$

and hence

$$\frac{h(e_t)}{1 - \eta h(e_t)} = \frac{h(0)}{1 - \eta h(0)} \exp[Be_t].$$

By imposing $h(0) = 1$, we conclude that

$$h(e_t) = \frac{\exp[Be_t]}{1 - \eta + \eta \exp[Be_t]}. \tag{7A.1}$$

Since $\eta \equiv \sigma / B$, equation (7A.1) corresponds to the logistic production function of human capital described by (7.4).

APPENDIX 7A.2 THE COUNTRY LIST

Algeria	Guatemala	Norway
Argentina	Guyana	Pakistan
Australia	Haiti	Panama
Austria	Honduras	Papua New Guinea
Belgium	India	Paraguay
Bolivia	Indonesia	Peru
Brazil	Iran, Islamic Republic of	Philippines
Cameroon	Ireland	Portugal
Canada	Israel	Rwanda
Central African Republic	Italy	Senegal
Chile	Jamaica	Sierra Leone
Colombia	Japan	South Africa
Congo	Kenya	Spain
Costa Rica	Korea, Republic of	Sri Lanka
Cyprus	Lesotho	Sudan
Denmark	Malawi	Sweden
Dominican Republic	Malaysia	Switzerland
Ecuador	Malta	Syria
Egypt, Arab Rep.	Mauritius	Thailand
El Salvador	Mexico	Togo
Finland	Nepal	Trinidad and Tobago
France	Netherlands	United Kingdom
Gambia, The	New Zealand	United States
Germany	Nicaragua	Uruguay
Ghana	Niger	Venezuela
Greece		

NOTES

* For helpful comments, I am grateful to W. Baumol, W. Brock, D. Fiaschi, A.M. Lavezzi, and seminar participants at the University of Pisa. The usual disclaimer applies.

1. A few examples of growth models in which human capital plays a central role in economic growth are: Nelson and Phelps (1966), Lucas (1988, 1990), Romer (1986, 1990), King and Rebelo (1990), Grossman and Helpman (1991).
2. For a detailed review of this literature see Venniker (2000).
3. This assumption is supported by several studies. For a rather detailed review of these studies see de Grip (2004).
4. Other theoretical models suggest that human capital may have a non-linear effect on economic growth. For example, by using an overlapping generation (OLG) model, Azariadis and Drazen (1990) explain the existence of multiple equilibria from threshold externalities in human capital accumulation. At the same time, Redding (1996) provides an endogenous growth model in which the presence of strategic complementarities between the accumulation of human capital and the investment in R&D sector may cause the existence of multiple equilibria in the economic growth path.
5. Obviously, the amount of time that individual *i* has already spent in leisure at time *t* will be $(1-u)t-e_{i,t}$. We abstract from the issue of optimal choice of allocation of time among work, education and leisure.
6. Since the focus of this study is on the relationship between education and growth, we abstract from the issue of human capital accumulation due to learning-by-doing, which clearly remains another important issue.
7. The main contributions to this literature are: Rosen (1976), Weiss and Lillard (1978), Johnson (1980), McPherson and Winston (1983), Neumann and Weiss (1995) and de Grip (2004).
8. Equation (6.3) is an autonomous differential equation also known as Verhulst's equation (from Verhulst, 1845). A formal derivation of this solution is provided in Appendix A.
9. Note that, in this model, the maximum level of human capital that an individual can accumulate $H_{max}=(B/s)$ does not depend on any biological consideration on the capacity of human brain, but it depends positively on the productivity of the education sector and negatively on the unitary variation of the depreciation coefficient of human capital.
10. Although, as suggested by van Leeuwen (2007), *B* is likely to be on occasion smaller than 1, in this context only too small a value of *B* may cause the absence of non-linearities.
11. In this work, we do not consider the implications of our model in terms of welfare analysis. Nevertheless, this consideration may represent an interesting starting point for future studies.
12. Formally, we will obtain $A_t=gA_t$ and $L_t=nL_t$.
13. The introduction of these complementarities in the accumulation of physical and human capital will allow us to explain the level of output only in terms of physical capital per unit of effective-labour, as in the Solow model. In this way, we will obtain a growth model in which non-linear dynamics in the economic growth path may appear.
14. Table 7.1 provides a set of the values of parameters consistent with a non-monotonic behaviour of $F(k_t)$.
15. As well discussed by Galor (1996), the non-monotonic behaviour of $F(k_t)$ is a necessary, but not sufficient, condition for the existence of multiple equilibria. For example, if *s* is sufficiently high (or $n+g+\delta$ is sufficiently low) the function $F(k_t)$ will match the function $(n+g+\delta)$ only once.
16. In order to obtain *b*, we regressed the logarithm of the average years of education, e_t, on the logarithm of the current stock of physical capital per capita, k_t. That is, by using the

OLS method, we estimated the following log-linear transformation of equation (6.12): $\ln(e_t) = b\ln(k_t)$.

17. In Figure 7.4 an increase in *b* has the same effect that an increase in the saving rate, *s*, has in Galor (1996). In both cases *F*(*k*) shifts up and only one equilibrium remains.
18. These values are rather standard in the growth accounting literature (see, e.g., Benhabib and Spiegel, 2002).
19. This approach is based on the idea that investment in education plays a central role in human capital accumulation and is known as 'educational stock-approach'. Of course, human capital includes many dimensions, but education is perhaps the most important component and, in any case, it can be measured more easily than other components such as on-the-job training, experience and learning-by-doing. Moreover, education can improve individual well-being not only through better economic conditions but also through non-market benefits such as improvements in health, nutrition, fertility, upbringing of children, opportunity for self-fulfillment, and development of individual capacities.
20. Since data on hours per worker are not available for most countries, we use the number of workers to measure the labour input.
21. Note that if $f(e_t) = 0$ for all e_t this is a standard production function with undifferentiated labour.
22. Josephson (2006) shows that since the hypothesis of homogeneity between TFP and human capital cannot be rejected, 'any changes in TFP growth is proportional to changes in human capital in a one-to-one relation'.
23. GLS estimates are obtained by using the *R* program provided by Abbey (1988).

REFERENCES

Abbey, S. (1988), 'Robust Measures and the Estimator Limit', *Geostandards Newsletter*, **12**, 241–48.

Arrazola, M., J. de Hevia, M. Risueño and J.F. (2005), 'A Proposal to Estimate Human Capital Depreciation: Some Evidence for Spain', *Hacienda Pública Española / Revista de Economía Pública*, **127**(1), 9–22.

Azariadis, C. and A. Drazen (1990), 'Threshold Externalities in Economic Development', *Quarterly Journal of Economics*, **105**(2), 501–26.

Barro, R.J. (1991), 'Economic Growth in a Cross Section of Countries', *Quarterly Journal of Economics*, **106**(2), 407–43.

Barro, R.J. and X. Sala-i-Martin (1995), *Economic Growth*. New York: McGraw-Hill.

Barro, R.J. and J.W. Lee (2001), 'International Data on Educational Attainment: Updates and Implications', *Oxford Economic Papers*, **53**(3), 541–63.

Benhabib, J. and M.M. Spiegel (1994), 'The Role of Human Capital in Economic Development: Evidence from Aggregate Cross-Country Data', *Journal of Monetary Economics*, **34**, 143–73.

Benhabib, J. and M.M. Spiegel (2002), 'Human Capital and Technology Diffusion', Federal Reserve Bank of San Francisco, mimeo.

Bils, M. and P.J. Klenow (2000), 'Does Schooling Cause Growth?', *American Economic Review*, **90**(5), 1160–83.

Cohen, D. and M. Soto (2007), 'Growth and Human Capital: Good Data, Good Results', *Journal of Economic Growth*, **12**(1), 51–76.

de Grip, A. (2004), 'Evaluating Human Capital Obsolescence', *Research Centre for Education and the Labour Market (R.O.A.) Working Papers*, no. 001, Maastricht University.

De la Fuente, A. and R. Domenech (2001), 'Schooling Data, Technological Diffusion and the Neoclassical Model', *American Economic Review*, **91**(2), 323–7.

Easterly, W. (2001), 'The Lost Decades: Developing Countries' Stagnation in Spite of Policy Reform 1980–1998', *Journal of Economic Growth*, **2**(6), 135–57.

Eurostat (2004), Oct. 18, <http://epp.eurostat.cec.eu.int>.

Galor, O. (1996), 'Convergence? Inferences from Theoretical Models', *Economic Journal*, **106**(437), 1056–69.

Glewwe, P. and H.G. Jacoby (2004), 'Economic Growth and the Demand for Education: Is There a Wealth Effect?', *Journal of Development Economics*, **74**(1), 33–51.

Grossman, G.M. and E. Helpman (1991), *Innovation and Growth in the Global Economy*, Cambridge, MA: MIT Press.

Hall, R. and C.I. Jones (1999), 'Why Do Some Countries Produce So Much More Output per Worker than Others?', *Quarterly Journal of Economics*, **114**(1), 83–116.

Isaksson, A. (2002), 'The Importance of Human Capital for the Trade-Growth Link', *SIN Working Paper*, no. 2, UNIDO.

Johnson, W.R. (1980), 'Vintage Effects in the Earnings of White American Men', *Review of Economics and Statistics*, **62**, 399–407.

Josephson, C. (2006), 'What Technical Change Really is in a Disaggregate Production Function', *The Business Review*, **5**(2).

King, R.G. and S. Rebelo (1990), 'Public Policy and Economic Growth: Developing Neoclassical Implications', *Journal of Political Economy*, **98**(5), S126–50.

Krueger, A.B. and M. Lindahl (2001), 'Education for Growth: Why and for Whom?', *Journal of Economic Literature*, **39**(4), 1101–36.

Lange, F. and R. Topel (2006), 'The Social Value of Education and Human Capital', in E. Hanushek and F. Welch (eds), *Handbook of Education Economics*, Vol. 1, Amsterdam: North Holland.

Lucas, R.E. (1988), 'On the Mechanics of Economic Development', *Journal of Monetary Economics*, **22**(1), 3–42.

Lucas, R.E. (1990), 'Why Doesn't Capital Flow from Rich to Poor Countries?', *American Economic Review, Papers and Proceedings*, **80**(2), 92–6.

Mankiw, N.G., D. Romer and D.N. Weil (1992), 'A Contribution to the Empirics of Economic Growth', *Quarterly Journal of Economics*, **107**(2), 407–37.

Mincer, J. (1974), *Schooling, Experience, and Earnings*, New York: Columbia University Press.

McPherson, M.S. and G.C. Winston (1983), 'The Economics of Academic Tenure: A Relational Perspective', *Journal of Economic Behavior and Organization*, **4**, 163–84.

Nelson, R.R. and S.E. Phelps (1966), 'Investment in Humans, Technological Diffusion, and Economic Growth', *American Economic Review*, **56**, 69–75.

Neumann, S. and A. Weiss (1995), 'On the Effects of Schooling Vintage on Experience-Earnings Profiles: Theory and Evidence', *European Economic Review*, **39**(5), 943–55.

Psacharopoulos, G. (1994), 'Returns to Investment in Education: A Global Update', World Development, **22**(9), 1325–43.

Redding, S. (1996), 'Low-Skill, Low-Quality Trap: Strategic Complementarities Between Human Capital and R&D', *Economic Journal*, **106**(435), 458–70.

Romer, P.M. (1986), 'Increasing Returns and Long-run Growth', *Journal of Political Economy*, **94**(5), 1002–37.

Romer, P.M. (1990), 'Endogenous Technical Change', *Journal of Political Economy*, **98**(5), S71–S102.

Rosen, S. (1976), 'A Theory of Life Earnings', *Journal of Political Economy*, **84**(4), 45–68.

Solow, R.M. (1956), 'A Contribution to the Theory of Economic Growth', *Quarterly Journal of Economics*, **70**(1), 65–94.

Stiglitz, J.E. and R.W. Boadway (1994), *Economics and The Canadian Economy*, New York: W.W. Norton & Company.

Temple, J.R.W. (2001), 'Generalizations that Aren't? Evidence on Education and Growth', *European Economic Review*, **45**(4–6), 905–18.

Trostel, A.P. (2004), 'Returns to Scale in Producing Human Capital from Schooling,' *Oxford Economic Papers*, **56**(3), 461–84.

van Leeuwen, B. (2007), 'Human Capital and Economic Growth in India, Indonesia, and Japan: A Quantitative Analysis, 1890–2000', Utrecht University, mimeo.

Venniker, R. (2000), 'Social Returns to Education: A Survey of Recent Literature on Human Capital Externalities', *CPB Netherlands Bureau for Economic Policy Analysis Report 00/1*, 47–50.

Verhulst, P.F. (1845), 'Recherches Mathématiques sur La Loi D'Accroissement de la Population', *Nouveaux Mémoires de l'Académie Royale des Sciences et Belles-Lettres de Bruxelles*, **18**(1), 1–45.

Weiss, Y. and L.A. Lillard (1978), 'Experience, Vintage, and Time Effects in the Growth of Earnings: American Scientists, 1960–1970', *Journal of Political Economy*, **86**(3), 427–47.

8. Child mortality decline, inequality and economic growth

Tamara Fioroni

8.1. INTRODUCTION

Through the last two centuries, economic development has gradually contributed to the increase in the human life span. In 1840 life expectancy at birth was 40 years in England, 44 years in Denmark and 45 years in Sweden (Livi-Bacci, 2001). According to recent life tables, in 2007 life expectancy at birth in the United Kingdom, Denmark and Sweden is 79, 78 and 81 years respectively. In most developed countries, life expectancy at birth is around 80 years (CIA, 2007). Developing countries have also shown a rapid increase in life expectancy, albeit prior to 1980. Indeed, in several poor countries the HIV/AIDS epidemic has reversed the positive trend in life expectancy (Becker et al., 2005, Cutler et al., 2006). Figure 8.1 shows how life expectancy rose from 1960 to 2004.

A large body of literature suggests that one of the most important factors for this rise in life expectancy is the increase in the level of education (Grossman, 1982; Schultz, 1999). Higher agent's education, indeed, implies a higher willingness to invest in health care either because education makes people better decision makers or because more educated people have better information about health. Education can improve health through a better choice of health inputs: it reduces smoking, improves eating habits and increases exercise (Adams, 2002). In addition, home environment and parents' schooling are correlated with lower child mortality (Grossman, 1982; Schultz, 1999). This a key point since the increase in life expectancy at birth mostly stems from the reduction in child mortality. At the same time as mortality rates decline there is a sharp decline in fertility rates. Figure 8.2 gives an insight into this relationship between child mortality rates and fertility rates. In addition, Figure 8.2 shows that fertility, especially in 1960, is increasing for low levels of income and decreasing for high levels of income.

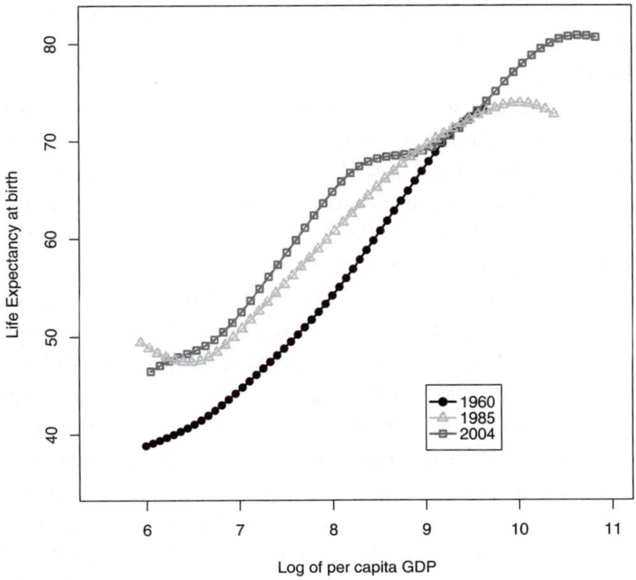

Source: Per capita GDP data are from Penn World Table 6.2. Life expectancy at birth data are from World Development Indicators CD-ROM, World Bank (2006).

Figure 8.1. Life expectancy versus log of GDP per capita (1960, 1985, 2004), non-parametric kernel smoother

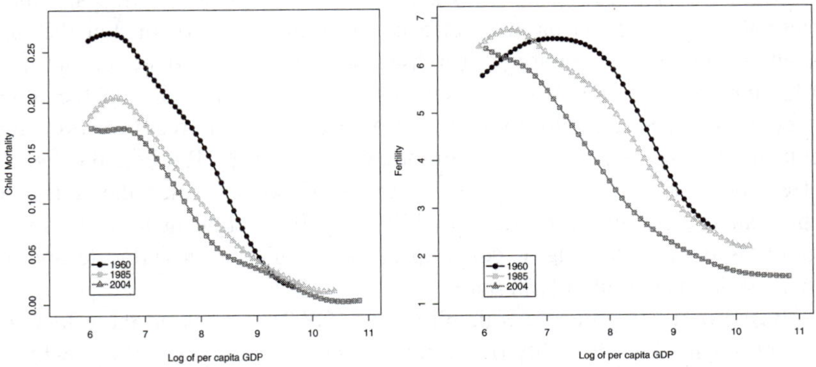

Source: Per capita GDP data are from Penn World Table 6.2. Fertility rate and child mortality data are from World Development Indicators CD-ROM, World Bank (2006).

Figure 8.2. Child mortality and fertility rate (1960, 1985, 2004), non-parametric kernel smoother

There are many theories which explain this path in mortality and fertility rates. In particular, we refer to the seminal paper by Becker et al. (1990) which analyzes the relationship between economic growth and fertility choice. This approach shows that initial levels of human capital and technology determine whether a country grows over time or stagnates at low income levels. Societies with low levels of human capital choose large families and invest little in each member since the return to human capital is scarce. On the other hand, in societies with high levels of human capital, the rate of return on human capital is high relative to the rate of return on children. Such societies choose to have small families and devote more resources to investment in education. Our work also links in with the papers by Galor and Weil (1999), Galor (2005) and Kalemli-Ozcan (2002). The first two papers describe the process of economic and demographic development of Western Europe as passing through three distinct regimes. The first is called the Malthusian Regime. Here the relationship between income per capita and population growth is positive: small increases in income lead to population growth. In the second regime, called the post-Malthusian regime, both per capita income and population present a positive growth rate and their relationship remains positive as in the Malthusian regime. The final stage of development is the Modern Growth Regime. In the latter, both income per capita and the level of technology present a positive growth rate whereas population growth declines. Galor and Weil (1999) focus on the technology, the population growth and output growth as the key elements which can explain the transition process through these three stages. They argue that technological progress raises the rate of return to human capital, inducing parents to invest in their children's education. In particular, technological progress has two effects on population growth. On the one hand, improved technology increases households' budget constraints, allowing them to spend more resources on raising children. On the other hand, it induces a reallocation of these increased resources toward child education, that is child 'quality'. In the Post-Malthusian Regime, the former effect dominates, and so population grows. However, since the return to child quality continues to rise, the shift away from child quantity becomes more significant, causing a reduction in the population growth rate and an increase in the output growth rate.

Based on this approach, Kalemli-Ozcan (2002) focuses on the effects of reductions in child mortality on fertility, education and economic growth. In particular, child mortality depends on parental income. At low levels of income per capita, population increases with income causing a reduction in income per capita. Thus, the economy is in a stable Malthusian steady state where fertility is high and human capital investment is low. At high levels of income per capita population growth falls as income per capita increases.

This leads to an unstable growth steady state with low fertility and high human capital investment.

Finally we refer to Lagerlöf (2003) who models demographic and economic long-run development in a setting where mortality depends on agents' human capital and is subject to epidemic shocks. The transition from the Malthusian trap to sustained growth is generated from a series of mild epidemic shocks. When the economy experiences a phase of relatively mild epidemic shocks, mortality rates fall leading to a positive population growth rate. However, birth rates remain unchanged and parents do not invest in children's education. When the education time becomes positive the economy shifts into the modern growth regime. In this regime, the economy experiences a quality–quantity substitution in children, i.e. birth rates fall since education time makes children more expensive. Once the growth rate of human capital is high, the impact of further epidemics becomes negligible and the economy remains in the modern growth regime. Our chapter departs from this strand by stressing the effect of different initial human capital endowments on fertility and education choices. We develop an overlapping generations model where altruistic parents care about the number of their surviving children and the future level of human capital of each of them. We assume that parents spend a proportion of their income on raising each child born and investing in the education of surviving children. The child's probability of survival through to adulthood is an increasing concave function of parents' human capital (see Figure 8.3).[1]

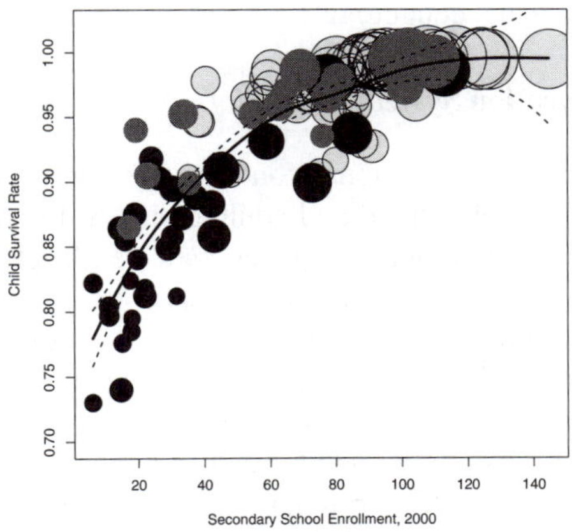

Note: Circles are proportional to the country's per capita income; black circles indicate Sub-Saharan countries and grey ones indicate East Asian and Pacific countries (WDI, 2006).

Source: World Development Indicators CD-ROM, World Bank (2006).

Figure 8.3. Child survival rate (under-5) versus secondary school enrolment, non-parametric kernel smoother, year 2000, n=127

This framework allows us to generate the demographic transition and has the effect of creating multiple development regimes such that the growth rate of the economy depends on initial human capital endowments.

The chapter is structured as follows. The model is set out in Section 8.2. Section 8.3 shows the optimal fertility and education choices. Section 8.4 contains the analysis of human capital accumulation. Finally, some concluding remarks are made in Section 8.5.

8.2. THE MODEL

Consider an overlapping-generations economy that operates in a perfectly competitive world. Activity extends over an infinite discrete time. In every period, the economy produces a single material good, the price of which is normalized to 1.

8.2.1. Production Technology

The production function is linear in the stock of human capital:[2]

$$Y_t = H_t. \tag{8.1}$$

Hence, firms employ the whole labour force to produce as long as the wage per unit of human capital is lower than or equal to one. The equilibrium in the labour market thus implies that the wage per unit of human capital is constant through time and equal to one, i.e., $w_t = 1$, for all t.

8.2.2. Private Education System

Consider an overlapping generations economy where members of generation t live for two periods: childhood and adulthood. All decisions are made in the adult period of life. Individuals have an endowed level of human capital h_t, determined from previous generations' decisions.

Parents have n_t children of which a fraction $1-\pi$ dies before reaching adulthood. We suppose that children's probability of reaching adulthood depends on their parents' human capital endowment, i.e. $\pi_t = \pi(h_t)$.

Individual preferences are defined for a consumption above a subsistence level $\tilde{c} > 0$, the number of surviving children $\pi(h_t)n_t$, i.e. children's quantity, and the human capital of children h_{t+1}, i.e. children's quality (see Galor, 2005). The utility function of an agent of generation t, U^t, is given by:

$$U^t = (1-\gamma)\log(c_t) + \gamma \log[\pi(h_t)n_t h_{t+1}], \tag{8.2}$$

where the parameter $\gamma > 0$ is the altruism factor.[3]

Agents allocate their income, i.e. h_t, between consumption c_t, child rearing and education spending per child e_t. In particular, raising each born child takes a fraction $\phi \in (0, 1)$ of an adult's income. This implies that having many children is more costly for parents who have high income. Investment in education e_t is devoted only to each surviving child. Thus the agent's budget constraint is given by:

$$c_t = h_t(1-\phi n) - \pi(h_t)e_t n_t. \tag{8.4}$$

The human capital of children h_{t+1} depends on the parents' human capital h_t and education spending e_t, that is:

$$h_{t+1} = (\theta + e_t)^{\alpha} h_t^{1-\alpha}, \tag{8.5}$$

where $\theta > 0$ and $\alpha \in (0, 1)$. The presence of θ implies that children's human capital is positive even if parents do not invest in education (de la Croix and Doepke, 2004).

8.2.3. Endogenous Child Mortality

Many contributions focus on the positive relationship between the parents' human capital and the child's health status. Schultz (1993), for example, shows that higher levels of parents human capital are correlated with lower child mortality, even after holding per capita income constant (see Figure 8.3). In particular, women's education is the most significant determinant of child mortality. A year of additional schooling for the mother is often associated, in a low-income country, with 5–10 per cent reduction in her child's probability of dying in the first five years of life.

Following empirical evidence (Figure 8.3) the survival probability of children is assumed to satisfy the following properties:

$$\partial \pi_t / \partial h_t > 0, \tag{8.6}$$

$$\partial^2 \pi_t / \partial h_t^2 < 0, \tag{8.7}$$

$$\lim_{h_t \to 0} = \underline{\pi} \geq 0, \tag{8.8}$$

$$\lim_{h_t \to \infty} \pi(h_t) = \overline{\pi} \leq 1. \tag{8.9}$$

Hence, we specify the children's probability of surviving as follows (see Blackburn and Cipriani, 2002):

$$\pi_t = \frac{\underline{\pi} + \overline{\pi}\delta(h_t)^{\eta}}{1+\delta(h_t)^{\eta}}, \tag{8.10}$$

where the parameters $0<\eta\leq 1$ and $\delta>0$ jointly determine both the turning point in $\partial\pi_t/\partial h_t$ and the speed at which $\pi(h_t)$ traverses the interval $(\underline{\pi}, \overline{\pi})$. For a given value of η, an increase (decrease) in δ reduces the turning point, while for a given value of such a point, an increase (decrease) in η raises the speed of transition (the limiting case of which is when $\pi(h_t)$ changes value from $\underline{\pi}$ to $\overline{\pi}$ instantaneously, which corresponds to the case of a step function. For simplicity we assume that $\eta=1$ and $\delta=1$:

$$\pi_t = \frac{\underline{\pi} + \overline{\pi}h_t}{1+h_t}. \tag{8.11}$$

8.3. FERTILITY AND EDUCATION CHOICES WITH PRIVATE EDUCATION

Members of generation t choose the number of children, the education spending for each of them and their own consumption. Substituting equations (8.4) and (8.5) into equation (8.2), the agents' maximization problem is given by:

$$U^t = (1-\gamma)\log\left[h_t(1-\phi n_t) - \pi(h_t)e_t n_t\right] + \gamma\log\left[\pi(h_t)n_t(\theta+e_t)^{\alpha} h_t^{1-\alpha}\right], \tag{8.12}$$

subject to:

$$h_t(1-\phi n_t) - \pi(h_t)e_t n_t \geq \tilde{c}, \tag{8.13}$$

$$(n_t,\ e_t) \geq 0. \tag{8.14}$$

For agents that have enough income so as to ensure a consumption above $\tilde{c}$, the optimal education level and the optimal number of children are given by:

$$n_t = \frac{\gamma h_t(1-\alpha)}{\phi h_t - \pi(h_t)\theta}, \tag{8.15}$$

and:

$$e_t = \frac{h_t\phi\alpha - \pi(h_t)\theta}{\pi(h_t)(1-\alpha)}. \tag{8.16}$$

In particular, the optimal consumption is above $\tilde{c}$ when human capital is above $\tilde{h}=\tilde{c}/(1-\gamma)$ (for the technical aspects see Appendix 8A.1). Hence, when $h_t>\tilde{h}$ a fraction $1-\gamma$ of h_t is devoted to consumption and a fraction γ of h_t is devoted to raising children and education spending for each child (see Figure 8.4). By contrast, when $h_t\leq\tilde{h}$, agents devote their income to ensure a consumption equal to $\tilde{c}$, and the remaining part, that is $h_t-\tilde{c}$, is devoted to raising children and the education spending for each child (see Figure 8.4), that is:

$$[\phi h_t+e_t\pi(h_t)]\ n_t=\begin{cases}\gamma h_t & \text{if } h_t>\tilde{h}\\ h_t-\tilde{c} & \text{if } h_t\leq\tilde{h},\end{cases} \tag{8.17}$$

from which we can see $h_t\geq\tilde{c}$.

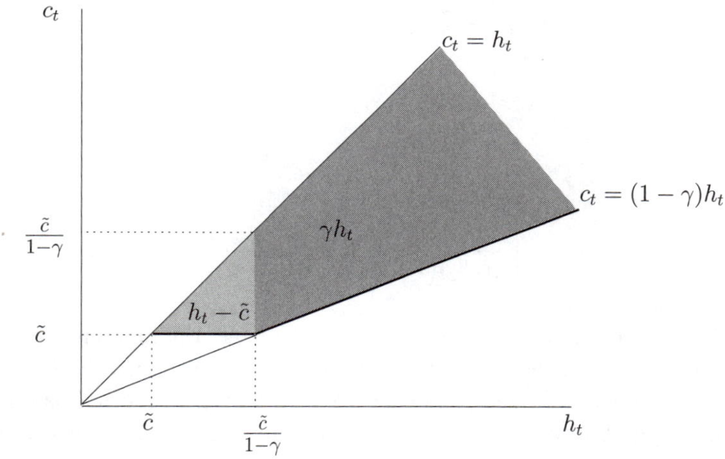

Figure 8.4. Consumption path

Given equation (8.16) we can see that there is an interior solution for the optimal education choice if agents have enough human capital such that $h_t>\bar{h}$ (the human capital level $\bar{h}$ is given in Appendix 8A.1). Hence, given the human capital level $\tilde{h}$, we can distinguish two cases depending on whether $\tilde{h}<\bar{h}$ or $\tilde{h}>\bar{h}$. However, we suppose that $\tilde{h}<\bar{h}$ on the consideration that only when income is sufficiently high so as to ensure consumption above the subsistence level, parents begin to invest in children's education (the case $\tilde{h}>\bar{h}$ is analyzed in Appendix 8A.1). Thus, given $\tilde{h}<\bar{h}$, there are the following regimes:

$$\tilde{c}\leq h_t\leq\tilde{h},$$

$$\tilde{h} < h_t \le \bar{h}, \qquad h_t > \bar{h}. \tag{8.18}$$

The optimal number of children and the level of education chosen by members of generation t, in the three regimes, are given by (see Appendix 8A):

$$n_t = \begin{cases} \frac{1}{\phi}\left(1 - \frac{\tilde{c}}{h_t}\right) & \text{if } \tilde{c} \le h_t \le \tilde{h}, \\ \frac{\gamma}{\phi} & \text{if } \tilde{h} < h_t \le \bar{h}, \\ \frac{\gamma h_t (1-\alpha)}{\phi h_t - \pi(h_t)\theta} & \text{if } h_t > \bar{h}. \end{cases} \tag{8.19}$$

and:

$$e_t = \begin{cases} 0 & \text{if } h_t \le \bar{h}, \\ \frac{h_t \phi\alpha - \pi(h_t)\theta}{\pi(h_t)(1-\alpha)} & \text{if } h_t > \bar{h}. \end{cases} \tag{8.20}$$

Therefore, when human capital is $\tilde{c} \le h_t \le \tilde{h}$, the optimal choice for education is zero while the optimal number of children increases in h_t, i.e. $\partial n_t / \partial h_t > 0$, $\partial^2 n_t / \partial h_t^2 < 0$ (see Appendix 8A.1.1). For less educated parents, indeed, the opportunity cost of raising children is low while providing education is expensive relative to their income.

When human capital is $\tilde{h} < h_t \le \bar{h}$, optimal education choice is zero while the optimal number of children ceases to increase in parents' human capital and becomes a constant.

When $h_t > \bar{h}$, the optimal number of children decreases in h_t, that is $\partial n_t / \partial h_t < 0$ (see Appendix 8A.1.1). Indeed, as income rises, the cost of having more children increases and parents choose to have a lower number of children and to give more education to each of them. Thus since for agents with a high human capital level, the rate of return on human capital is higher than the return on children, they choose to have a low number of children and to devote more resources to the education of each child. The lowest possible fertility rate is given by:

$$\lim_{h_t \to \infty} n_t = \frac{\gamma(1-\alpha)}{\phi}.$$

Fertility as a function of human capital is plotted in Figure 8.5.

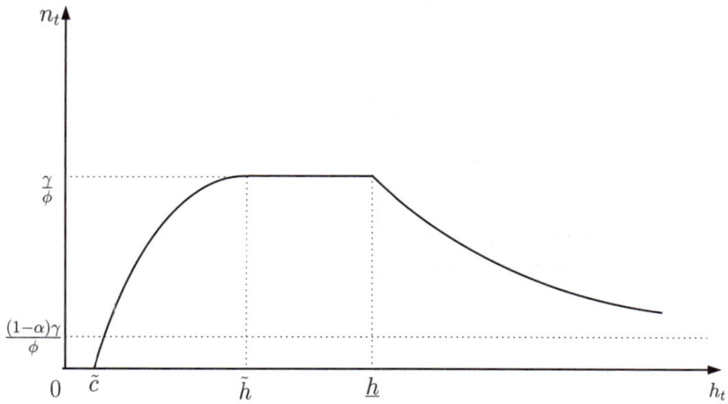

Figure 8.5. Fertility as a function of human capital

Equation (8.20) shows that the optimal education spending chosen by skilled parents is increasing concave with respect to parents' human capital, that is $\partial e_t / \partial h_t > 0$, $\partial^2 e_t / \partial h_t^2 > 0$ (see Appendix 8A.1.2).

Parents face a trade-off between the optimal number of children and the amount of resources to invest on the education of each child. For parents with a low level of human capital, the opportunity cost of raising children is low, while providing education is expensive relative to their income. Unskilled parents therefore prefer to have many children but invest little in the education of each child. As long as income is sufficiently high the optimal number of children decreases with income and investment in education increases with income. For parents with a sufficiently high level of human capital, the opportunity cost of child rearing is high and the rate of return in education is high. Hence, they prefer to invest in the education or 'quality' of a small number of children.

8.4. DYNAMIC OF HUMAN CAPITAL

Given the optimal education choice from equation (8.20) above, we can now characterize the dynamic of human capital accumulation as follows:

$$h_{t+1} = \begin{cases} (\theta)^{\alpha} h_t^{1-\alpha} & \text{if } h_t \leq \bar{h} \\ \left(\theta + \dfrac{h_t \phi \alpha - \pi(h_t)\theta}{\pi\left(h_t\right)\,(1-\alpha)}\right)^{\alpha} h_t^{1-\alpha} & \text{if } h_t > \bar{h}. \end{cases} \tag{8.21}$$

The economy shows multiple development regimes if the following condition holds (for technical details see Appendix 8A.2):

$$\phi < \frac{1}{\alpha}\left(\frac{\underline{\pi} + \bar{\pi}\theta}{1+\theta}\right). \tag{8.22}$$

Therefore, an economy which starts with a human capital level below $\bar{h}$, converges to a stable equilibrium $h_L = \theta$ which is a Malthusian steady state (see Appendix 8A.2). An economy with an initial human capital level above $\bar{h}$ grows in the long run if the following condition holds (for technical details see Appendix 8A.2):

$$\phi > \frac{\bar{\pi}(1-\alpha)}{\alpha}. \tag{8.23}$$

We collect these results in Proposition 1 below the technical aspects of which are proved in Appendix 8A.2.

Proposition 1 *An economy with an initial human capital level below* $\bar{h}$ *converges to a Malthusian steady state* h_L*. An economy with an initial human capital level above* $\bar{h}$ *grows in the long run.*

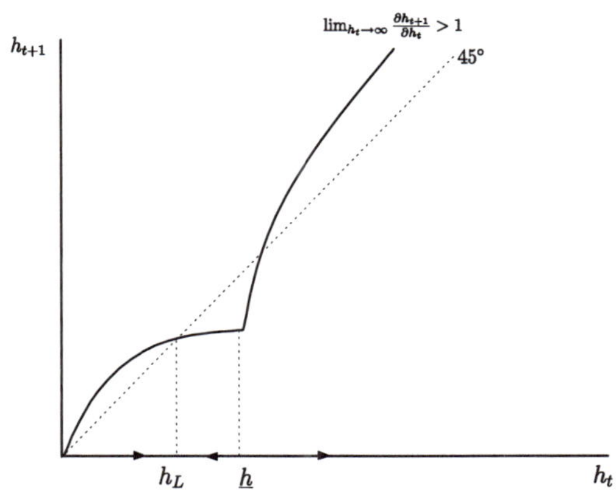

Figure 8.6. Multiple development regimes

Figure 8.6 depicts the dynamic of human capital. The initial stock of human capital determines the allocation of total resources between parents' consumption, education spending and the number of children. Given these initial conditions, the economy develops along one of two paths, either to the left or to the right of $\bar{h}$. Agents endowed with a low level of human capital do not invest in children's education and devote their income to the consumption and the number of children. This leads the economy to a Malthusian equilibrium where education is zero, fertility is high and the survival probability of children is low. When human capital is above $\bar{h}$, skilled agents choose to invest in the education of their children since the rate of return in the investment in human capital is higher than the rate of return on the number of children. A lower number of children with increased levels of human capital investment leads to endogenous growth.

8.5. CONCLUDING REMARKS

In this chapter we analyze the effect of income inequality on fertility, child mortality and education choices. This framework allows us to generate the demographic transition and has the effect of creating multiple development regimes such that the growth rate of the economy depends on initial conditions. The initial human capital endowment is the key factor in explaining the persistence in income inequality across households. For low levels of income, the optimal spending in children's education is zero, fertility increases in human capital and child mortality is high. Therefore, when income is below the subsistence level the economy converges to a Malthusian steady state where parents do not invest in children's education and choose to invest in the quantity of their children. When income is above the subsistence level, the economy is on a high development path: as income rises, child mortality decreases, and parents choose to have a lower number of children and to devote more resources to children's education.

APPENDIX

8A.1. Optimal Conditions

Given the agents' maximization problem from equations (8.12), (8.13) and (8.14), the first order conditions yield equations (8.15) and (8.16) for the optimal number of children and the optimal education spending, respectively. Substituting equations (8.15) and (8.16) into the budget constraint we obtain the optimal consumption as follows:

$$c_t = h_t(1-\gamma),$$

This consumption is above the subsistence level, i.e. $\tilde{c}$, if:

$$h_t \geq \frac{\tilde{c}}{(1-\gamma)}, \tag{8A.1}$$

where we define the human capital level $\tilde{h} = \tilde{c}/(1-\gamma)$ such that $c_t = \tilde{c}$.

When $c_t > \tilde{c}$ a fraction $1-\gamma$ of h_t is devoted to the consumption and a fraction γ of h_t is devoted to raising children and the education spending for each child, that is:

$$c_t = h_t(1-\gamma),$$

$$[\phi h_t + e_t \pi(h_t)]\ n_t = \gamma h_t.$$

When $c_t = \tilde{c}$, the difference between income and the subsistence consumption is devoted to raising children and the education spending for each child, that is:

$$c_t = \tilde{c},$$

$$[\phi h_t + e_t \pi(h_t)]\ n_t = h_t - \tilde{c}. \tag{8A.2}$$

Given equation (8A.16) there is a corner solution for education if:

$$h_t \leq \frac{\pi(h_t)\ \theta}{\phi\alpha},$$

where using equation (8A.11) we obtain the following solutions for h_t:

$$h_1 = \frac{-(\phi\alpha - \bar{\pi}\theta) + \sqrt{(\phi\alpha - \bar{\pi}\theta)^2 + 4\phi\alpha\underline{\pi}\theta}}{2\phi\alpha} > 0, \tag{8A.3}$$

$$h_2 = \frac{-(\phi\alpha - \pi\theta) - \sqrt{(\phi\alpha - \pi\theta)^2 + 4\phi\alpha\underline{\pi}\theta}}{2\phi\alpha} < 0, \tag{8A.4}$$

where $h_1 > 0$ and $h_2 < 0$.

We define the human capital $h_1 = \bar{h}$ such that when $h_t < \bar{h}$ the optimal choice for education is zero. Given the human capital level $\tilde{h}$, we distinguish two cases depending on whether $\tilde{h} < \bar{h}$ or $\tilde{h} > \bar{h}$. When $\tilde{h} < \bar{h}$ we have the three regimes given by (8.18). In the first regimes, i.e. $\tilde{c} \leq h_t \leq \tilde{h}$, the optimal choice for education is zero, that is:

$$e_t = 0$$

Substituting this solution into equation (8A.2) the optimal number of children is given by:

$$n_t = \frac{1}{\phi}\left(1 - \frac{\tilde{c}}{h_t}\right). \tag{8A.5}$$

When $h_t = \tilde{h}$, it follows that:

$$n_t = \frac{\gamma}{\phi}.$$

When $\tilde{h} < h_t \leq \bar{h}$, consumption is above the subsistence level $c_t > \tilde{c}$ and the optimal spending in education is zero. Hence, agents maximize the following utility function:

$$U^t = (1-\gamma)\log\left[h_t(1-\phi n_t)\right] + \gamma \log\left[\pi(h_t) n_t h^{1-\alpha}\theta^{\alpha}\right],$$

which yields the following optimal decision rule for the number of children:

$$n_t = \frac{\gamma}{\phi}.$$

When $h_t > \bar{h}$ the optimal number of children and the optimal choice for education are given by equations (8.15) and (8.16) respectively.

In the second case, i.e. $\tilde{h} < \bar{h}$, we have three regimes given by:

$$\tilde{c} \leq h_t \leq \bar{h},$$

$$\bar{h} < h_t \leq \tilde{h}, \tag{8A.6}$$

$$h_t > \tilde{h}.$$

The first-order conditions give the following solutions for the optimal number of children:

$$n_t = \begin{cases} \dfrac{\left(h_t - \tilde{c}\right)\,(1-\alpha)}{h_t\phi - \pi(h_t)\theta} & \text{if } \bar{h} < h_t \le \tilde{h}, \\[2ex] \dfrac{\gamma h_t\,(1-\alpha)}{\phi h_t - \pi(h_t)\theta} & \text{if } h_t > \tilde{h}. \end{cases} \tag{8A.7}$$

Thus fertility behaves as in the first case (see equation (8.19)) expect for $\bar{h} < h_t \le \tilde{h}$. In this regime, agents maximize the following utility function:

$$U^t = (1-\gamma)\log(\tilde{c}) + \gamma\log\left[\pi(h_t)\left(\frac{h_t - \tilde{c}}{h_t\phi - e_t\pi(h_t)}\right) h^{1-\alpha}\left(e+\theta\right)^{\alpha}\right].$$

The first-order conditions yield equation (8.16) for education, and the following solution for the optimal number of children:

$$n_t = \frac{\left(h_t - \tilde{c}\right)\,(1-\alpha)}{h_t\phi - \pi(h_t)\theta}.$$

8A.1.1. Optimal fertility

Given the optimal fertility in equation (8.19) when human capital is low, that is $\tilde{c} \le h_t \le \tilde{h}$, the optimal number of children increases in human capital and has a concave shape with respect to h_t, that is:

$$\frac{\partial n_t}{\partial h_t} = \frac{\tilde{c}}{\phi h_t^2} > 0, \tag{8A.8}$$

and:

$$\frac{\partial^2 n_t}{\partial h_t^2} = -\frac{2\tilde{c}}{\phi h_t^3} < 0. \tag{8A.9}$$

When $h_t > \bar{h}$ the optimal number of children decreases in h_t, that is:

$$\frac{\partial n_t}{\partial h_t} = -\frac{\gamma(1-\alpha)\theta\left[\pi(h_t) - \pi'(h_t)h_t\right]}{\left[\phi h_t - \pi(h_t)\right]^2} < 0, \tag{8A.10}$$

since $\pi(h_t) - \pi'(h_t)h_t > 0$.

If we suppose that $\tilde{h} > \bar{h}$ optimal fertility choice is given by equation (8A.7). The optimal number of children behaves as in the case $\tilde{h} < \bar{h}$ except for a human capital level $\bar{h} < h_t \leq \tilde{h}$. Indeed, in this regime fertility increases in human capital, that is:

$$\frac{\partial n_t}{\partial h_t} = \frac{(1-\alpha)\left[h_t^2(\phi\tilde{c} - \bar{\pi}\theta) + 2h_t(\phi\tilde{c} - \theta\underline{\pi}) + \phi\tilde{c} - \theta\underline{\pi} - \theta\tilde{c}(\bar{\pi} - \underline{\pi})\right]}{\left[\theta(\underline{\pi} + \bar{\pi}h_t) + (1+h_t)\ \phi h_t\right]^2} > 0,$$

where we suppose that:

$$\phi\tilde{c} - \bar{\pi}\theta > 0,$$

$$\tilde{c}\left[\phi - \theta(\bar{\pi} - \underline{\pi})\right] - \theta\underline{\pi} < 0.$$

We obtain the two solutions:

$$h_1 = \frac{(\phi\tilde{c} - \theta\underline{\pi}) + \sqrt{\theta\tilde{c}(\phi\tilde{c} - \theta\underline{\pi})\ (\bar{\pi} - \underline{\pi})}}{(\phi\tilde{c} - \bar{\pi}\theta)} > 0,$$

$$h_2 = \frac{(\phi\tilde{c} - \theta\underline{\pi}) - \sqrt{\theta\tilde{c}(\phi\tilde{c} - \theta\underline{\pi})\ (\bar{\pi} - \underline{\pi})}}{(\phi\tilde{c} - \bar{\pi}\theta)} < 0.$$

Thus when $h_t > h_1$ it follows that $\partial n_t / \partial h_t > 0$.

Finally when $h_t > \tilde{h}$, the number of children decreases in h_t as we can see in equation (8A.10).

8A.1.2. Optimal education

Given the optimal education choice in equation (8.20), when $h_t > \bar{h}$ the spending in education of each child increases in h_t and has a concave shape with respect to h_t, that is:

$$\frac{\partial e_t}{\partial h_t} = \frac{\phi\alpha[\pi(h_t) - h_t\pi'(h_t)]}{[\pi(h_t)]^2(1-\alpha)} > 0,$$

since $\pi(h_t) - h_t\pi'(h_t) > 0$.

The second derivative is given as follows:

$$\frac{\partial^2 e_t}{\partial h_t^2} = -\frac{\phi\alpha\underline{\pi}(\bar{\pi} - \underline{\pi})}{(1-\alpha)(\underline{\pi} + \bar{\pi}h_t)^3} < 0.$$

8A.2. Human Capital

Given human capital accumulation in equation (8.21), the economy shows multiple development paths if, when $h_t = \bar{h}$, we have:

$$h_{t+1}(\bar{h}) < \bar{h}. \tag{8A.11}$$

Hence, the economy shows multiple equilibria if the following condition holds:

$$\phi < \frac{1}{\alpha}\left(\frac{\underline{\pi} + \bar{\pi}\theta}{1+\theta}\right) \tag{8A.12}$$

When $h_t \leq \bar{h}$, the economy shows the stable steady state h_L, that is:

$$h_L = \theta,$$

where when $h_t = \theta$ we obtain:

$$\frac{\partial h_{t+1}}{\partial h_t} = (1-\alpha) < 1.$$

When $h_t > \bar{h}$, the economy grows in the long run at a constant rate if:

$$\lim_{h_t \to \infty} \frac{\partial h_{t+1}}{\partial h_t} > 1,$$

that is:

$$\lim_{h_t \to \infty} \frac{\partial h_{t+1}}{\partial h_t} = \frac{\alpha\phi}{\bar{\pi}(1-\alpha)} > 1,$$

which holds if:

$$\phi > \frac{\bar{\pi}(1-\alpha)}{\alpha}. \tag{8A.13}$$

NOTES

1. The confidence interval indicates the degree of variability in the estimate.
2. For simplicity we abstract from physical capital.
3. We use the preferences used by Galor (2005). However, introducing the subsistence consumption in the utility function, that is:

   $$U^t = (1-\gamma)\log(c_t - \tilde{c}) + \gamma \log\left[\pi(h_t) n_t h_{t+1}\right]$$

   the main results do not change.

REFERENCES

Adams, S.J. (2002), 'Educational Attainment and Health: Evidence from a Sample of Older Adults', *Education Economics*, **10**(1), 97–109.

Becker, G.S., K.M. Murphy and R. Tamura (1990), 'Human Capital, Fertility, and Economic Growth', *Journal of Political Economy*, **98**(5), S12–37.

Becker, G.S., T.J. Philipson and R.R. Soares (2005), 'The Quantity and Quality of Life and the Evolution of World Inequality', *American Economic Review*, **95**(1), 277–91.

Blackburn, K. and G.P. Cipriani (2002), 'A Model of Longevity, Fertility and Growth', *Journal of Economic Dynamics and Control*, **26**(2), 187–204.

CIA (2007), *The World Factbook*, https://www.cia.gov/library/publications/the-world-factbook/index.html.

Cutler, D., A. Deaton and A. Lleras-Muney (2006), 'The Determinants of Mortality', *Journal of Economic Perspectives*, **20**(3), 97–120.

de la Croix, D. and M. Doepke (2004), 'Public versus Private Education when Differential Fertility Matters', *Journal of Development Economics*, **73**(2), 607–29.

Galor, O. (2005), 'From Stagnation to Growth: Unified Growth Theory', in P. Aghion and S. Durlauf (eds), *Handbook of Economic Growth*, Vol. 1, Amsterdam: Elsevier, pp. 171–293.

Galor, O. and D.N. Weil (1999), 'From Malthusian Stagnation to Modern Growth', *American Economic Review*, **89**(2);150–54.

Grossman, M (1982), 'Government and Health Outcomes', *American Economic Review*, **72**(2), 191–5.

Kalemli-Ozcan, S. (2002), 'Does the Mortality Decline Promote Economic Growth?', *Journal of Economic Growth*, **7**(4), 411–39.

Lagerlöf, N.-P. (2003), 'From Malthus to Modern Growth: Can Epidemics Explain the Three Regimes?', *International Economic Review*, **44**(2), 755–77.

Livi-Bacci, M. (2001), *A Concise History of World Population*, Oxford: Blackwell.

Schultz, T.P. (1993), 'Mortality Decline in the Low-Income World: Causes and Consequences', *American Economic Review*, **83**(2), 337–42.

Schultz, T.P. (1999), 'Health and Schooling Investments in Africa', *Journal of Economic Perspectives*, **13**(3), 67–88.

World Bank (2006), *World Development Indicators 2006*, Washington, DC: International Bank for Reconstruction and Development and The World Bank.

9. Health funding, inequality and economic growth*

Davide Dottori

9.1. INTRODUCTION

9.1.1. Health and Economic Growth

Health is widely recognized to be an important component of human capital and a prerequisite for sustained economic growth (Hazan and Zoabi, 2006; Cervellati and Sunde, 2007). One stream of literature has stressed the positive effect of health on productivity growth: good health was found to have a positive and statistically significant effect on labour outcome. Fogel (1997) estimates that nutritional improvements alone contributed about 20–30 per cent of income growth per capita not explained by factor accumulation in Britain during 1780–1979. Shastry and Weil (2003) estimate that health differences can explain up to one-third of cross-country income per capita variation after controlling for other measures of factor accumulation. Mayer-Foulkes (2004) shows the positive effect of early child health and on the probability of obtaining a higher education later in life. In a recently released report, UNICEF (2004) find that the impacts of food deficiencies on mortality, sicknesses, and on early child, mother and adult cognitive ability are significant. Adult health contributes directly to adult income: healthier workers may be productive, or at least less likely to be absent due to illness (or illness of a family member). Howitt (2005) highlights the beneficial effects of health on creativity, learning capacity and copying skills.

Clearly, there exists a relation from income to health, since richer countries can afford better health services. Nevertheless, Devlin and Hansen (2001) find Granger causality running in both directions between health and GDP in OECD countries. Income is an important determinant of health expenditure first of all because people demand 'good' health since it brings them directly utility, even if the concept of health care is not narrowed to basic needs. Therefore health should be included as an argument of the utility function since it is important in itself for agents: when they demand health goods or facilities actually they demand healthy well-being. In this respect, Van Zon and Muysken (2001) suggest that health can even become a 'substitute for growth' insofar as resources potentially available for other kinds of consumption goods can be diverted towards the health sector. Aísa and Pueyo (2001) consider the trade-off between life expectancy effect and this kind of competition for resources, finding that a crucial role is played by longevity response to an increase in health expenditure. Not least, general health condition is a major aspect of the degree of a country's development, being included in the Human Development Index (UNDP, 1990).

Health also plays another non-negligible indirect role which can affect economic growth. Unlike any other element of human capital, it increases the lifespan thus lowering individuals' discount rate, that is they are effectively more patient and willing to invest, thereby boosting economic growth. The extension of life expectancy allows returns to be obtained over a longer period of time, thus encouraging accumulation of human capital (de la Croix and Licandro, 1999), while high mortality rates reduce returns in education, where risk is less diversifiable (Chakraborty, 2004; Kalemli-Ozcan et al., 2000). Savings and investment rates are generally low in high mortality societies because they are more risky and because the returns from them are expected to be received along a shorter horizon. Fuchs (1986) finds empirical evidence for the positive link between individual patience rates and health. Moreover, if economies with high childhood mortality are considered, the possibility itself of reaching adulthood or old age can be considerably influenced by health conditions. Hence in less developed countries, a reduction in mortality rates tends also to increase the labour force.[1] In this respect the situation is different for most developed countries where, as Aísa and Pueyo (2001) point out, improvements in life expectancy make the retirement period longer without increasing the labour force; de la Croix and Licandro (1999) suggest that this aging effect might also introduce some obsolescence in human capital if the economy consists of older agents who did their schooling a long time ago. Many models have highlighted the positive effect of increased lifespan on the incentive to accumulate human capital (e.g. see Ben-Porath, 1967; Cervellati and Sunde, 2005; Boucekkine et al., 2003).[2]

In Figure 9.1 data from the World Health Report (WHO, 2004) are used to plot the increasing relation between health expenditure and life expectancy at birth. Chakraborty and Das (2005), Chakraborty (2004) and Wang and Leung (2003) model the discount factor as a function of health investment, that exhibits properties consistent with such evidence.

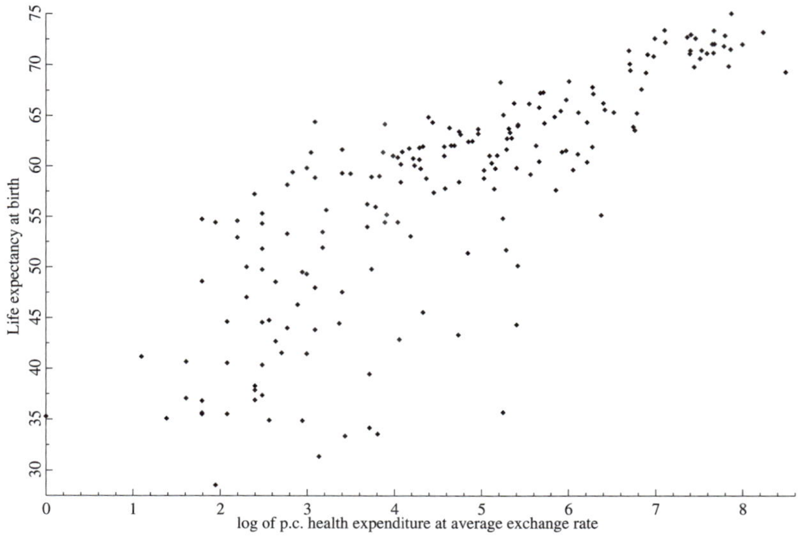

Source: WHO (2004).

Figure 9.1. Life expectancy and health expenditure per capita

As regards relations between health and inequalities, there is again a feedback between health and income inequalities: the causal direction from the inequalities in income to inequalities in health has been widely studied,[3] but less has been said about the opposite direction: Galor and Mayer-Foulkes (2004) show how health inequality may be a factor that explains persistence and increasing income inequalities, if health and education are complementary goods, but a minimum level of health is necessary and borrowing constraints are present. Chakraborty and Das (2005) point out that in the absence of perfect annuities markets[4] health shocks can have persistent effects on income distribution; Chakraborty (2004) shows how 'development traps' and persistent inequality may arise when mortality risk is endogenous and negatively dependent on health investment. Finally, de la Croix and Sommacal (forthcoming) study how differential mortality rates, inducing dissimilar propensities to save and bequeath, are a determinant of the path of inequality and of the relationship between inequality and growth.

Finally, health issues also exhibit many spillovers: for example, policies through investment in sanitation, vaccination and nourishment, and access to electricity, may reduce the impact and incidence of diseases, and the population size at risk of contacting such diseases (see Wang, 2003 for a survey). Whenever epidemics and diseases are a concrete obstacle to economic activity, improving the general health condition is an important condition to promote economic growth as well (Barro, 1996).

9.1.2. Private *vs* Public Health Funding, Inequality and Growth

In light of all these features of health, it seems interesting to investigate the effects on inequalities and on economic growth that two different regimes of health funding (public and private) may have. In the private system decisions over health spending are decentralized, whereas in the public regime health spending per capita is the same and chosen through voting by agents. A different approach was taken by Hosoya (2003) who focuses on the problem of the optimal tax rate to fund health in a public system; however, in his model health is an exogenous variable at the individual level, and there is no real comparison between the two systems. A comparison between public and private health funding systems is provided by Delfgaauw (2007) in a model which focuses on the differential altruism of physicians, finding that allowing for private provision of health care in addition to the public one is Pareto-improving; the framework is nevertheless a static one and hence growth issues are not concerned. Economic growth and funding systems for human capital were recently dealt with by Osang and Sarkar (2005). In an overlapping generations model, they study the impact on growth of different education funding systems whilst health is only public. The public education system proves outperformed as too many resources are diverted from health; inequality issues are not concerned, nor is the possibility of a private health system.

Our model follows the approach of Glomm and Ravikumar (1992; henceforth GR), which is applied to educational human capital in a model in which formal schooling is the engine of growth. They find that in the private case each agent devotes more time to schooling as he/she takes into account that any additional unit of time spent on education increases not only his/her earnings but also the bequests passed on to any offspring, whereas in the public case the latter effect is not internalized; hence, schooling in their model is always higher under a private regime. The analysis is extended by de la Croix and Doepke (2004) to a framework where also fertility decisions are endogenous: in such a context public education may have another channel to affect growth and inequality by reducing fertility differentials. Bénabou (1996) allows for complementarity in production and spillover effects, generating a trade-off between equalizing school budgets (which reduces heterogeneity) and sorting resources (which minimizes the growth loss at a given heterogeneity).

Health shares several features with education but it exhibits some peculiarities highlighted in Section 9.1.1.[5] Keeping a framework similar to

GR, some of these peculiarities are introduced in order to investigate whether and how the results change. In our model health plays mainly three roles: it is an argument of the utility function, it directly increases productivity and affects life expectancy. This last feature also affects the discount factor. Since time invested in education increases if agents discount the future less, the decision about how much to study in the private system is no longer the same across individuals as in GR, but it depends on the health investment they can afford. Agents with low income may be induced by public health provision to accumulate more human capital than they would do under the private system. On the other hand, in a private system more implications are taken into account, while in the public regime health spending turns out to be proportional to average income which is considered as exogenous by agents when voting for their preferred tax rate.

As far as inequalities are concerned, the public system turns out to reduce them more quickly than the private system. Actually in the private system inequalities are not reduced at all if long-run returns are not decreasing. Moreover, the model has an endogenous source of the poverty trap, which relies on the growth-enhancing – yet at a decreasing rate – effect of health on life expectancy: at low initial conditions health improvements have a big impact on survival probability and hence on the incentive to invest in human capital accumulation; further improvements in health have an increasingly small impact on life expectancy. This can cause a temporary convexity in the human capital map function, an unstable equilibrium and a poverty trap mechanism to take place.

The rest of the chapter is organized as follows: in Section 9.2 the basic framework for the model is illustrated; in Sections 9.3 and 9.4 optimizing choices and dynamics from the private and public system respectively are obtained. Section 9.5 deals with the comparison between the two regimes when agents are homogeneous, while in Section 9.6 the heterogeneous case is tackled. Section 9.7 provides some simulated examples after parameters have been calibrated. Finally in Section 9.8 there are some conclusive remarks.

9.2. THE BASIC FRAMEWORK

The model consists in an overlapping generations economy where agents live for two periods. The probability of living during the second part of life ($\phi \in (0, 1)$) depends positively on health expenditure during the first period.[6] In our context, we can regard ϕ also as the expected portion of second period lived. In the first period agents allocate their fixed amount of time between leisure and learning activities. At the end of the first period they have a child. During the second period they work, and allocate their income between consumption goods and health care facilities.

Each agent is endowed with a stock of human capital, which depends on the parents' stock of human capital, on time devoted to learning and on their health during their working period.[7] Agents are heterogeneous with respect to their endowments in human capital, whose distribution is initially given. Inequalities are measured by the variance of human capital distribution, that in this model coincides with the variance of income distribution.

Generations are linked through two channels: on one side every agent's stock of human capital depends on their parents' stock; on the other side, health expenditure of the household has a positive effect on life expectancy of the children. This introduces an externality since the parents do not internalize the benefit that their health expenditure has on the discount factor of the children through their life expectancy. Unlike the GR, there is no specific bequest motive in the utility function.[8] In the private system agents decide autonomously their preferred health expenditure; instead under a public regime health is provided by the government and is the same for all individuals. This health expenditure is financed by levying a proportional tax on labour income, with the tax rate determined through majority voting.

In order to keep things easy to handle, very simple functional forms are assumed: the logarithmic utility function, the Cobb–Douglas production function for human capital, and final good production linear in human capital so that the wage rate can be normalized to 1.[9] Agents receive utility from leisure and from a mix of health and consumption. Consumption and health in the first period are assumed to be variables beyond the agent's control since they are decided by parents: they can be considered as included in their parents' consumption and health. Hence, the objective function can be formalized as:

$$U = \ln n_t + \phi(h_t)[\ln c_{t+1} + \gamma \ln h_{t+1}] \tag{9.1}$$

where n_t, c_{t+1} and h_{t+1} are the control variables and denote respectively leisure, consumption and health. Parameter γ represents the weight of health relative to consumption: the greater is γ, the greater the importance of health relative to consumption.

Survival probability, $\phi(h_t)$, is a function of health investment during the first part of life. This health investment can be thought to occur through net food intake, personal care and hygiene, accessing clinical facilities and related medical expenditure that is the key to mortality reduction.[10] Subjective discounting is ignored to keep the notation as simple as possible, although it can be easily incorporated. Learning is assumed to have a time cost as it reduces the amount of disposable leisure. For the sake of simplicity we abstract from real costs of learning.[11]

Looking at the evidence from Figure 9.1, and following Chakraborty and Das (2005), the function $\phi(\cdot)$ should exhibit the following properties:

$$\phi(\cdot)\in(0;\,1),\ \phi'\geq 0,\ \phi''\leq 0,\ \text{and}\ \lim_{h\to\infty}\phi(h)=\bar{\phi}\leq 1.$$

Health investment augments lifespan, but at a decreasing rate, so that even when health expenditure is very high the limit for $\phi(\cdot)$ is finite and no greater than one since it is a probability. Some explicit forms for $\phi(h_t)$ are available in the literature. Chakraborty and Das (2005) use:

$$\phi(h)=\begin{cases} ah^{\varepsilon} & \text{if } h\in[0,\,\hat{h}] \\ \bar{\phi} & \text{otherwise} \end{cases} \tag{9.2}$$

where $\hat{h}\equiv(\bar{\phi}/a)^{1/\varepsilon}$, $\varepsilon\in(0;\,1)$ and a is a positive parameter related to exogenous medical progress.[12] Another example for an explicit $\phi(h)$ is available in Chakraborty (2004):

$$\varphi(h)=\beta\frac{h}{1+h} \tag{9.2a}$$

In this case, $\beta=\bar{\phi}$. Finally Wang and Leung (2003) propose

$$\varphi(h)=p_0+\bar{p}\sqrt{\frac{h}{1+h}} \tag{9.2b}$$

where p_0 represents the minimum level of longevity and $\bar{p}$ can be thought of as the state of the art of medical progress. In this case the supremum for $\phi(\cdot)$ is $\bar{\phi}=p_0+\bar{p}$.

As regards the evolution of human capital, ξ, the following functional form is assumed:

$$\xi_{t+1}=\psi(1-n_t)^{\lambda}h_{t+1}^{\theta}\xi_t^{v} \tag{9.3}$$

where $\psi>0$ is a productivity parameter; $(1-n_t)$ denotes time devoted to learning in youth and h_{t+1} represents the current health investment. The idea is that to accumulate human capital some favourable health conditions are necessary together with time devoted to study and the inherited stock of human capital. Evidence that good health is necessary to make education more effective is widely supported (see, among others, Lange and Bleakley, 2004 and Miguel and Kremer, 2004). The inclusion of lagged human stock is quite standard since it represents the intergenerational transfer of knowledge, skills and so on. As in GR, production technology is linear in human capital so that the wage rate can be normalized to one and every individual's income is equal to their human capital. The distribution of human capital is initially given. Dynamics of the variance will be used to measure dynamics of inequalities.

Before studying the private system, it may be worth briefly summarizing the three channels through which health plays a role in this simple model: it provides directly utility, it increases lifespans and finally it enhances productivity and income.

9.3. THE PRIVATE SYSTEM

In the private system, the optimization problem consists in maximizing (9.1) with respect to n_t, c_{t+1} and h_{t+1} under (9.3) and the budget constraint:[13]

$$\xi_{t+1} = c_{t+1} + h_{t+1} \tag{9.4}$$

with h_t and ξ_t given.

Using (9.4) to replace c_{t+1} in (9.1) and using (9.3) to substitute ξ_{t+1}, the constrained optimization problem is equivalent to maximizing with respect to n_t and h_{t+1} the following objective function:

$$\ln n_t + \phi(h_t)\{\ln[(\psi(1-n_t)^{\lambda} h_{t+1}^{\theta} \xi_t^{\nu} - h_{t+1}] + \gamma \ln h_{t+1}\} \tag{9.5}$$

Maximization with respect to n_t yields the first order condition:

$$\frac{1}{n_t} = \frac{\phi(h_t)\lambda\xi_{t+1}}{(\xi_{t+1} - h_{t+1})(1-n_t)} \tag{9.6}$$

while the first condition with respect to h_{t+1} amounts to:

$$\frac{h_{t+1} - \theta\xi_{t+1}}{\xi_{t+1} - h_{t+1}} = \gamma \tag{9.7}$$

The expression above can be solved for h_{t+1} getting:

$$h_{t+1} = \frac{\gamma + \theta}{\gamma + 1}\xi_{t+1} \equiv \alpha\xi_{t+1} \tag{9.8}$$

Hence the health share of consumption is denoted by α. Now it is straightforward to compute optimal consumption as:

$$c_{t+1} = \frac{1-\theta}{1+\gamma}\xi_{t+1} \equiv (1-\alpha)\xi_{t+1} \tag{9.9}$$

As expected, health investment is increasing (while c_{t+1} is decreasing) in γ and θ: this is not surprising since γ represents the preference for health over consumption; θ is related to the productivity effect of health.[14]

Because the utility function is homothetic, the optimal health-consumption ratio (χ) is independent of ξ_{t+1}, and amounts to:

$$\frac{h_{t+1}}{c_{t+1}} = \frac{\gamma+\theta}{1-\theta} \equiv \chi \tag{9.10}$$

Now, substituting (9.8) for h_{t+1} into (9.6), the optimal amount of time to devote to learning can be computed:

$$1-n_t = \frac{\phi(h_t)\lambda(\gamma+1)}{\phi(h_t)\lambda(\gamma+1)+(1-\theta)} \equiv \Delta \tag{9.11}$$

Denoting by Δ_i the partial derivative of Δ with respect to variable i, we have the following proposition:

Proposition 1 *Under the private regime, time devoted to learning is increasing in life expectancy, returns from instruction, returns from health and preference for health over general consumption:*

$$\Delta_\phi > 0, \quad \Delta_\lambda > 0, \quad \Delta_\theta > 0, \quad \Delta_\gamma > 0$$

Proof. Taking derivatives of (9.11), the sign of each inequality follows.

The sign of each derivative is as expected. The fraction of time that agents decide to invest in learning is increasing in the portion of the second period they expect to live, $\phi(h_t)$: if agents have a higher life expectancy, returns from human capital accumulation are worth more and hence it is preferable to consume less leisure. If λ increases, learning time is more productive such that it is optimal to increase it. As regards θ and γ, a direct and indirect effect can be detected, operating both in the same direction. The indirect effect works through (9.8) by increasing h_t and hence $\phi(h_t)$: when individuals live longer because they grew up in a healthier family environment they discount the future less and are more wiling to invest in human capital accumulation. The direct effect is instead related to the positive impact of γ and θ on the health share of outcome: from (9.6) it can be seen that the optimal leisure/learning ratio is increasing in the consumption share of income, which amounts to $1-\alpha \equiv (1-\theta)/(\gamma+1)$. If the health share decreases, individuals prefer to have more leisure; the opposite happens when an increase in γ or θ causes the health share to increase as well. The intuitive reason is as follows: either because returns from being healthy are higher (θ) or because health is more appreciated (γ) individuals devote more income to health investment. In order to keep the optimal technical rate of substitution between inputs in human capital technology, a higher amount of education is demanded as well.[15]

9.4. PUBLIC FUNDING

In the public funding regime, health investment is provided by government, which levies a proportional tax τ_t on wage income determined through majority voting, such that the common health investment is given by:

$$h_t = \bar{h}_t = \tau_t \bar{\xi}_t \tag{9.12}$$

where $\bar{\xi}_t$ denotes the average human capital.

Hence in the public regime constraint (9.4) is modified to:

$$\xi_{t+1}(1-\tau_{t+1}) = c_{t+1} \tag{9.13}$$

Since there is a common level of health, under the public system human capital is accumulated following:

$$\xi_{t+1} = \psi(1-n_t)^{\lambda} \bar{h}_{t+1}^{\theta} \xi_t^{v} \tag{9.14}$$

The agents maximize

$$U = \ln n_t + \phi(\bar{h}_t)[\ln c_{t+1} + \gamma \ln \bar{h}_{t+1}]$$

with respect to n_t, c_{t+1} and τ_{t+1} subject to (9.13) and (9.14). As in GR, we assume that individuals are aware of (9.12), but they take as given $\bar{\xi}_t$, since they see their contribution to average human capital as negligible.[16] Substituting the constraints in the expression above and maximizing with respect to n_t the following first order condition is obtained:

$$\frac{1}{n_t} = \frac{\phi(\bar{h}_t)\lambda}{1-n_t} \tag{9.15}$$

that can be solved to find optimal time devoted to human capital:

$$1-n_t = \frac{\phi(\bar{h}_t)\lambda}{1+\phi(\bar{h}_t)\lambda} \equiv \tilde{\Delta} \tag{9.16}$$

As in the private case, we derive a proposition for comparative statics on $\tilde{\Delta}$:

Proposition 2 *Under the public regime, time devoted to learning is increasing in life expectancy and returns from instruction; there is no effect by returns from health and preference for health except the one occurring through lifespan:*

$$\tilde{\Delta}_{\phi} > 0, \quad \tilde{\Delta}_{\lambda} > 0, \quad \tilde{\Delta}_{\theta} > 0, \quad \tilde{\Delta}_{\gamma} > 0$$

Proof. Taking derivatives of (9.16), the sign of each inequality follows.

The optimal tax rate is the result of the optimization with respect to τ_{t+1} of the following function:

$$\ln[(1-\tau_{t+1})\xi_{t+1}]+\gamma\ln(\tau_{t+1}\overline{\xi}_{t+1}) \tag{9.17}$$

First order condition gives:

$$\frac{-\xi_{t+1}+(1-\tau_{t+1})\theta\xi_{t+1}/\tau_{t+1}}{(1-\tau_{t+1})\xi_{t+1}}+\frac{\gamma}{\tau_{t+1}}=0 \tag{9.18}$$

From the equation above it is possible to find the optimal tax rate, which turns out to be:

$$\tau^{*}=\frac{\theta+\gamma}{1+\theta+\gamma} \tag{9.19}$$

As in GR, because of the functional forms chosen for utility, τ^{*} is independent of individual income[17] and constant over time. From (9.12) and (9.19), we have health investment under the public regime:

$$\overline{h}_{t+1}=\frac{\theta+\gamma}{1+\theta+\gamma}\overline{\xi}_{t+1} \tag{9.20}$$

In GR, the fraction of income devoted to health is $1/2$ in both regimes. This happens because in their model human capital investment affects productivity only starting from the next generation; parents have altruism investing in human capital for their children, but this bequest is totally independent of technology of human capital accumulation. Here, if agents invest in health, they directly improve their productivity and they are aware of human capital technology. GR's result can be seen as a particular case when $\gamma=1$ (as they implicitly assume) and $\theta=0$.

9.4.1. Dynamics

Under the private regime, equation (9.3) describes dynamics for human capital accumulation. Substituting for $(1-n_t)$ and h_{t+1} their optimal values and rearranging, a dynamic equation for human capital evolution can be found:

$$\xi_{t+1}=[\psi\alpha^{\theta}\Delta^{\lambda}\xi_t^{\nu}]^{\frac{1}{1-\theta}} \tag{9.21}$$

Inside Δ appears $\phi(h_t)$ which depends on health investment at time t, optimally chosen equal to $\alpha\xi_t$. Since agents' longevity is a function of health at time t which is a fraction of human capital at time t, a further channel of persistence is introduced in the human capital law of motion, that is not at work when only education is considered because it comes from a particular effect of health. In order to have an explicit dynamic equation a functional form for $\phi(h_t)$ should be chosen. For the sake of simplicity $\phi(\cdot)$ is chosen according to (9.2a). In Appendix 9A.1 results that would be obtained by using the specification as in (9.2) can be found. Then Δ, which represents optimal time devoted to learning, amounts to:

$$\Delta(\xi_t) = \frac{\beta\lambda\xi_t}{\left(\beta\lambda + \frac{1-\theta}{\gamma+1}\right)\xi_t + \frac{1-\theta}{\gamma+\theta}} \tag{9.22}$$

It is possible to highlight the role of the health share and health-consumption ratio, rewriting the expression above in a more compact form:

$$\Delta(\xi_t) = \frac{\beta\lambda\xi_t}{(\beta\lambda + 1 - \alpha)\xi_t + \chi^{-1}}$$

Actually, however $\phi(\cdot)$ is chosen between (9.2) and (9.2a), Δ exhibits the following properties:

1. $\Delta \in (0, 1)$;
2. $\frac{d\Delta}{d\xi_t} \geq 0;\ \frac{d^2\Delta}{d\xi_t^2} \leq 0$;
3. $\lim_{\xi \to 0} = 0;\ \lim_{\xi \to \infty} < 1$

Moreover, it is increasing in health expenditure measured as a share of income (α) and as ratio over consumption (χ). These results are consistent with the empirical evidence of a positive correlation between health expenditure and time devoted to human capital accumulation.

Under public funding dynamics of human capital can be studied by substituting optimal leisure from (9.16) and tax rate from (9.19) in (9.14):

$$\xi_{t+1} = \psi\tau^{*\theta}\tilde{\Delta}^{\lambda}\bar{\xi}_{t+1}^{\theta}\xi_t^{\nu} \tag{9.23}$$

Inside $\tilde{\Delta}$ appears $\phi(\bar{h}_t)$ which depends on health investment at time t, optimally given by $\tau^*\bar{\xi}_t$. As in the private case, in order to give an explicit dynamic equation a functional form for $\phi(\cdot)$, expression (9.2a) is used:

$$\tilde{\Delta}(\bar{\xi}_t) = \frac{\beta\lambda\tau^*\bar{\xi}_t}{(\beta\lambda + 1)\tau^*\bar{\xi}_t + 1} \tag{9.24}$$

However $\phi(\cdot)$ is chosen between (9.2) and (9.2a), $\tilde{\Delta}$ exhibits the same properties as Δ listed above.

9.5. HOMOGENEOUS AGENTS

In this section we compare the results from the previous section under the assumption that initial distribution of human capital is degenerate and agents are endowed with the same amount of human capital, such that each individual is equal to the average one.

With undifferentiated agents the following proposition on the health share of income holds:

Proposition 3 *If agents are homogeneous the share of income devoted to health is greater under the private regime.*

Proof. Follows by comparison of (9.8) and (9.20) when $\xi = \bar{\xi}$.

This comes from the fact that the effect on agent's own human capital (and hence income) is seen as negligible in the public regime. Note that the two systems yield the same share when $\theta = 0$.

Time devoted to human capital under private and public regimes is governed respectively by (9.11) and (9.16). If agents are homogeneous then $\xi_t = \bar{\xi}_t$, $\forall t$. The following result is readily available:

If agents are homogeneous, time devoted to learning is higher under the private regime:

$$\Delta > \tilde{\Delta}$$

Proof. See Appendix 9A.2.

This means that if agents are undifferentiated then in the private regime individuals devote more time to learning, thus boosting growth: this happens essentially because under public funding the same level of health investment is imposed across the board, and so h_{t+1} is seen only in the private regime as a fraction of agent's own human capital ξ_{t+1}, while in the public system it is a function of average human capital $\bar{\xi}_{t+1}$. This is by construction an advantage of the private system in terms of the growth rate. If a policy of mandatory schooling is enforced, then it would be possible to set time allocated to human capital investment as in (9.11) also in the public system, and this source of difference in the human capital law of motion would be eliminated, even if the private regime would remain preferable from a welfare viewpoint.

When agents are homogeneous, then $\xi_t = \overline{\xi}_t$ in every period. In other words it is possible to consider just a representative agent, focusing only on growth issues, abstracting from distributive ones. Since Δ and $\tilde{\Delta}$ share the same properties, analysis of the dynamics of human capital can be restricted without loss of generality to one of them, e.g. Δ. Since Δ depends positively on the cumulative factor ξ_t, it increases the marginal return of the cumulative factor and augments the persistence of dynamics. This effect is not at work in GR's model since in their context the discount factor is independent of human capital.

This further contribution of ξ_t through Δ on ξ_{t+1} is however only temporary since, as human capital is cumulated, Δ tends to a finite value, less than one, so that in the long run returns of cumulative factor are determined only by $\nu/(1-\theta)$. The intuition behind this is that at low levels of longevity, an increase in health investment not only makes workers more productive, but makes their children more likely to live longer, thus encouraging them to devote more time to learning because they discount the future less. Then productivity and hence income increase as well, so that agents can afford to augment their health investment as well. As income increases, health investment also increases, but as the improvements in life expectancy augment less than proportionally, the effect on discounting is progressively less important and at the limit it vanishes.

In other words, it is possible to consider the effects of health on optimal learning time as a positive externality that a generation has in the next due to its choice related to health care. Of course this can also be seen in a reverse perspective: if the health conditions worsen (which can be broadly seen as a negative investment in health) then the externality is negative and next generation has an incentive to discount the future more.

This effect is particularly interesting because it may give rise to poverty and underdevelopment traps. In the long run dynamics are governed by $\nu/(1-\theta)$. If the ratio is less than 1, i.e. $\nu+\theta<1$, but 'close enough' to 1, then, under compatible but reasonable values for parameters, there are two positive equilibria: the greater one is stable, the smaller one unstable.[18] Figure 9.2 provides a graphical example for such a case.

At low levels of human capital, the effect described above plays a role, increasing temporary returns of human capital. This can induce a temporary convexity on the map of ξ if the sum $(\nu+\theta)$ is not 'too low' and hence the map may intersect the 45 degrees line from below, in other words an unstable steady state is possible.

Moreover, if the economy starts with ξ_0 less than this unstable equilibrium, it will converge to zero, i.e. zero is a catching point for human capital dynamics;[19] while if ξ_0 is greater than the unstable equilibrium, then the economy will converge to the other positive equilibrium, that is stable and greater. The intuition behind this result comes from the evidence of virtuous and vicious circles that were mentioned in Section 9.1: even if a constant fraction of income is devoted to health, when human capital is too low, life expectancy is low too and agents have no incentive to devote much of their time to learning because they discount the future heavily, but in this way human capital cannot grow enough to escape the trap and the economy is condemned to a situation of poverty and insufficient health, which in its model counterpart is represented by the zero equilibrium. On the contrary, if initial conditions are high enough, virtuous circles made by more health – less discounting – more income, can take place.

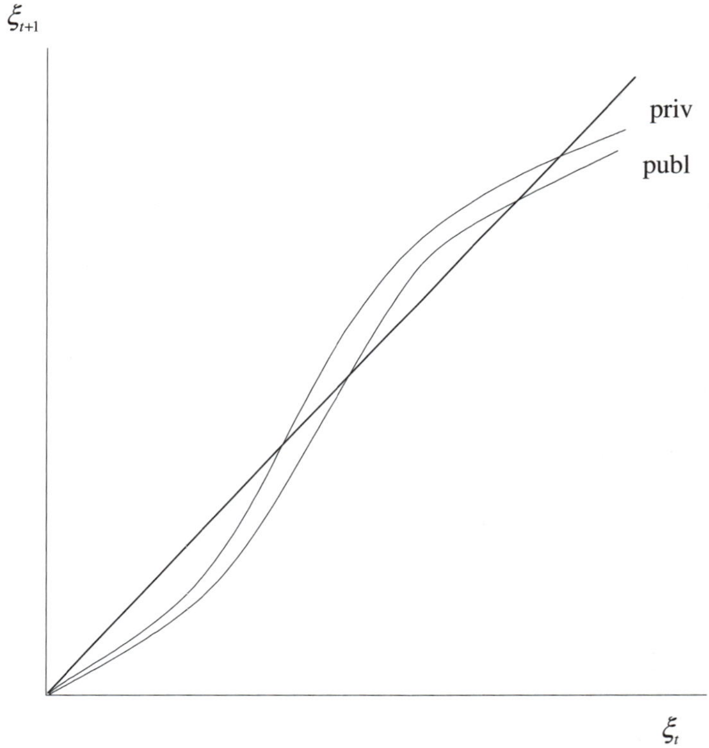

Figure 9.2. A human capital map with long-run decreasing returns

Constant long-run returns in cumulative factors, i.e. $\nu+\theta=1$, are a sufficient (but not necessary) condition to have convexity in the first part of the map of ξ. Then in the long run the map turns into a straight line. Under compatible and reasonable values of parameters the map intersects the 45 degrees line (see Figure 9.3). In this case there is a stable equilibrium in zero (catching point) and an unstable equilibrium at the positive intersection point. If the economy starts ξ_0 greater than the unstable equilibrium, it experiences long-run balanced growth; otherwise if it is lower the poverty trap mechanism described above takes place. It is worth noting that even under long-run constant returns of scale in cumulative factors, endogenous growth is not granted and historical conditions may determine the pattern of the economy.

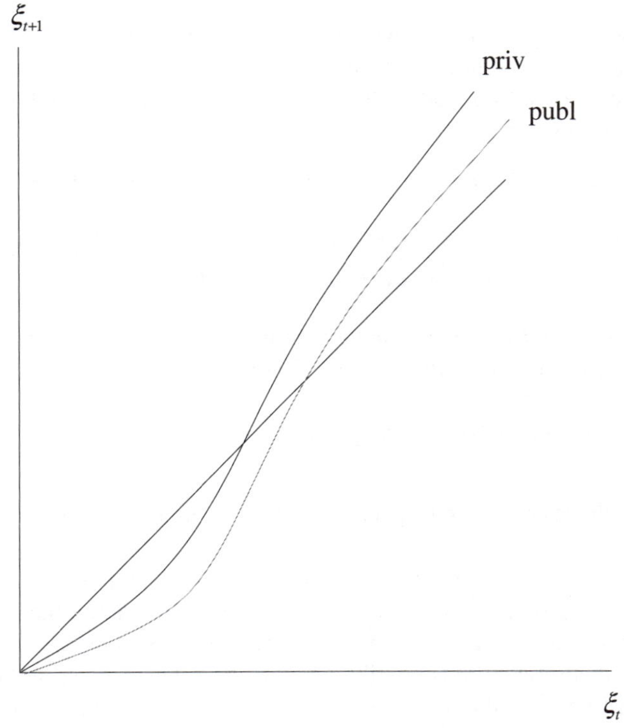

Figure 9.3. A human capital map with long-run constant returns

Finally, with increasing returns, i.e. $\nu+\theta>1$, under compatible but reasonable values for parameters, two equilibria exist: the zero stable equilibrium (catching point) and the positive unstable equilibrium, above which growth of human capital is explosive.[20] It is worth noting that the increasing returns condition is unable alone to grant long-run growth.

Let us now return to the comparison between the two regimes of health funding. Under the assumption of homogeneous agents, in order to assess which achieves the higher growth, we only need to compare (9.21) and its public counterpart (9.23), given that $\xi = \bar{\xi}, \forall t$. Since $\alpha > \tau^*$ for $\theta \in (0;1)$, a sufficient condition for private system to bring about higher growth is $\Delta > \tilde{\Delta}$. Indeed it is proved in Appendix 9A.1 that with homogeneous agents the inequality holds for both specifications of $\theta(\cdot)$ that are considered. Unlike GR's setting, even if a policy of mandatory schooling is chosen the gap in favour of the private system remains because learning time is not the only source of difference between the two regimes. The other source is that in private funding a bigger portion of income is devoted to health, which is an input of human capital technology.

Denoting by $\underline{\xi}_{pr}$ and $\underline{\xi}_{pu}$ the smallest positive (unstable) steady state in private and public regimes respectively, and by ξ^*_{pr}, ξ^*_{pu} the greatest positive (stable) steady state, the results can be summarized as in the following proposition:

Proposition 5 *With homogeneous agents, in the long run we have:*

- *If* $\nu + \theta < 1$ *and two positive steady states exist:* $\underline{\xi}_{pu} > \underline{\xi}_{pr}$; $\xi^*_{pr} > \xi^*_{pu}$. *The private system yields a greater stable steady state.*

- *If* $\nu + \theta = 1$ *and a positive steady state exists:* $\underline{\xi}_{pu} > \underline{\xi}_{pr}$. *The long-run constant growth rate under private funding is greater.*

- *If* $\nu + \theta > 1$ *and a positive steady state exists:* $\underline{\xi}_{pu} > \underline{\xi}_{pr}$.

Proof. Results follow from inspection of (9.21), (9.23) and Figure 9.3.

Some remarks can be made: first, whatever the assumption on returns, if $\underline{\xi}_{pr}$ and $\underline{\xi}_{pu}$ exist, then the latter is always greater, meaning that under the public system a higher ξ_0 is required to escape the poverty trap.

Second, theoretically it is possible that positive steady states and long-run growth exist only for the private system, since the human capital map in the private case is always above the map in the public case.

Third, these results hold under the hypothesis of homogeneity; bearing this in mind they are rather intuitive: in the public system fewer implications of health investment than in the private system are internalized. This introduces in the former regime an inefficiency, such that the latter performs better both in terms of growth and conditions to avoid poverty traps.

9.6. HETEROGENEOUS AGENTS

If agents are heterogeneous, the proposition that everyone devotes more time to learning under a private regime no longer necessarily holds. Instead we have:

Proposition 6 *If agents are heterogeneous, then time devoted to learning is greater under a public regime for those agents for whom:*

$$\phi(\bar{h}_t) > \frac{\gamma+1}{1-\theta}\phi(h_t) \equiv \frac{1}{1-\alpha}\phi(h_t)$$

Proof. See Appendix 9A.2.

Independently of how $\theta(\cdot)$ is chosen, a public regime is more likely to entail a higher time investment in learning if the health share of income is low. This can be seen as a direct consequence of the fact that under public regimes fewer effects of health are internalized. Those effects have the property to amplify the difference in lifespan due to the two regimes: if health becomes more important either because of preferences (γ) or because of a change in productivity (θ), the private system becomes likely to favour time investment in human capital to a greater extent than the public system.

In order to examine this issue in further detail it is necessary to choose an explicit form for $\phi(\cdot)$. We considered an explicit form as in (9.2a). The results from specification as in (9.2) can be found in Appendix 9A.1. Using this expression a condition on relative human capital can be derived. The amount of time devoted to learning is higher in a public regime for agents whose human capital is not much higher than the average:

$$\frac{\xi_t}{\bar{\xi}_t} < \frac{(1-\theta)(1+\gamma)}{(1+\gamma)(1+\theta+\gamma)+\bar{\xi}_t(\theta+\gamma)^2} \equiv \frac{\tau^*}{\chi\left(1+\bar{\xi}_t\tau^*\alpha\right)}$$

This relation means that if an agent's human capital is relatively low, then his/her children would choose to devote more time to human capital accumulation under the public regime. This occurs because if children's life expectancy depends on health investment that their parents can only privately afford it would be low and they would have less incentive to invest. Instead under a public regime their lifespan may benefit from the public health investment which is greater than what they could afford otherwise. At a low level of human capital this effect may overcome the advantage of a private regime in terms of internalization that have been highlighted above.

Keeping the ratio between agent-specific human capital and average human capital, $\xi_t/\bar{\xi}_t$, constant, the condition above becomes increasingly unlikely to occur as the level of average human capital increases. This happens essentially because of the concave shape of $\phi(\cdot)$: improvements in life expectancy are smaller as the health investment is augmented.

It is worth noting that however $\phi(\cdot)$ is chosen, the condition under which the public regime induces an agent to devote more time to human capital accumulation is more likely to occur if the agent's human capital is lower than average, if the optimal tax rate is high, and if the health share of income is low. The reason is that it is necessary to create a differential in favour of health investment in a public regime: this is affected positively by τ^* and $\bar{\xi}_t$ as can be seen from (9.12) and negatively by the private health share of income since it includes the advantage in terms of internalization that characterizes private funding. Note also that since both τ^* and α depend positively on γ and θ, an increase in these parameters has contrasting effects on conditions that assess whether the public regime promotes learning more than the private system.

Dynamics We now come to the dynamics in the heterogeneous case. Things are more complicated than in GR since here current human capital ξ_t plays a further role through Δ making fewer simplifications possible from the assumption of log-normality, and comparing the two regimes in terms of evolution of average log-human capital is not straightforward.[21] Furthermore one must also assess what happens when a poverty traps arises.

As far as the public system is concerned, applying logarithms to (9.23) and calling $\ell \equiv \ln \xi_t$, one obtains:

$$\ell_{t+1} = \nu \ell_t + \lambda \ln \tilde{\Delta}(\xi_t) + \theta \ln \bar{\xi}_{t+1} + \ln\left(\psi \tau^{*\theta}\right) \tag{9.25}$$

We assume the following initial distribution for human capital:

Assumption 1 *The initial distribution of human capital is log-normal.*

If human capital is log-normally distributed at time t with mean μ_t and variance σ_t^2, then human capital at time $t+1$ is also log-normally distributed with mean μ_{t+1} and variance σ_{t+1}^2, where

$$\mu_{t+1} = \nu \mu_t + \lambda \ln \tilde{\Delta}(\bar{\xi}_t) + \theta \ln \bar{\xi}_{t+1} + \ln\left(\psi \tau^{*\theta}\right) \tag{9.26}$$

$$\sigma_{t+1}^2 = \upsilon^2 \sigma_t^2 \tag{9.27}$$

As in GR's model, agents with low income experience higher growth rates than agents with high income because the growth factor, ξ_{t+1}/ξ_t, is a decreasing function of ξ_t in the public regime since $0<\nu<1$, hence inequalities tend to disappear. Expression (9.26) is complicated by the fact that the logarithm of the average human capital ($\ln\bar{\xi}$) and the average of the logarithm (μ) appear both at time t+1. The assumption of log-normality has an important implication in this sense since it provides a relation between μ_{t+1} and $\bar{\xi}_{t+1}$:[22]

$$\bar{\xi}_t = \exp\left(\mu_t + \frac{\sigma_t^2}{2}\right) \tag{9.28}$$

Using this property and (9.27), (9.26) can be rewritten as:

$$\mu_{t+1} = \frac{1}{1-\theta}\left[\nu\mu_t + \frac{\theta\nu^2}{2}\sigma_t^2 + \lambda\ln\tilde{\Delta} + \ln(\psi\tau^{*\theta})\right]$$

where $\tilde{\Delta}$ is a function of μ_t and σ_t^2 once $\bar{\xi}_t$ has been replaced.

A result of GR can now be replicated:

Proposition 7 *If two economies under the public regime start with the same per-capita income, the economy with lower inequality experiences higher growth.*

Proof. See Appendix 9A.3.

As far as the private system is concerned, it may be noted that by applying logarithms to (9.21) one gets:

$$\ell_{t+1} = \frac{\nu}{1-\theta}\ell_t + \frac{1}{1-\theta}[\lambda\ln\Delta(e^{\ell_t}) + \ln(\psi\alpha^\theta)] \tag{9.30}$$

Applying the expected value operator, the following expression is obtained:

$$\mu_{t+1} = \frac{\nu}{1-\theta}\mu_t + \frac{\lambda}{1-\theta}E[\ln\Delta(e^{\ell_t})] + \frac{1}{1-\theta}\ln(\psi\alpha^\theta) \tag{9.31}$$

Since Δ is a function of ℓ_t, the expression above cannot be reduced to a simple linear relation between μ_{t+1} and μ_t. Even if it is not straightforward to compute the law of motion for the variance in private regime in a short form as (9.27) for the public regime, it should be easy to see that in any period it will be greater than its public counterpart: the coefficient of ℓ_t in (9.30) is greater than in the public system (see (9.25)). Moreover, Δ is positively correlated with the first term in ℓ_t, and increasing in ℓ_t as well.

Thus for sure inequalities in the private system cannot decline faster than under the public regime.

The next sections provide further detail, examining cases with or without poverty traps from a theoretical point of view, while Section 9.7, after a calibration of parameters, provides some simulations for the case of constant long-run returns.

9.6.1. Inequalities and Growth Without Poverty Traps

In this section it is assumed that poverty traps do not arise.[23] We first consider decreasing returns in the long run. The following proposition on inequality dynamics and income growth holds:

Proposition 8 *Under long-run decreasing returns, inequality decreases in both regimes but is faster in the public one. Though the long-run positive steady state is higher under the private regime, during the transition the public system may feature higher growth.*

Proof. The results on inequalities dynamics follow from analysis in Section 9.6 comparing (9.25) and (9.30). As far as the transition result is concerned, note that by comparing (9.29) and (9.31) it can be seen that while a private regime has an advantage due to $\psi\tau^{*\theta} < \psi\alpha^{\theta}$ [24], as long as agents are heterogeneous, $\underset{\sim}{\mu}_{t+1}$ in the public system has a positive term in σ_t^2. Moreover, $\ln[\tilde{\Delta}(\xi_t)]$ can be greater than $E\{\ln[\Delta(\xi_t)]\}$: since functions ln and Δ are both concave, the inequality holds if $\Delta(\cdot)=\tilde{\Delta}(\cdot)$, but by continuity it still holds for some $\Delta(\cdot)>\tilde{\Delta}(\cdot)$. Since in the long run the human capital distribution is degenerate under both regimes, the ultimate result coincides with the homogeneous case, with a greater steady state under the private system.

Intuitively, if a society is very unequal, public health funding may induce some agents to accumulate more human capital than they would with private funding because in the public system their expected lifespan is higher since it benefits from an amount of health expenditure that they could not afford by themselves. The reduction in discount factor that they may benefit from is greater than the potential reduction the richest agents lose because improvements in life expectancy come at a decreasing rate. Since returns are decreasing in the long run, those who start with a lower level of human capital grow faster. Thus inequalities decrease progressively (even quicker under the public regime). As society becomes more equal, the condition under which the public system provides more incentive to human capital accumulation becomes increasingly restrictive and it is growth-enhancing to switch to the private regime, where more health implications are internalized. Inequalities continue to decrease but at a slower rate, until they finally vanish in the long run.

Proposition 9 *Under long-run constant returns, i.e.* $\nu+\theta=1$, *inequality declines only under the public system whereas in the private regime they initially increase and then stay steady. The long-run growth factor is higher under a private regime.*

Proof. In the public system there is again progressive reduction in inequalities, such that analysis of the homogeneous case for the endogenous balanced growth can be applied.

Under the private system inequalities are kept constant in the long run, but in the short run they increase since there is a temporary convexity in the map function. Hence long-run inequalities are higher than the initial ones.

The long-run growth factor in the private regime amounts to: $(\psi\alpha^{\theta}\Delta^{*\lambda})^{1/(1-\theta)}$ where $\Delta^{*}\equiv\lim_{\xi_t\to\infty}\Delta$ [25].

It can be easily seen that this growth factor is greater than that of the public regime: $(\psi\alpha^{*\theta}\tilde{\Delta}^{*\lambda})^{1/(1-\theta)}$.

Hence, at least in the long run, there is a trade-off between growth and equality in income distribution. Which system should be preferred from a welfare viewpoint cannot be said *a priori* without knowing the weight that the policy-maker assigns to equality. Under decreasing returns instead in the long run the private system is Pareto-superior since inequalities vanish in both systems but the private regime yields higher steady state income. During the transition also with constant returns the growth factor can be higher in the public regime, as shown by some examples in Section 9.7.

9.6.2. Growth and Inequalities with Poverty Traps

Let us consider the private regime first. With poverty traps, under decreasing returns, bi-polarization in human capital distribution is likely to take place: those who start below the threshold level (which is also the smallest steady state) converge to the zero equilibrium, while those who start above converge to the stable steady state equilibrium. Denoting by x the fraction of agents that are at the beginning in the poverty trap basin, the final average income is:[26] $(1-x)\xi^{*}_{pr}$. The steady state variance of the bipolar distribution can be easily computed: $\sigma^2=(1-x)x\xi^{*}_{pr}$. Hence at the aggregate level inequalities do not vanish despite decreasing returns because the poverty trap prevents the convergence mechanism from fully taking place. Inequality increases in ξ^{*}_{pr} because it augments the gap with the zero equilibrium; it also increases with x for $0<x<1/2$, then decreases: if exactly one half of the population is involved in the poverty trap there is a perfect bi-polarization and hence variance is at its maximum level.

A similar analysis can be made under constant returns, with the difference that the human capital of people avoiding the poverty trap then grow at rate $(\psi\alpha^{\theta}\Delta^{*\lambda})^{1/(1-\theta)}$. The economy growth rate is a weighted average between this rate and zero: $(1-x)(\psi\alpha^{\theta}\Delta^{*\lambda})^{1/(1-\theta)}$. This means that the long-run growth rate depends on initial conditions: if two economies where health is privately financed have the same deep parameters but start with a different portion of agents involved in poverty traps (for example because of a different distribution, mean or variance), then one will experience more growth than the other. If per-capita income is high, the economy that is more equal has more chances of growing further; the opposite occurs if per-capita income is low.

This happens because in private regime what determines long-run growth is the portion of agents that are outside the basin of attraction of poverty traps: if the average income is above that threshold and if the distribution is more concentrated around the mean then a greater portion of agents may escape the poverty trap; on the other hand, if the average income is very low, then growth may take place only if someone is outside the poverty trap basin, and this is more likely to happen if the variance of the distribution is high. Note that in this model without intra-generational spillover this does not help at all those who have been ‘caught’ in the zero catching point.

All this has important implications in terms of inequalities, since the distribution becomes bi-polar with only one group growing. Hence there is an ever-increasing disparity between the two groups and also for the economy; while the richest group experiences long-run growth, there is a part of the population that lives in stagnant misery. Unlike GR this happens even if long-run returns are not increasing, and is a direct consequence of the endogenous poverty trap.

How do these conclusions change under the public system?

It can be expected that some results of the analysis with no poverty trap can still hold: the public regime reduces inequalities more than the private system, whatever the assumption on long-run returns; if an economy has high inequality, then the public system may yield higher growth, at least for some periods. With poverty traps the fact that health is provided at a common level could help several agents to escape from the basin of attraction of the zero equilibrium if human capital distribution exhibits some skewness (e.g. if average human capital is above the median human capital), as happens for the log-normal distribution, and average human capital is high enough. This occurs because ξ_{t+1} depends on a mix of average and agent-specific human capital. On the other hand, the risk is that, especially at a low level of per-capita income, the relatively more endowed agents, who would own enough resources to escape from the poverty trap, cannot grow either since they are forced to rely on too low a common health provision.[27]

Even if closed-form solutions are hard to find, it is possible to provide examples showing how income distribution moves for different initial conditions. In order to do so, parameters have to be calibrated; this is done in the next section.

9.7. SIMULATIONS

9.7.1. Calibration

First of all it is necessary to approximately fit the periods to real years. We can assume the lifespan to be split at the age of 33. In the very first part of life agents' decisions are taken by their parents. Then they have to choose how much to study in order to accumulate human capital; in this sense leisure includes everything that is not learning. They then work for 30 years. The lifespan can then be expressed as $33+\phi(h_t)30$: the bottom level for life expectancy matches closely enough what the data show (Figure 9.3). The top level is slightly underestimated, thus suggesting the possibility of extending the model by including a third age where agents spend money saved during adulthood. For the sake of simplicity only two periods are assumed and $\phi(\cdot)$ is chosen according to (9.2a). All this implies that setting $\beta=1$ can be reasonable.

The health share of income α can be used to calibrate γ and θ. Empirically, the health expenditure share of GDP is between 4.3 per cent (the average for Africa) and 11.7 per cent (Europe), with a maximum in the USA of 13.9 per cent (WHO, 2004). Actually, due to the simplifying assumption of non-physical capital, the figure that α should match should be the share of health expenditure over total consumption, or at least over GDP net of physical investment. In this sense calibrating $\gamma=0.05$ and $\theta=0.1$ implies a reasonable value for the health expenditure share of 14.3 per cent, while τ^* amounts to 13 per cent. This choice of θ also allows for the effects of θ on productivity, based on Bloom et al. (2004) and WHO (2001).[28]

As for the learning coefficient λ, the main implication is that in general the higher the value of λ the more the human capital map is likely to exhibit initial convexity: in order to allow for poverty traps λ should not be too low; In de la Croix and Doepke (2004) a conservative estimate is set at 0.6, which is kept here. Moreover, it is assumed to have balanced growth in the long run; this implies that $\nu+\theta=1$, so that $\nu=0.9$.[29] The productivity parameter ψ can then be fixed so as to have a long-run reasonable growth rate, i.e. 2 per cent a year, given the choice of θ, γ, λ and the number of years for which individuals produce: the computation gives ψ=3.531. A relevant issue is that in the presence of poverty traps the average growth rate depends on historical conditions because a portion x of the population is caught by the poverty trap. Hence the growth rate on which the calibration of ψ is based should be intended as the rate of growth for the group of agents starting after the unstable steady state.

9.7.2. Simulated Dynamics

Figure 9.4 shows the map functions in this benchmark framework under the assumption of homogeneous agents. The results predicted in Section 9.5 are confirmed: the private system grows more than the public system and the basin of attraction to the poverty trap equilibrium is larger under the public regime. This means that in a society of perfectly equal agents there is a region for initial conditions such that the public system leads to poverty whereas the private regime can sustain endogenous growth.

What happens now if heterogeneity is allowed? Some numerical experiments were run, keeping the benchmark parameterization and varying the mean and variance of the normal distribution of log-human capital, for a population of 150 individuals. Below we report the main regularities that emerge.

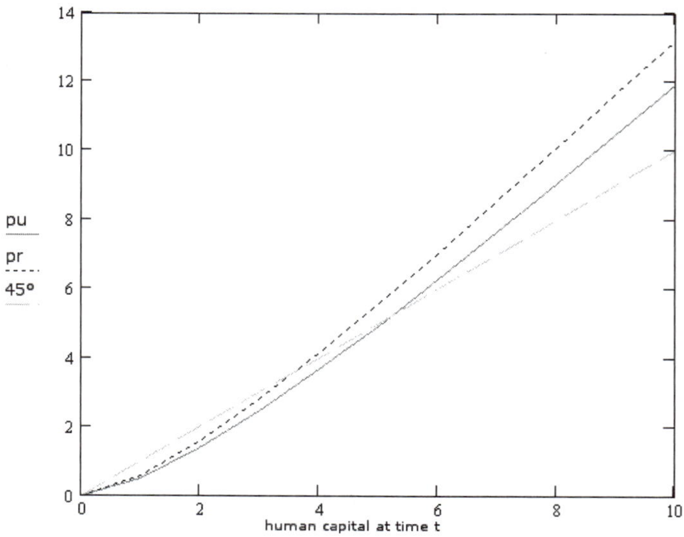

Figure 9.4. A human capital map with homogeneous agents

First of all, we present the comparison for a situation in which average initial log human capital is high enough that *basically nobody is involved in the poverty trap mechanism*, for example μ=8. When variance is zero, i.e. the homogeneous case, the private system brings about higher growth. The variance is then fixed at 4. It can be observed in Figure 9.5 that the public system reduces inequalities whereas in the private regime they rise at the beginning and then remain constant. From (9.28), $\ln(\overline{\xi}_t)$ in the two economies can be computed, and then a comparison of how growth factors evolve over time can be represented in Figure 9.6.

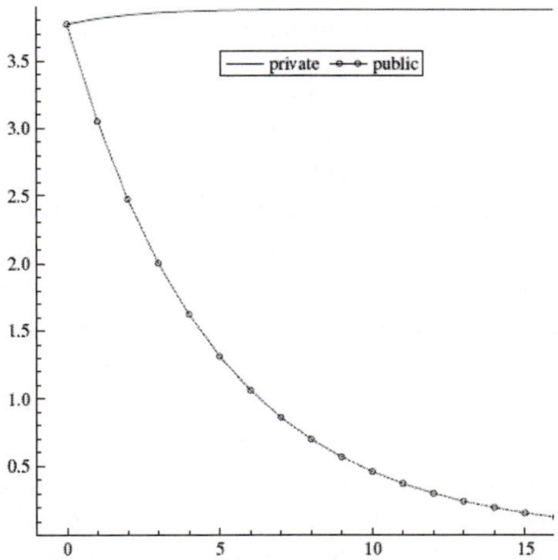

Figure 9.5. Dynamics of variance for μ=8 and σ^2=4

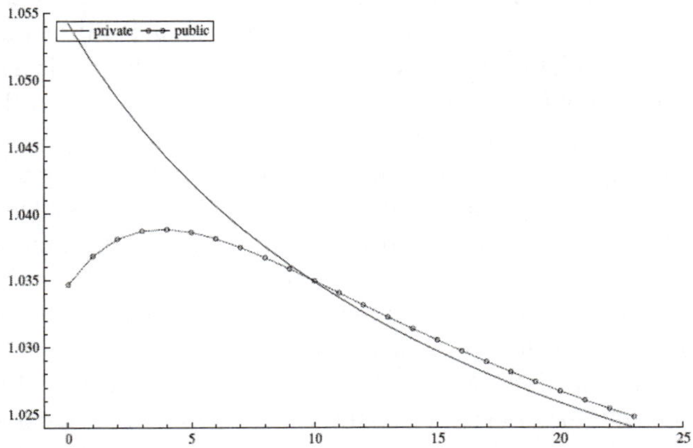

Figure 9.6. Dynamics of growth factors of log per-capita income for μ=8 and σ^2=4

Simulation Regularities 1 *When no poverty trap occurs, the following regularities emerge:*

- *the private regime initially yields higher growth rates but, provided the initial distribution is sufficiently unequal, during the transition the public regime may experience higher growth factors*
- *if two societies start with the same per-capita income but different variance then the more equal society grows more, whatever the regime.*
- *if two societies start with the same per-capita income but different variance, then the span during which the public system exhibits higher growth factors is longer in the more unequal society.*

These regularities are now commented upon, with the help of graphics from the simulations. If two economies start with the same μ, the private system leads at the beginning to higher growth rates in per-capita income: the growth-enhancing mechanism related to health effects on life expectancy works immediately. Then as this effect decreases because of properties of Δ the private regime's growth factor converges exponentially to its long-run value. Note that the rise in the initial variance contributes to augment per-capita income in a lognormal distribution (see (9.28)).[30] In the public system the mechanism is slower because a redistributive channel is at work, but when the growth slows down it takes more time to decrease as well. Interestingly, inequality introduces a hump-shape in the growth rate of log per capita income in the public economy: if the initial inequality is large enough, redistribution slows down growth immediately, but then while it continues to reduce inequalities the growth-enhancing mechanism operating through $\tilde{\Delta}$ is triggered and the public economy converges to its long-run path where agents are increasingly homogeneous. Hence during transition a public regime may experience higher growth factors than the private regime. By varying the initial inequalities it can be seen that to have this result initial variance should not be too low. For small values of σ^2 the growth factor in the private economy is always greater.

All this suggests that in an equal society, the private regime should be preferable, whereas in an unequal society the public system, though statically less efficient from a growth viewpoint, in a dynamic sense can combine lower inequalities and higher growth rates.

The second point of simulation regularities 1 shows that, *ceteris paribus*, a lower inequality can be desirable also from a growth perspective. It has been claimed in Section 9.6 that if two public systems start with the same μ but different σ^2 then the more equal society grows more; simulations show that the same happens if two private economies are involved, even if this difference proves less than in the public regime. The intuitive reason is that in the more equal society, more agents are close to the mean income and thus their average will be higher than the unequal society's because of concavity of Δ and $\tilde{\Delta}$, and of human capital accumulation technology with respect to each input.[31]

Finally, if two societies start with the same per-capita income but a different degree of inequality, then the length of the period over which the public system yields greater growth factors than the private system is larger in the more equal society. This just comes about by extending the findings from the first point. Not only does the time interval turn out to be longer when the initial inequality is greater, but also the quantitative gap turns out to be larger at every step.

Poverty Traps If the initial distribution is chosen with a lower mean or a higher variance, then *some agents may be involved in the poverty trap mechanism.* This has a direct impact on inequalities dynamics since in the private regime inequalities become explosive, as explained in Section 9.6.2. As shown in Figure 9.7, in the public system there is a continuous link between the poor and the rich since they share the same health provision which depends on average income, thus offsetting the endogenous force toward increasing inequalities which characterizes private regimes.

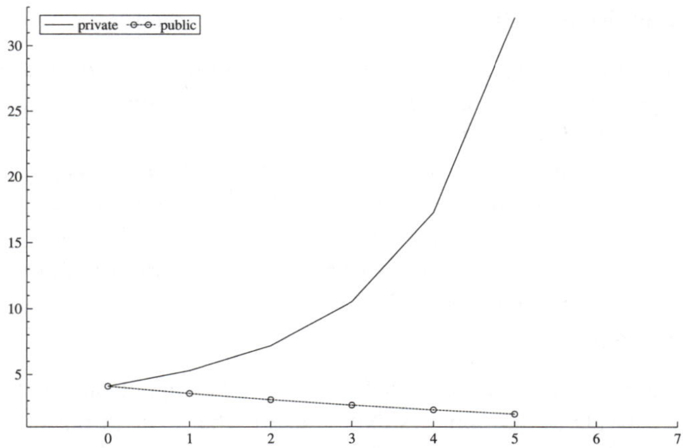

Figure 9.7. Dynamics of variance for $\mu=4$ *and* $\sigma^2=4$

In order to assess growth issues under poverty traps, the initial distribution is centred on a relatively low level, e.g. $\mu=4$, so that some agents are involved in a poverty trap because they are in the catching point basin. In the private regime every agent that has a lower endowment the poverty trap threshold converges to the zero equilibrium, while the others grow. What happens from an economic growth viewpoint? Figure 9.8 is concerns growth factors in this case.

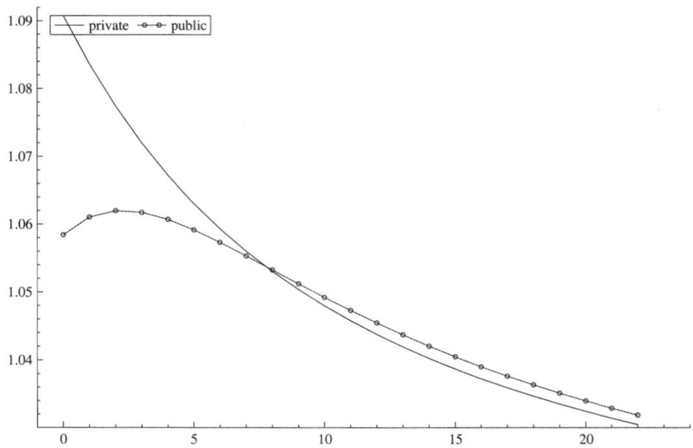

Figure 9.8. Dynamics of growth factors of log per-capita income for μ=4 *and* σ^2=4

The following regularities emerge:

Simulation Regularities 2 *When a poverty trap occurs:*

- *at a given variance, a decline in* μ *increases the initial advantage of the private system, but usually the span for which the public system features higher growth factors increases as well*
- *at a given mean, a decline in* σ *decreases the initial gap. A change in initial inequality does not substantially affect the span over which the public system grows faster, but affects the size of this gap.*
- *if initial per capita income is very low, then the public regime can grow faster than the private regime in the future only if initial inequality is high enough.*

On the first point, it may be added that only when agents are perfectly equal does the private system always experience higher growth rates. When there are inequalities, in a situation with low average income, the stickiness in the motion of human capital in the public regime increases, and, through this channel, the period over which this regime yields higher growth is longer.

As regards the second point, the dynamics shown in Figure 9.9 when σ^2=6 roughly exhibit the behaviour illustrated before for Figure 9.6. Varying σ^2 has no significant effect on the length of the interval for which the public system outperforms the private system in terms of growth factors, but affects the impact of this exceedance: if a society is more unequal at the beginning, then when the public system's growth rate overtakes the private system's growth rate, it does that to a greater extent.

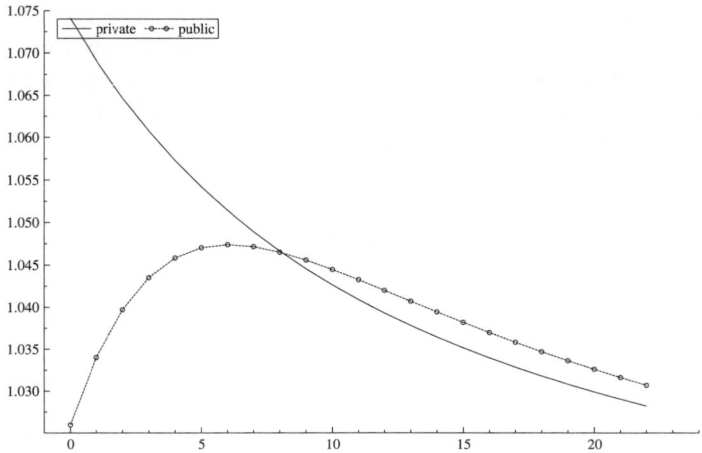

Figure 9.9. Dynamics of growth factors of log per-capita income for μ=4 *and* σ^2=6

With regard to the third point, we consider what happens by choosing for μ a value such that in the homogeneous case only the private regime escapes poverty trap. By looking at Figure 9.4 and considering that μ is expressed in logarithmic scale, the chosen value is 1.65. As expected if agents are perfectly equal, only the private system is able to escape the poverty trap.[32] Then heterogeneity is introduced by increasing progressively the initial variance, running the experiment several times for each value of σ^2. By continuity it turns out that in order to have the public system able to escape the poverty trap σ^2 should not be too low. At this very low level of income, where poverty trap is the rule more than the exception for many agents, initial inequality has an important impact on timing of those dynamics: in the private system the growth mechanism is triggered soon for those who can afford it, while in the public system it may take more time, because it comes through a redistributive mechanism, but then it involves more people. The higher is σ^2 the longer is the interval for which the growth rate is higher in the public regime than in the private regime. Nevertheless, if σ^2 is high enough, human capital begins to move more quickly and the relative gap between the two regimes shrinks. A comparison of growth dynamics for two different σ can be found in Figure 9.10.

To conclude, in poor societies, the trade-off between the immediate advantage in growth terms yielded by the private regime and the advantage in a longer perspective yielded by the public regime with inequality reduction and higher growth rates seems reinforced. If the society is very poor, but the income distribution is relatively equal, the model predicts that the private regime is preferable; if instead income distribution is sufficiently unequal, the public regime can bring about longer periods of sustained growth. Beginning with a private regime may be preferred when only under the private regime some agents may escape the poverty trap and hence accumulate human capital.

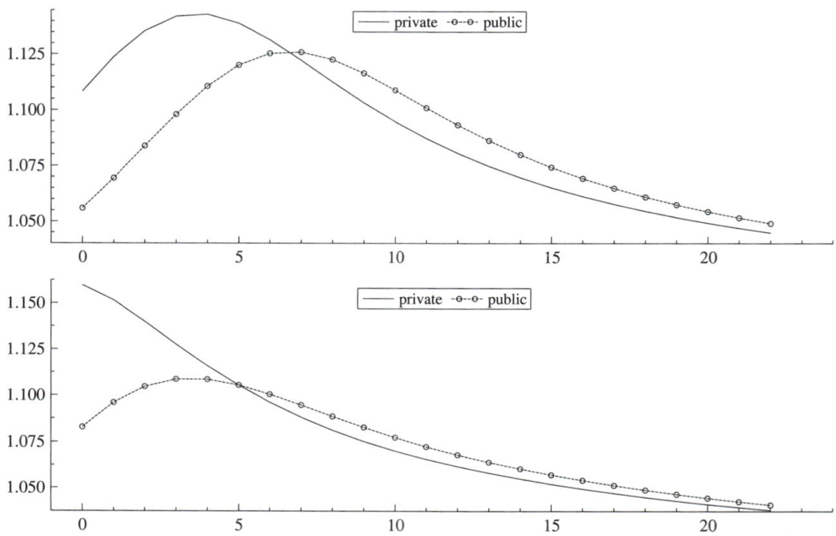

Figure 9.10. Dynamics of growth factors of log-per capita income for μ=1.654 *and* σ^2=0.5 *(top) and* σ^2=2 *(bottom)*

9.8. CONCLUSIVE REMARKS

A model of economic growth was presented in an OLG setting to focus on differences in terms of growth and inequalities between private and public health funding. Health enters directly into the utility function, but it is important also indirectly because it improves productivity and increases life expectancy, thus reducing the discount factor and encouraging human capital investment. In the private system agents decide in a decentralized way how much to spend on health, while in the public regime health is provided by government and financed through proportional taxation with the tax rate determined through majority voting.

The fact that health is provided in the same amount in the public regime means that less positive effects of health are internalized since agents see their contribution to average income as negligible. Nevertheless, it is worth emphasizing that even providing the private system with such advantages in terms of internalization, it does not follow that the private regime yields anyhow sustained higher growth rates than the public regime.

The public system turns out to be more effective in reducing inequalities and, unlike the GR model, may induce poor agents to devote more time to learning since their survival probability may be higher due to public provision of health care. Since improvements in lifespan come at a decreasing rate, this positive effect is greater than the negative one borne by the richest. It is found that if initial income inequality is not too large, the private system always yields higher growth, but if initial variance is large enough the private system may be overtaken for several periods by the public system in terms of growth factors. Simulations show that it is more likely to happen as initial inequality increases.

All this suggests that it could be a growth-enhancing switching regime in time: when inequalities are high, a public health system contributes to reduce them and could even bring about higher growth rates than a private regime. As inequalities are reduced and agents are increasingly homogeneous, the balanced growth path of a private regime is higher and – as long as the economy is sufficiently rich to avoid poverty trap – inequalities are not increased. Clearly, although changing a health regime entails considerable switching costs which generally makes complete switching prohibitive, rather than a complete switch we can look at this implication as a variation in the share of public/private provision of health-care. In this sense, the model's implications appear consistent with what historically occurred in Western countries, as the initial establishment of the public health system took place in highly unequal societies and developed with a progressive reduction in inequality; nowadays many countries are experiencing an ongoing reduction in the public share of health expenditure.[33] It is worth adding that the reasons for having a public health system might go beyond those related to economic prosperity and income inequality, on which this chapter focused. The results and implications of the model should be seen as complementary to the contribution of the other social sciences in evaluating the choice of a public versus private health-care system.

The model is also able to account for endogenous poverty traps. They are due to the temporary convexity induced in the human capital map by the effect of lifespan on human capital investment. When a poverty trap is at work, the private regime exhibits ever-increasing inequalities in the endogenous growth case. Generally, although the growth factor proves initially higher in a private regime, it may later be overtaken by public systems for several periods.

The health effect on lifespan acts like an inter-generational externality. It might also be interesting to consider intra-generational externalities, since improving general health conditions reduces the risk of contracting contagious epidemics and diseases. The beneficial effect on economic growth of the public system in the presence of a highly unequal society would be arguably reinforced in the presence of such an intra-generational externality: when for everyone's human capital it is important that everyone else's health condition is also sufficiently high (e.g. so that the risk of contagion with diseases can be limited), then public provision of a common standard of health care in an unequal context has another channel to positively affect economic growth and reduce inequality.[34] However, the fact that voters do not internalize all the effects would still be true, thus continuing to represent a departure from a social planner's solution. Therefore, though we still evoke for further research the investigation of the issue of intra-generational externality, the implication of the basic model suggesting that the larger the inequalities the better a public system of health provision performs in terms of economic growth seems robust and only reinforced by such an extension: i.e. even at a smaller level of inequality the public system can perform better. An interesting line of research could be to allow for internalization of the static intra-generational externality, which could induce a trade-off between a public regime which could better internalize the intra-generational externality and a private system which better internalizes the inter-temporal individual-specific effect of health spending.

Finally, another line along which the model can be extended is to include in the analysis a third period, old age, which should realistically represent another important component of health demand and give rise to an increase in health expenditure, without having necessarily positive effects on growth, as has happened in Western economies. This would also provide a natural framework in this OLG setting to include savings and physical capital accumulation. All these possible extensions represent suggestions for further research.

APPENDIX

9A.1. Alternative specification of $\phi(\cdot)$

If $\phi(\cdot)$ is chosen according to (9.2), we have for Δ:

$$\Delta(\xi_t)=\begin{cases}\dfrac{\lambda a\left(\dfrac{\gamma+1}{\gamma+\theta}\right)^{1-\varepsilon}}{\lambda a\left(\dfrac{\gamma+1}{\gamma+\theta}\right)^{1-\varepsilon}+\dfrac{1-\theta}{\gamma+\theta}\xi_t^{-\varepsilon}} & \text{if } \xi_t<\hat{\xi}_t\\[2ex] \dfrac{\lambda\bar{\phi}}{\lambda\bar{\phi}+\dfrac{1-\theta}{\gamma+1}} & \text{otherwise}\end{cases}$$

where the threshold level $\hat{\xi}_t$ is defined as $(\bar{\phi}/a)^{1/\varepsilon}(\gamma+1)/(\gamma+\theta)$.

The expression above can be rewritten more briefly as:

$$\Delta(\xi_t)=\begin{cases}\dfrac{\lambda a\alpha^{\varepsilon-1}}{\lambda a\alpha^{\varepsilon-1}+\chi^{-1}\xi_t^{-\varepsilon}} & \text{if } \xi_t<\hat{\xi}_t\\[2ex] \dfrac{\lambda\bar{\phi}}{\lambda\bar{\phi}+\chi^{-1}} & \text{otherwise}\end{cases}$$

In the public regime we have:

$$\tilde{\Delta}(\bar{\xi}_t)=\begin{cases}\dfrac{\lambda a\bar{\xi}_t^{\varepsilon}}{\lambda a\bar{\xi}_t^{\varepsilon}+(\tau^*)^{-\varepsilon}} & \text{if } \bar{\xi}_t<\tilde{\hat{\xi}}_t\\[2ex] \dfrac{\lambda\bar{\phi}}{\lambda\bar{\phi}+1} & \text{otherwise}\end{cases}$$

where the threshold level $\tilde{\hat{\xi}}_t$ is defined as $(\bar{\phi}/a)^{1/\varepsilon}(\gamma+\theta+1)/(\gamma+\theta)$.

In order to assess conditions under which an agent devotes more time to learning under the public regime, three possible situations may arise:

- Both average and agent-specific human capital are below the threshold levels of health investment.[35] In this case a relation between ξ_t and $\bar{\xi}_t$ can be found, stating a condition for public funding to enhance learning investment more than in the private system:

$$\frac{\xi_t}{\bar{\xi}_t} < \frac{(1-\theta)^{1/\varepsilon}}{(1+\gamma+\theta)(1+\gamma)^{\frac{1-\varepsilon}{\varepsilon}}} \equiv (1-\alpha)^{1/\varepsilon}\frac{\tau^*}{\alpha}$$

- An agent's health investment in the private system is below the threshold level while public health investment is above. In this case public funding yields higher time for learning if

$$\xi_t < \frac{\gamma+1}{\gamma+\theta}\left(\frac{\bar{\phi}(1-\theta)}{a(\gamma+1)}\right)^{1/\varepsilon} \equiv \frac{1}{\alpha}\left(\frac{\bar{\phi}(1-\alpha)}{a}\right)^{1/\varepsilon}$$

- If an agent's health investment in the private regime is above the threshold level then learning is higher in the private system whatever the average human capital. Intuitively this happens because the lifespan is already at its maximum so that there is no chance that the public system closes the gap with the private regime by increasing life expectancy.

9A.2. Proof of Propositions 4 and 6

If agents are homogeneous then $\Delta > \tilde{\Delta}$, whatever the specification of $\phi(\cdot)$.

$$\Delta > \tilde{\Delta} \Leftrightarrow \frac{\phi(h_t)\lambda(\gamma+1)}{\phi(h_t)\lambda(\gamma+1)+(1-\theta)} > \frac{\phi(\bar{h}_t)\lambda}{1+\phi(\bar{h}_t)\lambda}$$

The inequalities above hold if and only if:

$$\phi(h_t)\lambda(\gamma+1)+\phi(h_t)\phi(\bar{h}_t)\lambda^2(\gamma+1)-\phi(h_t)\phi(\bar{h}_t)\lambda^2(\gamma+1)-\phi(\bar{h}_t)\lambda(1-\theta)>0$$

$\Leftrightarrow$

$$\phi(h_t)\lambda(\gamma+1)-\phi(\bar{h}_t)\lambda(1-\theta)>0$$

The inequality above always holds if agents are homogeneous, i.e. $\xi = \bar{\xi}$, since $\gamma,\ \theta \in (0;\ 1)$ and

$$h_t = \frac{\gamma+\theta}{\gamma+1}\bar{\xi}_t > \frac{\theta+\gamma}{1+\theta+\gamma}\bar{\xi}_t = \bar{h}_t$$

9A.3. Proof of Proposition 7

Proof of comparison between two public economies in Section 9.6: *If two public economies start with the same per-capita income, if $\sigma_t'^2 > \sigma_t^2$ then $\bar{\xi}_{t+1} > \bar{\xi}'_{t+1}$.*

Since $\bar{\xi}_{t+1} = \mu_t + \sigma_t^2$, using (9.29) and (9.27), $\bar{\xi}_{t+1} > \bar{\xi}'_{t+1}$ if and only if

$$\frac{\nu}{1-\theta}\mu_t+\frac{\nu^2}{2(1-\theta)}\sigma_t^2>\frac{\nu}{1-\theta}\mu_t'+\frac{\nu^2}{2(1-\theta)}\sigma_t'^2$$

Now, because $\overline{\xi}_t=\overline{\xi}_t'$ we have:

$$\frac{\nu}{1-\theta}(\mu_t-\mu_t')=\frac{\nu}{2(1-\theta)}(\sigma_t'^2-\sigma_t^2)>\frac{\nu^2}{2(1-\theta)}(\sigma_t'^2-\sigma_t^2) \text{ since } \nu<1.$$

The same reasoning holds for every t that follows.

9A.4. Further Issues

9A.4.1. Childhood health productivity

Human capital is likely to be positively affected by the health condition in childhood. If the human capital accumulation function (9.3) is modified to

$$\xi_{t+1}=\psi(1-n_t)^{\lambda}h_t^{\theta}\xi_t^{\nu}$$

for the private system and

$$\xi_{t+1}=\psi(1-n_t)^{\lambda}\overline{h}_t^{\theta}\xi_t^{\nu}$$

for the public regime. This specification is even closer to GR. The main implication is that in the maximization problem the only control variable that affects ξ_{t+1} is the learning time $(1-n_t)$ since h_t is chosen by parents. In the private regime, optimization of (9.1) subject to (9.4) and (9.34) yields

$$h_{t+1}=\frac{\gamma}{1+\gamma}\xi_{t+1}\equiv\alpha'\xi_{t+1}$$

In the public regime, optimization of (9.1) subject to (9.13) and (9.35) yields:

$$\tau_{t+1}'=\frac{\gamma}{1+\gamma}$$

It may be noted that $\tau'=\alpha'$ and that $\alpha=\alpha'=\tau'^{*}$ if $\theta=0$: considering childhood health on the one hand increases the impact of the intergenerational externality, on the other hand implies the loss of an advantage of private regime in terms of internalization: whatever the regime, the choice of health has no direct impact on income, since only the human capital of the next generation is affected. Hence the share of income devoted to health in both systems is less than in the case with adulthood health in human capital accumulation. This reduction is nevertheless greater under the private regime and the share of income devoted to health proves the same.

The condition under which an agent devotes more time to learning under the public than under the private regime becomes:

$$\frac{\xi_t}{\overline{\xi}_t} < \frac{\alpha'}{\gamma(1+\alpha'^2\overline{\xi}_t)}$$

The threshold is bigger than in the adulthood health case, hence under this specification the number of agents investing more time in human capital is likely to be greater under the public regime.

If agents are homogeneous, the private regime yields higher stable steady state or long-run growth factors (depending on long-run returns). It can be seen by comparing the laws of motion of human capital accumulation under private and public regimes, which are respectively:

$$\xi_{t+1} = \psi\alpha'^{\theta}\Delta'^{\lambda}\xi_t^{\nu+\theta}$$

$$\xi_{t+1} = \psi\alpha'^{\theta}\tilde{\Delta}'^{\lambda}\overline{\xi}_t^{\theta}\xi_t^{\nu}$$

If agents are homogeneous (i.e. $\xi_t = \overline{\xi}$) the private regime yields higher stable steady state or long-run growth factors (depending on long-run returns). However, now the gap is completely determined by Δ and $\tilde{\Delta}$, and the advantage of the public regime, albeit lower than before, is confirmed. As in GR, a policy of mandatory school is able to cancel out this source of advantage for the private regime.

Analysing the human capital dynamics, one can see that now the model is closer to GR's prediction. For the private regime:

$$\mu_{t+1} = (\nu+\theta)\mu_t + \lambda E[\ln\Delta(e^{\ell_t})] + \ln(\psi\alpha'^{\theta})$$

For the public regime:

$$\mu_{t+1} = (\nu+\theta)\mu_t + \frac{\theta}{2}\sigma_t^2 + \lambda\ln\tilde{\Delta}(e^{\mu_t+\sigma_t^2}) + \ln(\psi\alpha'^{\theta})$$

The law of motion of log per capita income under the private regime becomes:

$$\ln\overline{\xi}_{t+1} = (\nu+\theta)\mu_t + \frac{\sigma_{t+1}^2}{2} + \lambda E[\ln\Delta(e^{\ell_t})] + \ln(\psi\alpha'^{\theta})$$

In the public regime:

$$\ln\overline{\xi}_{t+1} = (\nu+\theta)\mu_t + \frac{\theta+\nu^2}{2}\sigma_t^2 + \lambda\ln\tilde{\Delta}(e^{\mu_t+\sigma_t^2}) + \ln(\psi\alpha'^{\theta})$$

With respect to GR, here the concavity of log function and $\Delta(\cdot)$ plays a role in favour of the public system, i.e. $\ln(\tilde{\Delta}(\overline{\xi}_t))$ can be greater than $E[\ln(\Delta(\xi_t))]$: since functions ln and Δ are both concave, the inequality holds if $\Delta(\cdot)=\tilde{\Delta}(\cdot)$, but by continuity it still holds for some $\Delta(\cdot)>\tilde{\Delta}(\cdot)$. On the other hand, we know that in the private regime $\sigma_{t+1}^2>(\theta+\nu)^2$, as it is in GR. Hence it cannot be said unambiguously if the public system is more likely to bring about higher per-capita income than in GR.

Compared to the benchmark specification (adulthood health), the main qualitative result is that the gap between private and public regimes is reduced. Both childhood and adulthood health in the human capital production function can be allowed for as follows:

$$\xi_{t+1}=\psi(1-n_t)^{\lambda}h_{t+1}^{\delta\theta}h_t^{(1-\delta)\theta}\xi_t^{\nu}$$

where $\delta\in(0;\,1)$. Maximization yields analogous results of the case with only adulthood health, since the health share of income now amounts to $(\gamma+\delta\theta)/(\gamma+1)$ and $\tau^*=(\gamma+\delta\theta)/(\gamma+1+\delta\theta)$. Then the dynamics are between the two extreme cases: the closer to the benchmark case the higher is δ.

NOTES

* The author is thankful to Prof. David de la Croix and Prof. Henri Sneessens for helpful comments on a previous version of this chapter, and also to Prof. Renato Balducci and the participants at the workshop 'Economic Growth: Social and Institutional dynamics' held in Pisa, 26–28 April 2007 for further beneficial and useful suggestions on the newer version. The usual disclaimer applies.

1. The differences on improvements in child and adult health are discussed among others by Soares (2005).
2. This view is not shared by Hazan and Zoabi (2006) who point out the beneficial effect of health on human capital accumulation is mostly via the channel of complementarity with education in production of human capital.
3. See Deaton (2003) for a critical survey, or Leigh and Jencks (2007) for a recent investigation.
4. Perfect annuities markets mean that all savings are intermediated through mutual funds that invest them in assets. The gross returns from these investments are then distributed among the surviving old.
5. In particular, the effect on discounting and propensity to invest through life expectancy, and the relevance in utility. Also education can provide utility directly ('pleasure of studying'), but reasonably this direct effect is much more important for health.
6. The importance of childhood and youth health care in determining life expectancy is well supported. See for example de la Croix and Licandro (2007).
7. In Section 8.1 it was stressed also that health before the productive age has an influence on labour productivity. However, this would amount to adding a further dimension to the optimization problem, making the model less tractable without adding any decisive insight.

8. Aguiar-Conraria (2005) shows that the conclusion that the private system leads to higher growth is not necessarily true if altruism is not allowed.
9. Bénabou (1996) stresses the possible role of complementarities in production and peer group effects, which can alter the choice of the funding system of human capital, possibly in favour of public provision. Maintaining the formulation of GR allows the model to be kept relatively simple and highlights the peculiar effect of health on schooling decisions.
10. Actually an 'innate' component given by nature should play a role as well: $\phi^i = \phi(h^i, \kappa^i)$ where κ^i is the innate health capital of agent i. Nevertheless, it is assumed for the sake of simplicity that $\kappa^i = 1$ for all i, such that $\phi(h^i) \equiv \phi(h^i, 1)$.
11. This assumption which is made for the sake of simplicity since our primary focus is on health, has the shortcoming of ignoring possible budgetary tensions between health and education expenditure. See Osang and Sarkar (2005).
12. Actually it is a little weird to assume medical progress exogenous to health investment; in any case, a_t can be seen as a parameter reflecting all the factors involved in life expectancy not directly related to health investment.
13. Here it is assumed that the only specific cost of learning is in terms of time, or equivalently that the real cost of children's education is included in parents' consumption.
14. In this model, elasticity of health with respect to income is constant and equal to one: health is a normal good, but neither a primary nor a luxury good. This can be a good approximation since 'health' is considered in a broad sense. The increased taste for health that has occurred in Western economies in recent decades can be interpreted in this context as an increase in γ. See Hall and Jones (2007) for a model which stresses demand for health care as a superior good.
15. In GR the optimal amount of time is $\lambda/(1/2+\lambda)$. It is easy to see this result as a particular case of (8.11) when $\gamma=1$ and $\phi(h_t)=1$, as it is in their model, and $\theta=0$: in their framework human capital investment is a mere bequest and it affects productivity only starting from the next generation. Hence the technology parameter (i.e. θ) describing marginal returns of this investment is not taken into account.
16. This follows from the fact that electors are an atomistic part of the whole society, which is commonly assumed in the literature. A remarkable exception is Bénabou (1996) who assumes perfectly rational dynastic voters internalizing all the effects; this makes the public solution closer to a first best.
17. Hence this tax rate is preferred not only through majority voting, but also unanimously.
18. If parameters are such that no intersection occurs at a positive value of human capital, the only (stable) equilibrium is the trivial one: 0; while if parameters are such that even for small value of ξ, the map is above the 45 degrees line, then there is only one positive (stable) steady state and the zero equilibrium is unstable. In Section 8.7 it is found that values of parameters implying a poverty trap are a relevant empirical case.
19. 0 is a catching point for x if, for small x, $g(x)<x$, where $g(x)$ denotes the map function of x.
20. The other possible scenario is that zero equilibrium is not a catching point: in this case it is the only steady state, it is unstable and for any positive ξ_0 the economy experiences long-run explosive growth.
21. Moreover ξ_{t+1} in the public system depends on its concurrent average $\overline{\xi}_{t+1}$, while in GR's model the lagged average appears.
22. Moreover, for the log-normal distribution, the Gini coefficient depends only on the standard deviation σ_t. Hence under the assumption of log-normality, inequalities may be measured also through the Gini coefficient without adding other parametric specifications to the distribution.

23. In graphical terms this means that either the human capital map function does not cross in its convex tract the 45° degrees line or that even the lowest endowed agent is above the poverty trap threshold (the unstable steady state). Note that these assumptions do not preclude any case about long-run returns $(\nu+\theta)$.
24. Note that if $\theta=0$, the two expressions are equal. Hence the lower is θ, the lower is this advantage of the private regime.
25. With $\phi(\cdot)$ specified as in (9.2a) this limit is $\beta\lambda/[\beta\lambda+(1-\theta/\gamma+1)]$ for Δ and $\beta\lambda/(\beta\lambda+1)$ for $\tilde{\Delta}$, while under (9.2) it amounts to $\lambda\bar{\phi}/[\lambda\bar{\phi}+(1-\theta/\gamma+1)]$ for Δ and $\lambda\bar{\phi}/(\lambda\bar{\phi}+1)$ for $\tilde{\Delta}$.
26. It is implicitly assumed that no agent is at the beginning exactly in the unstable steady state.
27. If this is the case, beginning from a private system in order to foster growth and then switching to a public system to decrease inequalities when the average income is high enough to make this policy effective can be considered.
28. In fact, it may be a little too high but I think it can be reasonable for this benchmark representation. If a lower θ is chosen, the main qualitative effect is to make the human capital map flatter.
29. Maybe it is worth recalling that in this model ξ_t is not a simple externality of human capital on its next level but more broadly characterizes persistence in the level of knowledge. Therefore the chosen value for ν does not seem exaggerated.
30. In fact μ_t tends to grow more, at least at the beginning, under the public regime, but this effect is overcome by the simultaneous decrease in variance in the public regime compared to the variance of the private system.
31. Since Δ is 'less concave' than $\tilde{\Delta}$ (in the private system agents see higher returns from devoting time to learning), then this result is mitigated in the private regime: this explains the last part of the second point in Simulation Regularities 1.
32. It is worth noting that for this very low average initial value also the growth rate of the private regime exhibits a hump-shape.
33. Between 1993 and 2003 the average growth rate per year in OECD countries of the public share of health expenditure was negative for all countries but the USA (0.3 per cent), Turkey (3.90 per cent) and Portugal (0.35 per cent). Turkey and the USA had relatively high levels of inequality.
34. See Bénabou (1996, 2000) for a model with complementarity among agents' human capital.
35. These threshold levels expressed in terms of human capital are

$$\frac{\gamma+1}{\gamma+\theta}\left(\frac{\bar{\phi}}{a}\right)^{1/\varepsilon}$$

for ξ_t under the private regime and

$$\frac{\gamma+\theta+1}{\gamma+\theta}\left(\frac{\bar{\phi}}{a}\right)^{1/\varepsilon}$$

for $\bar{\xi}_t$ under the public regime.

REFERENCES

Aguiar-Conraria, L. (2005), 'Public vs Private Schooling in an Endogenous Growth Model', *Economics Bulletin*, **9**(10), 1–6.

Aísa, R. and F. Pueyo (2001), 'Endogenous Longevity, Health and Economic Growth: a Slow Growth for a Longer Life', *Economics Bulletin*, **9**(3), 1–10.

Barro, R. (1996), 'Health and Economic Growth', Paper prepared for the Pan American Health Organization, mimeo.

Bénabou, R. (1996), 'Heterogeneity, Stratification, and Growth: Macroeconomic Implications of Community Structure and School Finance', *American Economic Review*, **86**(3), 584–609.

Bénabou, R. (2000), 'Unequal Societies: Income Distribution and the Social Contract', *American Economic Review*, **90**(1), 96–129.

Ben-Porath, Y. (1967), 'The Production of Human Capital and the Life Cycle of Earnings', *Journal of Political Economy*, **75**(4), 352–65.

Bloom, D.E., D. Canning and J. Sevilla (2004), 'The Effect of Health on Economic Growth: A Production Function Approach', *World Development*, **32**(1), 1–13.

Boucekkine, R., D. de la Croix and O. Licandro (2003), 'Early Mortality Declines at the Dawn of Modern Growth', *Scandinavian Journal of Economics*, **105**, 401–18.

Cervellati, M. and U. Sunde (2005), 'Human Capital Formation, Life Expectancy, and the Process of Development', *American Economic Review*, **95**(5), 1653–72.

Cervellati, M. and U. Sunde (2007), 'Human Capital, Mortality and Fertility: A Unified Theory of the Economic and Demographic Transition', *CEPR Discussion Papers 6384*.

Chakraborty, S. (2004), 'Endogenous Lifetime and Economic Growth', *Journal of Economic Theory*, **116**(1), 119–37.

Chakraborty, S. and M. Das (2005), 'Mortality, Human Capital and Persistent Inequality', *Journal of Economic Growth*, **10**(2), 159–92.

Deaton, A. (2003), 'Health, Inequality, and Economic Development', *Journal of Economic Literature*, **41**(1), 113–58.

de la Croix, D, and M. Doepke (2004), 'Public versus Private Education when Differential Fertility Matters', *Journal of Development Economics*, **93**, 1091–113.

de la Croix, D. and O. Licandro (1999), 'Life Expectancy and Endogenous Growth', *Economic Letters*, **65**, 255–63.

de la Croix, D. and O. Licandro (2007), '"The Child is Father of the Man": Implications for the Demographic Transition', *CEPR Discussion Paper 6493*.

de la Croix, D. and A. Sommacal (forthcoming), 'A Theory of Medical Effectiveness, Differential Mortality, Income Inequality and Growth for Pre-industrial England', *Mathematical Population Studies*.

Delfgaauw, J. (2007), 'Dedicated Doctors: Public and Private Provision of Health Care with Altruistic Physicians', *Tinbergen Institute Discussion Papers*, no. 07-010/1.

Devlin, N. and Hansen, P. (2001), 'Health Care Spending and Economic Output: Granger Causality', *Applied Economic Letters*, **8**(8), 561–64.

Fogel, R. (1997), 'New Findings on Secular Trends in Nutrition and Mortality: Some Implications for Population Theory', in M. Rosenzweig and O. Stark (eds),

Handbook of Population and Family Economics, Amsterdam: Elsevier Science Publishers, pp. 433–81.

Fuchs, V. (1986), *The Health Economy*, Cambridge, MA: Harvard University Press,

Galor, O. and D. Mayer-Foulkes (2004), 'Food for Thought: Basic Needs and Persistent Educational Inequality', *EconWPA*, no. 0410002.

Glomm, G. and B. Ravikumar (1992), 'Public versus Private Investment in Human Capital: Endogenous Growth and Income Inequality', *Journal of Political Economy*, **100**(4), 818–34.

Hall, R.E. and C.I. Jones (2007), 'The Value of Life and the Rise in Health Spending', *Quarterly Journal of Economics*, **122**(1), 39–72.

Hazan, M. and H. Zoabi (2006), 'Does Longevity Cause Growth? A Theoretical Critique', *Journal of Economic Growth*, **11**(4), 363–76.

Hosoya, K. (2003), 'Tax Financed Government Health Expenditure and Growth with Capital Deepening Externality?', *Economics Bulletin*, **5**(14), 1–10.

Howitt, P. (2005), 'Health and Economic Growth: Findings and Policy Implications', in G. López-Casasnovas, B. Rivera and L. Currais (eds), *Health, Human Capital and Economic Growth: a Schumpeterian Perspective*, Cambridge, MA: MIT Press, pp. 19–24.

Kalemli-Ozcan, S., H.E. Ryder and D.N. Weil (2000), 'Mortality Decline, Human Capital Investment, and Economic Growth', *Journal of Development Economics*, **62**(1), 1–23.

Lange, F. and H. Bleakley (2004), 'The Impact of Chronic Disease Burden on Education, Fertility and Economic Growth. Evidence from the American South', *Econometric Society 2004 North American Winter Meetings Series*, no. 513.

Leigh, A. and C. Jencks (2007), 'Inequality and Mortality: Long-run Evidence from a Panel of Countries', *Journal of Health Economics*, **26**(1), 1–24.

Mayer-Foulkes, D. (2004), 'Human Development Traps in Mexico', Centro de Investigacion y Docencia Economicas (CIDE), Division de Economia, mimeo.

Miguel, E and M. Kremer (2004), 'Worms: Identifying Impacts on Education and Health in the Presence of Treatment Externalities', *Econometrica*, **72**(1), 159–217.

Osang, T. and J. Sarkar (2005), 'Endogenous Mortality, Human Capital and Endogenous Growth', Southern Methodist University, *Department of Economics Working Papers*, no. 0511.

Shastry, G.K. and D.N. Weil (2003), 'How Much of Cross-Country Income Variation is Explained By Health?', *Journal of the European Economic Association*, **1**(2–3), 387–96.

Soares, R.R. (2005), 'Mortality Reductions, Educational Attainment, and Fertility Choice', *American Economic Review*, **95**(3), 580–601.

UNDP (1990), *Human Development Report*, New York and Oxford: Oxford University Press.

UNICEF (2004), *Vitamin and Mineral Deficiency: A Global Progress Report*, available at http://www.micronutrient.org/reports/.

Van Zon, A. and J. Muysken (2001), 'Health and Endogenous Growth', *Journal of Health Economics*, **20**, 169–85.

Wang, L. (2003), 'Determinants of Child Mortality in LDCs. Empirical Findings from Demographic and Health Surveys', *Health Policy*, **65**(23), 277–99.

Wang, Y. and M.C.M. Leung (2003), 'Endogenous Health Care, Life Expectancy, and Economic Development', *Royal Economic Society Annual Conference 2003 Paper no. 218*.
WHO (2001), *Macroeconomics and Health: Investing in Health for Economic Development*, Technical Report of the Commission on Macroeconomics and Health, Geneva: World Health Organization.
WHO (2004), *The World Health Report*, Geneva: World Health Organization.

10. Education, change in consumer preferences and growth*

Renato Balducci

10.1. INTRODUCTION

The idea that investment in education, whether public or private, can promote economic growth was recognized by New Growth Theory,[1] contrary to the neoclassical theory that preceded it.[2] Lucas (1988) argued that investment in (that is, time dedicated to) schooling increases the stock of human capital and the long-run rate of growth. Similarly, government spending on research and development (Romer, 1990), on schooling (Mincer, 1974; Willis and Rosen, 1979; Willis, 1986; Glomm and Ravikumar, 1992; Becker, 1993), on health (Barro, 1996; Bloom et al., 2001; Van Zon and Muyshen, 2001; Howitt, 2002; Mayer, 2002; Galor and Hosoya, 2003; de la Croix and Doepke, 2004) and on public infrastructures fosters economic development, introducing an externality into private decisions on production. In particular, education has a positive effect on labour productivity (Bloom et al., 2001), improving creativity, learning capacity and skills (Howitt, 2002).[3]

A different approach derives from Barro (1990).[4] The basic hypothesis of this model is that the government provides free public services to firms, such as defence of property rights, spending on justice, health, education and so on. Public spending, financed with proportional taxes on income, affects the production function, which is with constant returns to scale in two production factors: physical capital stock and public investment.[5] On maximizing the utility of private consumption, one obtains a constant steady-state growth rate which is influenced by public spending on education. An increase in the tax rate and in public investment in education fosters economic growth up to a threshold (Barro, 1990, p. 109); beyond this value the growth rate decreases.

An extension of this important result has been advanced by Barro (1990, p. 117) himself: 'We could also allow for public consumption services as an influence on households' utility'. However, public consumption slows economic growth because it reduces private income net of taxes without increasing the productivity of the capital stock.

In this chapter I examine the effect on the growth rate of both private and public investment in health, schooling and culture: in short, *education*. Investment in education exerts two effects on the economic growth: (i) it increases the productivity of the capital stock, and (ii) modifies household saving decisions through substitutability (Flessig and Rossana, 2003) between education and consumption. I do not follow Lucas's (1988) approach, according to which the engine of (or the binding constraint on) economic growth is the time share dedicated to the accumulation of human capital: the effective binding constraint for growth consists in the financial resources available to invest in schooling. This financial constraint could be relaxed only if perfect capital markets were willing to finance private investment in schooling. In reality this does not happen. Financial resources determine a person's possibility of continuing his or her studies. For this reason, I consider the methodological approach taken by Barro's (1990) model most interesting, according to which public spending on schooling produces externalities for firms which support economic growth.

In this chapter I analyze whether public or private financing of education is equivalent in relation to long-run economic growth. In general the answer is negative. Public financing of education for the entire school-age population exerts an important positive externality on labour productivity and gives rise to a positive steady-state rate of growth. However, public education provision does not produce such income differentials as to change private preferences in favour of education. Otherwise, in the case of private financing of education, there will be a share of individuals who first achieve a higher level of education and obtain higher per capita income (see Griliches, 1977; Erickson and Ichino, 1992; Bénabou, 1994; Lucifora, 1994; Psacharopoulos, 1994; Card, 1999; Harmon and Walzer, 1995; Galor and Tsidon, 1997; Epple and Romano, 1998; Manacorda, 2000; Miguel, 2005; Sala-i-Martin, 2005). Their preferences shift towards higher levels of education, which in turn generates further investment in education and higher earnings. However, this cumulative process encounters a limit: the greater the share of the higher educated population, the more rapidly education becomes an externality, exactly as happens with public schooling.

Section 10.2 presents a model of endogenous growth like Barro's (1990) model in which the engine of economic growth is private investment in education. Section 10.3 extends this model to the case of public financing of education and compares the two optimal rates of growth. Section 10.4 describes the evolution of individual preferences engendered by investment in education and illustrates the differences between the private and public financing of education. Section 10.5 concludes.

10.2. A MODEL OF GROWTH WITH PRIVATE INVESTMENT IN EDUCATION

I shall construct a simple model of endogenous growth with expenditure on education $h(t)$[6] in the utility function and in the production function. The production function, in terms of constant labour units,[7] is a Cobb–Douglas with constant returns to scale in physical capital stock $k(t)$ and investment in education $h(t)$:

$$y(t)=k(t)^{\alpha}h(t)^{1-\alpha} \qquad y_k(t)=\alpha x(t)^{1-\alpha}, \qquad y_h(t)=(1-\alpha)x(t)^{-\alpha} \tag{10.1}$$

where $x(t)=h(t)/k(t)$.

The disposable income of a representative household is spent on consumption and investment in physical capital and in education:

$$y(t)=c(t)+\dot{k}(t)+h(t) \tag{10.2}$$

The arguments of the household utility function are consumption $c(t)$, with weight $(1-\beta)$, and education $h(t)$, with weight $0\leq\beta<1$:

$$u(t)=\frac{\left\{c(t)^{1-\beta}\left[\gamma h(t)\right]^{\beta}\right\}^{1-\sigma}}{1-\sigma}, \; u_c(t)=(1-\beta)(1-\sigma)\frac{u(t)}{c(t)}, \; u_h(t)=\beta(1-\sigma)\frac{u(t)}{h(t)} \tag{10.3}$$

where γ indicates the value in terms of the utility of the investment in education.

Households maximize the current value of future flows of utility, choosing both consumption $c(t)$ and investment in education $h(t)$ in respect of the dynamic constraint (10.2), given a positive initial capital stock: $k(0)=k0>0$. In Appendix 10A.1 this optimal control problem is solved and the steady state growth rate is obtained as the solution of the following implicit equation:

$$Z(g)=\left[B(\beta)-\beta\right]g-\left(\frac{\sigma g+\rho}{\alpha}\right)^{\frac{1}{1-\alpha}}+B(\beta)\rho=0 \tag{10.4}$$

where $B(\beta)=\sigma[(1-\alpha)/\alpha+\beta]$.

Note that if $\beta<[\sigma(1-\alpha)]/[(1-\sigma)\alpha]$ (*sufficient condition*), the term in the square brackets, $B(\beta)-\beta$, is positive. I assume that this condition is satisfied. Then $Z(g)$ is a concave function of g increasing up to $g_{\min}$ and thereafter decreasing:

$$\frac{\partial Z(g)}{\partial g}=[B(\beta)-\beta]-\frac{\sigma}{\alpha(1-\alpha)}\left(\frac{\sigma g+\rho}{\alpha}\right)^{\frac{\alpha}{1-\alpha}}<0 \qquad \text{for } g>g_{\min}$$ [8]

It is interesting to study the relation between the value g^* such that $Z(g^*)=0$ and the preference for education β:

$$\frac{\partial g^*}{\partial \beta}=\frac{(1-\sigma)g^*-\rho}{\frac{\partial Z(g)}{\partial g}}>0 \qquad \text{if } g_{\min}<g^*<\frac{\rho}{1-\sigma}$$

Therefore, if households consider $h(t)$ to be useful, i.e. $\beta>0$, the steady state rate of growth increases with β (see Figure 10.1). But, when $\beta=0$, the value of $x^*(\beta=0)$ (see Appendix 10A.1) is minimum and the rate of growth is lowest, as in Barro (1990):

$$g^*(\beta=0)=\frac{1}{\sigma}\left[\alpha(1-\alpha)^{\frac{1-\alpha}{\alpha}}-\rho\right] \tag{10.5}$$

In general, the following proposition holds:

Proposition 1: *When the optimal investment in education is privately financed, the steady state rate of growth is an increasing function of household preferences for education through the optimal ratio between investment in education and physical capital stock:* $g^*=g[x^*(\beta)]$.

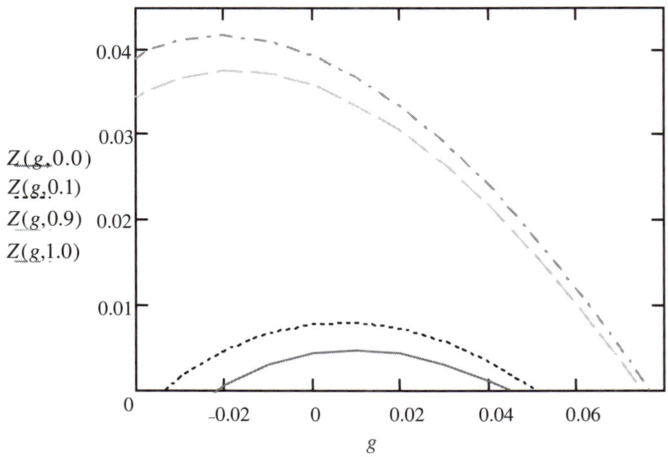

Figure 10.1. Steady state rate of growth g as function of the preferences for education. Values of the parameters: α=0.3, σ=0.75, ρ=0.05*

The steady state utility of a representative household, taking into account the optimal constant ratio between education and consumption $(\gamma h/c)^*$, may be written as follows:

$$u[c(t),h(t)]=\left[\frac{\left(\frac{\gamma h^*}{c^*}\right)^{\beta} c_0 e^{g(\beta)t}}{1-\sigma}\right]^{1-\sigma}$$

The effect of a change in household preferences for education is then given by the sum of two components: (i) change in the optimal ratio between education and consumption $(\gamma h/c)^*$, and (ii) change in optimal consumption, which grows at the rate $g(\beta)$. Thus, in the long run, a shift in household preferences towards education increases utility, given that the effect of β on the rate of growth is positive.

10.3. PUBLIC INVESTMENT IN EDUCATION AND GROWTH

10.3.1. Now consider the same previous framework assuming that the government imposes a proportional income tax rate, $0<\tau<1$, to finance public investments in education $h(t)=\tau y(t)$. The government is a benevolent planner which maximizes the household utility function by choosing the optimal income tax rate τ^*. The household utility function is the same as that hypothesised in Section 10.2.

The production function, in terms of constant labour units, with $N(t)=1$, is the same Cobb–Douglas function as introduced in equation (10.1). If economic agents know the public budget constraint: $h(t)=\tau y(t)$, the production function can be written as follows:

$$y(t)=k(t)^{\alpha}h(t)^{1-\alpha}=k(t)^{\alpha}[\tau y(t)]^{1-\alpha}=A(\tau)k(t) \qquad (10.6)$$

where: $A(\tau)=\tau^{(1-\alpha)/\alpha}$, $A_{\tau}=A(\tau)[(1-\alpha)/\alpha\tau]$.

Given that education is freely provided by the public sector, the disposable income of a representative household is spent on private consumption and physical investment only:

$$(1-\tau)A(\tau)k(t)=c(t)+\dot{k}(t) \qquad (10.7)$$

In Appendix 10A.1 this optimal control problem is solved and the steady state growth rate is obtained as the solution of the following implicit equation:

$$V(g)=[B(\beta)-\beta]g-\left(\frac{\sigma g+\rho}{\alpha}\right)^{\frac{1}{1-\alpha}}+B(\beta)\rho=0 \tag{10.8}$$

Note that this solution of the government's optimum control problem is identical to equation (10.4) obtained as a solution of the households' optimum control problem. Therefore the steady state rate of growth is the same in both cases of public and private education financing. When households do not consider education to be useful, $\beta=0$, the corner solution of the problem envisages only private consumption. The optimal tax rate is $\tau^*=1-\alpha$, and from equation (10A.18) in Appendix 10A.2 the same minimum optimal rate of growth as in equation (10.5) is obtained.

In general, the following proposition holds:

Proposition 2: *When the optimal investment in education is decided by a benevolent planner and financed by general taxation, the steady state growth rate is an increasing function of household preferences for education through the optimal tax rate:* $g^*=g[\tau^*(\beta)]$.

There are two main channels through which public expenditure on education influences the rate of growth: (i) it increases the productivity of physical capital, and (ii) it modifies the saving decisions of households. If we consider public expenditure on education in the household utility function, then such expenditure almost partially substitutes for private consumption, freeing resources to increase saving and investment.

10.3.2. By equalizing $Z(x)=V(t)$ (equation (10A.9) in Appendix 10A.1 and equation (10A.20) in Appendix 10A.2), the relation between the optimal tax rate τ^* and the optimal ratio x^* between investments in education and physical capital stock can be determined:

$$x^*=\tau^{1/\alpha} \quad \text{or} \quad \tau^*=x^\alpha \tag{10.9}$$

It is easy to verify that for these values of τ^* and x^*, the growth rates g(x*) and g(τ*) are equal.

Proposition 3: *There exists an optimal tax rate τ^* which makes the rate of growth in the case of public financing of education equal to the rate of growth in the case of private investment in education.*

Are, then, both private and public investments in education perfectly equivalent? The answer is negative. The next section explains the differences between private and public financing of education.

10.4. INVESTMENT IN EDUCATION AND CHANGE IN CONSUMER PREFERENCES

10.4.1. To understand the differences between public and private financing of education, let us hypothesize a process of economic development in three phases.

Phase 1. A neoclassical growth model with physical capital only

At time $t=0$, each household possesses a stock of capital $k_0>0$ and a basic level of education (e.g. *compulsory schooling*) normalized to 1: $h_0=1$. In the household utility function the value assigned to h_0 is $\beta_0=0$. In fact, education can be considered a *superior good*, such that below a minimum level of income $y°$ the optimal choice is a corner solution with nil investment in education. All income is devoted to consumption and investment in physical capital. Given this *Ramsey framework*, the solution of the optimum problem of the representative household yields the following steady-state equilibrium:

$$E_0^*: \left\{ k_0^* = \left(\frac{\alpha}{\rho}\right)^{\frac{1}{1-\alpha}}, \qquad y_0^* = (k_0^*)^{\alpha}, \qquad g_0^* = 0 \right\}$$

If k_0^* is greater than initial k_0 there will be a phase of transition during which the economy grows at a decreasing rate until it reaches the steady state equilibrium E_0^*. However, households may differ in their abilities to utilize their capital stock, such that the steady state equilibrium will be approached at different speeds. Thus at time t there will be a distribution on individual incomes because each household will be at a different point on the path leading from y_0 to y_0^*.

Phase 2. Change in preferences. A growth model with physical and human capital

Suppose that at time $t=t_1$ $n_1(<1)$ households exceed the threshold value $y°$ of per capita income and then change their preferences regarding education from $\beta_0=0$ to $\beta_1>0$. These households n_1 decide to spend a share of their incomes on education for themselves (or for their children) and achieve an intermediate level of education (e.g. *secondary school*): $h_1>h_0=1$. The optimal control problem faced by these n_1 households is described by the model in Section 10.2. The steady-state equilibrium E_1^* is the following (see equation (10A.8), Appendix 10A.1):

$$E_1^*: \left\{ x(\beta_1) > x(\beta_0) = 0,\ g_1(t > t_1) = \frac{1}{\sigma}\left[\alpha x(\beta_1)^{1-\alpha} - \rho\right],\ y_1(t > t_1) = y(t_1)e^{g_1(t-t_1)} \right\}$$

For the economy as a whole, the steady-state equilibrium is given by the weighted average of n_1 economic agents with an intermediate education h_1 and $(1-n_1)$ agents with a basic education h_0:

$$y(t > t_1) = n_1 y_1(t) + (1-n_1) y_0$$

$$g(t > t_1) = n_1 g_1 + (1-n_1) g_0 = n_1 g_1$$

$$h(t > t_1) = n_1 h_1 + (1-n_1) h_0 = 1 + n_1(h_1 - 1)$$

Because higher-educated agents earn an income $y_1(t)$ greater than that of lower-educated agents y_0, let us suppose that their number increases according to the following rule:

$$n_1(g_1, t) = 1 - \frac{y_0}{y_1(t)} = 1 - e^{-g_1(t-t_1)}$$

where g_1 is the rate of growth corresponding to β_1. As a consequence, the economy's growth rate and the level of per capita income become:

$$g(t) = n_1(g_1, t).g_1 \qquad \text{for } t > t_1$$

$$y(t) = \left[1 - n_1(t)\right] y_0 + n_1(t) y(t_1) e^{g_1(t-t_1)}$$

With the passing of time, $n_1(g_1, t) \to 1$: that is to say, all households will acquire an intermediate level of education $h_1 > 1$, and income disparities will diminish. This higher average level of education improves the efficiency of the economy, but it transforms education into a positive externality. Therefore no agent is able to obtain a positive income differential which offsets the investment made.

Phase 3. The limit to growth entailed by investment in education

Suppose that at time $t_2 > t_1, n_2 (< 1)$ households will switch their preferences to a higher level of education: $\beta_2 > \beta_1 > \beta_0 = 0$. They will devote a greater share of their income to education so that they can attain a higher schooling level (*university education*): $h_2 > h_1 > h_0 = 1$. Given that $x(\beta)$ is an increasing function of β,[9] the new growth rate $g(\beta_2)$ will be higher than the previous one, $g(\beta_1)$. The greater is per capita income y_2 of the higher-educated people, the more rapid will be the increase in the share of the population which invests in education. Income differentials will reduce and higher education will become a positive externality which improves the economy's efficiency. However, this cumulative evolution of household preferences driven by income differentials will encounter a *limit*. As shown in Appendix 10A.1, when $x(t)$ exceeds x_M, further investments in education reverse the trend, so that the economy grows at a lower steady state rate.

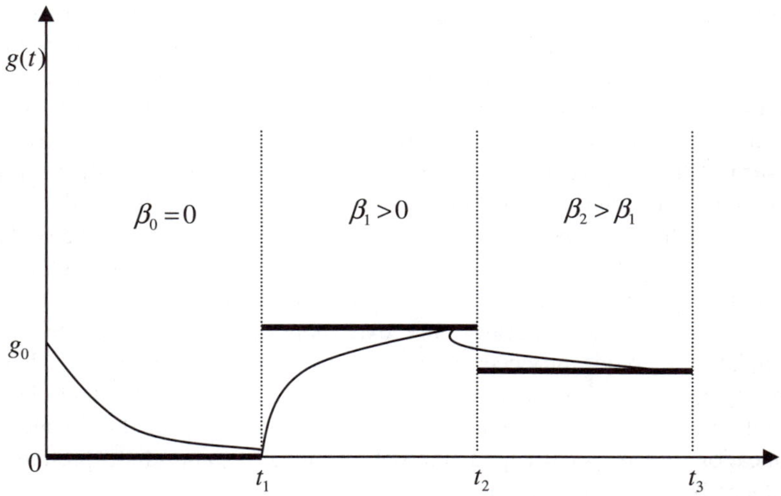

Figure 10.2. Evolution of preferences for education β and growth rate g(t)

10.4.2. What happens when education is financed by the government? The neoclassical phase 1 is like that described above. There will be convergence to the steady state equilibrium E_0^*, with an exogenous nil rate of growth. Households spend their net income on consumption and investment in physical capital. As soon as per capita income has sufficiently increased, the government supplies (historically 'imposes' on) all citizens with an education level $h_1 > h_0 = 1$ financed by income taxation. In this case the positive externality due to public education will have a very strong impact on the entire population (i.e. it will be equivalent to setting $n_1 = 1$). The generalized level of education does not increase income differentials and there is no incentive for economic agents to shift their preferences for education from $\beta_0 = 0$ to $\beta_1 > 0$. The only effect is an increase in labour efficiency. If household preferences for education β do not change, there will be no willingness to pay more taxes to finance a higher level of education.[10] Given that the rate of growth is an increasing function of the optimal tax rate

$\tau^*(\beta)$ (see Appendix 10A.2), the public financing of education may be insufficient to sustain a higher optimal rate of growth.

10.5. CONCLUSIONS

The possibilities and limits of a growth process driven by investment in education were examined. This investment is well known to promote economic growth not only by increasing labour productivity, but also by shifting household preferences to education. As a consequence, expenditure on education partly substitutes for consumption, thus freeing resources for investment in physical capital. This cumulative process is bounded, and its limit is determined by production technology, specifically by the substitutability between physical capital and education. Thereafter, further investments in education slow down growth rather than accelerate it.

The differences between a growth process driven by a benevolent government and one driven by individual choices were highlighted. A process led by the government would be more efficacious in the first phase of economic take-off because the extension of education to the entire population would produce a strong positive externality on labour productivity. In subsequent phases, a process driven by individual choices would be more long-lasting, and it would establish the optimal ratio between education and physical capital through a change in household preferences induced by income differentials.

Briefly, in the initial phase of an economy's take-off, public investment in education on behalf of all people is preferable. Thereafter, I believe it advisable to leave individuals free to make their own optimal decisions on investment in education.

APPENDIX 10A.1: THE STEADY STATE GROWTH RATE g^* WITH PRIVATE FINANCING OF EDUCATION

The solution of the optimization problem is obtained by deriving from the Hamiltonian function the following first-order maximum conditions:

$$e^{-\rho t}u_c(t)-\mu(t)=0 \qquad (10A.1)$$

$$e^{-\rho t}u_h(t)-\mu(t)+\mu(t)(1-\alpha)x(t)^{-\alpha}=0 \qquad (10A.2)$$

$$-g_\mu(t)=\alpha x(t)^{1-\alpha} \qquad (10A.3)$$

$$g_k(t)=x(t)^{1-\alpha}-\frac{c(t)}{k(t)}-x(t) \qquad (10A.4)$$

where $\rho>0$ is the intertemporal discount rate, and $g_y(t)=\dot{y}(t)/y(t)=g(y)$ indicates the growth rate of the variable $y(t)$.

Moreover, the following transversality condition must occur

$$\lim_{t\to\infty}\mu(t)h(t)=0.$$

Equations (10A.1) and (10A.2) define the optimal time path of the control variables $c(t)$ and $h(t)$, setting it in relation to the time path of the *costate* variable $\mu(t)$; equations (10A.3) and (10A.4) define the rate of variation of the *costate* variable and capital stock respectively.

Substituting equation (10A.1) in equation (10A.2) yields the optimal ratio between $c(t)$ and $k(t)$:

$$\frac{c(t)}{k(t)}=\frac{1-\beta}{\beta}(x(t)-(1-\alpha)x(t)^{1-\alpha})>0 \text{ if } \quad x(t)>x_m=(1-\alpha)^{\frac{1}{\alpha}} \qquad (10A.5)$$

The optimal growth rate of the capital stock is derived by substituting equation (10A.5) into equation (10A.4):

$$g(k)=\frac{1}{\beta}\left[(1-\alpha+\alpha\beta)x(t)^{1-\alpha}-x(t)\right] \qquad (10A.6)$$

In steady state the ratio $x(t)$ as well as the growth rate of the capital stock must be constant; by differentiating (10A.4) with respect to time, and taking account of (10A.5), the following steady state condition is obtained:

$$g(k)=g(h)=g(c)=g(y)=g \qquad (10A.7)$$

The growth rate of consumption is derived from condition (10A.1) (taking the logarithm and deriving it with respect to time), taking equation (10A.3) into account:

$$g = \frac{1}{\sigma}\left[\alpha x^{1-\alpha} - \rho\right] \tag{10A.8}$$

or

$$x = \left(\frac{\sigma g + \rho}{\alpha}\right)^{\frac{1}{1-\alpha}} \tag{10A.8A)'$$

On equalising equations (10A.6) and (10A.8), the following implicit equation is obtained:

$$Z(x) = x^{1-\alpha}[\sigma(1-\alpha+\alpha\beta)-\alpha\beta]-\sigma x+\beta\rho = 0 \tag{10A.9}$$

where: $(\partial Z/\partial x)<0$.[11]

The optimal constant value x^* is obtained by solving equation (10A.9); by substituting x^* in equation (10.8A), we obtain the steady state growth rate of income:

$$g^* = \frac{1}{\sigma}\left[\alpha(x^*)^{1-\alpha} - \rho\right] \tag{10A.10}$$

where g^* is an increasing function of x^*.

We define the relation between x and the preference for education β from implicit equation (10A.9):

$$sign\frac{\partial x(\beta)}{\partial \beta} = sign\frac{\partial Z}{\partial \beta} = \frac{\rho R - x}{\sigma R - \beta} >< 0 \quad \text{for } x <> x_M = \rho R \quad \text{where } R = \frac{1-\alpha}{\alpha(1-\sigma)}$$

Finally, the limit condition is satisfied if:

$$h_0 < \left(\frac{\rho}{\alpha(1-\sigma)}\right)^{\frac{1}{1-\alpha}} k_0$$

A different way to present the same result consists in substituting equation (10A.8)′ in equation (10A.6), obtaining an implicit equation in g^* as a function of deep parameters (σ, ρ, α) and the preferences for education β (see equation (10.4) in the text).

APPENDIX 10A.2: PROOF OF EXISTENCE OF THE STEADY STATE EQUILIBRIUM GROWTH RATE g^* WITH PUBLIC FINANCING OF EDUCATION

I introduce the first-order maximum conditions obtained by deriving the Hamiltonian function with respect to the control variable $c(t)$ and $\tau(t)$ and the state variable $k(t)$:

$$e^{-\rho t}u_c(t)-\mu(t)=0 \tag{10A.11}$$

$$e^{-\rho t}u_\tau+\mu(t)A(\tau)k(t)\frac{1-\tau-\alpha}{\alpha\tau}=0 \tag{10A.12}$$

$$-\dot{\mu}(t)=e^{-\rho t}u_k(t)+\mu(t)(1-\tau)A(\tau) \tag{10A.13}$$

$$g_k(t)=-\frac{c(t)}{k(t)}+(1-\tau)A(\tau) \tag{10A.14}$$

Equations (10A.11) and (10A.12) define the optimal time path of the control variables $c(t)$ and $\tau(t)$, setting it in relation to the time path of the *costate* variable $\mu(t)$; equations (10A.13) and (10A.14) define the variation rate of the *costate* variable and capital stock respectively.

Note that in steady state the rate of growth of the capital stock must be constant; therefore, by differentiating (10A.14) with respect to time, it must be: $g_c(t)=g_k(t)=g_y(t)=g$.

Substituting equation (10A.11) in (10A.12) and (10A.13) yields the rate of growth of the *costate* variable and the optimal ratio between consumption and capital:

$$-g_\mu(t)=\frac{\beta}{1-\beta}\frac{c(t)}{k(t)}+(1-\tau)A(\tau) \tag{10A.15}$$

$$\frac{c(\tau)}{k(\tau)}=\frac{1-\beta}{\beta}(\tau+\alpha-1)A(\tau)>0 \quad \text{for} \quad \tau>tm=1-\big|\,\tau>\tau_m=1-\alpha \quad (10A.16)^{12}$$

Then, given the optimal ratio between consumption and capital, the growth rate of the *costate* variable is defined:

$$-g_\mu(t)=\alpha A(\tau) \tag{10A.17}$$

I take the logarithm of the condition (10A.11) and derive it with respect to time. Taking account of the above equality between rates of growth, and equation (10A.17), the growth rate of consumption is derived as:

$$g(c)=g=\frac{1}{\sigma}[\alpha A(\tau)-\rho] \tag{10A.18}$$

or

$$\tau=\left(\frac{\sigma g+\rho}{\alpha}\right)^{\frac{\alpha}{1-\alpha}} \tag{10A.18$'$}$$

The optimal growth rate of the capital stock can be obtained by substituting equation (10A.16) in equation (10A.14):

$$g(k)=g=\frac{A(\tau)}{\beta}[(1-\alpha+\alpha\beta)-\tau] \tag{10A.19}$$

Finally, by equalizing equations (10A.18) and (10A.19), we obtain the following implicit relation which defines the optimal income tax rate:

$$V(\tau)=\alpha A(\tau)[B(\beta)-\beta]-\sigma\tau A(\tau)+\beta\rho=0\,; \qquad \frac{\partial V(\tau)}{\partial\tau}<0 \qquad \text{(10A.20)}^{13}$$

Note that $V(\tau)$ is a concave function of τ which decreases for $\tau>\tau_m$. There will be an optimal τ^* such that $V(\tau^*)=0$. Moreover, it is easy to ascertain from (10A.18) that g is an increasing function of τ.

We can define the relation between the optimal tax rate and the preferences for education β from the implicit equation (10A.20):

$$sign\frac{\partial\tau(\beta)}{\partial\beta}=sign\frac{\partial V}{\partial\beta}=-\alpha(1-\sigma)A(\tau)+\rho><0 \quad \text{for: } \tau<>\tau_M=\left(\frac{\rho}{\alpha(1-\sigma)}\right)^{\frac{\alpha}{1-\alpha}}$$

A different way to present the same result consists in substituting equation (10A.18)′ in equation (10A.19), obtaining an implicit equation in g as a function of deep parameters (σ, ρ, α) and the preferences for education β (see equation (10.8) in the text).

NOTES

* I thank all participants at the workshop on *Economic Growth: Institutional and Social Dynamics*, Lucca, 10–12 December 2008, financed by PRIN 2005, for their useful comments. All remaining errors and opinions are entirely my responsibility.

1. The authors and studies that have given rise to New Growth Theory are the following: Romer (1986, 1990, 1994); Lucas (1988); Barro (1990); Rebelo (1991); Aghion and Howitt (1992); Barro and Sala-i-Martin (1992, 1995); Alesina and Rodrik (1994).
2. As regards neoclassical growth theory, reference is made principally to Robert Solow's (1956) model. On the economic policy implications of new growth theory see the following works: Scott (1992); Shaw (1992); Bajo-Rubio (2000).

3. For an interesting survey of the literature on fiscal policy and economic growth, see Zagler and Durneker (2003). In a recent paper, Peretto (2003) shows that in a model of endogenous growth that does not exhibit the scale effect, the level and composition of public expenditure have no effect on steady-state growth, but only on per capita income. See also Futagami et al. (1993); Turnovsky (1996, 2000); Greiner and Hanush (1998); Bajo-Rubio (2000).
4. See also Barro and Sala-i-Martin (1992, 1995). Public investments are non-rival and non-excludable, like public goods.
5. That is, an 'AK' production function as defined by Rebelo (1991).
6. Note that $h(t)$ is the annual flow of investment in schooling, and not the stock of human capital as in Lucas (1988).
7. For simplicity, the units of population at the initial date are normalised to 1, $N(t)=1$, and the growth rate of the population is assumed to be nil: $n=0$.
8. Note that $g_{\min}$ is the value of g such that $[\partial Z(g)]/\partial g=0$.
9. As long as the ratio between investment in education and physical capital $x(\beta)$ is less than the maximum value x_M: (see Appendix 10A.1).
10. Note that the optimal tax rate τ^* is an increasing function of β (see Appendix 10A.2).
11. In fact, we have:

$$x\frac{\partial Z}{\partial x}=(1-\alpha)x^{1-\alpha}\left[\sigma(1-\alpha+\alpha\beta)-\alpha\beta\right]-\sigma x=-\alpha\sigma x-(1-\alpha)\beta\rho<0$$

for every value of root x of equation $V(x) = 0$.
12. Note that in order to have *positive* private consumption $c(t)/k(t)$, this constraint must be satisfied.
13. In fact:

$$sign\frac{\partial V(\tau)}{\partial \tau}=sign\left[\alpha(1-\alpha)(1-\sigma)(\sigma R-\beta)-\sigma\tau\right]<0 \quad \text{for} \quad \tau=\tau_m=(1-a)$$

REFERENCES

Aghion, P. and P. Howitt (1992), 'A Model of Growth through Creative Destruction', *Econometrica*, **60**(2), 323–51.

Alesina, A. and D. Rodrik (1994), 'Distributive Policies and Economic Growth', *Quarterly Journal of Economics*, **109**(2), 465–69.

Bajo-Rubio, O. (2000), 'A Further Generalization of the Solow Growth Model: the Role of the Public Sector', *Economic Letters*, **68**(1), 79–84.

Barro, R.J. (1990), 'Government Spending in a Simple Model of Endogenous Growth', *Journal of Political Economy*, **98**(2), 103–25.

Barro, R.J. (1996), 'Health and Economic Growth', Paper prepared for the Pan American Health Organization, Washington, 4 October.

Barro, R.J. and X. Sala-i-Martin (1992), 'Public Finance in Models of Economic Growth', *Review of Economic Studies*, **59**(4), 645–61.

Barro, R.J. and X. Sala-i-Martin (1995), *Economic Growth*, New York: McGraw-Hill.

Becker, G.S. (1993), *Human Capital. A Theoretical and Empirical Analysis with Special Reference to Education*, Chicago: University of Chicago Press.

Bénabou, R. (1994), 'Human Capital, Inequality and Growth: the Local Perspective', *European Economic Review*, **38**(3–4), 817–26.

Bloom, D.E., D. Canning and J. Sevilla (2001), 'The Effect of Health on Economic Growth: Theory and Evidence', *NBER Working Paper no.8587*.

Card, D. (1999), 'The Causal Effect of Education on Earnings', in O. Ashenfelter and D. Card (eds), *Handbook of Labor Economics*, vol. 3, pp. 1801–63.

de la Croix, D. and M. Doepke (2004), 'Public versus Private Education when Differential Fertility Matters', *Journal of Development Economics*, **73**(2), 607–29.

Epple, D. and R. Romano (1998), 'Competition between Private and Public Schools, Vouchers, and Peer-group Effect', *American Economic Review*, **88**(1), 33–62.

Erickson, C.L. and A. Ichino (1992), 'Wage Differential in Italy: Market Forces, Institutions, and Inflation', in R. Freeman and L. Katz (eds), *Difference and Changes in the Wage Structure*, Chicago: University of Chicago Press.

Flessig, A.R. and R.J. Rossana (2003), 'Are Consumption and Government Expenditures Substitutes or Complements? Morishima Elasticity Estimates from the Fourier Flexible Form', *Economic Inquiry*, **41**(1), 132–46.

Futagami, K., Y. Morita and S. Akihisa (1993) 'Dynamic Analysis of an Endogenous Growth Model with Public Capital', *Scandinavian Journal of Economics*, **95**(4), 607–25.

Galor, O. and D. Tsiddon (1997), 'The Distribution of Human Capital and Economic Growth', *Journal of Economic Growth*, **2**(1), 93–124.

Galor, O. and D. Mayer (2002), 'Food for Thought: Basic Needs and Persistent Educational Inequality', Paper prepared for the Pan American Health Organization, Washington, 4 October.

Glomm, G. and B. Ravikumar (1992), 'Public versus Private Investment in Human Capital: Endogenous Growth and Income Inequality', *Journal of Political Economy*, **100**(4), 818–34.

Greiner, A. and H. Hanusch (1998), 'Growth and Welfare Effects of Fiscal Policy in an Endogenous Growth Model with Public Investment', *International Tax and Public Finance*, **5**(3), 249–61.

Griliches, Z. (1977), 'Estimating the Returns to Schooling: Some Econometric Problems', *Econometrica*, **45**(1), 1–22.

Harmon, C. and I. Walker (1995), 'Estimates of the Economic Return to Schooling for the United Kingdom', *American Economic Review*, **85**(5), 1278–86.

Hosoya, K. (2003), 'Tax Financed Government Health Expenditure and Growth with Capital Deepening Externality', *Economic Bulletin*, **5**(14), 1–10.

Howitt, P. (2002), 'Health, Human Capital and Economic Growth: a Schumpeterian Perspective', in G. López-Casasnovas, B. Rivera and L. Currais (eds), *Health and Economic Growth. Findings and Policy Implications*, Cambridge, MA: MIT Press.

Lucas, R. (1988), 'On the Mechanics of Economic Development', *Journal of Monetary Economics*, **22**(1), 3–42.

Lucifora, C. (1994), 'Determinazione del salario in Italia: una rassegna della letteratura empirica. Il contributo dell'analisi con microdati', in C. Dell'Aringa (ed.), *La determinazione del salario*, Napoli: Edizioni Scientifiche Italiane.

Manacorda, M. (2000), 'The Evolution of Return to Education in Italy, 1978–1992: Changing Institutions or Changing Supply and Demand?', in R.B. Freeman (ed.), *Inequality Around the World*, New York: Palgrave Macmillan.

Miguel, E. (2005), 'Health, Education, and Economic Development', in G. López-Casasnovas, B. Rivera and L. Currais (eds), *Health and Economic Growth. Findings and Policy Implications*, Cambridge, MA: MIT Press.

Mincer, J (1974), *Schooling, Experience, and Earnings*, New York: NBER.

Peretto, P.F. (2003), 'Fiscal Policy and Long-run Growth in R&D-based Models with Endogenous Market Structure', *Journal of Economic Growth*, **8**(3), 325–47.

Psacharopoulos, G. (1994), 'Returns to Investment in Education: a Global Update', *World Development*, **22**(9), 1325–43.

Rebelo, S.T. (1991), 'Long-Run Policy Analysis and Long-Run Growth', *Journal of Political Economy*, **99**(3), 500–521.

Romer, P.M. (1986), 'Increasing Returns and Long-Run Growth', *Journal of Political Economy*, **94**(5), 1002–37.

Romer, P.M. (1990), 'Endogenous Technological Change', *Journal of Political Economy*, **98**(5), 71–101.

Romer, P.M. (1994), 'The Origins of Endogenous Growth', *Journal of Economy Perspective*, **8**(1), 3–22.

Sala-i-Martin, X. (2005), 'On the Health-Poverty Trap', in G. López-Casasnovas, B. Rivera and L. Currais (eds), *Health and Economic Growth. Findings and Policy Implications*, Cambridge, MA: MIT Press.

Scott, M.F. (1992), 'Policy Implications of a New View of Economic Growth', *Economic Journal*, **102**(412), 622–32.

Shaw, K.G. (1992), 'Policy Implications of Endogenous Growth Theory', *Economic Journal*, **102**(412), 611–21.

Soares, R.R. (2005), 'Mortality Reductions, Educational Attainment, and Fertility Choice', *American Economic Review*, **95**(3), 580–601.

Solow, R. (1956), 'A Contribution to the Theory of Economic Growth', *Quarterly Journal of Economics*, **70**(1), 65–94.

Turnovsky, S.J. (1996), 'Optimal Tax, Debt and Expenditure Policies in a Growing Economy', *Journal of Public Economics*, **60**(1), 21–44.

Turnovsky, S.J. (2000), 'Fiscal Policy, Elastic Labour Supply, and Endogenous Growth', *Journal of Monetary Economics*, **45**(1), 185–210.

Van Zon, A. and J. Muyshen (2001), 'Health and Endogenous Growth', *Journal of Health Economics*, **20**(2), 169–85.

Willis, R.J. and S. Rosen (1979), 'Education and Self-selection', *Journal of Political Economy*, **87**(5), S7–S36.

Willis, R.J. (1986), 'Wage Determinants: A Survey and Reinterpretation of Human Capital Earnings Function', in O. Ashenfelter and R. Layard, *Handbook of Labor Economics*, Amsterdam: North Holland.

Zagler, M. and G. Durneker (2003), 'Fiscal Policy and Economic Growth', *Journal of Economic Surveys*, **17**(3), 397–418.

11. Unemployment in a system of labour-managed firms

Bruno Jossa

11.1. INTRODUCTION

The problem we set out to discuss in this chapter is the idea that worker control tends to increase, rather than reduce, unemployment. This idea seems to be prevailing in the published literature and is grounded on four main assumptions (in the chapter democratic firms, labour-managed firms and cooperative firms are considered to be synonyms).

The first of these is the argument that the higher capital–labour ratios required for (short-term) equilibrium in labour-managed versus capitalistic firms at equal capital accumulation conditions will result in higher unemployment levels in a system of democratically managed firms (see Ward, 1958 and Vanek, 1970 ch. 2).[1]

The second is the idea that the supply curve of a producer cooperative operating in conditions of perfect competition has a decreasing slope for in such a situation unemployment may increase, rather than diminish, at each rise in demand. In fact, although extensive criticism by several authors has deprived Ward's 'perverse' supply curve theory of much of its former clout (see, among others, Domar, 1966; Sen, 1966; Horvat, 1967; Berman, 1977; Steinherr and Thisse, 1979a and 1979b; Conte, 1980; Brewer and Browning, 1982; Sertel, 1982 and 1987; Miyazaki and Neary, 1983 and Hansmann, 1996, pp. 84–5), the argument that every upsurge in demand in a labour-managed system actually generates fewer jobs than it would in a system of capitalistic firms is still accepted in the economic literature.[2]

Thirdly, the assumed higher unemployment levels of a labour-managed economy are traced to a tendency to underinvest which results in diminished job creation. Although Furubotn and Pejovich's (1970a, 1970b, 1972 and 1973) criticism of the labour-managed firm with respect to this problem has been even more forcefully confuted than the previous one, the opinion that a system of democratic firms tends to generate structural unemployment is nonetheless still widely shared.

The fourth, even stronger argument is the investment funding issue, i.e. the obstacles that democratic firms are assumed to face when it comes to raising funds (see Drèze, 1989, chapter IV and 1993, pp. 257–62; Bowles and Gintis, 1993; Putterman, 1993; Dow, 1993 and 1998).

To clarify this point, we recall Meade's well-known contention (see Meade, 1972 and 1979) that employment opportunities for those in search of jobs in a labour-managed economy are even more directly linked to the creation of new firms than they are in a capitalistic system. While it is true that rises in aggregate demand, far from generating fresh jobs, may induce existing firms to lay off some of their workers, it is first and foremost by setting up new business firms that a worker-controlled system can create more employment opportunities. And theorists of the funding difficulties of a labour-managed firm hold these difficulties to be particularly severe at the start-up stage.

For all these reasons, labour management is said to exacerbate, rather than help solve the employment issue. But is this position correct? The case of Yugoslavia, where unemployment rose after the collapse of self-management, would rather speak in support of the opposite view (Horvat, 2000, p. 18). Be that as it may, this chapter is intended to discuss the complex facets of this issue from a theoretical point of view and in order to do so, we will separately address the following three cases: 1) high-wage unemployment, 2) Keynesian unemployment, and 3) structural unemployment.

The chapter is organised as follows: The second section deals with high-wage unemployment, and makes it clear that most of today's unemployment would be non-existent in a system of labour-managed firms since these do not pay wages proper. The third section discusses the assumption that the applicability of (what Keynes termed) the 2nd postulate of classical theory to a labour-managed economy would rule out Keynesian unemployment altogether. Section 11.4 analyses the obstacles to full employment as theorised by Kalecki for a capitalistic system, while Section 11.5 dwells on the effects of the absence of a Phillips curve in a system of producer cooperatives. Sections 11.6 and 11.7 analyse forms of structural unemployment in a system of democratic firms with the aim of providing evidence that in a system entirely formed of labour-managed firms structural unemployment would not exceed its present level in a capitalistic system. Section 11.8 sets forth our conclusions.

11.2. CLASSICAL UNEMPLOYMENT

As is well known, mainstream theorists tend to assume that in capitalistic systems unemployment is mainly caused by high labour costs. From among the best-known theoretical approaches to high-wage unemployment, let us mention the following three:

a) efficiency wage theory;
b) insider–outsider theory;
c) path-dependence theory;

and argue that none of the types of unemployment theorised by these approaches would apply under labour management, a system which by definition incurs no labour costs.

To start with, we sum up the main points of efficiency wage theory as reported in Yellen (1984), Stiglitz (1986) and Weiss (1990). As suggested by these authors, one reason why wages are deliberately kept high is to induce personnel to work hard and with great commitment, for workers who are well paid feel rewarded and – as Akerlof and others put it – tend to remunerate the 'partial gift' of a higher pay with the 'partial gift' of greater commitment to their tasks. This is termed the *incentive effect* (see, among others, Akerlof, 1982 and 1984 and Burow and Summers, 1986). The second major element of this theory is the *turnover effect*, according to which firms pay high wages in an effort to retain the personnel they have, i.e. to avoid incurring the substantial training and other costs associated with hiring new workers (see, among others, Stiglitz, 1974 and 1985; Hall, 1975; Schlicht, 1978 and Salop, 1979). An even more important factor seems to be the *selection effect*, which stems from the firm's wish to attract, and retain, the best workers available (see, among others, Weiss, 1980 and Malcomson, 1981). These three effects concordantly entail fixing the equilibrium wage above the level at which labour demand would equal labour supply.

Both capitalistic and labour-managed firms tend to avert personnel turnovers and sundry other costs incurred in replacing workers with others and to attract and retain the best labour force available. However, unlike what happens in capitalism a labour-managed firm cannot attain these ends by paying its partners higher wages since these earn, not wages proper, but a predetermined percentage rate of the firm's income. It goes without saying that a labour-managed firm cannot attract given workers by assigning them a greater rate of its income than it has originally agreed to pay that category of workers without automatically reducing the percentage rate assigned to the remaining workforce.

Moreover, while the discipline effect stemming from the workers' fear of being laid off is certainly no less an option in democratic firms than in capitalistic ones, no discipline effect can be generated by increasing the income levels of the partners of a cooperative and no high-wage unemployment of the type suggested in efficiency wage theory is consequently envisaged in a worker-controlled economy.

As to the insider–outsider approach, it is known to conceive of the labour market as split into two parts and assume that wage levels are determined by insiders only. As the dominant position of insiders is generally explained with high layoff and hiring costs, the existence of trade unions is not an essential prerequisite for the validity of this theoretical approach. An additional point to be emphasised is that outsiders do not automatically become insiders on first joining a firm. As layoffs are generally governed by the 'last in, first out' rule, it is only those who have been working for the firm for some time that can feel safe from layoff risks when wages begin to rise. And this is why wages will often soar to levels far above those that would guarantee full employment.

The main rationale behind this theoretical approach is that cooperation within the manufacturing process increases in proportion to the team spirit prevailing within the firm. In the opinion of Lindbeck and Snower, this may account for the observation that even in periods of high unemployment workers face little unfair competition from workers prepared to put up with lower pay. The reason why firms seldom deem it expedient to replace existing workers with others ready to accept lower wages, they argue, is the fear that insiders resenting this unfair practice may prove less cooperative with the newcomers. As Lindbeck and Snower put it, outsiders themselves refrain from underbidding on the assumption that they would be harassed by insiders and treated as scabs intending to 'steal other people's jobs'. In other words, the fact that insiders may fail to cooperate with newcomers may greatly affect the productivity rates of newcomers, which means that not only workers, but even firms will assume that wage cuts are not in their best interests (see Lindbeck and Snower, 1982, 1985, 1986a, 1986b, 1988a and 1988b and Lindbeck, 1993). In the opinion of Solow (1990, p. 37), this formidable finding accounts for most classical unemployment from high wages.

As is well known, one major point of Ward and Vanek's producer cooperative theory is the opposition of insiders to the hiring of more workers for reasons of self-interest, i.e. to avoid cuts on their incomes. At first sight, this would appear to back up the assumption that the insider–outsider approach can be extended to a system of democratic firms as well. In fact, as incomes in a producer cooperative are determined by the market, insiders in these firms can hardly be assumed to step up their incomes to levels that would stand in the way of the entry of more workers.

The point that these reflections are intended to make is that even insider–outsider theorists associate unemployment with high labour costs and that this is in itself enough to rule out that the kind of unemployment they theorise is an option in a system of democratic firms.

Turning to path-dependence theory, one major assumption behind this approach is that the rate of growth in money wages tends to be fixed at exactly that level at which the earnings of the existing workforce can be maximised without entailing layoffs of insiders or new hires. In other words, based on this theory it is assumed that those in employment drive up wages to levels at odds with the creation of new jobs (see Blanchard and Summers, 1986, 1987 and 1988).

The favourable reception of this and the previous two theoretical approaches (along with others that have not been mentioned in this chapter) is ultimately responsible for the widespread opinion, in economic thought, that most of today's unemployment is to be traced to high wages.

A preliminary conclusion possible at this stage is that a democratic firm system would offer the far from negligible advantage of doing away with all the unemployment which, based on these theories, is assumed to stem from high labour costs.

11.3. KEYNESIAN UNEMPLOYMENT

Distinguishing between 'cooperative economies' and 'entrepreneur economies', in the 1933 version of what was later to develop into *The General Theory* Keynes argued that the former were governed by Say's law and were not subject to fluctuations in aggregate demand. This would appear to justify the assumption that involuntary unemployment is typical of a market economy founded on hired labour. In Keynes's opinion, in a cooperative economy 'the factors of production are rewarded by dividing up in agreed proportions the actual output of their cooperative effort' (Keynes, 1933, p. 77), and when this happens, the second postulate of classical theory will apply and the number of hours worked tends to equate the marginal productivity of labour with its marginal disutility level (Keynes, 1933, pp. 77 and 101).

This belief in the validity of the law of markets in a cooperative economy induced Keynes to argue that 'the distinction between a co-operative economy and an entrepreneur economy bears some relation to a pregnant observation made by Karl Marx' which runs that 'the nature of production in the actual world is not, as economists seem often to suppose, a case of C-M-C', that is, of exchanging commodities (or effort) for money in order to obtain another commodity or effort, 'but an instance of M-C-M', i.e. a situation in which money is exchanged for commodities in order to obtain more money (1933, p. 81). Keynes' categorisation of a cooperative economy as an instance of C-M-C sheds added light on his belief that overproduction crises were closely associated with capitalistic economies and were impossible in cooperative economies.

In fact, Keynes likened the system he had termed a 'cooperative economy' to a 'natural economy'; but although he failed to expatiate on this subject and his reflections on this point are, admittedly, all but easy to interpret, it seems clear that his definition of a cooperative economy does not appreciably depart from what today is termed a system of production cooperatives or labour-managed firms.

Coming to Keynes's train of reasoning in 1933, it is worth emphasising that it is shared by more than one author (see, *inter alia*, Rotheim, 1981 and D'Acunto, 2000) and that Rotheim went so far as to contend that most of the criticisms against *The General Theory* would never have been raised if Keynes had opted for the publication of its 1933 version (Rotheim, 1981, p. 571). For our part, there can be little doubt that fluctuations in aggregate demand are possible both in worker-controlled and in capitalistic economies since the investment function of a democratic firm (of the LMF type) does not substantially differ from that of a capitalistic firm. Nonetheless, no Keynesian unemployment will normally arise in a system of democratic firms due to the applicability of the 2nd postulate of classical theory.

The 2nd postulate of classical theory applies to a system of democratic firms because workers who are free to organise their firm at their will tend to work exactly that number of hours at which their satisfaction is maximised, i.e. at which the income generated by the last hour of work equates the marginal disutility entailed in the effort required by the last hour of work (as stated by this postulate).

However, as the 2nd postulate of classical theory is fully applicable to a labour-managed firm only if workers are found to have the same preferences, its application is restricted to workers with average preferences and, as such, representative of all the firm's partners. This begs the question: what if the preferences of partners diverge? In this case, the firm will have the option of leaving individual workers free to work the amount of hours that best suits their respective needs, or passing a majority resolution to impose a fixed working day on the whole of the workforce. In the former case, the firm will face obvious difficulties; above all, if expectations of individual workers concerning the responses of the other partners are of the Cournot type (i.e. if they think that their own choices will hardly influence those of their fellow-workers), the firm's equilibrium and efficiency levels are likely to be seriously undermined. As pointed out by Berman (1977) in this case those partners who are paid in proportion to the hours worked will not deem it in their interests to work until the marginal disutility of their labour equals the marginal utility of their product (see Berman, 1977). Hence, the most reasonable conclusion seems to be that firms will opt for an equal working day for the whole workforce (although this determines that the 2nd postulate will only apply to partners representative of the average preferences of the workforce as a whole).[3]

In the light of these reflections, we will now ask ourselves what would happen in a democratic firm system that is subject to the 2nd postulate (with the above limitations) but not to Say's law. How would a cooperative firm respond to a fall in aggregate demand?

In a system not subject to Say's law but whose national income is determined in Keynesian terms, each fall in aggregate demand will reduce the equilibrium value of the aggregate hours worked. Provided layoff resolutions are adopted at meetings or, in other words, in the best interests of the workforce, in such a system it is difficult to think that workers will consent to the dismissal of their fellow-partners. Indeed, as a lay-off resolution passed by the majority of the partners of a labour-managed firm would trigger tensions and mutual mistrust within the team and interfere with regular work processes, it is far more probable that the meeting would not authorise any layoffs for fear of undermining the climate of solidarity within the firm (see Vanek, 1972, pp. 144–55; Neuberger and James, 1973 and Berman, 1997, p. 130).[4] Thus there are reasons to assume that a democratic firm will sooner opt for a shorter working week than dismiss any of its workers. No involuntary unemployment will ensue in this case; on the contrary, those already in employment will preserve their jobs, though all of them will be working fewer hours.

When Meade (1980, pp. 93–6), Steinherr and Thiesse (1979a and 1979b) and Brewer and Browning (1982) investigated the implications of layoff resolutions in cooperative firms, they took it for granted that the length of the working day would be fixed by law; but although they did not tackle the team solidarity issue, they concluded that the workers of a democratic firm would generally not find it convenient to authorise any layoffs. In particular, Brewer and Browning suggested that candidates for layoffs would have to be designated by drawing lots and that the magnitude likely to be maximised in the workers' layoff resolution was not the average income of those expected to be employed in the firm at the end of the process, but the average income of the partners on the payroll at the time of the vote. In their opinion, if those at risk of layoff had material prospects of getting jobs elsewhere or could safely rely on state subsidies, the magnitude that the voting partners were likely to maximise upon passing a layoff resolution was the firm's (post-layoff) income plus the prospective incomes of those laid off. As demonstrated by Brewer and Browning (but it is also intuitively obvious) in such a case, if all the workers have equal prospects of getting jobs outside the firm,[5] a layoff resolution would only be adopted when the marginal productivity of work in the labour-managed firm comes short of the income level estimated for those facing layoff.

A simpler, but probably even more interesting case is that in which workers facing layoff are thought to have no prospects of earning incomes in the future. Based on the above-mentioned rule, no layoffs will be deemed expedient in this case so long as the marginal productivity of work is more than nil. In other words, in the case under review the labour-managed firm will pass a layoff resolution only when the resulting lower employment level would not result in a drop in the firm's aggregate output; and, as there are reasons to believe that the marginal productivity of labour will remain positive even in a recessionary phase, in such a situation the workers will not resolve to lay off any of their partners.

The rationale behind this conclusion is simple and intuitive: if the partners of a labour-managed firm face the same layoff risks and have reasons to assume that those dismissed will be unable to earn incomes outside the firm, they will quite naturally think it in their interests to maximise the expected average income level of all voters.

As pointed out above, the most interesting hypothesis is a variable working week whose length would be left to the decision of the individual partners based on their respective needs. In such a case, as we have argued, in periods of slack demand the workers of a democratic firm opt for a reduced working week for all of them, rather than lay off their partners.[6]

The reflections developed so far concordantly suggest the conclusion that no involuntary Keynesian unemployment can exist in a system of democratic firms.[7]

11.4. KALECKI'S APPROACH TO FULL EMPLOYMENT

Coming back to efficiency-wage and discipline-effect theory, its authors might have drawn it from a 1943 article by Kalecki which is often rated as 'deservedly famous' (see, *inter alia*, Salvati, 1981), but which they hardly ever take the trouble of quoting. This article, which Caffé (1979, p. 14)[8] has described as 'acute and revealing', will be discussed in a separate section because it includes a cogent argument in support of the employment-boosting potential of a labour-managed system. Kalecki's starting-point is the fact that industrialists, though welcoming wider markets for their goods, often oppose demand-boosting public spending policies launched to further employment because they are inimical to public policies. To account for this apparent contradiction, Kalecki ascribes the resistance of industrialists to employment-boosting spending policies to three main causes: a) an aversion to public intervention in the economy in general; b) a strong dislike of measures purposely aiming to regulate employments levels and the labour market; c) the social and political changes associated with long periods of full employment. Let us emphasise straight away that none of these oppositions to public policies would apply in a cooperative system, for as soon as the government is no longer felt to be the expression of the capitalistic class, the workers of democratic firms operating in a class-conflict-free context would not only deem it in their interests not to oppose public intervention in the economy, but would even welcome any such intervention provided it aims to further full employment.

In greater detail, Kalecki's comments on the arguments against public spending in a) and b) are as follows. To a large extent – Kalecki argued – employment levels in a *laissez-faire* system are positively related to trust, since economic crises are often caused by lack of confidence in the future development of the economy and concomitant falls in private investment. As a result, capitalists are indirectly able to exercise powerful control over government policies: any moves that may interfere with this feeling of confidence should be carefully avoided for fear of depressing the economy (Kalecki, 1943, p. 166). And it is possible to add that one major effect of the close link between confidence and employment is to refrain workers and their unions from stepping up their demands on the assumption that risks of strikes may alarm entrepreneurs and that these may respond to excessive rises in labour costs by cutting investment resources. Kalecki's conclusion was that a generalised belief in the power of the government to boost employment at will would deprive industrialists of their control over government policies (for in periods of faltering confidence the government could easily restore a climate of trust by means of boosts in public spending).

Kalecki's argument with regard to point c) is even more forceful. Assuming that the government could effectively handle the opposition of the industrial class, he argued, 'the social and political changes likely to be triggered by the maintenance of full employment would promptly fuel fresh protests from the business world' (Kalecki, 1943, p. 168). Consistent with this rationale, modern efficiency wage theorists have made it clear that no discipline effect will result from layoff risks in conditions of full employment, since workers losing their jobs would easily find employment elsewhere. Moreover, in long-term full employment conditions trade unions would gain in power, workers would look to the future with greater confidence and the working class and its union representatives would step up their demands.

In Kalecki's opinion (ibid.), brisk demand in markets, the prerequisite for full employment, undoubtedly adds to profits, but as industrial operators value order in the workplace even higher than rewarding bottomline results, at least in the short term they will put up with slack demand and lesser profits so long as this will enable them to secure control and trim down demand for higher wages.

To the extent Kalecki's line of reasoning is correct, the added strength the working class is thought to gain in periods of boom goes to confute the Marxian argument that the revolutionary thrust of the working class is inversely related to levels of prosperity. Hence it is not surprising that Kalecki's arguments have been described 'as a direct refutation of Marx's argument that thriving trade and industrial activities weaken the confrontational spirit of workers' (Morley-Fletcher, 1986, p. XIV).

11.5. UNEMPLOYMENT AND THE PHILLIPS CURVE

The argument that a system of cooperatives is likely to ensure full employment may receive confirmation from the debate on the Phillips curve.

One of the generally accepted macroeconomic principles is the idea that the short-term Phillips curve is decreasing, i.e. that an inverse relation exists between wage rate increases and unemployment levels (see Mankiw, 2001). There is less agreement concerning the long-period Phillips curve, because Tobin (1972) and others continue to hold its slope to be decreasing, instead of vertical, even in the long run.

As a rule, a decreasing Phillips curve entails that unemployment and inflation are two antithetical ills and that there is no way of reducing one without accelerating the other. And as inflation is generally held to be a danger, it has long been customary to shape monetary policies geared towards controlling inflation even at the cost of driving up unemployment. As a result, it may be argued that unemployment is often the effect of economic policies which drive up unemployment for the sake of inhibiting inflation.

Today, there is widespread agreement that a vertical long-period Phillips curve identifies an equilibrium income level at which inflation and deflation are both ruled out. However, while monetarists hold that this level is the NRU, a natural rate of unemployment almost concordantly assumed to be voluntary (i.e. caused by the search for jobs), most Keynesians tend to argue that this equilibrium income level is a NAIRU ('non-accelerating inflation rate of unemployment'), at which unemployment is, for the most part, involuntary.

The Phillips curve with a NAIRU reflects social conflict between capital and labour and has been elucidated by Rowthorn (1977) and Carlin and Soskice (1990), among others. It rests on the assumption that the 'equilibrium' income at which prices neither increase nor diminish is the unemployment level at which wage-driven price increases make up for productivity-driven price drops. From this perspective, equilibrium unemployment is involuntary because the bargaining power of unions increases at each rise in employment and wages are driven up beyond levels that would be compatible with labour productivity rates of growth. In such a situation the full employment hypothesis becomes unrealistic because the deflationary policies that the government would have to launch in order to reduce the rises in wages and prices resulting from the added power of organised workers would promptly generate unemployment.

From what has been stated so far it follows that one major advantage of a system of cooperatives is to rule out the Phillips curve altogether. In the absence of wages, any rise in incomes would reduce unemployment without driving up monetary wages and prices in their wake. And in a conflict-free context the government could shape expansionist monetary and fiscal measures and employment–boosting policies without igniting those social conflicts which trigger inflation.

In short, in the light of the Phillips curve theory Kalecki's 1943 argument can be re-formulated in line with the idea that Keynesian expansionist policies can be used to secure full employment in a system of cooperatives because rises in income in such a system do not generate levels of social conflict at which inflation must necessarily accelerate (and do not oblige the government to put in place deflationary policies).

In even more general terms, it may be argued that full employment would be the rule in a cooperative system. Given the absence of a Philips curve, it would no longer be necessary to put up with rises in unemployment for the sake of reducing inflation, for unemployment and inflation would cease to be antithetical ills and governments would always be free to launch full employment policies.

11.6. STRUCTURAL UNEMPLOYMENT AND OBSTACLES TO CAPITAL ACCUMULATION IN THE DEMOCRATIC FIRM

From the reflections developed in the previous section it may be concluded that structural unemployment is the only possible type of unemployment in a system of democratic firms. This begs the question: would structural unemployment exceed the present level? As mentioned in the opening section, there is widespread agreement that structural unemployment in a system of democratic firms would soar far above its present levels in capitalistic systems for two reasons: a) the assumed tendency of democratic firms to underinvest; and b) the difficulties democratic firms are held to face in raising investment funds.

Based on the abundant literature on the underinvestment issue (Furubotn and Pejovich, 1970a, 1970b, 1972 and 1973; Furubotn, 1971, 1976 and 1980; Vanek, 1970, pp. 296–303, 1971a, 1971b and 1975), today it seems correct to argue that firms of the LMF type do not underinvest (see Jensen and Meckling, 1979; Jossa, 1988 and Jossa and Casavola, 1993).

The difficulties faced by democratic firms in raising investment funds have been investigated in less detail. Two main arguments acquire relevance in this regard. Firstly, it is argued, non-capitalist borrowers such as the partners of democratic firms offer insufficient assurance to prospective financers; secondly, the labour-managed firm can neither issue equities nor freely self-finance itself (without becoming like a capitalistic firm), and there is ample evidence that financers are all the more willing to provide loans, the more the borrowing firm funds its investments out of its own resources (for those prepared to risk their own capital resources are obviously confident in the success of their business projects).

Although this objection has doubtless solid grounds, to attenuate its weight it is possible to argue that a self-managed firm can raise investment funds by issuing bonds in exchange for retained earnings and allotting them to its partners. In line with a celebrated distinction proposed by Vanek, self-financing firms are termed WMFs if they fund their investments out of their retained earnings and do not distribute labour incomes and capital incomes separately, and are classed as LMFs if they issue bonds for raising investment funds. As mentioned above, the underinvestment hypothesis applies to WMF-type firms only, but the debate on Vanek's WMF/LMF distinction has made it clear that a self-managed firm does not become a WMF solely because it funds its investments by retained earnings with the concurrent issuing of bonds underwritten by its partners.

Neither is there any need for the firm's bonds to be entirely purchased by the partners at their free will, for nothing can prevent a firm from passing a majority resolution providing for the allotment of part of its earnings to the partners in the form of bonds. This is a self-financing method which will neither change the firm from an LMF into a WMF nor generate underinvestment.

An additional way to tackle funding difficulties is to issue non-voting equities *or* variable-income bonds, as suggested by numerous authors (see, among others, Nutzinger, 1975, p. 181; Drèze, 1976, pp. 433–5; Vanek, 1977, pp. 226–8; McCain, 1977, p. 365; Jay, 1980; Thomas, 1990, pp. 176 ff.; Thomas and Defourny, 1990; Major, 1996 and Smith and Waldman, 1999). Voting equities only are incompatible with self-management, since the voting rights they vest in shareholders are quite naturally at odds with the principle that power to run the firm's business must be vested in workers on an exclusive basis.

Non-voting equities are also fully consistent with Drèze's approach to the investment funding difficulties discussed in this chapter, i.e. with his proposal that firms should enter into 'financing agreements' which would transfer part of the risks from the firm's partners to its financers. Based on Kalecki's 'increasing risk' principle, the risks taken by providers of funds increase in proportion to the part of the investment that is funded with loan capital (see Kalecki, 1937), so that risks of failure will be maximised in self-managed firms which fund their investments solely with loan capital.

In this connection, Drèze drew attention to the basic idea behind 'implicit contract theory'. In capitalistic firms it is known to be the rule for workers (who are less prepared to share risks with capitalists) to enter into implicit contracts whereby they tacitly accept lower wages in exchange for the employer's commitment to abstain from wage cuts in periods of crisis, i.e. in exchange for his/her acceptance of all the risks associated with business crises. Starting from the existence of implicit contracts in capitalism, Drèze argued that just as workers in capitalistic systems deem it in their interests to self-insure themselves against income fluctuation risks by renouncing part of their earnings, so the workers of a labour-managed economy could find it expedient to change their variable incomes into fixed incomes by entering into financing contracts that shift business risks onto capitalistic providers of funds.[9]

On closer analysis, however, the most forceful argument that goes to confute, if not altogether reverse, the assumption that investment funding difficulties are maximised in a labour-managed economy is associated with the reversal of the capital–labour relationship in labour-managed firms.

As is well known, whereas in a capitalistic economy it is 'capital' that hires labour, pays it a fixed income and appropriates the 'residual', in a democratic firm of the LMF type it is the workers that borrow capital, pay a fixed interest rate thereon and appropriate the 'residual'. As a result,

- in capitalistic systems, it is workers that take precedence over shareholders, in terms that they cash their wages during the production process and shareholders are only remunerated out of the residual, if any;
- in a labour-managed economy, it is loan capital providers that take precedence over workers, insofar as they are remunerated prior to workers and the latter are only paid after them, i.e. out of the residual.

Accordingly, providers of loan capital are better protected in a labour-managed system versus a capitalistic system;[10] and with all else assumed constant and unchanged, this single fact would suffice, in itself, to diminish the risks of loans to self-managed firms and make them appear more profitable than loans to capitalistic firms.

In our opinion, the long-ingrained idea that labour-managed firms face greater investment funding difficulties than capitalistic firms is first and foremost due to the lack of importance given to this weighty argument in the published literature.

11.7. SECOND-LEVEL COOPERATIVES

A common business risk hedging method today is portfolio diversification; and the issuance of equities is one way to attain this end. However, a similar risk diversification system could also be devised for a labour-managed system despite the ban on the issuance of equities.

Financers in a capitalistic system tend to diversify their investment portfolios by underwriting securities issued by several firms facing different levels of risk. Conversely, in a system of democratic firms workers living on the residual income of their firm appear indissolubly tied to the latter since they cannot work for more than one firm at the same time. In point of fact, to enable the partners of a democratic firm to participate in the lives of several firms it would be possible to devise a very simple institutional mechanism providing for the formation of 'second level' or 'holding' cooperative firms whose members are not individual workers, but cooperative firms themselves.

The second-level cooperative's workforce would consist of staff seconded to it from the affiliated cooperatives. Part of the earnings of this second-level cooperative would be distributed based on the quantity and specialization of the workforce thus seconded; the remaining income would be distributed to the affiliated cooperatives themselves. This method would help partition aggregate risks among all of them.

The second-level cooperative's capital resources would be raised in accordance with the procedures adopted in the first-level cooperative, but in the resulting pyramid of firms the second-level cooperative's financing problems would be eased since the firm would be in a position to rely on direct financing by its affiliates and/or on security lodged by them. A second-level cooperative negotiating a financing agreement would be doing so on behalf of the whole group and the business diversification thus achieved would reduce both the group's aggregate risk profile and the risks taken by the financers of the second-level cooperative's individual business projects.

Thanks to these second-level cooperatives, first-level LMF firms wishing to venture into high-risk business projects and/or boost their activities through capital-intensive productions otherwise beyond their reach would benefit from a protection mechanism analogous with the portfolio diversification method adopted by capitalistic entrepreneurs.[11]

Due to the risk diversification potential inherent in its approx. 71,000 member group structure, the Mondragon complex of cooperatives in Spain has never experienced any financing problems and has always had access to financial resources far in excess of its needs. The substantial funds managed by the group bank, the Caja Laboral Popular, have at all times been more than enough to meet the financing requirements of the whole complex. A 1994 report by the Caja provides evidence that no fewer than 16 concerns of the current size of the existing group could have been financed out of the resources it had available (see Lutz, 1997, pp. 1413–14).

11.8. CONCLUSION

In Marshall's words, a system of labour-managed firms offers two main advantages: 'the production of fine human beings' (Marshall, 1889, p. 228) and a more effective use of the working capabilities of most members of the working population. The cooperative movement – Marshall wrote – 'sets itself to develop the spontaneous energies of the individual while training him to collective action by the aid of collective resources and for the attainment of collective ends' (ibid., p. 227); and as the character of a human being 'has been moulded by his everyday work, and the material resources which he thereby procures, more than by any other influence, unless it be that of his religious ideals' (see Marshall, 1890, p. 1), this may act as a great character-forming stimulant to the working partners. Another basic advantage of cooperation emphasised by Marshall is the use of all those work capabilities that capitalism tends to waste. In a cooperative firm – he wrote – a worker produces, not for the benefit of another, but for his own, and this mobilises a huge potential for accurate and high-quality work that capitalism tends to stifle. 'In the world's history there has been one waste product, so much more important than all others that it has a right to be called THE WASTE PRODUCT. It is the higher abilities of many of the working classes' (see Marshall, 1889, p. 229; upper case in the original).

In point of fact, before we support the view that democratically managed firms can make the most of human abilities we would have to provide material evidence that a system of labour-managed firms is actually in a position to provide jobs to all those seeking employment and ensure full employment much more effectively than a capitalistic firm system can do. Marshall failed to provide any such evidence in the belief that the market vouchsafes full employment by its very nature. In the meantime, though, Keynesian theory has shown that this optimistic attitude is unrealistic and contemporary theory of producer cooperatives has generated the widespread belief that democratic firms offer fewer employment opportunities than their 'capitalistic twins'.

Hence, we have tried to offer the evidence that Marshall failed to provide by examining three possible types of involuntary unemployment:

a) high-wage unemployment;
b) Keynesian unemployment;
c) structural unemployment.

Our conclusions can be summed up as follows. The first of the above three types of unemployment does not apply to a system of democratic firms by definition; neither does Keynesian unemployment in consequence of the validity of the 2nd postulate of classical theory in a labour-managed economy. As far as structural unemployment is concerned, our reflections would suggest that it would not exceed its present levels in capitalistic economies. In point of fact, there is no denying that a system of self-managed firms will employ fewer workers than a system of capitalistic firms in analogous capital accumulation conditions, and it is also true that this additional source of structural unemployment might *prima facie* appear to be as serious an issue as the funding difficulties discussed in the previous sections of this chapter. However, these objections can be countered by emphasising that higher capital–labour ratios are required for short-term equilibrium only (see Vanek, 1970, pp. 27–34 and Drèze, 1985) and that production coefficients are now for the most part fixed and are likely to be all the more so in future; but it is especially thanks to the refutation of the investment funding difficulties hypothesis that we feel in a position to deny that structural unemployment would be higher in a labour-managed system.

The above reflections suggest a general, though fairly obvious conclusion which we nevertheless wish to set forth at this stage. Insofar as it is true that employment is a primary goal to be steadily and consistently pursued, and provided our approach in this chapter has been correct, it seems barely possible to argue that a capitalistic system as near as possible to the perfect-competition ideal is to be prioritised over worker control. In fact, the perfect-competition ideal is far from being realised either in a capitalistic economy or in a worker-controlled system. However, if a higher employment level is a goal to be pursued by any means, a system capable of attaining this end in the real-case scenario of today's world should take precedence despite the higher *per capita* incomes vouchsafed by capitalism (see, *inter alia*, Dahl, 1989, pp. 330–31).

NOTES

1. In a short-term perspective, it is commonly assumed that democratic firms operating in a perfect-competition environment tend to hire fewer workers than capitalistic firms under the same circumstances. In point of fact, there are reasons to believe that the opposite may apply in conditions of uncertainty and when workers look upon democratic firms as entailing greater risks than capitalistic companies (see Muzondo, 1979 and 1980).
2. Although Weitzman (1984) strongly recommends profit sharing, he strongly argues against worker participation in firm control on the assumption (suggested by Ward) that insiders tend to discriminate against outsiders.
3. For a more detailed analysis of this point, see Jossa and Cuomo (1997, pp. 193–202).
4. In the opinion of Ward (see Ward, 1958), implied, though widely accepted rules require that no majority resolutions should undermine the solidarity feelings linking worker to worker. This contention was countered by Robinson (1967). As a matter of fact in ex-Yugoslavia both hiring and layoff criteria were generally fixed by workers' councils.
5. This is especially the case when the only prospect offered to workers outside the firm is an unemployment subsidy paid by the government.
6. The idea that in periods of slack demand labour-managed firms will rather shorten the working week than reduce employment levels was first set forth in Berman (1977) and is consistent with the remark that in Italy and elsewhere 'cooperatives arose with the aim of controlling cases of excess labour supply and apportioning available work opportunities among the working population in such a way as to guarantee employment to everybody' (Becchio, 2001, p. 146).
7. It is argued by some that the retention of the excess workforce in periods of crisis may add to the risks taken by external providers of funds (Zafiris, 1986, p. 44).
8. Both this and the previous quote have been drawn from Morley-Fletcher (1986, p. XIII).
9. In Drèze's words, a 'paradoxical' or 'surprising' finding was that a self-managed firms could indifferently enter into a financing agreement fixing the dividends owed to providers of funds under given circumstances or into a labour contract specifying the work loads and wage rates of individual workers in the same situations (Drèze, 1989, pp. 92–3, and 1993, p. 260). In conditions of perfect information, either contract could be entered into on terms that would vouchsafe the same result, but in the event of an unanticipated business crisis the actuals-versus-budget shortfall would be charged to the account of financers in one case, and to the account of workers in the other.
10. 'The residually remunerated resource suppliers can be thought of as 'insuring' the suppliers of contractually paid resources for some of their risks' (Zafiris, 1986, p. 37).
11. This idea, which is based on the experience of the Spanish Mondragon group, was first suggested to me by Gaetano Cuomo.

REFERENCES

Akerlof, G.A. (1982), 'Labor Contracts as a Partial Gift Exchange', *Quarterly Journal of Economics*, **96**(4), 543–69.

Akerlof, G.A. (1984), 'Gift Exchange and Efficiency-Wage Theory: Four Views', *American Economic Review, Papers and Proceedings*, **74**(2), 79–83.

Becchio, G. (2001), 'Attilio Cabiati fra socialismo cooperativo e marginalismo', in M.E.L. Guidi and L. Michelini (eds), *Marginalismo e socialismo nell'Italia liberale: 1870–1925*, Milan: Feltrinelli.

Berman, M.D. (1977), 'Short Run Efficiency in the Labour-managed Firm', *Journal of Comparative Economics*, **1**(3), 1309–14.

Blanchard, O.J. and L.H. Summers (1986), 'Hysteresis and European Unemployment Problem', *NBER Macroeconomics Annual*, Cambridge, MA.

Blanchard, O.J. and L.H. Summers (1987), 'Hysteresis in Unemployment', *European Economic Review*, **31**, 288–95.

Blanchard, O.J. and L.H. Summers (1988), 'Beyond the Natural Rate Hypothesis', *European Economic Review*, **78**, 182–87.

Bowles, S. and H. Gintis (1993), 'Post-Walrasian Political Economy', in S. Bowles, H. Gintis and B. Gustafsson B. (eds), *Markets and Democracy: Participation, Accountability and Efficiency*, Cambridge: Cambridge University Press.

Brewer, A.A. and M.J. Browning (1982), 'On the Employment Decision of a Labour-managed Firm', *Economica*, **49**(194), 141–6.

Burow, J.I. and L.H. Summers (1986), 'A Theory of Dual Labor Markets with Applications to Industrial Policy, Discrimination, and Keynesian Unemployment', *Journal of Labor Economics*, **4**(3), 376–41.

Caffé, F. (1979), 'Prefazione' in A. Burchardt, M. Kalecki et al. (1979), *L'economia della piena occupazione*, Turin: Rosenberg e Sellier.

Carlin, W. and D. Soskice (1990), *Macroeconomics and the Wage Bargain*, Oxford: Oxford University Press.

Conte, M.A. (1980), 'On the Economic Theory of the Labour-Managed Firm in the Short Run', *Journal of Comparative Economics*, **4**(2), 173–83.

D'Acunto, S. (2000), 'Genesi ed evoluzione della domanda effettiva', *Studi economici*, **55**(70), 103–28.

Dahl, R.A. (1989), *Democracy and its Critics*, New Haven: Yale University Press.

Domar, E.D. (1966), 'The Soviet Collective Farm as a Producer Cooperative', *American Economic Review*, **56**(4), 734–57.

Dow, G. (1993), 'The Appropriability Critique of Transaction Cost Economics', in C. Pitelis (ed.), *Transaction Costs, Markets and Hierarchies*, Oxford: Blackwell.

Dow, G. (1998), 'Review of B. Jossa and G. Cuomo, "The Economic Theory of Socialism and the Labour-Managed Firm"', *Journal of Economic Literature*, **36**, 992–94.

Drèze, J.H. (1976), 'Some Theory of Labour Management and Participation', *Econometrica*, **44**(6), 1125–39.

Drèze, J.H. (1985), 'Labor Management and General Equilibrium', in D.C. Jones and J. Svejnar (eds), *Advances in the Economic Analysis of Participatory and Labor-Managed Firms*, Greenwich, CT: JAI Press, pp. 3–20.

Drèze, J.H. (1989), *Labour-Management, Contracts and Capital Markets. A General Equilibrium Approach*, Oxford: Basil Blackwell.

Drèze, J.H. (1993), 'Self-Management and Economic Theory: Efficiency, Funding and Employment', in P. Bardhan and J.E. Roemer (eds), *Market Socialism: The Current Debate*, New York: Oxford Economic Press, pp. 253–65.

Furubotn, E.G. (1971), 'Toward a Dynamic Model of the Yugoslav Firm', *Canadian Journal of Economics*, **4**(2), 182–97.
Furubotn, E.G. (1976), 'The Long-run Analysis of the Labor-managed Firm: an Alternative Interpretation', *American Economic Review*, **66**(1), 104–23.
Furubotn, E.G. (1980), 'The Socialist Labor-managed Firm and Bank-financed Investment: Some Theoretical Issues', *Journal of Comparative Economics*, **4**(4), 184–91.
Furubotn, E.G. and S. Pejovich (1970a), 'Tax Policy and Investment Decision of the Yugoslav Firm', *National Tax Journal*, **23**, 335–48.
Furubotn, E.G. and S. Pejovich (1970b), 'Property Rights and the Behavior of the Firm in a Socialist State: the Example of Yugoslavia', *Zeitschrift für Nationalökonomie*, **30**(5), 431–54.
Furubotn, E.G. and S. Pejovich (1972), 'Property Rights and Economic Theory: a Survey of Recent Literature', *Journal of Economic Literature*, **10**(4), 1137–62.
Furubotn, E.G. and S. Pejovich (1973), 'Property Rights, Economic Decentralization and the Evolution of the Yugoslav Firm 1965–72', *Journal of Law and Economics*, **16**(2), 275–302.
Hall, R.E. (1975), 'The Rigidity of Wages and the Persistence of Unemployment', *Brookings Papers in Economic Activity*, **6**(2), 301–50.
Hansmann, H. (1996), *The Ownership of Enterprise*, London: Harvard University Press.
Horvat, B. (1967), 'A Contribution to the Theory of the Yugoslav Firm', *Economic Analysis*, **1**(1–2), 7–28.
Horvat, B. (2000), 'Social Ownership', report presented at the 10th Conference of IAFEP, Trient, 6–8 July.
Jay, P. (1980), 'The Workers' Cooperative Economy', in A. Clayre (ed.), *The Political Economy of Cooperation and Participation: a Third Sector*, Oxford: Oxford Economic Press, pp. 9–45.
Jensen, M.C. and W.J. Meckling (1979), 'Rights and Production Functions: an Application to Labor-Managed Firms and Codetermination', *Journal of Business*, **52**(4), 469–506.
Jossa, B. (1988), 'Sul problema del sottoinvestimento delle imprese gestite dai lavoratori', preprint in Atti del V Convegno Scientifico Annuale dell'Associazione Italiana per lo Studio dei Sistemi Economici Comparati, Pavia (14–16 September), published in B. Jossa, *La democrazia nell'impresa*, Naples: Edizioni Scientifiche, 1999.
Jossa, B. and P. Casavola (1993), 'The Problem of Under-Investment in Firms Managed by Workers', in A.B. Atkinson (ed.), *Alternatives to Capitalism: The Economics of Partnership*, London: Macmillan.
Jossa, B. and G. Cuomo (1997), *The Economic Theory of Socialism and the Labour-Managed Firm*, Cheltenham, UK and Brookfield, USA: Edward Elgar.
Kalecki, M. (1937), 'The Principle of Increasing Risk', *Economica*, **4**(3), 440–47.
Kalecki, M. (1943), 'Political Aspects of Full Employment', *Political Quarterly*, **14**(4), 322–31, reprinted in *The Last Phase in the Transformation of Capitalism*, New York: Monthly Review Press.

Keynes, J.M. (1933), 'The Distinction Between a Cooperative Economy and an Entrepreneur Economy', in J.M. Keynes, *The Collected Writings of John Maynard Keynes*, vol. XXIX, London: Macmillan, 1979.

Lindbeck, A. (1993), *Unemployment and Macroeconomics*, Cambridge, MA: MIT Press.

Lindbeck, A. and D.J. Snower (1982), 'Involuntary Unemployment as an Insider–Outsider Dilemma', revised and reprinted under the title 'Wage Rigidity, Union Activity, and Unemployment', in W. Beckerman (ed.), *Wage Rigidity and Employment*, London: Duckworth, 1986.

Lindbeck, A. and D.J. Snower (1985), 'Explanations of Unemployment', *Oxford Review of Economic Policy*, **1**(2), 34–59.

Lindbeck, A. and D.J. Snower (1986a), 'Efficiency Wages versus Insiders-Outsiders', *European Economic Review*, **31**(1–2), 407–16.

Lindbeck, A. and D.J. Snower (1986b), 'Wage Setting, Unemployment and Insider–outsider Relations', *American Economic Review*, **76**(2), 235–39.

Lindbeck, A. and D.J. Snower (1988a), 'Cooperation, Harassment, and Involuntary Unemployment: an Insider–outsider Theory Approach', *American Economic Review*, **78**(1), 167–88.

Lindbeck, A. and D.J. Snower (1988b), *The Insider–Outsider Theory of Employment and Unemployment*, Cambridge, MA: MIT Press.

Lutz, M.A. (1997), 'The Mondragon Cooperative Complex: an Application of Kantian Ethics to Social Economics', *Journal of Social Economy*, **24**(12), 1404–21.

Major, G. (1996), 'Solving the Underinvestment and Degenerations Problem of Workers' Cooperatives: Non-voting and Vote-Weighted Value-Added Residual Shares', *Annals of Public and Cooperative Economics*, **6**(4), 545–601.

Malcomson, J.M. (1981), 'Unemployment and the Efficiency Wage Hypothesis', *Economic Journal*, **91**(364), 848–66.

Mankiw, N.G. (2001), 'The Inexorable and Mysterious Trade-off between Inflation and Unemployment', *Economic Journal*, **111**(471), C45–C61.

Marshall, A. (1889), 'Cooperation', reprinted in Marshall (1925).

Marshall, A. (1890,) *Principles of Economics*, 9th edn, London: Macmillan.

Marshall, A. (1925), edited by A.C. Pigou, *Memorials of Alfred Marshall*, London: Macmillan.

McCain, R.A. (1977), 'On the Optimum Financial Environment for Worker Cooperatives', *Zeitschrift für Nationalökonomie*, **37**(3–4), 355–84.

Meade, J.E. (1972), 'The Theory of Labour-Managed Firms and of Profit Sharing', *Economic Journal*, **82**(Supplement), 402–28.

Meade, J.E. (1979), 'The Adjustment Processes of Labour Cooperatives with Constant Returns to Scale and Perfect Competition', *Economic Journal*, **89**(356), 781–8.

Meade, J.E. (1980), 'Labour Cooperatives, Participation and Value-Added Sharing', in A. Clayre (ed.), *The Political Economy of Cooperation and Participation: a Third Sector*, Oxford: Oxford Economic Press, pp. 88–108.

Miyazaki, H. and H.N. Neary (1983), 'The Illyrian Firm Revisited', *Bell Journal of Economics*, **14**(1), 259–70.

Morley-Fletcher, E. (1986), 'Certezze per rischiare, competere per cooperare: una introduzione', in S. Veca et al., *Cooperare e competere*, Milan: Feltrinelli.

Muzondo, T.R. (1979), 'On the Theory of the Competitive Labor-Managed Firm under Price Uncertainty', *Journal of Comparative Economics*, **3**(2), 127–44.

Muzondo, T.R. (1980), 'On the Theory of the Competitive Labor-Managed Firm under Price Uncertainty: Reply', *Journal of Comparative Economics*, **4**(3), 342–44.

Neuberger, E. and E. James (1973), 'The Yugoslav Self Managed Enterprise: a Systematic Approach', in M. Bornstein (ed.), *Plan and Market: Economic Reforms in Eastern Europe*, New Haven: Yale University Press.

Nutzinger, H.G. (1975), 'Investment and Financing in a Labour-managed Firm and its Social Implications', *Economic Analysis and Workers' Management*, **9**(3–4), 181–201.

Putterman, L. (1993), 'Incentive Problems, Favoring Noncentralized Investment Fund Ownership', in P. Bardhan and J.E. Roemer (eds), *Market Socialism: The Current Debate*, New York: Oxford Economic Press.

Robinson, J. (1967), 'The Soviet Collective Farm as a Producer Cooperative: Comment', *American Economic Review*, **57**(1), 222–3.

Rotheim, R.J. (1981), 'Keynes' Monetary Theory of Value (1933)', *Journal of Post-Keynesian Economics*, **3**, 568–85.

Rowthorn, B. (1977), 'Conflict, Inflation and Money', *Cambridge Journal of Economics*, **1**(3), 215–39.

Salop, S.C. (1979), 'Strategic Entry Deterrence', *American Economic Review*, **69**, 335–8.

Salvati, M. (1981), 'Ciclo politico e onde lunghe. Note su Kalecki e Phelps Brown', *Stato e mercato*, **1**, 9–45.

Schlicht, E. (1978), 'Labour Turnover, Wage Structure and Natural Unemployment', *Zeitschrift für die Gesamte Staatswissenschaft*, **134**, 337–46.

Sen, A.K. (1966), 'Labour Allocation in a Cooperative Enterprise', *Review of Economic Studies*, **33**(4), 361–71.

Sertel, M.R. (1982), *Workers and Incentives*, Amsterdam: North Holland.

Sertel, M.R. (1987), 'Workers' Enterprise are not Perverse', *European Economic Review*, **31**(8), 1619–25.

Smith, S.C. and R.J. Waldmann (1999), 'Investment and Supply Effects of Industry-indexed Bonds: the Labor Managed Firm', *Economic Systems*, **23**(3), 245–67.

Solow, R. (1990), *The Labor Market as a Social Institution*, Oxford: Basil Blackwell.

Steinherr, A. and J.F. Thisse (1979a), 'Are Labour-Managers Really Perverse?', *Economic Letters*, **2**, 137–42.

Steinherr, A. and J.F. Thisse (1979b), 'Is There a Negatively-sloped Supply Curve in the Labour-Managed Firm?', *Economic Analysis and Workers' Management*, **13**, 23–33.

Stiglitz, J.E. (1974), 'Wage Determination and Unemployment in LDCs: the Labor Turnover Model', *Quarterly Journal of Economics*, **88**(2), 194–227.

Stiglitz, J.E. (1985), 'Equilibrium Wage Distribution', *Economic Journal*, **95**(379), 595–618.

Stiglitz, J.E. (1986), 'Theories of Wage Rigidity', in J.L. Butkiewicz, K.J. Koford and J.B. Miller (eds), *Keynes' Economic Legacy*, New York: Prager.

Thomas, A. (1990), 'Financing Worker Cooperatives in EC Countries', *Annals of Public and Cooperative Economics*, **61**, 175–211.

Thomas, H. and J. Defourny (1990), 'Financing Workers' Cooperatives and Self-managed Enterprises', *Special Issue of Annals of Public and Co-operative Economics*, **61**(2–3).

Tobin, J. (1972), 'Inflation and Unemployment', *Economic Journal*, **82**(327), 853–82.

Vanek, J. (1970), *The General Theory of Labor-Managed Market Economies*, Ithaca: Cornell University Press.

Vanek, J. (1971a), 'Some Fundamental Considerations on Financing and the Form of Ownership under Labor Management', reprinted in Vanek (1977, pp. 171–85).

Vanek, J. (1971b), 'The Basic Theory of Financing of Participatory Firms', reprinted in Vanek (1977, pp. 186–98).

Vanek, J. (1972), 'A General Theory of an Efficient Participatory Society', mimeo.

Vanek, J. (ed.) (1975), *Self-Management: Economic Liberation of Man*, Harmondsworth: Penguin Books.

Vanek, J. (1977), *The Labor Managed Economy: Essays by J. Vanek*, Ithaca: Cornell University Press.

Ward, B. (1958), 'The Firm in Illyria: Market Syndacalism', *American Economic Review*, **48**(4), 566–89.

Weiss, A. (1980), 'Job Queues and Layoffs in Labor Markets with Flexible Wages', *Journal of Political Economy*, **88**(3), 526–38.

Weiss, A. (1990), *Efficiency Wages: Models of Unemployment, Layoffs and Wage Dispersion*, Princeton, NJ: Princeton University Press.

Weitzman, M.L. (1984), *The Share Economy*, Cambridge, MA: Harvard University Press.

Yellen, J.J. (1984), 'Efficiency Wage Models of Unemployment', *American Economic Review, Papers and Proceedings*, **74**, 200–205.

Zafiris, N. (1986), 'The Sharing of the Firm's Risks between Capital and Labour', *Annals of Public and Cooperative Economics*, **57**(1), 35–46.

12. Regulated wage economy and taxation systems: a long-run welfare and growth theoretical analysis and a policy exercise

Luciano Fanti and Luca Gori

12.1. INTRODUCTION

There has been a protracted debate around the macroeconomic effects of the regulation of wages and the introduction of unemployment insurance benefits. Conventional wisdom, dating back to the seminal paper by Stigler (1946), holds that both may be harmful, mainly because they tend to reduce output, employment, labour supply and welfare. However, higher wages for non-specialised workers and benefits for unemployed people are often advocated for equity reasons. Another controversial debate in economics, especially in Italy in recent years, has concerned the taxation of capital income. Although some recent literature[1] has relaxed the efficiency-equity trade-off by showing that in some cases a minimum wage could even be welfare-improving regardless of its negative effect on unemployment, we note, however, that these models are neither concerned with standard public policies such as unemployment insurance systems and income taxation nor are they framed in the basic dynamic overlapping generations (OLG) model adopted in this chapter. Therefore, to the best of our knowledge there is no literature that formally explores the joint role played by policy interventions on the labour market on the one side – e.g., regulation of wages and unemployment insurance mechanisms – and on the tax system on the other. We explore how different taxation systems used to finance unemployment benefits as well as an amount of unproductive public expenditure affects both long-run output and welfare. We show that while taxing the income of young people (either in the form of wage taxes or in the form of lump-sum taxes) and applying tax burdens on firms (as a proportional-to-the-net-wage tax rate) always reduce output and welfare, switching from competitive-wage economies to regulated-wage economies with tax systems based on proportional consumption taxes, capital income taxes or lump-sum taxes incurred by the old to fund unemployment benefits may result in output and welfare gains. As an illustrative exercise, motivated by a recent political debate in Italy, in this chapter we only focused on the effects of an increased tax burden on capital income from 12.5 per cent to 20 per cent on output and welfare. In this work we evaluate a balanced budget fiscal reform according to which the increase in the capital income tax is accompanied by the introduction of both binding minimum wages and unemployment insurance benefit with a fixed replacement ratio. The revenues from the increased capital income tax are used to finance the unemployment benefit scheme rather than fund an additional amount of unproductive public expenditure. Under plausible values of technology and preference parameters, we show that our fiscal exercise improves the steady-state representative individual's lifetime welfare even with slightly higher minimum wages than the market-clearing wage.

However, the increased welfare in spite of a higher unemployment rate is only part of the story. By taking into account the important leisure values associated with unemployed time (for instance, leisure time, self-enrichment activities, education, home production and so on) it is easy to see that unemployment should be considered as a resource instead of damage for the whole economy. In other words, in our model a 50 per cent unemployment rate simply means that each individual working only for six months rather than the entire year is able to reach higher welfare levels than in the competitive-wage economy: in this sense the large amount of free time created by legislated wage minima may be thought to be a further step towards the realization of a 'utopia', namely liberation from the pain of working. In particular, the leisure time associated with unemployment may have straightforward economic effects as in the case of employing the unemployed time either for educational activities or for exploiting an existing backyard technology. For exploring the effects of the proposed fiscal reform even with an economic use of the leisure time associated with unemployment, we assume the existence of a home production technology with constant productivity (assumed to be lower than both the marginal productivity in the production sector and the binding minimum wage, such that nobody makes use of the home production technology unless they are unemployed). We show in this case that the higher the productivity of the home technology, the higher is the individual's welfare gain.

To sum up, our findings show that accompanying the increased capital income tax with legislated wage minima along with a sufficiently high replacement rate, by keeping the government budget balanced, may raise the long-run lifetime welfare. This result is magnified when a backyard technology exists. The chapter is structured as follows. In Sections 12.2 and

12.3 we present competitive-wage and regulated-wage economies, respectively, along with the corresponding steady state results. In Section 12.4 we introduce our proposal for reforming the labour market and then we compare minimum-wage and competitive-wage economies. In Section 12.5 we introduce a home technology. Finally, Section 12.6 makes some concluding comments.

12.2. THE MARKET-WAGE ECONOMY

We consider a standard dynamic general equilibrium OLG economy (e.g., Samuelson, 1958; Diamond, 1965) with a young population N_t growing at the constant rate n and closed to international trade, and where goods, capital and labour markets are competitive (as reference textbooks see Azariadis, 1993 and De La Croix and Michel, 2002).

12.2.1. Individuals

Each generation is represented by identical individuals who live for two periods. Only young individuals join the workforce supplying inelastically one unit of time and receiving wage income at the rate w_t. This income is used to consume and to save. During the second period of life they are retired and live on the proceeds of their savings (s_t). Old individuals earn a return (net of taxes) $1+r_{t+1}(1-\tau_{t+1,pc})$ on their investments when young, where r_{t+1} is the gross rate of return on savings from period t to period $t+1$ and $\tau_{t+1,pc}$ represents the capital income tax. The subscript pc is for perfect competition.. The lifetime utility of the representative individual born at time t is $U_t(c_t^y, c_{t+1}^o) = (c_t^y)^{1-\phi}(c_{t+1}^o)^{\phi}$, where c_t^y and c_{t+1}^o represent young-aged and old-aged consumption, and $0<\phi<1$ captures the importance in the welfare function of consuming when old relative to the utility of young-aged consumption. Each generation takes wage and interest rate on savings as given. Therefore, the maximisation of U_t subject to the intra-temporal constraints $c_t^y + s_t = w_t$ and $c_{t+1}^o = [1+r_{t+1}(1-\tau_{t+1,pc})]s_t$ gives

$$c_t^y = (1-\phi)w_t, \tag{12.1}$$

$$c_{t+1}^o = \phi\left[1+r_{t+1}\left(1-\tau_{t+1,pc}\right)\right]w_t. \tag{12.2}$$

The solution of the problem may also be expressed in terms of the savings function as:[2]

$$s_t = \phi\ w_t. \tag{12.3}$$

12.2.2. Firms

Identical firms in the economy act competitively and own a constant returns to scale Cobb–Douglas technology through which capital and labour are transformed into consumption goods. The representative profit-maximising firm hires aggregate capital stock (K_t) and labour supplied by young agents $(L_t = N_t)$ to determine aggregate production $Y_t = AK_t^{\alpha} L_t^{1-\alpha}$, where $A > 0$ is a scale parameter and $0 < \alpha < 1$ is the capital's weight in technology. Defining $k_t := K_t / N_t$ and $y_t := Y_t / N_t$ as capital and output per-capita respectively, the intensive form production technology is $y_t = Ak_t^{\alpha}$. Assuming total depreciation of capital at the end of each period and a unit price of total output, profit maximisation leads to the following marginal conditions for capital and labour, respectively:

$$r_t = \alpha A k_t^{\alpha-1} - 1, \tag{12.4}$$

$$w_t = (1-\alpha) A k_t^{\alpha}. \tag{12.5}$$

12.2.3. Government

The government levies and adjusts capital income taxes to fund at a balanced budget a fixed amount of unproductive public expenditure (g) per young individual. Therefore, the per-capita time-t government constraint is:

$$g = T_t, \tag{12.6}$$

where $T_t := \tau_{t,pc} \cdot r_t \cdot k_t$ are per-capita tax revenues.

12.2.4. Equilibrium

Using equation (12.6), the equilibrium in goods as well as in capital markets is:

$$(1+n) k_{t+1} = s_t, \tag{12.7}$$

and combining (12.7) with (12.3) and (12.5), the dynamic equilibrium sequence of capital is given by:

$$k_{t+1} = \frac{\phi}{1+n} (1-\alpha) A k_t^{\alpha}, \tag{12.8}$$

Steady-state implies $k_{t+1} = k_t = k^*$. Hence, the long-run (per-capita) stock of capital is:[3]

$$k_{pc}^{*}=\left(\frac{\phi(1-\alpha)A}{1+n}\right)^{\frac{1}{1-\alpha}}. \tag{12.9}$$

Substituting out k_{pc}^{*} into the intensive form production function and into equations (12.4) and (12.5) we get:

$$y_{pc}^{*}=A\left(\frac{\phi(1-\alpha)A}{1+n}\right)^{\frac{\alpha}{1-\alpha}}, \tag{12.10}$$

$$r_{pc}=\alpha A\left(k_{pc}^{*}\right)^{\alpha-1}-1, \tag{12.11}$$

$$w_{pc}=(1-\alpha)A\left(k_{pc}^{*}\right)^{\alpha}. \tag{12.12}$$

From equation (12.8), the transitional rate of economic growth is:

$$g_{pc}(k_t)=\frac{\phi}{1+n}(1-\alpha)Ak_t^{\alpha-1}-1. \tag{12.13}$$

An increase in the stock of capital reduces the transitional rate of long-run growth, and $g_{pc}(k)$ converges asymptotically to zero as k_t approaches to the steady-state.

12.3. THE REGULATED-WAGE ECONOMY

We consider an economy where the only departure from the model built up in the previous section is an imperfect labour market due to the existence of wage minima $(\underline{w})$[4] introduced by law. Therefore, the labour market does not clear and unemployment occurs.

12.3.1. Individuals

For any given minimum wage, depending on the demand for labour, the supplied workforce may be partially unemployed. If employed, the wage income is $\underline{w}$. If unemployed, the government provides an hourly unemployment insurance benefit such that $b(\underline{w}):=\gamma\ \underline{w}$, where $0<\gamma<1$ is the so-called replacement rate.[5] The aggregate unemployment rate is defined as $u_t=(N_t-L_t)/N_t$, where $L_t=(1-u_t)=N_t$ is labour demand. Thus, the individual maximisation problem for agents of generation t changes to become:

$$\max_{\{c_t^y, c_{t+1}^o\}} U_t\left(c_t^y, c_{t+1}^o\right) = \left(c_t^y\right)^{1-\phi}\left(c_{t+1}^o\right)^{\phi}$$

subject to

$$\begin{aligned} c_t^y + s_t &= \underline{w}(1-u_t) + \gamma \underline{w} u_t \\ c_{t+1}^o &= \left[1 + r_{t+1}\left(1-\tau_{t+1,mw}\right)\right]s_t \end{aligned}.$$

In this context a capital income tax at the rate $\tau_{mw} > \tau_{pc}$ is levied in each period by the government and used to fund the unemployment benefit system as well as the same amount of per-capita public spending as that of the competitive-wage economy (g) at balanced budget. The subscript *mw* is for minimum-wage economy.

Therefore, young-aged and old-aged consumption are given by:

$$c_t^{\,y}(\underline{w}) = (1-\phi)W_t(\underline{w}), \tag{12.14}$$

$$c_{t+1}^{\,o}(\underline{w}) = \phi\left[1 + r_{t+1}\left(1-\tau_{t+1,mw}\right)\right]W_t(\underline{w}), \tag{12.15}$$

where $W_t(\underline{w}) := \underline{w}[1-u_t(1-\gamma)]$ is the total income of the current young (given by the sum of the minimum wage for each employed hour plus the unemployment benefit for each unemployed hour).

The savings function therefore is simply:

$$s_t(\underline{w}) = \phi\ W_t(\underline{w}). \tag{12.16}$$

12.3.2. Firms

Equilibrium in the labour market implies $L_t = (1-u_t)N_t$. Therefore, the Cobb–Douglas technology changes to:

$$y_t = Ak_t^{\,\alpha}(1-u_t)^{1-\alpha}. \tag{12.17}$$

Standard profit maximisation leads to the following marginal conditions:

$$r_t = \alpha A\left(\frac{k_t}{1-u_t}\right)^{\alpha-1} - 1, \tag{12.18}$$

$$\underline{w} = (1-\alpha)A\left(\frac{k_t}{1-u_t}\right)^{\alpha}. \tag{12.19}$$

Once the wage has been fixed the real interest rate is exogenous, i.e., it does not depend on the level of the current stock of capital. In fact, exploiting (12.18) and (12.19) we get:

$$r(\underline{w})=\alpha A(\psi/\underline{w})^{\frac{1-\alpha}{\alpha}}-1, \tag{12.20}$$

where $\psi:=(1-\alpha)A$. An increase in $\underline{w}$ always reduces the real interest rate. Moreover, $r(\underline{w})<r_{pc}$ for any $\underline{w}>w_{pc}$. Using (12.19) the endogenous current unemployment rate is:

$$u_t(k_t,\underline{w})=1-(\psi/\underline{w})^{\frac{1}{\alpha}}\cdot k_t, \tag{12.21}$$

which is positively related with the minimum wage and strictly decreasing in the capital stock.

12.3.3. Government

Introducing minimum wages causes unemployment. Therefore, if the government has a publicly provided unemployment benefit scheme, there is the need to finance the payment of benefits. There are many ways to raise revenues to fund such a scheme. The extent to which a long-run welfare gain will be successful depends crucially upon the type of taxation used. Though without exhaustively exploring the entire range of possible taxation systems, we show that taxation systems burdening on the income of young people (e.g., a wage tax or a lump-sum tax) as well as burdening on firms (e.g., a proportional-to-wage contribution rate) always result in a reduction of both output per-capita and welfare (see Appendix 12A.1). By contrast, taxation systems based on consumption taxes, capital income taxes or lump-sum taxes incurred by the elderly may entail both output and welfare gains despite a positive unemployment rate.[6]

In this chapter we use only capital income taxes to assess the effects of our proposed fiscal reform on output per capita and individual welfare. In particular, we suppose that an increase in such a tax from 12.5 per cent to 20 per cent is accompanied both by wage minima as well as unemployment insurance benefits with a fixed replacement rate financed at balanced budget.

The government's strategy is to adjust capital income tax receipts so as to balance out the unemployment benefit expenditure and the same amount of per-capita unproductive public spending as that funded in the competitive-wage economy. Therefore, the time-t government constraint changes to:

$$\gamma\underline{w}\ u_t+g=\tau_{t,mw}\cdot r(\underline{w})\cdot k_t, \tag{12.22}$$

where $g=T_t=\tau_{t,pc}\cdot r_t\cdot k_t$.

12.3.4. Equilibrium

Given equation (12.22), the market clearing condition in goods as well as in capital markets is:

$$(1+n)k_{t+1}=s_t(\underline{w}), \tag{12.23}$$

and combining (12.23) with (12.16) we find:

$$(1+n)k_{t+1}=\phi\underline{w}\left[1-u_t(k_t,\underline{w})\cdot(1-\gamma)\right]. \tag{12.24}$$

Substituting out for $u_t(k_t,\underline{w})$ from (12.21), capital evolves over time according to the following first order linear difference equation:

$$k_{t+1}=\frac{\phi}{1+n}(1-\gamma)\psi^{\frac{1}{\alpha}}\underline{w}^{-\frac{1-\alpha}{\alpha}}k_t+\frac{\phi}{1+n}\gamma\underline{w}. \tag{12.25}$$

Steady state implies $k_{t+1}=k_t=k^*$. Therefore, the long-run unemployment rate, capital stock and output per-capita are given by:

$$u^*(\underline{w})=\frac{\underline{w}^{\frac{1-\alpha}{\alpha}}(1+n)-\phi\psi^{\frac{1}{\alpha}}}{\underline{w}^{\frac{1-\alpha}{\alpha}}(1+n)-\phi(1-\gamma)\psi^{\frac{1}{\alpha}}}, \tag{12.26}$$

$$k^*(\underline{w})=\frac{\phi\gamma\underline{w}^{\frac{1}{\alpha}}}{\underline{w}^{\frac{1-\alpha}{\alpha}}(1+n)-\phi(1-\gamma)\psi^{\frac{1}{\alpha}}}, \tag{12.27}$$

$$y^*(\underline{w})=\frac{A\phi\gamma\psi^{\frac{1-\alpha}{\alpha}}\underline{w}}{\underline{w}^{\frac{1-\alpha}{\alpha}}(1+n)-\phi(1-\gamma)\psi^{\frac{1}{\alpha}}}, \tag{12.28}$$

which are defined for any $\underline{w}\neq w_T$, where $w_T:=(1-\gamma)^{\alpha/(1-\alpha)}\cdot w_{pc}<w_{pc}$.[7]

It is possible to demonstrate[8] that: (1) a threshold minimum wage value which guarantees a higher steady-state stock of capital per capita in the minimum-wage economy than in the competitive-wage economy always exists; (2) provided that $\alpha>1-\gamma$ then the capital stock in the minimum-wage economy is always higher than in the competitive-wage economy whatever the minimum wage. The following Figures 12.1a and 12.1b display the behaviour of the long-run stock of capital and output per-capita for increasing minimum wages.

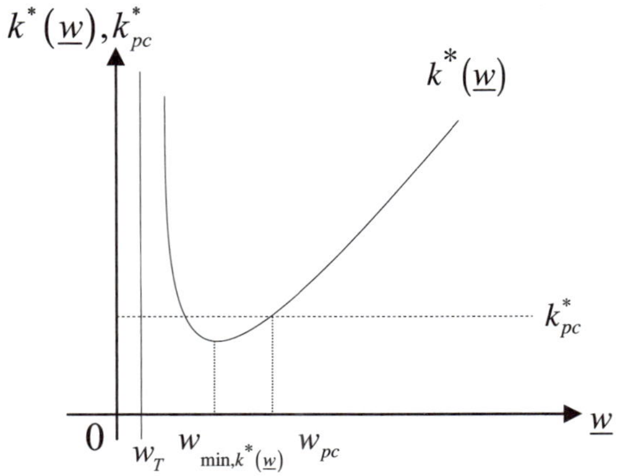

Figure 12.1a. Steady-state capital stock in regulated and market wage economies

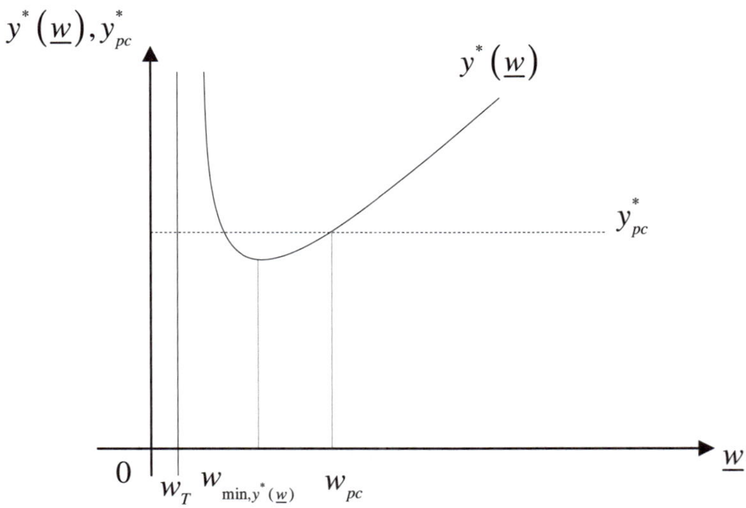

Figure 12.1b. Steady-state income in regulated and market wage economies

Solving equation (12.25) yields:

$$k_t = k_0 d^t + k^*(\underline{w}). \tag{12.29}$$

with $k_0 > 0$ given and $d := [\phi(1-\gamma)\psi^{(1/\alpha)}] / [(1+n)\underline{w}^{(1-\alpha)/\alpha}]$. Stability requires $d < 1$, that is $\underline{w} > w_T$. In this case $\lim_{t \to +\infty} k_t = 0^+$ and the economy converges towards the steady-state equilibrium, $k^*(\underline{w})$.

Multiplying both sides of (12.25) by $1/k_t$, the transitional rate of economic growth in the minimum-wage economy is given by:

$$g(k_t, \underline{w}) = \frac{\phi\gamma\underline{w}}{(1+n)k_t} + \frac{\phi(1-\gamma)\psi^{\frac{1}{\alpha}}}{(1+n)\underline{w}^{\frac{1-\alpha}{\alpha}}} - 1. \qquad (12.30)$$

As k_t approaches the steady state, $g(k, \underline{w})$ converges asymptotically to zero.

Figure 12.2 shows the locus of dynamic capital accumulation $k_{t+1} = f(k_t)$ in both competitive-wage and minimum-wage economies (see equations (12.8) and (12.25), respectively).

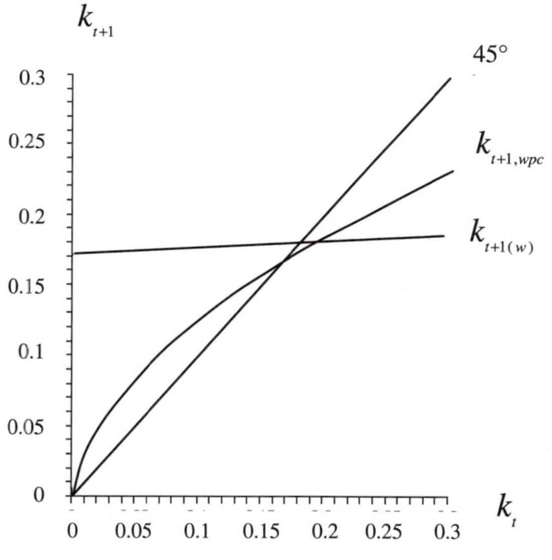

Figure 12.2. The dynamics of capital in competitive and minimum-wage economies. Parameter set: $A = 10$, $\alpha = 0.55$, $\phi = 0.10$, $\gamma = 0.95$ *and* $n = 0$

Figure 12.3 shows the behaviour of the transitional growth rate both in competitive-wage and regulated-wage economies (see equations (12.13) and (12.30), respectively): as can easily be seen during the transition towards the steady state the regulated-wage economy always grows at a rate higher than the competitive-wage economy and thus the corresponding steady-state stock of capital is greater. Note that along all the points of the transitional path, the minimum wage is always binding, that is, at any time t the condition $\underline{w} > w_{t,pc}$ holds.

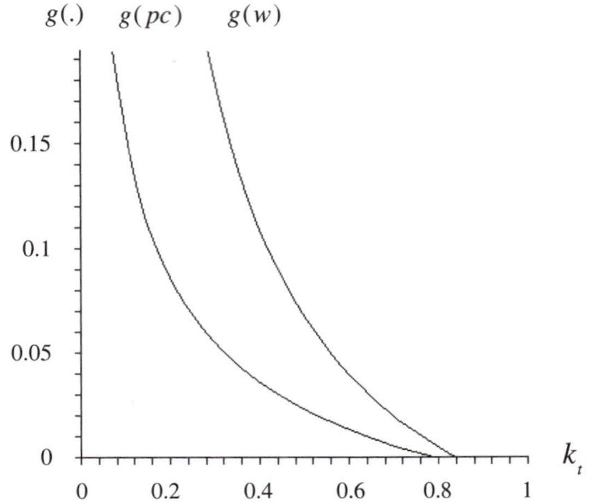

Figure 12.3. The transitional growth rates of k in regulated-wage and competitive-wage economies, $g_{mw}(k_t,\underline{w})$ and $g_{pc}(k_t)$ respectively. Parameter set: $A=10$, $\alpha=0.55$, $\phi=0.20$, $\gamma=0.95$ and $n=0$

Therefore, provided the capital's weight in technology (α) and the replacement rate (γ) are high enough, the equilibrium stock of capital per capita is increased by the introduction of minimum wages. However, the increased accumulation of capital is only part of the story: it is possible to show that there exists another condition which also ensures a higher long-run per-capita output in the minimum-wage economy than in the competitive-wage economy, that is, $\alpha > 1/(1+\gamma)$. A graphical illustration of an increasing equilibrium income function is displayed in Figure 12.1b.

Hence, if the capital's weight in production and the replacement rate are high enough, the increased accumulation of capital induced by wage minima also leads to a higher per-capita output so as to create a virtuous growth mechanism. Moreover, the higher the minimum wage, the higher are both the long-run stock of capital and income per capita.

To sum up, under some plausible conditions: (1) an increase in the regulated wage may lead to a higher transitional rate of capital per capita than in the competitive-wage economy, and (2) interestingly, this positive effect on capital can be beneficial for the long-run income per capita provided the capital's weight in production and the replacement rate are high enough.

These results sharply contrast with the common wisdom about the effects of minimum wage on macroeconomic variables.

12.4. WELFARE ANALYSIS AND NUMERICAL EXAMPLES

In this section we compare two different capital income tax regimes, evaluating their effects on the steady-state representative individual's lifetime welfare in market-wage and regulated-wage economies.

12.4.1. The Market-Wage Economy

The steady-state young-aged and old-aged consumption are given by:

$$c^y\left(w_{pc}\right)=(1-\phi)w_{pc}\,, \tag{12.31}$$

$$c^o\left(w_{pc}\right)=\phi\left[1+r_{pc}\left(1-\tau_{pc}\right)\right]w_{pc}\,. \tag{12.32}$$

Assuming the government levies a capital income tax $\tau_{pc}=0.125$, the pre-reform long-run lifetime welfare is evaluated as follows:

$$V\left(w_{pc}\right)=(1-\phi)\ln\left\{(1-\phi)w_{pc}\right\}+\phi\ln\left\{\phi\left[1+r_{pc}(1-0.125)\right]w_{pc}\right\}. \tag{12.33}$$

12.4.2. The Regulated-Wage Economy

The steady-state young-aged and old-aged consumption are now given by:

$$c^y\left(\underline{w}\right)=(1-\phi)W\left(\underline{w}\right), \tag{12.34}$$

$$c^o\left(\underline{w}\right)=\phi\left[1+r\left(\underline{w}\right)\left(1-\tau_{mw}\right)\right]W\left(\underline{w}\right). \tag{12.35}$$

We assume the public expenditure g is kept at the same steady-state pre-reform level $\overline{g}=\tau_{pc}\cdot r_{pc}\cdot k^*_{pc}$ and the additional revenue generated by the increased tax rate is used to fund the unemployment benefit scheme at balanced budget. The steady-state government constraint thus becomes:

$$\gamma\underline{w}\;u^*\left(\underline{w}\right)+\overline{g}=\tau_{mw}\cdot r\left(\underline{w}\right)\cdot k^*\left(\underline{w}\right)\Rightarrow\tau\left(\underline{w}\right)=\frac{\gamma\underline{w}\;u^*\left(\underline{w}\right)}{r\left(\underline{w}\right)k^*\left(\underline{w}\right)}+\frac{\overline{g}}{r\left(\underline{w}\right)k^*\left(\underline{w}\right)}\,. \tag{12.36}$$

Equation (12.38) is a non-linear function of $\underline{w}$. Thus, solving implicitly (12.36) with respect to the minimum wage yields:

$$w^{\circ} = w^{\circ}(\bullet). \quad (12.37)$$

Equation (12.37) determines the minimum wage at which the government budget is balanced as a function of the key parameters of the model, the capital income tax and the replacement ratio.

Assuming now the government levies a capital income tax $\tau_{mw} = 0.2$, the post-reform long-run lifetime welfare evaluated at w° is:

$$V(w^{\circ}) = (1-\phi)\ln\{(1-\phi)W(w^{\circ})\} + \phi\ln\{\phi[1+r(w^{\circ})(1-0.20)]W(w^{\circ})\}. \quad (12.38)$$

Since (12.36)–(12.38) are not tractable in a neat analytical form, we shall run simulations that basically make use of equations (12.33) and (12.38) in order to compare the pre- and post-reform individual welfare. In fact, numerical simulations using typical Italian values for the capital's share in technology and the propensity to save lead to clear-cut results as regards the welfare effects of the introduction of the assumed reform which is, however, only illustrative: our purpose is to show that within a 'calibrated' standard OLG model increasing capital income taxes, and introducing wage minima along with unemployment benefits could lead to higher long-run welfare gains than in the competitive-wage framework.

Recently, Jones (2003, 2005) provided estimates for the capital's share in OECD countries. He reported two types of measures: (1) a measure constructed as one minus the employees' compensation divided by GDP; and (2) the employees' compensation share corrected for self-employment. As regards Italy, the evidence reported in Jones (2003, p. 8) shows that recently the capital's share belongs either to 0.55 and 0.60 according to the first measure or to 0.37 and 0.42 when self-employment is taken into account.

As regards the propensity to save, Italy experienced a decrease in the decade from about 20 per cent to about 10 per cent, as reported in Table 12.1.

Finally, as regards the replacement rate, Italy shows a hybrid form of unemployment insurance system including different types of benefits, which can be summarised only approximately by using a single replacement rate (see Appendix 12A.2). In any case, without any loss of realism, we assumed a replacement rate lying between 0.50 and 0.99.

In what follows we resort to numerical simulations to compare the pre- and post-reform representative individual's steady-state lifetime welfare, i.e., equation (12.33) versus equation (12.41), for increasing values of γ. As regards the capital's share in technology we used values without self-employment correction (as reported in Jones, 2003) since we think that in our model the workforce only includes non-specialised labour and the capital input may be thought of in its broad concept, including physical and human components. In such a case, as is known, the coefficient α may be fairly about 0.6 and 0.8.[9]

Table 12.1. Household saving rates 1990–2000 (in percentage points) for some OECD countries

	Canada	United States	Italy	United Kingdom	Germany	Spain	France
1990s peak	13.2	8.7	18.7	11.4	13.1	14.4	16.2
Year of peak	1991	1992	1991	1992	1991	1993	1997
2000	3.2	–0.1	10.4	4.4	9.8	11.6	15.8
Change[1]	–10.0	–8.8	–8.3	–7.0	–3.3	–2.8	–0.4

[1] From 1990s peak to 2000.

Source: Our elaboration from Table II.3, Bank of International Settlement (BIS), 71st Annual Report (2001, p. 30), OECD national data.

In Tables 12.2–12.5 we present the behaviour of macroeconomic variables and the individual's welfare – as regards market-wage and minimum-wage economies for the plausible parameter values mentioned above – by showing the gain of our fiscal reform. The only difference between the tables[10] concerns the values used for α and ϕ, which are respectively the minimum and maximum approximated values for the recent decade. Clearly, in all cases both accumulation and welfare are significantly improved (see Table 12.4) by introducing a minimum wage quite close to the market one (from about +8 per cent to about +15 per cent). Moreover, the higher the replacement ratio, the higher the improvement in the steady-state lifetime welfare and the capital stock. Note that, although wage regulation caused unemployment rates between 7 per cent and 13 per cent, the long-run welfare is higher than in the competitive-wage case.

Despite the common wisdom in the economic literature which considers wage regulation harmful due to output losses, we have shown that the introduction of a slightly binding minimum wage, whilst generating unemployment, may also, surprisingly, create production as well as welfare gains in the long run.

To better understand the reason why the minimum wage may raise long-run output per capita and welfare, suffice it to say that it acts as a reversed social security scheme: that is, it transfers resources from old to young

Table 12.2. Macroeconomic variables and welfare in market-wage and regulated-wage economies. Parameter set: $A=10$, $\alpha=0.55$, $\phi=0.10$, $n=0$, $\tau_{pc}=0.125$ *and* $\tau_{mw}=0.20$

	$\gamma=0.60$	$\gamma=0.80$	$\gamma=0.90$	$\gamma=0.99$
w°	1.8593	1.8679	1.8709	1.8732
w_{pc}	1.6957	1.6957	1.6957	1.6957
$V(w^{\circ})$	0.4705	0.5032	0.5149	0.5238
$V(w_{pc})$	0.4411	0.4411	0.4411	0.4411
w°/w_{pc}	+9.64%	+10.15%	+10.33%	+10.46%
$u^{*}(w^{\circ})$	0.1153	0.093	0.085	0.078
$u^{*}(w_{pc})$	0	0	0	0
$k^{*}(w^{\circ})$	0.1773	0.1833	0.1855	0.1871
$k^{*}(w_{pc})$	0.1695	0.1695	0.1695	0.1695

Table 12.3. Macroeconomic variables and welfare in market-wage and regulated-wage economies. Parameter set: $A=10$, $\alpha=0.55$, $\phi=0.20$, $n=0$, $\tau_{pc}=0.125$ *and* $\tau_{mw}=0.20$

	$\gamma=0.60$	$\gamma=0.80$	$\gamma=0.90$	$\gamma=0.99$
w°	4.2986	4.3148	4.3206	4.3248
w_{pc}	3.9562	3.9562	3.9562	3.9562
$V(w^{\circ})$	1.2274	1.2564	1.2668	1.2747
$V(w_{pc})$	1.2148	1.2148	1.2148	1.2148
w°/w_{pc}	+8.65%	+9.06%	+9.20%	+9.31%
$u^{*}(w^{\circ})$	0.104	0.084	0.076	0.070
$u^{*}(w_{pc})$	0	0	0	0
$k^{*}(w^{\circ})$	0.8236	0.8484	0.8574	0.8643
$k^{*}(w_{pc})$	0.7912	0.7912	0.7912	0.7912

Table 12.4. Macroeconomic variables and welfare in market-wage and regulated-wage economies. Parameter set: $A=10$, $\alpha=0.59$, $\phi=0.10$, $n=0$, $\tau_{pc}=0.125$ *and* $\tau_{mw}=0.20$

	$\gamma=0.60$	$\gamma=0.80$	$\gamma=0.90$	$\gamma=0.99$
w°	1.2963	1.3064	1.3100	1.3127
w_{pc}	1.1365	1.1365	1.1365	1.1365
$V(w^{\circ})$	0.1149	0.1559	0.1709	0.1822
$V(w_{pc})$	0.0571	0.0571	0.0571	0.0571
w°/w_{pc}	+14.06%	+14.94%	+15.26%	+15.50%
$u^{*}(w^{\circ})$	0.137	0.1127	0.103	0.096
$u^{*}(w_{pc})$	0	0	0	0
$k^{*}(w^{\circ})$	0.1224	0.1276	0.1296	0.1311
$k^{*}(w_{pc})$	0.1136	0.1136	0.1136	0.1136

Table 12.5. Macroeconomic variables and welfare in market-wage and regulated-wage economies. Parameter set: $A=10$, $\alpha=0.59$, $\phi=0.20$, $n=0$, $\tau_{pc}=0.125$ *and* $\tau_{mw}=0.20$

	$\gamma=0.60$	$\gamma=0.80$	$\gamma=0.90$	$\gamma=0.99$
w°	3.4747	3.4974	3.5055	3.5115
w_{pc}	3.0814	3.0814	3.0814	3.0814
$V(w^{\circ})$	1.0338	1.0706	1.0840	1.0941
$V(w_{pc})$	0.9969	0.9969	0.9969	0.9969
w°/w_{pc}	+12.76%	+13.49%	+13.76%	+13.95%
$u^{*}(w^{\circ})$	0.126	0.103	0.094	0.087
$u^{*}(w_{pc})$	0	0	0	0
$k^{*}(w^{\circ})$	0.6597	0.6850	0.6944	0.7017
$k^{*}(w_{pc})$	0.6162	0.6162	0.6162	0.6162

people by raising the income of the current young (savers) and by decreasing the interest rate, and this intergenerational transfer channel could be further favoured if the unemployment benefit system is funded with lump-sum taxes incurred only by the retired.

Note that in this section we did not take account of the important leisure values associated with unemployment. In the next section we will fill this gap.

12.5. THE HOME PRODUCTION MODEL

12.5.1. Individuals

Home-produced goods are assumed to be created with the following linear technology in the (unemployed) labour factor: $h_t = Bu_t$, where B is the constant average and marginal productivity of the 'backyard' technology.[11]

The reason why home production employs only the unemployed workforce is simple: if we assume the return to labour in home technology to be always smaller than the regulated wage in the 'firms' sector (that is, $B<\underline{w}$), then the hours worked in the home sector are only those left unemployed by the introduction of wage minima.[12] Furthermore, we also make the technical assumption that the physical marginal productivity of labour in the home sector is always smaller than the physical marginal productivity of labour in the firms sector in the market-wage economy, that is, $B<w_{pc}$.[13]

With home-produced goods, the representative individual is faced with the following programme:

$$\max_{\{c_t^y, c_{t+1}^o\}} U_t\left(c_t^y, c_{t+1}^o\right) = \left(c_t^y\right)^{1-\phi}\left(c_{t+1}^o\right)^{\phi},$$

subject to

$$c_t^y + s_t = \underline{w}(1-u_t) + \gamma \underline{w}\ u_t + h_t$$

$$c_{t+1}^o = \left[1 + r_{t+1}\left(1-\tau_{t+1,mw}\right)\right]s_t$$

Therefore, young-aged consumption, old-aged consumption and the savings path are, respectively:

$$c_t^y(\underline{w}, B) = (1-\phi)W_t(\underline{w}, B), \tag{12.39}$$

$$c_{t+1}^o(\underline{w}, B) = \phi\left[1 + r_{t+1}\left(1-\tau_{t+1,mw}\right)\right]W_t(\underline{w}, B), \tag{12.40}$$

$$s_t(\underline{w},B)=\phi W_t(\underline{w},B), \tag{12.41}$$

where $W_t(\underline{w},B):=\underline{w}(1-u_t)+(B+\gamma\underline{w})u_t=W_t(\underline{w})+Bu_t$ is the total income of the young, as given by the sum of labour income, unemployment benefits and the income received from home production.

12.5.2. Government

The government strategy is to adjust the capital income tax rate so as to balance out unemployment benefit expenditures with tax receipts in each period. Thus, the per-capita time-t government constraint is given exactly by equation (12.22).

12.5.3. Equilibrium

The market clearing condition in goods as well as in capital markets is given by:

$$(1+n)k_{t+1}=s_t(\underline{w},B). \tag{12.42}$$

Therefore, the dynamic equilibrium sequence of capital is now given by:

$$k_{t+1}=\frac{\phi}{1+n}(B+\gamma\underline{w})+\frac{\phi}{1+n}\psi^{\frac{1}{\alpha}}\underline{w}^{-\frac{1}{\alpha}}\left[\underline{w}(1-\gamma)-B\right]k_t. \tag{12.43}$$

Steady state implies $k_{t+1}=k_t:=k^*$, such that the long-run unemployment rate, capital stock and total production $(q=y+h)$ per capita are given by:

$$u^*(\underline{w},B)=\frac{\underline{w}^{\frac{1}{\alpha}}(1+n)-\phi\underline{w}\psi^{\frac{1}{\alpha}}}{\underline{w}^{\frac{1}{\alpha}}(1+n)-\phi\left[\underline{w}(1-\gamma)-B\right]\psi^{\frac{1}{\alpha}}}, \tag{12.44}$$

$$k^*(\underline{w},B)=\frac{\phi(B+\gamma\underline{w})\underline{w}^{\frac{1}{\alpha}}}{\underline{w}^{\frac{1}{\alpha}}(1+n)-\phi\left[\underline{w}(1-\gamma)-B\right]\psi^{\frac{1}{\alpha}}}, \tag{12.45}$$

$$q^*(\underline{w},B)=y^*(\underline{w},B)+h^*(\underline{w},B)=\frac{\underline{w}^{\frac{1}{\alpha}}(1+n)B+\phi\psi^{\frac{1}{\alpha}}\underline{w}\left(\frac{\alpha B+\gamma\underline{w}}{1-\alpha}\right)}{\underline{w}^{\frac{1}{\alpha}}(1+n)-\phi\left[\underline{w}(1-\gamma)-B\right]\psi^{\frac{1}{\alpha}}}. \tag{12.46}$$

If $B=0$, equations (12.44)–(12.46) collapse to (12.26)–(12.28), respectively.

As regards stability, analysis of (12.43) yields more interesting findings than in the minimum-wage economy without home production. In particular, as is known, the general condition for stability requires that $-1<\partial k_{t+1}/\partial k_t<1$. Differentiating (12.48) with respect to k_t yields $\partial k_{t+1}/\partial k_t=\phi/(1+n)\psi^{1/\alpha}\underline{w}^{-1/a}[\underline{w}(1-\gamma)-B]$.

Therefore, stability requires that $-1<\phi/(1+n)\psi^{1/\alpha}\underline{w}^{-1/a}[\underline{w}(1-\gamma)-B]<1$.[14] The latter derivative may be positive or negative depending on the sign of the difference $\underline{w}(1-\gamma)-B$. If $B<\underline{w}(1-\gamma)$, then $0<\partial k_{t+1}/\partial k_t<1$ holds. In this case, the trajectory is stable and converges monotonically towards the steady-state equilibrium. If, instead, $B>\underline{w}(1-\gamma)$, then $-1<\partial k_{t+1}/\partial k_t<0$. In this latter case, the dynamics of capital is oscillatory and convergent to the steady state. Thus, the model with home technology gives the noteworthy property of generating dumped economic fluctuations. Figure 12.4 shows the dynamics of capital $k_{t+1}=f(k_t)$ with and without home production. The parameter set chosen is that presented previously in Table 12.4, with in addition $B=1$. In this case, we see that the steady-state capital stock is higher in the home production economy and that noteworthy fluctuations may occur.

The existence of a backyard technology used only by unemployed workers modifies the steady-state results of the minimum-wage economy presented in the previous section in a clear-cut way. The new results, compared with those of the model without such technology, can be formally summarised in the following proposition:

Proposition 1. *The existence of a home production technology implies that in steady state,* ceteris paribus *as regards* α, ϕ *and* $\underline{w}$, *1)* $k^*(\underline{w},B)>k^*(\underline{w})$; *2)* $u^*(\underline{w};B)<u^*(\underline{w})$; *3)* $q^*(\underline{w},B)>y^*(\underline{w})$; *4)* $c^y(\underline{w},B)>c^y(\underline{w})$; *5)* $\tau(\underline{w};B)<\tau(\underline{w})$; *6)* $c^o(\underline{w},B)>c^o(\underline{w})$; *and 7)* $V(\underline{w},B)>V(\underline{w})$ *for any* $\underline{w}>w_{pc}$ *and* $B>0$.

Proof. Since $W(\underline{w},B)>W(\underline{w})$ for any $\underline{w}>w_{pc}$ and $B>0$ holds by definition, then 1) given that $\partial k^*(\underline{w},B)/\partial B>0$ for any $\underline{w}>w_{pc}$, and if $B=0$ then $k^*(\underline{w},B)=k^*(\underline{w})$, it follows that $k^*(\underline{w},B)>k^*(\underline{w})$ for any $\underline{w}>w_{pc}$ and $B>0$; 2) by looking at equation (12.21), it can be easily seen that the rate of unemployment is a decreasing function of the per-capita stock of capital. Since $k^*(\underline{w},B)>k^*(\underline{w})$, then $u^*(\underline{w};B)<u^*(\underline{w})$ for any $\underline{w}>w_{pc}$ and $B>0$; 3) since

$$y^*(\cdot)=f\left(\overbrace{k^*(\cdot)}^{+},\overbrace{u^*(\cdot)}^{-}\right),$$

then given points 1) and 2) we have $y^*(\underline{w},B)>y^*(\underline{w})$ for any $\underline{w}>w_{pc}$ and $B>0$. Therefore, $q^*(\underline{w},B):=y^*(\underline{w},B)+Bu^*(\underline{w},B)>y^*(\underline{w})$ holds *a fortiori*; 4)

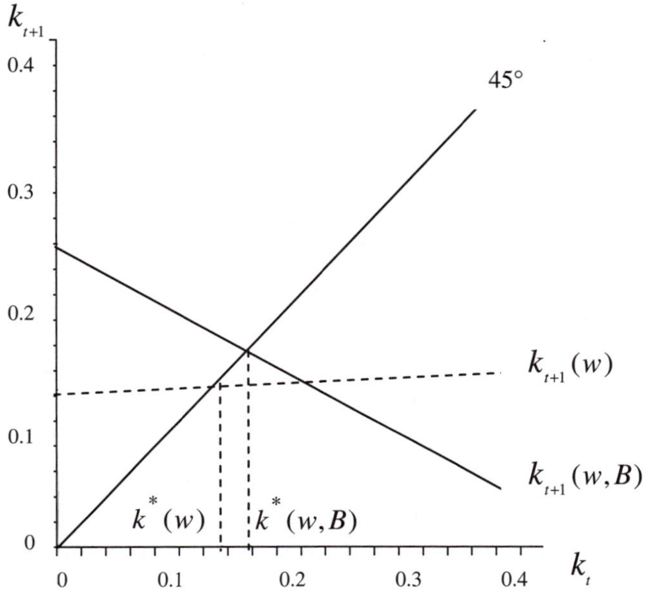

Figure 12.4. Capital dynamics with and without home production, $k_{t+1}(B,\underline{w})$ *and* $k_{t+1}(\underline{w})$*, respectively. Parameter set:* $A=10$*,* $\alpha=0.59$*,* $\phi=0.10$*,* $\gamma=0.95$*,* $B=1$ *and* $n=0$

since $c^{y}(\underline{w},B)=(1-\phi)W(\underline{w},B)$ and $c^{y}(\underline{w})=(1-\phi)W(\underline{w})$, and knowing that $W(\underline{w},B)>W(\underline{w})$, it follows that $c^{y}(\underline{w},B)>c^{y}(\underline{w})$ for any $\underline{w}>w_{pc}$ and $B>0$; 5) since the real rate of interest, equation (12.21), does not depend on B, and given points 1) and 2), equations (12.38) and (12.52) yield $\tau(\underline{w};B)<\tau(\underline{w})$ for any $\underline{w}>w_{pc}$ and $B>0$, that is the capital income tax rate balancing out the government budget is smaller with home production than in the case in which $B=0$; 6) since $c^{o}(\underline{w},B)=\phi\{1+r(\underline{w})[1-\tau(\underline{w},B)]\}W(\underline{w},B)$ and $c^{o}(\underline{w})=\phi\{1+r(\underline{w})[1-\tau(\underline{w})]\}W(\underline{w})$, knowing that $W(\underline{w},B)>W(\underline{w})$ and given point 5) it follows that $c^{o}(\underline{w},B)>c^{o}(\underline{w})$ for any $\underline{w}>w_{pc}$ and $B>0$; 7) given points 4) and 6), it follows directly that $V(\underline{w},B)>V(\underline{w})$ for any $\underline{w}>w_{pc}$ and $B>0$. **Q.E.D.**

To sum up, the following remark holds: in the presence of a minimum wage, the higher the productivity of the home technology, the more likely the welfare gain is.

Figures 12.5 and 12.6 illustrate the comparison between minimum-wage economies with and without home production technology for the same parameter sets used above for Italy and show the welfare gain which home technology may create.

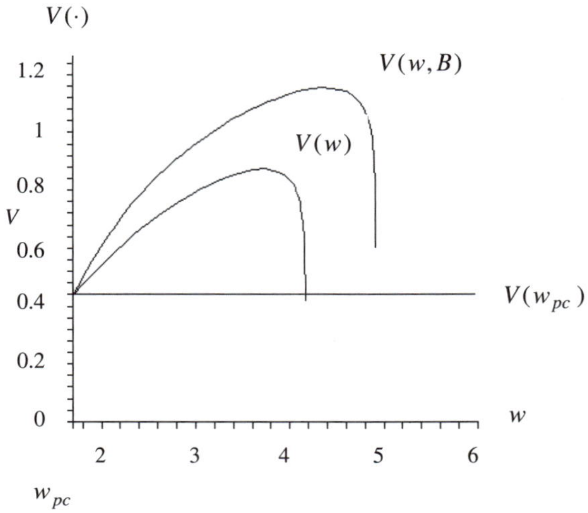

Figure 12.5. Lifetime with and without home technology as a function of the minimum wage, $V(\underline{w},B)$ *and* $V(\underline{w})$*. respectively. Parameter set:* $A=10$, $\alpha=0.55$, $\phi=0.10$, $B=1$, $\gamma=0.95$ *and* $n=0$

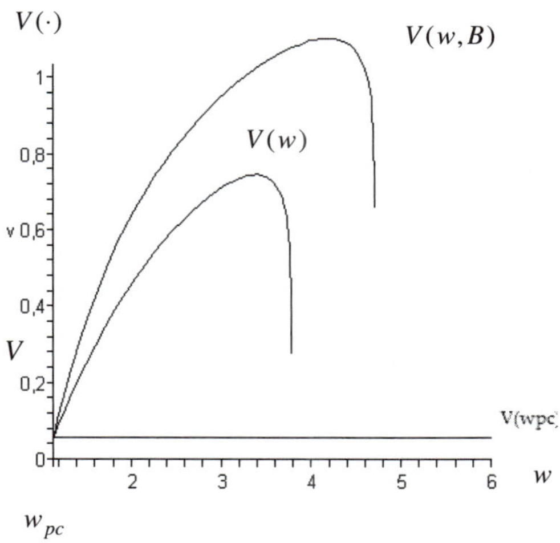

Figure 12.6. Lifetime with and without home technology as a function of the minimum wage, $V(\underline{w},B)$ *and* $V(\underline{w})$*, respectively. Parameter set:* $A=10$, $\alpha=0.59$, $\phi=0.10$, $B=1$, $\gamma=0.95$ *and* $n=0$

12.6. CONCLUDING COMMENTS

In this chapter we showed that minimum wage legislation, though generating market inefficiencies and unemployment, may also, surprisingly, create production as well as welfare gains in the long run. From a policy point of view, motivated by the recent political debate in Italy about increasing capital income taxes from 12.5 per cent to 20 per cent, we studied the impact on the long-run lifetime welfare of a theoretical fiscal policy reform which consists in introducing wage minima and unemployment insurance benefits funded with an increase in capital income tax at balanced budget. The results depend crucially on the size of the capital's weight in technology, the propensity to save and the replacement ratio. Indeed, our simulation exercises show that, in contrast with the prevailing common wisdom in the economic literature, positive effects of minimum wage on macroeconomic variables and on individual lifetime welfare always appear when 'calibrating' parameters that largely correspond to the current situation in Italy.

Moreover we pointed out that unemployment time should be considered as an additional resource instead of damage, since there exist important leisure values associated with unemployment (for instance, leisure time, self-enrichment activities, education, home production and so on). To further explore the effects of our fiscal reform with an economic use of the leisure time associated with unemployment, we assumed the existence of a home production technology with constant productivity and we then showed that the higher the productivity of the home sector, the higher is the welfare gain due to the introduction of minimum wages.

Our conclusions are reached within a standard dynamic general equilibrium overlapping generations model where agents live two periods and where the only departure from the textbook OLG model is the assumption of legislated wage minima. Finally, while we made much progress in understanding the effects of the regulation of wages in a standard OLG dynamic context, there remain many other interesting research topics which should be considered in future papers. For instance, how do these findings regarding a closed economy change when the economy is open to international trade? What occurs when there is an efficiency-wage mechanism in the labour market?

APPENDIX 12A.1

In this appendix we show that taxation systems used to fund unemployment insurance systems borne by the income of young people as well as by firms always result in a reduction of output and welfare. In particular we investigate the following three cases: (1) a wage tax; (2) a lump-sum tax levied on young people; and (3) a contribution rate (proportional to the net wage received by employees) paid by firms. Firstly, as regard the firms' behaviour, we note that for the first two cases equations (12.17)–(12.21) in the main text still hold.

Tax on Workers' Labour Income

Individuals

The individual maximisation problem for agents at time t is:

$$\max_{\{c_t^y, c_{t+1}^o\}} U_t\left(c_t^y, c_{t+1}^o\right) = \left(c_t^y\right)^{1-\phi}\left(c_{t+1}^o\right)^{\phi}$$

subject to

$$c_t^y + s_t = \underline{w}\left(1-\tau_t^w\right)\left(1-u_t\right) + \gamma\underline{w}\ u_t$$

$$c_{t+1}^o = \left(1+r_{t+1}\right)s_t$$

Solving the maximisation program yields:

$$c_t^y\left(\underline{w}\right) = (1-\phi)\left[\underline{w}\left(1-\tau_t^w\right)\left(1-u_t\right) + \gamma\underline{w}u_t\right], \tag{12A.1}$$

$$c_t^y\left(\underline{w}\right) = \phi\left(1+r_{t+1}\right)\left[\underline{w}\left(1-\tau_t^w\right)\left(1-u_t\right) + \gamma\underline{w}u_t\right], \tag{12A.2}$$

$$s_t\left(\underline{w}\right) = \phi\left[\underline{w}\left(1-\tau_t^w\right)\left(1-u_t\right) + \gamma\underline{w}u_t\right]. \tag{12A.3}$$

Government

The government adjusts the labour income tax so as to balance out unemployment benefit expenditures with tax receipts in each period. Thus, the per-capita time-t government constraint is:

$$\gamma\underline{w}\ u_t = \tau_t^w\ \underline{w}\left(1-u_t\right). \tag{12A.4}$$

Equilibrium
Given equation (12A.4), the market clearing condition in goods as well as in capital markets is:

$$(1+n)k_{t+1}=s_t(\underline{w}). \tag{12A.5}$$

Combining (12A.5) with (12A.3) the dynamic equilibrium sequence of capital is:

$$k_{t+1}=\frac{\phi}{1+n}\psi^{\frac{1}{\alpha}}\underline{w}^{\frac{1-\alpha}{\alpha}}k_t. \tag{12A.6}$$

Equation (12A.6) implies there is no steady state. Differentiating (12A.8) with respect to the minimum wage yields:

$$\frac{\partial k_{t+1}}{\partial \underline{w}}=-\frac{1-\alpha}{\alpha}\frac{\phi}{1+n}\psi^{\frac{1}{\alpha}}\underline{w}^{-\frac{1}{\alpha}}k_t<0. \tag{12A.7}$$

Equation (12A.7) clearly shows that introducing minimum wages and unemployment benefits financed at balanced budget by levying labour income taxes on the income of the young always reduces the capital stock.

Lump-Sum Tax on the Young

Individuals
The individual maximisation problem changes to

$$\max_{\{c_t^y,c_{t+1}^o\}}U_t(c_t^y,c_{t+1}^o)=(c_t^y)^{1-\phi}(c_{t+1}^o)^{\phi}$$

subject to

$$c_t^y+s_t=\underline{w}(1-u_t)+\gamma\underline{w}\ u_t-\tau_t$$

$$c_{t+1}^o=(1+r_{t+1})s_t.$$

Therefore

$$c_t^y(\underline{w})=(1-\phi)\left[\underline{w}(1-u_t)+\gamma\underline{w}u_t-\tau_t\right], \tag{12A.8}$$

$$c_t^y(\underline{w})=\phi(1+r_{t+1})\left[\underline{w}(1-u_t)+\gamma\underline{w}u_t-\tau_t\right], \tag{12A.9}$$

$$s_t(\underline{w})=\phi\left[\underline{w}(1-u_t)+\gamma\underline{w}u_t-\tau_t\right]. \tag{12A.10}$$

Government

The government adjusts the lump-sum tax so as to balance out unemployment benefit expenditures with tax receipts in each period. Thus, the per-capita time-t government constraint is

$$\gamma \underline{w}\ u_t = \tau_t . \qquad (12A.11)$$

Equilibrium

The dynamic equilibrium sequence of capital is given by equation (12A.6). Thus, introducing minimum wages and unemployment benefits financed at balanced budget with lump-sum tax burdens on the young always reduces the capital stock.

Tax Burden on Firms

In this section we consider an unemployment benefit scheme financed with a labour tax paid by the representative firm. The model is outlined as follows.

Individuals

The individual maximisation problem for agents of generation t is:

$$\max_{\{c_t^{\,y}, c_{t+1}^{\,o}\}} U_t\left(c_t^{\,y}, c_{t+1}^{\,o}\right) = \left(c_t^{\,y}\right)^{1-\phi}\left(c_{t+1}^{\,o}\right)^{\phi}$$

subject to

$$c_t^{\,y} + s_t = \underline{w}(1-u_t) + \gamma \underline{w}\ u_t$$

$$c_{t+1}^{\,o} = (1+r_{t+1})s_t .$$

The optimal young- and old-age consumption functions become:

$$c_t^{\,y}(\underline{w}) = (1-\phi)\left[\underline{w}(1-u_t) + \gamma \underline{w} u_t\right], \qquad (12A.12)$$

$$c_t^{\,y}(\underline{w}) = \phi(1+r_{t+1})\left[\underline{w}(1-u_t) + \gamma \underline{w} u_t\right], \qquad (12A.13)$$

$$s_t(\underline{w}) = \phi\left[\underline{w}(1-u_t) + \gamma \underline{w} u_t\right]. \qquad (12A.14)$$

Firms

Standard profit maximisation $\max_{\{K_t, L_t\}} Y_t - \underline{w}(1+\tau_t^f)L_t - (1+r_t)K_t$ leads to the following marginal conditions for capital and labour, respectively:

$$r_t = \alpha A \left(\frac{k_t}{1-u_t} \right)^{\alpha-1} - 1 \tag{12A.15}$$

$$\underline{w} = \frac{(1-\alpha)A}{1+\tau_t^f} \left(\frac{k_t}{1-u_t} \right)^{\alpha} \tag{12A.16}$$

Therefore, the equilibrium interest rate and the unemployment rate are given by:

$$r(\underline{w}) = \alpha A \left[\frac{\psi}{\underline{w}(1+\tau_t^f)} \right]^{\frac{1-\alpha}{\alpha}} - 1 \tag{12A.17}$$

$$u_t(k_t, \underline{w}) = 1 - \left[\frac{\psi}{\underline{w}(1+\tau_t^f)} \right]^{\frac{1}{\alpha}} \cdot k_t \tag{12A.18}$$

Government
The government strategy is to adjust the contribution rate paid by firms such as to balance out unemployment benefit expenditures with tax receipts in each period. Thus, the per-capita time-t government constraint is:

$$\gamma \underline{w}\, u_t = \tau_t^f\, \underline{w}(1-u_t). \tag{12A.19}$$

Equilibrium
The dynamic equilibrium sequence of capital is now given by:

$$k_{t+1} = \frac{\phi}{1+n} \psi^{\frac{1}{\alpha}} \left[\underline{w}(1+\tau_t^f) \right]^{-\frac{1-\alpha}{\alpha}} k_t \tag{12A.20}$$

Equation (12A.20) implies there is no steady state. It can be seen that the dynamics of capital depend negatively both on the minimum wage and the labour tax. Thus, in this case, introducing minimum wages, *a fortiori*, confirms the finding of endogenous reductions in the transitional rate of economic growth.

The analysis developed in this appendix can be summarised as follows: introducing minimum wages and unemployment benefits financed by 1) a wage tax, 2) a lump-sum tax on young people, 3) a contribution rate proportional to the net wage received by employees paid by firms, always depresses the long-run output per capita and lifetime welfare.

APPENDIX 12A.2

The Unemployment Insurance System in Italy

In the Italian social welfare system there exist various kinds of unemployment insurance benefits. In particular the ordinary unemployment benefits are payable for a maximum of seven months for beneficiaries aged 50 or older. Daily benefits are equal to 50 per cent of the gross average daily wage for the first six months and 40 per cent for the seventh month. Beneficiaries aged 50 or older receive 50 per cent of the gross average daily wage during the first six months, 40 per cent for the next three months, and 30 per cent for the tenth month. The gross average daily wage is based on earnings of the previous three months. *Mobility allowances*: 80 per cent of the insured's last earnings are paid for up to twelve months; thereafter, 64 per cent. The maximum duration of the allowance varies from 12 months to 36 months, and it is dependent on the age of the worker and the location of the place of employment. In addition to unemployment benefits, Italy has a state fund for employees in industry whose companies put them on temporary redundancy through no fault of their own (e.g., market crisis, natural disaster, etc.), called Cassa Integrazione Guadagni (CIG), which is designed to integrate employees' earnings until work is resumed. There are two types of CIG: *Ordinary CIG* comprises 80 per cent of the wage for hours not worked. This cannot exceed a monthly maximum amount. *Extraordinary CIG* has a benefit equal to 80 per cent of the wage designed to cover special situations, e.g. when a production line is being reorganised or converted, and work must temporarily cease. To sum up loosely, we can say that in Italy the 'replacement ratio' lies between 50 and 80 per cent and is only temporary.

NOTES

1. For instance, monopsonistic labour markets (e.g., West and McKee, 1980), education as a signalling device (Lang, 1987), schooling (Cahuc and Michel, 1996) or training on the job (Ravn and Sorensen, 1999) as an engine of human capital accumulation, efficiency wages (Rebitzer and Taylor, 1985), imperfect information and job search (Swinnerton, 1996).
2. In this context taxing capital income does not affect savings, since the Cobb–Douglas utility hypothesis gives a zero elasticity of savings with respect to the interest rate. Anyway, by considering a more general CIES utility function, where the capital income tax affects saving behaviour, it can be seen that the main findings of this chapter are numerically confirmed.
3. Using (12.8) and (12.9) it can be shown that the equilibrium is always stable.
4. For simplicity we assume the hourly minimum wage to be constant over time.
5. Notice that we treat $\underline{w}$ and γ as policy parameters, whereas the quantity of employed labour force is endogenous.

6. For economy of space, we do not report here the analysis of tax systems based on consumption taxes and lump-sum taxes incurred by the elderly.
7. If the minimum wage is not binding, i.e. $\underline{w} = w_{pc}$, then equations (12.27) and (12.28) collapse to equations (12.9) and (12.10) respectively and the unemployment rate is zero.
8. We do not report here the complete proof which is available on request.
9. In fact, Mankiw et al. (1992, p. 417) suggested that since the minimum wage: (1) could be interpreted as a proxy of the return to labour without human capital, and (2) it has averaged about 30 to 50 per cent of the average wage in manufacturing – so that 50 to 70 per cent of total labour income represents the return to human capital – then if the physical capital's share of income is expected to be about 1/3, the human capital's share of income should be between 1/3 and 1/2. In sum, with the broad concept of capital the coefficient α may be fairly about 0.6 and 0.8.
10. Since our purpose in this chapter is limited to the current increase in the capital income tax from 12.5 per cent to 20 per cent, we do not report simulations for different tax rates. However, it is worth noting that increasing the capital income tax further may increase lifetime welfare further as well.
11. A seminal contribution on home production in macroeconomic models may be found in Benhabib et al. (1991).
12. It is important to note that since (1) the unemployment created by the introduction of the minimum wage is only involuntary, and (2) the government pays wage-indexed unemployment insurance benefit for the hours left unemployed, then the condition preserving the incentive to supply labour in firms is that the average and marginal productivity in the home technology must be no greater than the regulated wage.
13. Note that, as regards the production side, firms behave just as explained in the previous section.
14. This condition is always satisfied but the algebraic proof is rather cumbersome and omitted here for economy of space.

REFERENCES

Azariadis, C. (1993), *Intertemporal Macroeconomics*, Oxford: Basil Blackwell.

Bank of International Settlement (BIS) (2001), *71st Annual Report*, available at http://www.bis.org/publ/arpdf/ar2001i2.pdf.

Benhabib, J., R. Rogerson and R. Wright (1991), 'Homework in Macroeconomics: Household Production and Aggregate Fluctuations', *Journal of Political Economy*, **99**(6), 1166–87.

Cahuc, P. and P. Michel (1996), 'Minimum Wage, Unemployment and Growth', *European Economic Review*, **40**(7), 1463–82.

De La Croix, D. and P. Michel (2002), *A Theory of Economic Growth. Dynamics and Policy in Overlapping Generations*, Cambridge, UK: Cambridge University Press.

Diamond, P.A. (1965), 'National Debt in a Neoclassical Growth Model', *American Economic Review*, **55**(5), 1126–50.

Jones, C.I. (2003), 'Growth, Capital Shares and a New Perspective on Production Functions', available at http://elsa.berkeley.edu/~chad.

Jones, C.I. (2005), 'The Shape of Production Functions and the Direction of Technical Change', *Quarterly Journal of Economics*, **120**(2), 517–49.

Lang, K. (1987), 'Job Signalling and Welfare Improving Minimum Wage Laws', *Economic Inquiry*, **26**(3), 525–32.

Mankiw, N.G., D. Romer and D.N. Weil (1992), 'A Contribution to the Empirics of Economic Growth', *Quarterly Journal of Economics*, **107**(2), 407–37.

Ravn, M.O. and J.R. Sorensen (1999), 'Schooling, Training, Growth and Minimum Wages', *Scandinavian Journal of Economics*, **10**(3), 441–57.

Rebitzer, J. and L. Taylor (1995), 'The Consequences of Minimum Wage Laws: Some New Theoretical Ideas', *Journal of Public Economics*, **56**(2), 245–55.

Samuelson, P.A. (1958), 'An Exact-Consumption Loan Model of Interest With or Without the Social Contrivance of Money', *Journal of Political Economy*, **66**(6), 467–82.

Stigler, G.J. (1946), 'The Economics of Minimum Wage Legislation', *American Economic Review*, **36**(3), 358–65.

Swinnerton, K.A. (1996), 'Minimum Wages in an Equilibrium Search Model with Diminishing Returns to Labor in Production', *Journal of Labor Economics*, **14**(2), 340–55.

West, E.G. and M. McKee (1980), 'Monopsony and "Shock" Arguments for Minimum Wages', *Southern Economic Journal*, **46**(3), 883–91.

13. Sustainable development and energy trends

Simone Borghesi and Alessandro Vercelli*

13.1. INTRODUCTION

In this chapter, we will discuss to what extent the recent trends in energy consumption are compatible with the requirements of sustainable development. The current model of energy production, distribution and consumption is very vulnerable. This is because it is based almost exclusively on the use of fossil fuels (coal, natural gas and, above all, oil) whose reserves are strictly limited, although the experts are divided on the size of these limits. There is, however, unanimous agreement on the fact that the age of fossil fuels is bound to decline during this century, progressively giving way to renewable energy sources such as wind power, photovoltaic energy and, according to some experts, nuclear energy. Nevertheless, opinion is divided on what the characteristics of the new energy model should be, as regards the timing and the ways of making changes and therefore as regards also the best economic, environmental and energy policies to guide the pace for the transition process.

Today's energy model is vulnerable not only because fossil fuels are scarce, but also because their reserves are remarkably concentrated in terms of location and ownership.[1] This exposes energy production and distribution to considerable geopolitical dangers which clearly emerged in the 1970s when the two oil shocks of 1973 and 1979 caused serious economic turmoil in the world economy due to the simultaneous increase of inflation and unemployment (stagflation).

Furthermore, the geographical concentration of reserves has led to the consolidation of centralized and hierarchical energy infrastructures (Rifkin, 2002, p. 9) which accentuate the vulnerability of the energy model. World energy supplies depend on a network of oil and gas pipelines and petrol tankers – a network which has its head and 'pumping heart' in the Middle East. Any problem occurring at the heart of the fossil fuel circulatory system which animates the 'body' of the world economy, would have devastating repercussions for the entire circulation of the lymph of vital energy. This has contributed to dangerous conflicts for economic and political leadership over the area of the Middle East with serious consequences for this 'circulation of energy'; consequences which could become even more serious in the future.

Lastly, the very high costs linked to prospecting, extracting, refining and distributing oil and other fossil fuels require colossal investments which only mega-enterprises can manage. This has created an oligopolistic market dominated by eight multinational energy giants on whose strategies depend the world energy supply and the oil price which in turn strongly affects the performance of the world economy.

For all these reasons, the current energy model is extremely vulnerable and risks endangering not only the sustainability of development but also the progress of world economic development.

In this chapter we will limit ourselves to considering to what extent the transition process under way towards a new model of energy production and consumption is compatible with sustainable development. This analysis will provide some indications on the desirable characteristics of the future energy model and on the most opportune policies to make the transition process consistent with the sustainability requirements.

For this reason, after having illustrated the conventional position on energy production and consumption (Section 13.2), we examine it more carefully from a critical viewpoint (Section 13.3). Applying to the energy sector the approach adopted in a previous work (Borghesi and Vercelli, 2003), we derive a few analytical requirements for long-term energy sustainability and examine whether they are satisfied on the basis of the currently available data and projections for the future (Section 13.4). The conclusions, summarized in Section 13.5, stress the need for a new model of energy production and consumption based on energy saving and on the systematic use of renewable energy sources.

13.2. THE CONVENTIONAL POSITION

First of all, we intend to discuss the dominant position concerning the production and consumption of energy – a position held by the main energy producers and most energy agencies, although with different nuances, and often reported by the mass media. For ease of reference, we will call this the 'conventional position'.

The 'conventional position' is characterized by a marked optimism in the capacity of the market, assisted by market-oriented technical progress, to resolve energy problems quickly and efficiently. This also applies to energy sources that have an unavoidable physical scarcity, such as fossil fuels which represent the pillar of today's energy production and consumption model. This position is often corroborated by tables and figures illustrating the paradox whereby proven reserves of oil and natural gas are supposed to have gradually increased in the last few decades (see Figure 13.1).[2] Therefore the expected lifespan, *T*, of many exhaustible resources, including fossil fuels, has been upwardly revised over the years (Table 13.1). This has often been used to accuse the Club of Rome (Meadows et al., 1972) of being excessively pessimistic and its forecasts systematically wrong. As some authors have underlined (e.g. Georgescu-Roegen, 1977), however, this argument derived from a quick and partially biased look that many analysts gave at only the first few chapters of the original contribution by the Club of Rome (Meadows et al., 1972). As a matter of fact, the often-mentioned 'wrong' forecasts of the Club of Rome were actually the output of a scenario analysis performed through computer simulations. Subsequent updates by the Club (Meadows et al., 1992 and 2004) revised and integrated the original version, showing that many of the original scenarios actually turned out to be overly optimistic.[3]

The paradox of an increase over time of these depletable resources is normally explained in terms of technical progress whereby more and more reserves are found as a result of increasingly sophisticated methods of prospecting. Furthermore, technical progress should allow the exploitation – at competitive costs – of reserves that are increasingly difficult to use, for reasons of location (e.g. under the sea), depth, and quality of the raw

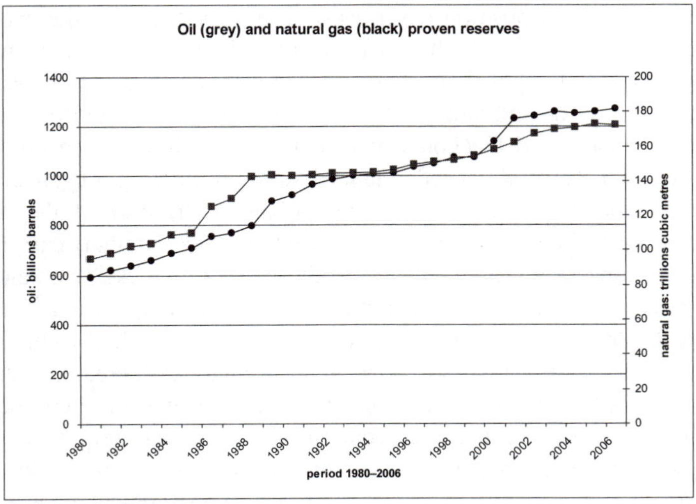

Source: Authors' elaboration on British Petroleum data (British Petroleum, 2007).

Figure 13.1. Proven reserves of oil and natural gas

Table 13.1. Expected lifespan of fossil fuel reserves measured in number of years (T) starting from different base years (1970, 1994 and 2006)[4]

Fossil fuels	T_{1970} (*Source*: Meadows et al., 1972)	T_{1994} (*Source*: British Petroleum 1995)	T_{2006} (*Source*: British Petroleum 2007)
Coal	111	139	147
Natural gas	22	42	63.3
Oil	20	35	40.5

material. The observed increase over time of fossil fuel reserves and the underlying explanation have generated the widespread conviction that the age of fossil fuels will not exhaust its leading role in the next half century and that the transition towards an alternative energy model could be managed by the 'spontaneous' forces of the market and technical progress. Sheikh Yamani, the powerful OPEC leader, used to say that the Stone Age did not come to an end because there were no more stones and that the Age of Oil will not come to an end for the lack of oil. From this standpoint, the transition will come about spontaneously as soon as the cost of one kilowatt-hour (kWh) produced from fossil fuels exceeds the cost of one kWh produced by renewable energy.[5] In this view the transition towards an alternative technology (so-called 'backstop technology') is not expected to occur before the middle of this century.

The conventional position described above does not deny the economic scarcity of fossil fuels, which generates from time to time a tendency for demand to exceed supply. However, the dominant viewpoint is that these situations are to be interpreted as essentially episodic instances (such as during the widespread blackouts of recent years). They can be defined as 'cyclical' when demand exceeds planned supply following a cyclical boom in national income, or as 'extra-economic' as in the case of the two oil shocks of the 1970s. They depend on a scarcity which is in any case limited in time and space; a scarcity to which the market responds spontaneously with a prompt and congruent increase in the price of the scarce fuel. The increase in price of the scarce fuel is expected to stimulate technological progress to find alternative solutions. In particular, an increase in the fuel price shifts the demand towards suppliers or reserves which, in consequence of such a price increase, become economically convenient. So, for example, the rapid increase in the price of oil provoked by the two shocks in the 1970s, made it worthwhile to extract oil in other geographical areas, such as the North Sea, the USA, Russia and Mexico, where average production costs were considerably higher than in the OPEC countries.[6] This resulted in a reduction over time in OPEC's share of world oil production which led the member countries to reduce the price they had established in order to gain back the share they had lost.[7]

As regards pollution, the conventional position maintained a rather optimistic attitude in the 1990s, one which is still held today. On the basis of a reduction in energy intensity observed in those years and in the carbon content per unit of consumption, the conviction grew that the pollution generated by energy consumption had started to stabilize. In this spirit, from the Environmental Kuznets Curve (EKC) applied to energy consumption, some have drawn the hurried conclusion that in order to resolve the environmental problems raised by energy consumption, it would suffice to promote economic growth (cf. Colombo, 1992).[8]

The conventional position is the dominant one in all the industrialized countries but opinion is divided on the best environmental and energy policy to make the transition to a new model of energy consumption as painless as possible. In some countries, mainly European ones, it is thought that command and control instruments and environmental taxation are often necessary to accelerate the transition to a new energy model, while in other countries, notably in the USA, it is considered preferable to negotiate permits and voluntary agreements between enterprises and the environmental authorities to reduce the pollution and the wasting of resources that characterize the current energy model.

13.3. LIMITS TO THE CONVENTIONAL POSITION

The conventional position is reassuring but not very convincing. Above all, it risks underestimating the physical scarcity of fossil fuels. The latest data at our disposal do not support the paradox of their growing availability. For example, as regards oil, its estimated availability seems to have reached its peak in the mid-1990s after which it began to fall. Moreover, there are many indications that the residual reserves may have been overestimated by 'creative' geological accounting. The proponents of these estimates, in fact, may have an interest in inflating them. The producer countries do so in order to obtain higher production quotas and better conditions for the large loans they contract with the banks and international organizations. In the same way, the oil multinationals who participate in the data-gathering process and in the estimates of the residual reserves, have an interest in overestimating the reserves under their control in order to improve the performance of their shares on the stock exchange and to increase their bargaining power.

In any case, leaving aside the limited reliability of the data on residual reserves, there is a general agreement on the fact that the age of fossil fuels must come to an end before very long. Opinion is quite strongly divided, however, on the energy production and consumption model to adopt, as well as on when and how to change over to the new model. The speed and nature of the transition depends crucially on the evolution of the cost of production per kWh for the single energy sources. Everyone agrees that renewable energy sources must have a predominant role in the new energy model. As we have seen, according to the conventional position, this cannot happen before the middle of the century. Nevertheless, this assessment, which is crucial for steering energy choices, is not only a question of fairly accurate forecasting but it is also a question of energy policy. If the large state subsidies granted to the production and distribution of energy from fossil fuel were abolished, this could considerably accelerate the transition to the use of renewable energy sources. Further acceleration could be achieved by channelling the above-mentioned subsidies to the renewable energies sector to encourage the immediate utilization of the potential economies of scale which would considerably hasten the transition process. On the contrary, current energy subsidies are still mainly directed to exhaustible resources. In the US energy market, for instance, 88.5 per cent of total energy subsidies went to nuclear and fossil fuels, whereas only 5.4 per cent of the whole subsidy policy was devoted to emerging renewables (non-ethanol biomass, solar, wind, geothermal etc.) and to increasing demand efficiency (Koplow, 1993).

Nevertheless, there are some very powerful economic, financial and political interests that are trying to slow down the transition. All states and enterprises with large interests in the fossil fuel sector would like to exploit the economic opportunities it offers for as long as possible. Paradoxically, the physical scarcity of fossil fuel reserves means that all those who have an interest in the sector are trying to maximize profits from their use as quickly as possible, before they run out or before they become too costly to exploit and, in any case, before the already fragile political stability of producer countries comes to an end.[9] If we interpret the available resources as a relatively illiquid financial asset, it seems clear that an owner will try to liquidate this asset as soon as possible before its value is undermined by the lower price per kWh of renewable energy sources. Alternatively, to maintain their own position in the energy market, the owners of fossil fuel reserves could try and invest in backstop technology, getting ahead of any other competitors in research terms, so as to keep on meeting the demand for energy when the price of fossil fuel exceeds that of renewable resources. This could help to explain why some large oil companies (e.g. Shell) have, in recent years, invested in renewable energy sources such as, for example, solar energy. Furthermore, even the states which import most of the available fossil fuels are reluctant to take direct steps to reduce consumption due to the sizeable tax revenues earned from fossil fuel consumption.

As to the market optimism displayed by the conventional position, it could be claimed that in the energy field the myth of the invisible hand in the competitive market is particularly groundless. The allocation of resources and the prices for their use are moved by hands that are both visible and easy to identify: multinational oil companies, OPEC, and the energy policies of the richest countries.

13.4. THE TRANSITION UNDER WAY AND SUSTAINABLE DEVELOPMENT

In this section we intend to discuss to what extent the current trends of energy production and consumption are compatible with sustainable development. To analyze this point, let us now apply to the energy sector the well-known IPAT identity originally proposed by Holdren and Ehrlich (1974) and recently reformulated by Borghesi and Vercelli (2003) to examine whether the globalization process can be considered sustainable. Following previous authors (Kaya, 1990; Yamaji et al., 1991) the IPAT identity can be applied to the energy sector as follows:

$$D = yPed \tag{13.1}$$

where D represents environmental degradation, $y = Y/P$ is per capita income, P is the population level, $e = E/Y$ is energy intensity (that is, global demand for primary energy E per unit of output Y) and $d = D/E$ represents the intensity of environmental degradation (i.e. environmental degradation D per unit of primary energy consumption E). From (13.1) it is possible to derive the following modified identity:

$$D^* = y^* + P^* + e^* + d^* \tag{13.2}$$

where the star above each variable indicates the growth rate of the variable (i.e. its logarithmic derivative with respect to time).[10]

It should be stressed that identity (13.1) and the resulting condition (13.2) are, by definition, unfit for a causal analysis. Indeed, as some authors have argued (e.g. MacKellar et al., 1995), the IPAT model omits to analyse the interactions between the exogenous variables assuming that each is independent of the others, while in reality this is obviously not the case. Thus, for instance, the per capita income growth rate y^* affects the demographic growth rate P^* as well as the technological change (proxied by the terms e^* and d^*). By using conditions (13.1) and (13.2), however, total environmental degradation can be decomposed according to a few of its constituent parts and important constraints that any causal analysis has to comply with may be set.

The growth rate of environmental degradation D^* is measured, as a first approximation, with the growth rate of CO_2 emissions in that CO_2 is considered to be the main cause of the greenhouse effect among the gases produced by fossil fuels (IPCC, 2001) and a reference parameter for the aggregation of the other greenhouse gases (often measured in terms of tons of CO_2 emissions equivalent). Furthermore, given that emissions of carbon dioxide are specific to the use of fossil fuels, their measurement can be considered as a proxy, even if only a rough one, for the environmental degradation generated by the current energy model.

To ensure the sustainability of the planet, global environmental degradation should not increase with time but be reduced or at least remain constant. If it increases, we will move further away from sustainability, while if it decreases, we will move closer towards it.

Global environmental degradation tends to increase, other things being equal, with an increase in per capita income, unless the sum of the growth rates of population (P^*), energy intensity (e^*) and environmental degradation intensity (d^*) is negative and greater in absolute terms than the growth rate of per capita income (y^*). Therefore, to reduce global environmental degradation (and thus achieve sustainability) it is not sufficient that energy intensity follows an Environmental Kuznets Curve as some representatives of the conventional position have suggested (see Section 13.2 above). This can only ensure that e^* (but not D^*) would eventually become negative. Environmental degradation in the energy sector also depends on the trends of income, population and polluting emissions intensity, as explained by identity (13.2).

This can clearly be seen by looking at Figures 13.2 and 13.3 that report the annual growth rates of environmental degradation (as measured by total CO_2 emissions, D) and of its constituent parts (the terms on the right-hand side of equation (13.2)) over the period 1970–2000. As Figure 13.2 shows, the annual growth rates of degradation intensity (d^*) and, particularly, of energy intensity (e^*) have been negative most of the time during the three decades under consideration.[11] This seems *prima facie* to support the optimistic viewpoint that energy problems may be solved by technological progress alone. As Figure 13.3 shows, however, this optimism induced by the mainly negative values of d^* and e^* is somewhat misleading. Despite the steady (but slow) reduction of the demographic growth rate P^*, the annual growth rate of D was positive most of the time during the period 1970–2000. From Figure 13.3, moreover, it emerges that the trend followed by D^* is generally closely related to that followed by y^* which clearly plays a major role among the decomposition factors taken into account.

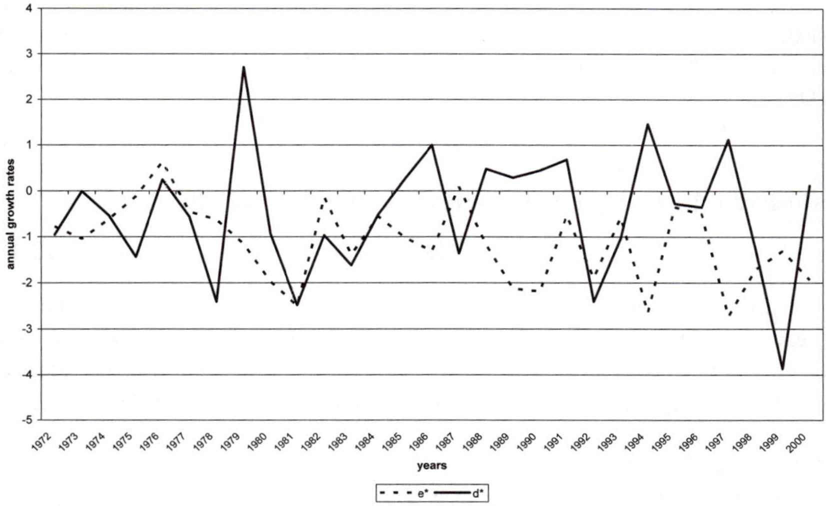

Source: Authors' elaboration on World Bank data (World Bank, 2007).

Figure 13.2. Energy intensity (e) and emission intensity (d*) annual growth rates, 1970–2000*

Source: Authors' elaboration on World Bank data (World Bank, 2007).

Figure 13.3. Total emissions (D), per capita income (y*) and population (P*) annual growth rates, 1970–2000*

From (13.2) we derive the following condition for long-term energy sustainability, namely, the condition that the growth rate of per capita income should satisfy to be consistent with a non-increasing path of CO_2 emissions ($D^* \leq 0$):

$$y^* \leq (e^* + P^* + d^*) \tag{13.3}$$

which can also be expressed in terms of total income as follows:

$$Y^* \leq (e^* + d^*) \tag{13.4}$$

On the basis of these identities, it is possible to analyze what happened in the world in the last three decades of the previous century and the forecasts of the Energy Information Administration (EIA) for the first three decades of the new century (EIA, 2006). The basic data are summarized in Table 13.2.[12]

Table 13.2. EIA scenario

World	Y*	P*	y*	E*	e*	D*	d*
1971–1980	4.1	1.9	2.2	3.0	–1.1	2.8	–0.2
1981–1990	3.2	1.9	1.3	2.1	–1.1	1.6	–0.5
1991–2000	3.4	1.6	1.8	1.6	–1.8	1.4	–0.2
1971–2000	3.3	1.7	1.6	2.1	–1.2	1.8	–0.3
2003–2030	3.8	1.0	2.8	2.0	–1.8	2.1	0.1

Legend: Y = income, P = population, y = per capita income, E = primary energy demand, e = E/Y = energy intensity, D = environmental degradation, d = D/E = environmental degradation intensity. The star above each variable indicates the growth rate of the variable.

Source: Authors' elaboration on EIA (2006) data.

According to the EIA's forecasts based on the 'business-as-usual' (BAU) scenario, global energy demand is destined to increase until 2030 at an average rate of 2 per cent, while in the same period fossil fuels will increase their share of demand and international trade. Global energy intensity is destined to fall by 1.8 per cent as a result of technical progress but this is not enough to reduce CO_2 emissions which will increase on average by 2.1 per cent, partly because in the meantime the intensity of polluting emissions will slightly increase (+ 0.1 per cent) (EIA, 2006). Therefore, the estimated trends do not comply with the minimum requirements of environmental sustainability.

In addition, the energy trends do not comply with the requirements of social sustainability (see Borghesi and Vercelli, 2003). According to the forecasts of the International Energy Agency (IEA, 2004) in 2030 there will still be 1.4 billion people without electricity, the effects of which will progressively feed into the vicious circle of poverty and inequality. Furthermore, in the developing countries 2/5 of energy consumption will still be based on traditional biomass which is a particularly inefficient and polluting source of energy. Lastly, inequality in terms of per capita energy distribution is expected to remain very marked which will strongly influence access to economic opportunities on the part of the most disadvantaged populations, further increasing inequality and poverty.

These forecasts, which are based on the current economic, energy and environmental policies, expect a worsening of energy trends as compared with those registered over the last three decades. Energy trends were incompatible with sustainable development in the latter period. Nevertheless, as can be seen in Table 13.2, the trends gradually improved over the last three decades of the 20th century, while they are expected to worsen over the next three. In particular, energy intensity e has fallen ever more rapidly from 1.1 per cent in the 1970s and 1980s to 1.8 per cent in the 1990s. This was the result of greater attention being paid to energy saving following the oil shocks of the 1970s which was then consolidated by increasingly rigorous energy policies in the 1980s and '90s. Above all in the 1990s, a significant contribution to this virtuous trend was provided by the systematic introduction of information and communication technologies. The progressive reduction in energy intensity, however, might be unable to continue in the next few decades with respect to the 1990s, due to the more rapid growth of developing economies such as India and China. These economies generally have a high energy intensity (and thus also high carbon intensity) which may cause high growth rates of CO_2 emissions in the future as their GDP grows.

Moreover, the energy intensity of polluting emissions d, which had fallen significantly in the 1980s and '90s, is expected to grow in the next 25 years, albeit at a very low rate (0.1 per cent). This suggests a worsening of the sustainable development scenario despite the expected reduction in the rate of demographic growth. This deterioration of development sustainability can also be expressed by defining a sustainability gap g in the energy sector based on the identity (13.4):

$$g = y^* - y^*_{max} = Y^* - Y^*_{max} = Y^* + e^* + d^* \qquad (13.5)$$

where y^*_{max} and Y^*_{max} define the maximum growth rate respectively of per capita income and total income that are compatible with sustainable development (i.e. the growth rates corresponding to zero environmental deterioration).

With this definition, we can see that the sustainability gap in the energy sector falls from 2.8 per cent in the 1970s to 1.6 per cent in the '80s and to 1.4 per cent in the '90s, but the EIA forecasts that the value will rise in the next 25 years to 2.1 per cent (EIA, 2006). Behind these negative trends there is an overly slow transition process towards an alternative model based on the massive use of renewable energies: the share of world energy consumption met by all renewable sources has increased very slowly (from 14 per cent to 19.7 per cent) between 1973 and 2004 (IEA, 2006).[13] Similarly, the total share of renewable energy sources in world electricity generation is expected to increase by only 1 per cent (from 18 per cent to 19 per cent) between 2002 and 2030 (IEA, 2004). The explanation set forth for such a slow transition process is generally that energy produced from fossil fuels costs less and will continue to do so for the whole period. This explanation, however, seems only partly valid. Indeed, this affirmation is based on a very unsatisfactory way of calculating the cost per kWh. First of all, no account is taken of external costs which in the case of fossil fuels are particularly high. The increase in carbon dioxide is destined considerably to worsen global warming with all its dire consequences for the climate, the melting of glaciers, and atmospheric variability. In the second place, the production of fossil fuels can be just as dangerous in itself. It has been calculated, for example, that coal-mining alone accounts for some 10,000 deaths a year. Finally, there are also high political and economic risks connected with the predominant use of fossil fuels in that their availability is very concentrated geographically-speaking, thus creating strong tensions for the economic and political control of these areas (the Middle East in the first place). Given that the forecasts for the costs of each energy source are crucially dependent on the hypotheses made about economic, energy, and environment policies, these tensions could lead in the future to a much higher cost of energy production with fossil fuels than that being forecast today.

13.5. CONCLUSIONS

In this chapter we have argued that the conventional position concerning the energy trends and their impact on sustainable development appears to be excessively optimistic. This optimism is mainly based on the observed increase in the reserves of fossil fuels over the years; on the capacity of the market price to signal the scarcity of the resources and thus induce a shift towards alternative energy sources; and on the existence of an Environmental Kuznets Curve in energy intensity, so that the latter variable will eventually fall in the long run. Each of these arguments, however, presents serious shortcomings. The estimated increase in the reserves of fossil fuels might have been partially overestimated by the current data sources (mainly OPEC and oil multinationals). Moreover, market price signals are often distorted by large state subsidies for the production and distribution of energy from fossil fuels, that deeply modify the speed and the nature of the transition to renewable energy sources. Finally, as pointed out above, the existence of an Environmental Kuznets Curve in energy intensity is not sufficient *per se* to ensure a decrease in the environmental degradation generated by the current energy model.

Despite these drawbacks, the conventional position has so far greatly influenced energy and environmental policies, favouring an overly slow transition process towards a new way of producing, distributing and consuming energy based on the use of renewable sources. This stance is destined to further widen the sustainability gap which has characterized the last 30 years, albeit at decreasing rates. This is confirmed by the recent EIA estimates that forecast a future inversion of the decreasing trend in energy and emission intensity observed over the last three decades.

In recent years, the growing optimism in the market capacity to resolve spontaneously the problems of energy scarcity and pollution produced by energy consumption, has manifestly weakened policies aimed at promoting energy-saving and renewable sources. The estimates proposed in this chapter indicate the urgency of strengthening the above-mentioned policies in order to accelerate the convergence towards compatibility between energy consumption and sustainable development. In particular, the priority is to make provisions to accelerate the transition towards an alternative model for the production, distribution and consumption of energy that should be based on energy saving and on incentives for the adoption of renewable sources in proportion to their external economies.

NOTES

* The authors would like to thank seminar participants at the Workshop 'Crescita economica: dinamiche sociali ed istituzionali' (Lucca, 10–12 July, 2007) for helpful comments and suggestions. The usual disclaimer applies.

1. More than 60 per cent of the world's oil production is concentrated in only five countries (Saudi Arabia, the United Arab Emirates, Iraq, Kuwait and Iran). If we exclude the North Sea and the USA, the remaining percentage is mainly concentrated in areas of high tension and political instability such as the west coast of Africa, Libya, Algeria, Russia and the post-Soviet republics of the Caspian.
2. Using the terminology adopted by British Petroleum (2007), the term 'proven reserves' indicates those quantities that, on the basis of the geological and engineering information available, can be recuperated in the future with reasonable certainty from the known reserves under existing economic and operating conditions.

3. Adopting the notion proposed by Wackernagel and Rees (1996), for instance, the authors argue that the human ecological footprint is already about 20 per cent beyond the Earth's carrying capacity.
4. The expected lifespan T is calculated by British Petroleum as the ratio between the remaining proven reserves at the end of the year and that year's output, assuming that output will continue at the same level in the future.
5. Since fossil fuels are by nature depletable resources the corresponding cost is bound to rise in the long term.
6. It has been estimated, for example, that the average production cost in the Arab countries is between 1 and 2 dollars a barrel, while in the North Sea it ranges between 7 and 10 dollars a barrel.
7. In a similar way, the observation that the productive capacity of the North Sea could have reached its upper limit led OPEC to cut its own production by about 1.7 million barrels a day in the period 1999–2000. Together with the embargo on Iraq, this increased the price from 15 to over 34 dollars a barrel. The relationship between the OPEC cartel and the non-OPEC countries (the so-called 'cartel-fringe' relationship) is the subject of numerous theoretical models that analyze OPEC's production decisions in relation to those of its competitors and the consequent changes in the leadership of the productive market (see for example Ulph and Folie, 1980; Geroski et al., 1987).
8. Various empirical studies have analyzed the hypothesis of the Environmental Kuznets Curve in the case of energy (e.g. Cole et al., 1997; Suri and Chapman, 1998; Galeotti and Lanza, 1999; Sun, 1999; Focacci, 2003). See Cleveland et al. (2000) and Soytas and Sari (2003) for an analysis of the causality links between energy consumption and income growth, and Borghesi (2001) for a general survey of the literature on the EKC. See also Luzzati and Orsini (2006) for an estimate of the EKC on energy use which contains innovative elements both in the evaluation of the econometric critiques of the EKC literature and in the comparison among different econometric techniques and different levels of analysis (world, time series/cross-country, single country).
9. Boyce (1994) argues that in countries with high levels of inequality (such as the oil-producing countries) the richest individuals and enterprises apply a higher discount rate for the risk of political instability generated by this inequality. For this reason, they would prefer to exploit their own resources as fast as possible to invest the resulting profits abroad where political instability and the consequent investment risks are lower.
10. Notice that, following the terminology adopted in the literature on the Environmental Kuznets Curve, the terms on the right-hand side of equation (13.2) can be interpreted as a measure of the scale effect ($y^* + P^*$), the composition effect (e^*) and the technological effect (d^*) that economic growth has on environmental degradation.
11. The values for d^* and e^* were computed using the World Development Indicators (World Bank, 2007). As no observations are available in this dataset on total energy use at the world level up to 1971, the trends of d^* and e^* in Figure 13.2 start from 1972.
12. Similar results apply if we use the forecasts of the International Energy Agency (IEA, 2006) for the same period. Notice that Table 13.2 also reports data concerning two variables (Y^* and E^*) that do not appear in equations (13.1) and (13.2) as these help to determine the values of the remaining variables. Thus, for instance, the values of e^* can be derived from the difference between E^* and Y^*. The same applies to y^* that is given by $Y^* - P^*$.
13. Notice, moreover, that if we exclude nuclear energy the share of total energy produced from the other renewable resources increased by only 0.1 per cent (from 13.1 per cent to 13.2 per cent) in the same period (IEA, 2006).

REFERENCES

Borghesi, S. (2001), 'The Environmental Kuznets Curve: A Survey of the Literature', in M. Franzini and A. Nicita (eds), *Economic Institutions and Environmental Policy*, Aldershot: Ashgate, pp. 201–24. Previously published as *Nota di Lavoro no.85.99*, Milan: Fondazione ENI Enrico Mattei, 1999.

Borghesi, S. and A. Vercelli (2003), 'Sustainable Globalisation', *Ecological Economics*, **44**(1), 77–89.

Boyce, J.K. (1994), 'Inequality as a Cause of Environmental Degradation', *Ecological Economics*, **11**(3), 169–78.

British Petroleum (1995), *BP Statistical Review of World Energy*, London: BP plc.

British Petroleum (2007), *BP Statistical Review of World Energy*, London: BP plc.

Cleveland, C.J., R.K. Kaufman and D.I. Stern (2000), 'Aggregation and the Role of Energy in the Economy', *Ecological Economics*, **32**(2), 301–17.

Cole, M.A., A.J. Rayner and J.M. Bates (1997), 'The Environmental Kuznets Curve: An Empirical Analysis', *Environment and Development Economics*, **2**(4), 401–16.

Colombo, U. (1992), 'Sustainable Energy Development', in *IIASA*, pp. 95–119.

EIA – Energy Information Administration (2006), *International Energy Outlook 2006*, Office of Integrated Analysis and Forecasting, Washington DC: U.S. Department of Energy.

Focacci, A. (2003), 'Empirical Evidence in the Analysis of the Environmental and Energy Policies of a Series of Industrialised Nations, During the Period 1960–1997, Using Widely Employed Macroeconomic Indicators', *Energy Policy*, **31**(4), 333–52.

Galeotti M. and A. Lanza (1999), 'Desperately Seeking (Environmental) Kuznets', *Nota di lavoro no.2.99*, Milan: Fondazione ENI Enrico Mattei.

Georgescu-Roegen, N. (1977), 'The Steady State and the Economic Salvation', *Bioscience*, **27**(4), 266–70.

Geroski, P., A. Ulph and D. Ulph (1987), 'A Model of the Crude Oil Market in which Conduct Varies', *Economic Journal*, **97**(388a), 77–86.

Holdren, J.P. and P.R. Ehrlich (1974), 'Human Population and the Global Environment', *American Scientist*, **62**, 282-292.

IIASA - International Institute for Applied Systems Analysis (1992), *Science and Sustainability*, Vienna: Novographic.

IEA – International Energy Agency (2004), *World Energy Outlook 2004*, Paris: OECD/IEA.

IEA – International Energy Agency (2006), *World Energy Outlook 2006*, Paris: OECD/IEA.

IPCC – Intergovernmental Panel on Climate Change (2001), *Third Assessment Report – Climate Change*, Geneva, Switzerland.

Kaya, Y. (1990), 'Impact of Carbon Dioxide Emission Control on GNP Growth: Interpretation of Proposed Scenarios', paper presented to *IPCC Energy and Industry Sub-Group*, Response strategies Working Group.

Koplow, D. (1993), *Federal Energy Subsidies: Energy, Environmental and Fiscal Impacts*, Alliance to Save Energy, Washington DC.

Luzzati T. and M. Orsini (2006), 'The Natural Environment and Economic Growth: Looking for the Energy-EKC', Economic Growth: Institutional and Social Dynamics, PRIN 2005, *Working Paper No. 7.*

MacKellar, F.L., W. Lutz, C. Prinz and A. Goujon (1995), 'Population, Households and CO_2 Emissions', *Population and Development Review*, **21**(4), 849–65.

Meadows, D.H., D.L. Meadows, J. Randers and W. Behrens (1972), *The Limits to Growth*, New York: Universe Books.

Meadows, D.H., D.L. Meadows and J. Randers (1992), *Beyond the Limits: Confronting Global Collapse, Envisioning a Sustainable Future*, White River Junction, VT: Chelsea Green Publishing Company.

Meadows, D.H., D.L. Meadows and J. Randers (2004), *Limits to Growth: The 30-Year Update*, White River Junction, VT: Chelsea Green Publishing Company.

Rifkin, J. (2002), *The Hydrogen Economy*, New York: Tarcher/Putnam.

Soytas, U. and R. Sari (2003), 'Energy Consumption and GDP: Causality Relationship in G-7 Countries and Emerging Markets', *Energy Economics*, **25**(1), 33–7.

Sun, J.W. (1999), 'The Nature of CO_2 Emission Kuznets Curve', *Energy Policy*, **27**(2), 691–94.

Suri V. and D. Chapman (1998), 'Economic Growth, Trade and Energy: Implications for the Environmental Kuznets Curve', *Ecological Economics*, **25**(2), 195–208.

Ulph, A. and M. Folie (1980), 'Exhaustible Resources and Cartels: An Intertemporal Nash-Cournot Model', *Canadian Journal of Economics*, **13**(4), 645–58.

Wackernagel, M. and W. Rees (1996), *Our Ecological Footprint: Reducing Human Impact on the Earth*, Philadelphia: New Society Publishers.

World Bank (2007), *World Development Indicators*, Washington DC.

Yamaji, K., Y. Matsuhashi, Y. Nagata and Y. Kaya (1991), *An Integrated System for C02/Energy/GNP Analysis: Case Studies on Economic Measures for CO_2 Reduction in Japan*', Workshop on CO2 Reduction and Removal: Measures for the Next Century, 19–21.3.1991, Luxemburg, Austria: International Institute for Applied Systems Analysis.

14. Human needs, sustainable development and public policy: learning from K.W. Kapp (1910–1976)*

Tommaso Luzzati

14.1. INTRODUCTION

The role and extent of public intervention in the economy, more than any other topic, has polarized the various traditions of economic thought. Karl William Kapp (1910–1976) was among those who strongly advocated public intervention. However, his analysis and the prescriptions involved were rather peculiar. His approach was rooted in (old) institutionalism and his attention focused on economic development and its processes. He maintained that economic analysis and policy have to be centred on the satisfaction of human needs and ensure continuation of human life on Earth. He saw himself as an advocate of 'rational humanism'. Ahead of his time, in the 1950s he was already aware that unregulated economic processes deeply impair the human environment (both the social and natural environment). Given these premises, he saw public intervention as being aimed at protecting the human environment, both in the short and long run. It must not be thought, however, that he suggested top-down/paternalistic methods for choosing goals, strategies and policies. On the contrary, he advocated a dialectic between ends and means, guided by the interplay between science and participatory processes.

This chapter will outline K.W. Kapp's position, with reference both to the analytical framework he elaborated and to one of its origins, Myrdal's approach. The next section shortly introduces the life and works of Kapp. The third section focuses on circular cumulative causation, a notion that he mainly derived from Myrdal and that was central to his thought. Section 14.4 shows in what respect Kapp moved beyond Myrdal, Section 14.5 seeks to give a unitary picture of his thought, while his position on development policies is explored in Section 14.6.

14.2. A BIOGRAPHICAL NOTE

Kapp was born in 1910 at Königsberg in Germany, and graduated in Economics and Law at the University of Berlin. Forced to leave Germany in 1933 to flee Nazi persecutions, he settled in Geneva where he obtained his PhD with a thesis on 'Planwirtschaft und Aussenhandel' (Economic planning and international commerce). He then lectured at various universities in the USA, the country to where he moved in 1939. In 1957, as a Fulbright research fellow, Kapp moved with his wife to the Gokhale Institute of Politics and Economics at Poona in India. From 1961 to 1962, he visited the University of Rajasthan in Jaipur and in 1964 the University of the Philippines in Quezon City. In 1965, he went back to Switzerland, at the University of Basel. Kapp contributed to the first United Nations Conference on the Human Environment held at Stockholm in 1972 as an expert in environmental problems (for more details, see the profile by Steppacher (1994)).

His thought belongs to the institutionalist tradition, influenced in particular by T. Veblen, J.M. Clark, G. Myrdal, A. Lowe, F. Perroux and K. Polanyi. With Polanyi, in particular (for a detailed comparison see Swaney and Evers, 1989), he shared the idea of an individual embedded in social relations and of an economy as an open system, tied by a double strand to the natural and cultural context. As a consequence, Kapp advocated the need to integrate the study of economic, physical and social spheres. As we will see in the following, Kapp, influenced by Myrdal's notion of cumulative causation and by the developments of system theory in the 1960s, adopted a systemic and evolutionary perspective. Such a perspective led him to reject the 'boundary conditions' normally defined by economic theory, that is, the hypothesis of exogenous preferences, technology and institutions. Above all, Kapp believed that the focus of economic inquiry should be human beings and their needs – at least partly definable with objective and broadly shared parameters, that is, a corpus of 'existential social minima' which is open and to be determined in time.

Publication in 1950 of the book *The Social Costs of Private Enterprise*[1] may be considered the first significant stage in Kapp's thinking. In subsequent years, in several books and articles, he progressively refined his key concepts. His ideas matured and were summarised in publications in the late 1960s and early 1970s, many of which appeared in *Kyklos*. Unfortunately, the mature stage of his scientific production was suddenly interrupted when he suffered a heart attack during a conference on ecological development at the University of Dubrovnik in Croatia and died the day after on 10 April 1976.

14.3. MYRDAL'S CIRCULAR CUMULATIVE CAUSATION AS A KEY ELEMENT IN KAPP'S THOUGHT

In his collection of readings in the history of economic thought, Kapp includes a part on 'social or institutional economics' (Kapp and Kapp, 1963, p. 381). In the introduction to that part he traces a concise picture of the distinguishing features of institutional economics – a picture which is very close to subsequent papers on the nature of institutional economics both by himself (Kapp 1968, 1976b) and by others, such as Myrdal (1978). In particular, two ideas are central, that 'the economy is more than the market' and that '[it] is always a process of becoming' (Samuels, 1995, p. 580), which Kapp expresses as the need to take 'account of the open and dynamic character of the economy' (Kapp and Kapp, 1963, p. 382).

The first claim, that 'economic problems must be viewed within a broad social and political framework' (Kapp and Kapp, 1963, p. 381), is entailed by a systemic perspective that views the economy as an open system. As a subsystem of the social system, the economy is part of a large web of interconnected elements so 'it becomes, indeed, difficult to perceive what precisely should be meant by the "economic factor" as distinct from the others, and still less understandable how it can be "basic", as everything is cause to everything else in an interlocking circular manner' (Myrdal, 1957, p. 19, also in Kapp and Kapp, 1963, p. 418).

The second claim, that the economy has to be viewed in continuous change, is a matter of 'process philosophy' – an approach that began with the ancient Greeks (Heraclitus of Ephesus) and continues to this day (modern process philosophers include H. Bergson, J. Dewey, A.N. Whitehead). Within economics, J.S. Mill in his *System of Logic* (1843) had already focused on processes by identifying cumulative circularity – both between causes and effects and between humans and their context – as the driving force behind social change.

> The circumstances in which mankind are placed ... form the characters of the human beings; but the human beings, in their turn, mould and shape the circumstances for themselves and for those who come after them. From this reciprocal action there must necessarily result either a cycle or a progress. One of the thinkers who earliest conceived the succession of historical events as subject to fixed laws, and endeavoured to discover these laws by an analytical survey of history, Vico, the celebrated author of Scienza Nuova, adopted the former of these opinions. [On the contrary Mill thought that] ... in each successive age the principal phenomena of society are different from what they were in the age preceding ... [and that] ... what we now are and do is in a very small degree the result of the universal circumstances of the human race, or even of our own circumstances acting through the original qualities of our species, but mainly of

> the qualities produced in us by the whole previous history of humanity (Mill, 1843, Book 6, Ch. 10, Sect. 3).

In short, 'history matters' and human societies are mainly the result of their own history. The key mechanism is the principle of sequential, related and cumulative process on which is based the present notion of 'path-dependence' and 'lock-in'. Cumulative change is pivotal in Veblen's writings, who used it to build his non-teleological evolutionism, where neither ultimate causes nor final states can be considered in an unending process of change that replaces the traditional equilibrium idea (see, e.g., Hodgson, 1994). Veblen's concept is held (see Hodgson, 1994; Argyrous and Sethi, 1996) as highly influential both on the circular cumulative causation (CCC) approach followed by Young in 1928 and subsequently by Kaldor, and, more in general, on evolutionary economics (Mayhew, 2001, p. 243). To be fair, however, as Berger and Elsner (2007, p. 529) noted, 'approaches dealing with "cumulative causation" were common in England, Germany and Sweden in the 1920s'. Actually Kapp took Myrdal's approach as the main reference for CCC, pointing out, among others, that Myrdal 'draws the logical inferences and the practical conclusions from Veblen's earlier notion of cumulative change and drift'[2] (Kapp and Kapp, 1963, p. 385).

With the help of many excerpts taken from Myrdal's *Economic Theory and Underdeveloped Regions*, Kapp and Kapp (ibid., pp. 417–34) draw attention to 'the notion of a circular casual relationship of all relevant factors in a social system' (ibid., p. 384) and its cumulative character that makes the idea of stable equilibrium of low empirical relevance. One important application of circular cumulative causation is to explain the drift toward regional and interregional inequality. More specifically, 'backwash' effects largely dominate spread effects in underdeveloped regions, so that even absolute inequality may increase.[3]

Given the insufficiency of self-correcting market forces, and given the aim of spurring development and increasing equality, Myrdal calls for public action. Circular cumulative causation is 'bound to encourage the reformer' since 'it promises final effects of very much greater magnitude than the efforts and cost of the reforms themselves', which 'is, in one sense, a demonstration, and also a measure, of the earlier existing "social waste"'. (Myrdal, 1957, p. 20, also in Kapp and Kapp, 1963, pp. 418–19). This allows Myrdal (and Kapp as well) to understand policy as a broad complex of measures inducing and controlling a cumulative process of change. Myrdal (1957, p. 90) notes that 'the price system as a part of a very irrational whole, namely the economy of a backward and stagnating country, can hardly have any great claim on rationality' to guide the formation of policies.

> The plan and its targets have in the final analysis to be determined by decisions which represent choices made among different, alternatively possible, sets of goals and means. These choices are policy decisions, reached in terms of national development goals as determined by the political process (Myrdal, 1957, p. 89).[4]

Kapp fully endorsed Myrdal's position. He did it to such an extent that he would write that 'with Myrdal's formulation of the principle of circular causation we finally arrive at the core of institutional economics which sets it apart from earlier and contemporary non-institutionalist approaches and particularly from mechanistic equilibrium analysis' (Kapp, 1976b, p. 217).

The thought of J.S. Mill is very relevant to institutionalism in general, and to Myrdal's and Kapp's positions in particular. For this reason it is helpful to read some passages again from J.S. Mill's *System of Logic*.

> [Man] has, to a certain extent, a power to alter his character. Its being, in the ultimate resort, formed for him, is not inconsistent with its being, in part, formed by him as one of the intermediate agents. His character is formed by his circumstances, (including among these his particular organisation), but his own desire to mould it in a particular way is one of those circumstances, and by no means one of the least influential (Mill, 1843, Book 6, Ch. 2, Sect. 3).
>
> ... the character, that is, the opinions, feelings, and habits of the people, though greatly the results of the state of society which precedes them, are also greatly the causes of the state of society which follows them (Mill 1843, Book 6, Ch. 9, Sect. 4).
>
> ... we must remember that a degree of knowledge far short of the power of actual prediction is often of much practical value. There may be great power of influencing phenomena, with a very imperfect knowledge of the causes by which they are in any given instance determined. It is enough that we know that certain means have a tendency to produce a given effect, and that others have a tendency to frustrate it. When the circumstances of an individual or of a nation are in any considerable degree under our control, we may, by our knowledge of tendencies, be enabled to shape those circumstances in a manner much more favourable to the ends we desire than the shape which they would of themselves assume. This is the limit of our power, but within this limit the power is a most important one (Mill 1843, Book 6, Ch. 5, Sect. 4).

Mill was pointing to the power of human action to induce change, the importance of social/institutional factors, the practical value (involved by a dynamic approach) of knowing the quality/direction of the feedbacks. These features lie at the core of the institutionalist paradigm, albeit with different emphasis in each author. Differently from Veblen, Myrdal and Kapp emphasised the possibility and need for action. Moreover, Kapp was also very concerned with the individual level and adopted Mill and Veblen's notion of human agency according to which individuals are not passive recipients of pleasure and pain, 'a bundle of desires that are to be saturated

… but rather a coherent structure of propensities and habits which seeks realisation and expression in an unfolding activity' (Veblen, 1898, p. 390). In other words, Kapp took individuals as active, learning and social beings.[5] Actually, he was rather optimistic since he believed that 'man, with his specifically human intelligence, is capable of using reason and science for the exploration of goals and as a basis for judgements as to the kind and direction of action to be followed' (Kapp, 1965, pp. 76–7).

14.4. EXTENDING MYRDAL

Myrdal's position is generally summarised by three core ideas (e.g. Panico and Rizzo, 2008) – the cumulative causation approach, the consideration of socio-cultural factors and the impossibility of value-free theory, which involves the need of explicit value premises. Myrdal's main value premise was equality such that his analysis developed as a theoretical foundation of egalitarian policies. Kapp took some steps further thanks to a basic analytical extension of Myrdal's approach. The extension was to further 'open' the economic system, not only to the society system, but also to the bio-physical system; in other words he maintained the need to analyse the economy not only as part of society but also of the natural environment.

Such an idea was originated by Kapp's early interest and adherence to general system theory, substantially supported[6] in the 1960s and which was to assume a key role in ecology and had a distinguished predecessor in Erwin Schrödinger. Kapp was aware of the thermodynamic nature of the living organisms that keep themselves alive by exchanging matter with their environment (e.g. Kapp, 1961, p. 93). Moreover, like Georgescu Roegen, he was well aware that societies also have a physical metabolism that cannot be left out of the analysis. As pointed out by Berger and Elsner (2007, pp. 532–3), Kapp and Georgescu refer to bio-physical knowledge not for analogical/metaphorical purposes, rather 'in a direct integration, as far as this is directly applicable to the biological open character of man and the material level of the economic process', that is 'to establish a causal analysis, which directly takes physical and institutional chains into account' and 'to deal with discontinuous nonlinear feedbacks, which characterize the dynamic interdependencies between the different subsystems, as well as of each subsystem with the composite whole'. Later on, when doing research on China, Kapp found such an approach consistent with Taoism:

> the Taoist component of Chinese culture has always held that man and society are integral parts of nature and hence marked by interdependencies which, if ignored by human action and innovation without adequate assessment of their consequences, must give rise to grave perturbations of man's social and natural

environment. … The term environment will be interpreted in the broad sense in which it is used in the Chinese literature. That is to say, it includes both the social and the physical components of the human environment as it affects the quality of life in the wider sense of the term (Kapp, 1974a, p. 10).

It is the very consciousness of the biophysical dimension that makes Kapp's analysis and his policy prescriptions very peculiar and broad. For instance, social costs, a major cause for concern among institutional economists,[7] acquire a special light. They are seen as very extensive interdependencies.[8] transferred by means of physical non-market exchanges, which feed complicated circuits of cumulative causality. The traditional meaning of externality becomes therefore irrelevant, since social costs are not a secondary (or, at any rate, limited) phenomenon[9] and cannot be reduced to simple cause–effect[10] mechanisms.

As a result, while Myrdal had to derive his belief on the irrationality in the market by observing stagnation (as evidenced in the quote in Section 14.3), Kapp could go much further, maintaining that 'the organising principles of economic systems guided by exchange values are incompatible with the requirements of ecological systems and the satisfaction of basic human needs' (Kapp, 1976a, p. 95).

Combining social costs with CCC, Kapp attacked positions like Hirschman's according to which ecological protection is a 'luxury' so that 'planners would be well advised to follow the old "capitalist trick" of shifting social costs to society at large' (Kapp, 1977a, p. 205). The recipe of 'first the economy, then the environment' is held by Kapp to be ineffective and dangerous since 'environmental disruption and social costs are important causal factors that play a significant negative role in the cumulative process of development … The false dichotomy of economic and socio-environmental objectives' (ibid., p. 209) has to be abandoned (see also Kapp 1974b, p. 105). In other words, preventing environmental degradation in Kapp is not a matter of environmental ethics, rather a need arising from the awareness that the economic processes, via extra-market physical flows, 'threaten the economic process, its social reproduction, and hence the continued guarantee of human well-being and survival' (Kapp, 1976a, p. 91; see also Kapp, 1977a, p. 205).

The material nature of human beings made him focus on basic needs.[11] He strongly believed that public policy has to be guided 'by the social and *moral* imperative of minimizing human suffering' (Kapp, 1977b, p. 538). He maintained that

economic decision-making will have to be guided by a substantive concept of rationality; such a concept would be based upon a direct social evaluation (at the political level) of essential human needs and their relative social importance and the real costs evaluated in terms of available, unutilized and potential resources …

> as well as the possibility of sharply restricting or abandoning the pursuit of less essential objectives. Among these objectives we would list the production of luxury goods, the pursuit of costly programs of space travel and nuclear weapon systems the relative social importance of which has never been evaluated and compared with the social need of safeguarding the dynamic equilibrium of the environment. Instead of exchange values, social use values (values which are socially i.e. politically appraised and determined) would begin to guide the process of production and allocation while calling simultaneously for the setting-up of the necessary institutional arrangements (Kapp, 1974c, p. 136).[12]

Finally, his consideration for humans prevented him from suggesting top-down/paternalistic methods for choosing goals, strategies and policies. On the contrary, he advocated a dialectic between ends and means, guided by the interplay between science and participatory processes within the constraints given by the ethical goal of human needs satisfaction. This actually shows the pride of place given by Kapp to ethics and politics. The decision as to which avenues to follow and instruments to use is the actors' task, both for a question of legitimacy and because the actors are those who best know the context of their action and their ability to set in train the strategies that have been worked out. 'External' agents, even if experts (scientists/technicians), must not and cannot provide solutions and remedies; rather, they should offer instruments capable of improving the soundness of actors' decisions.[13]

14.5. A SYNTHESIS OF KAPP'S APPROACH

Having sketched Kapp's approach, this section will gather his more recurrent and significant ideas within a unitary framework, which is tentatively illustrated in Figure 14.1

The cornerstone is, in my opinion, the very consideration of the biophysical dimension of society and life. On it Kapp based the very central notion of 'the economy as an open system' – a notion from which, in turn, most of Kapp's analytical concepts follow (see Kapp, 1976a). Such a systemic perspective, that also takes account of the social and physical environment, involves not only interdisciplinary research (e.g. Kapp, 1977b, p. 528) but also the acknowledgement that phenomena under observation both unravel on various spatial-temporal scales (e.g. Kapp, 1976a, p. 99; Kapp, 1977b, pp. 529 ff.) and require non-equivalent descriptions (see, e.g., Giampietro, 2003).

From these methodological premises four (interconnected) veins branch off, that is, system dynamics, social change, incommensurability, and relevance of social costs. Within a biophysical systemic perspective, phenomena continuously change and show the typical non-linearity of complex systems (such as threshold effects and synergies, see e.g. Kapp, 1976a, pp. 97 ff., or Kapp, 1977b, pp. 529 ff.). Human society makes no exception, which involves acknowledging change in preferences, technology and institutions (e.g. Kapp, 1976a, p. 102). Incommensurability follows straight from the multiplicity of scales and descriptions needed; despite a common material and energy base[14] (see Kapp, 1977b, pp. 531–2), phenomena show epistemological and ontological incommensurability that cannot be reduced to a common denominator.[15] Finally openness to physical and social systems makes the extent of the social costs in current competitive market economies very visible.[16]

On social costs his starting point was a detailed pioneering analysis (Kapp, 1950) of the many sources of social 'waste' induced by the working of the capitalist economy. Refining his critique, in the years to follow, he defined it as 'a 'system of non-paid costs' which generates high social costs and where 'power' of shifting costs onto others (*cost shifting*) is highly relevant'[17] (e.g. Kapp, 1969, p. 335). It was the inclusion of the bio-physical dimension that made Kapp conclude that an unregulated market leads to a systematic and substantial degradation of the physical and social environment through relevant cost-shifting that represent 'a "socialization", so to speak, of an important part of the actual costs of production' (Kapp, 1977b, pp. 529 ff.).[18]

As a consequence, defending society and social reproduction against social costs, i.e., against the spontaneous disorder of an unregulated market, is for Kapp an ethical must. To implement social control we should define aims that are both socially desirable and that guarantee 'the maintenance of dynamic states of ecological and economic balance' (Kapp, 1976a, p. 101). According to Kapp, such objectives need be defined through the joint action of technical aspects and politico-ethical aspects:

> in order to satisfy these human needs and to arrive at a substantive rationality in the utilization of society's scarce resources, these requirements (environmental requirements) will have been defined as objectively as our present knowledge permits and evaluated by means of a deliberate collective, i.e., political decision in comparison to other public goals to be pursued (Kapp, 1963, p. 317).

In other words, social control has to be implemented through democratic processes[19] which should ensure a compromise among the many interests and conflicting aims (see, e.g., Kapp, 1976a, p. 100; or Kapp, 1977b, pp. 536–7), guarantee social reproduction (intergenerational equity), and adhere to 'the social and *moral* imperative of minimizing human suffering' (Kapp, 1977b, p. 538) (intragenerational equity).

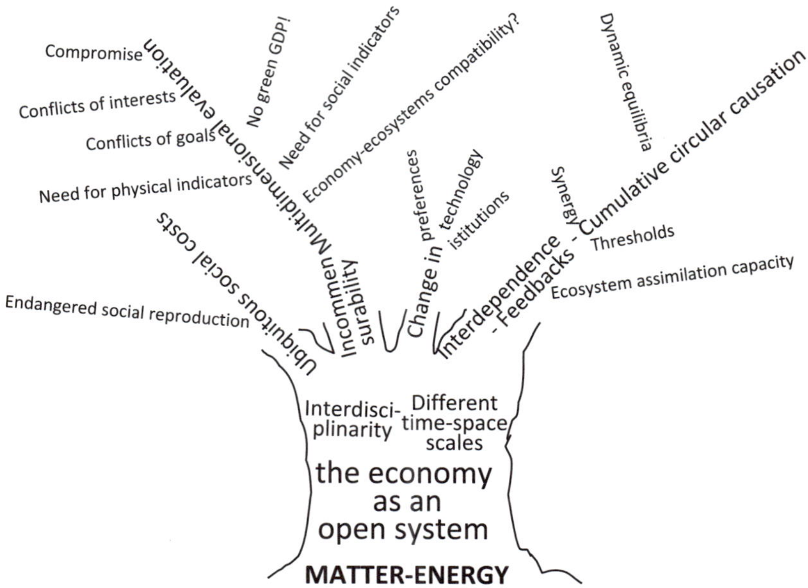

Note: Important epistemological tenets follow from acknowledging the material nature of human systems – to take into account of the openness (both to nature and society) of the economy, to use a systemic perspective, to look at several (and appropriates) time-space scales, to do interdisciplinary research. Having in mind these founding premises, Kapp's more recurrent and significant ideas can be gathered, as explained in details in the text, within a unitary framework made of four major branches.

Figure 14.1. The economy as an open system and its implications

A basic need for his proposal is, of course, a wide range of social and physical indicators[20] (see e.g. Kapp, 1977b, p. 538) for which Kapp makes a plea. Aware of the incommensurability of the various spheres, however, Kapp maintains the need of an integrated multidimensional approach (Kapp, 1976a, p. 97) showing that, in the context of social evaluation, 'all monetary evaluations' are 'problematical if not indeed unacceptable and cognitively irrelevant' (ibid., p. 101). Kapp argues that economic calculation cannot be extended beyond its normal field of application, that is, cannot be used in order to express the 'relative social importance in the sense of value to society (and individuals) both in the short and in the long run' (ibid.) of the environmental damage and of the public goods and services. Kapp, in other words, considers it neither sensible nor effective (see e.g. Kapp, 1977b, p. 534) to reduce real-world complexity merely to an economic dimension, expressing, for example, serious doubts about the 'current proposal of "deducting" social costs from gross or net national product measurements'

(Kapp, 1976a, p. 104). Like Georgescu Roegen, Kapp criticises the use of synthetic indexes to express, for instance, the 'true' value of goods and services.[21] Such indexes instead, 'upon closer analysis, can be shown to reflect either the subjective preferences and valuations of the experts and/or powerful vested interests' (Kapp, 1976a, p. 100).

14.6. ECONOMIC DEVELOPMENT POLICY

The focus on the physical and social environment played a key role for Kapp's analysis of economic development. In particular, two of his last articles (Kapp, 1974b, 1977a) show very effectively the need for integration between development and human environment.

Kapp personally experienced, during his lengthy study periods in Asia, the negative effects of traditional development policies, focussing on the technical and economic efficiency of investment projects and paying little heed to the institutional and cultural context or to impacts on social and physical equilibria. Such a one-dimensional vision, focused only on the economic sphere, has produced policies poorly connected to local situations and the socio-institutional context, often bringing about 'new dependencies and domination effects' between developing countries and their industrialised 'partners' (Kapp, 1977a, p. 206). The green revolution was an example taken by Kapp of a misguided transfer of capital and technologies to less developed countries – technologies which, for having being developed by and for the industrial world, have 'turned out to be problematic and in fact inappropriate solutions for the problems of the less-developed countries'. Kapp held that most development policies failed, producing instead

> high social costs not only in terms of ecological imbalances and overexploitation of resources but also in terms of socioeconomic disruption ... including social and personal relationships ... and a general dehumanization of the conditions of individual existence and group relations, which tends to cumulatively undermine the fabric of society and culture (Kapp, 1977a, p. 208).

Still today the LDCs are particularly fragile, entering 'the process of economic and social change under conditions which are in several respects less favourable than those which prevailed in today's advanced economies two hundred years ago', whether for intrinsic reasons, or due to the presence of already affluent and powerful economies (Kapp, 1974b, p. 103). The outcome envisaged by Kapp is 'a division of labour highly problematical for the LDCs in the long run' (Kapp, 1974b, p. 103) – the usual division of labour in which poor countries export low value-added products, with little effect on local development, within a context of growing economic dependence and high environmental, and hence social, impacts.

In dealing with such fragility, Kapp believed as 'essential that the less developed countries consider the process of development from the very outset as a multi-purpose undertaking' to be defined not 'exclusively in terms of national income … [i.e.] in terms of a single monetary denominator' (Kapp, 1974b, p. 106). The challenge thus becomes one of working out strategies for development, social planning and control capable of re-directing resource allocation 'with a more comprehensive economic calculus, taking into account the short and long term social costs and potential social benefits of alternative patterns of resource allocation' (Kapp, 1974b, p. 104).

In the previous section, the importance attributed by Kapp to indicators was mentioned. The first step for building a development strategy (Kapp, 1974b, pp. 106 ff.; Kapp, 1977a, pp. 209 ff) – as is now fairly consolidated – is to monitor the environmental and socio-economic situation using a sort of 'inventory' which gathers indicators and indexes on various scales, each expressed in the most appropriate unit of measurement regarding living conditions, the satisfaction of primary needs, the employment situation, pollution, the state of resources, technologies, the location of economic activities, and institutional factors.

This 'incommensurable complex' makes the next step, i.e., the process of identifying aims to pursue and possible lines of intervention, particularly difficult. While for the individual firm the objectives 'may be said to be quantifiable and more or less unproblematic inasmuch as they can be expressed in terms of one common denominator (i.e. money and the maximization of profits)' (Kapp, 1977a, p. 212), when dealing with society the means and the ends – for which Kapp, like Myrdal, rejects the traditional dichotomy (Kapp, 1965, pp. 57 ff.) – cannot be conceived as predetermined. Rather, they 'need to be discovered and defined in a continuous interaction of factual research and the formulation of goals and priorities …; they are under discussion and need to be explored and can be defined only in the process of an action- or policy-oriented process of research' (Kapp, 1977a, p. 213). What Kapp suggests, consistently with the general purpose of satisfying human primary needs and maintaining ecological equilibria and social reproduction) is to formulate aims both in terms of safety standards and of social minima.

Once social priorities are chosen (via a democratic and transparent process), the next two steps are the definition of control policies able to steer the competitive economic process towards social objectives, and development planning, i.e., the phase in which general aims and objectives are translated into specific plans and detailed projects. For the former, Kapp was in favour of a large number of instruments (e.g. Kapp, 1974b, pp. 115

ff.). For development planning, he stressed the importance of feasibility studies: to be able to carry out sound planning 'such surveys must establish in considerable detail the technical and institutional interdependencies and implications of alternative plans' and include 'the selection of the technology as well as the choice of institutional and administrative arrangements needed to implement the project at reasonable levels of technical and economic efficiency' (Kapp, 1965, p. 71). As for the contents of the plans, Kapp again shows his institutionalist spirit, maintaining the need both to pay concrete attention to the local context and its characteristics (which is crucial in choosing, say, which technology to promote) and to strive towards relative self-sufficiency, encouraging the ability to self-protect from social costs deriving from the international division of labour and reduce economic and political dependence.

It is not a question of aiming towards autarky, but rather of

> relying, as far as possible, upon the country's own resources as well as upon public participation in the political decision-making process … [through] a policy that stresses the use of available resources and techniques and their modernization ... A policy of self-reliance facilitates and increases the capacity of the population to develop, invent, and absorb new tools and technologies; it will thus support their confidence in their ability to increase productivity and to come to terms with the problems before them without surrendering their independence, their autonomy of decision making, and their choice of policy options in harmony with their own values and preferences. For these reasons, too, a policy of self-reliance and resistance to submission to foreign control must remain an essential objective of every viable national entity' (Kapp, 1997a., pp. 215–17).

14.7. CONCLUSIONS

One of the aims of this work was to introduce Kapp's approach and show its strong links with Myrdal's work and in general with the evolutionary-institutionalist tradition. Kapp maintained that circular cumulative causation has to be applied also to the bio-physical environment, not only to society and economy. This allowed him to show, in a coherent logical manner, the damage arising from an unregulated competitive system, especially, but not exclusively, for less developed countries. The role of public intervention appears then as crucial – especially under the moral imperative that Kapp assigned to economics and to economic policy, that is, to minimise human suffering and ensure continuation of human life on Earth.

Kapp's awareness of the highly complex nature of society prevented him falling into naïve top-down prescriptions. On the contrary, he demanded governance practices that favoured interaction between science and stakeholders within a transparent democratic process aimed at defining goals and means dialectically.

It is my hope, in conclusion, to have given an adequate picture of Kapp's main ideas. If this is so, readers should now be persuaded that Kapp's work is interesting not only for the history of economic thought. His ideas are still topical and offer a consistent and original framework both for reflection on the role of public intervention and for the implementation of successful strategies and practices of sustainable development.

NOTES

* I wish to thank S. Berger, R. Gaskins, G. Freni, P. Frigato, J. Martinez Alier, P. Meoli, L. Michelini, M. Orsini, C. Panico, S. Pochini, A.Opocher, and R. Steppacher for their invaluable criticisms and suggestions. I also received very helpful comments from the participants at a seminar held at the UAB in Barcelona, at the 5th ISEE Conference (New Dehli, 3-6 December 2006), at the 7th ESEE Conference (Leipzig, 5-8 June 2007) and in the workshops organised by the research group 'Economic Growth: Institutional and Social Dynamics' (PRIN 2005). Special thanks are due to Antonio G. Calafati for having brought Kapp's work to Italy via the publishers Otium and for having personally taught me to appreciate it. Any mistake or oversight is entirely my responsibility.

1. A second edition was published in 1963. The title was changed to *Social Costs of Business Enterprise* to testify to the new-found awareness that business in general gives rise to social costs, often in contradiction with its own institutional purpose. Both theoretical and empirical contents were modified and broadened. In 1971, a second edition of the 1950 book was published. Kapp added a new, and very interesting, introduction.
2. To my knowledge, Myrdal never clarified whether he was influenced by Veblen, although the similarity is high. Fujita (2006), reassessing Myrdal's CCC, shows the differences with the more successful Young-Kaldor's CCC and with the Veblenian one. See also Angresano (1997, p. 85).
3. Fujita (2006) maintains that the consideration of 'spread effects' makes Myrdal's approach more than a simple theory of polarization process.
4. See also Kapp and Kapp (1963, p. 430).
5. On human agency within the Veblenian institutionalist tradition see Mayhew (2001).
6. For example, Ackoff (1960) and von Bertalanffy (1968), both cited by Kapp and with whom he corresponded (Berger and Elsner, 2007, p. 533).
7. For his *History of Economic Thought*, Kapp selected many excerpts by Veblen and Myrdal that focus on social waste.
8. 'Problems of environmental disruption confront the social scientist with an unusually complex set of interdependencies and delayed cumulative effects' (Kapp, 1970, p. 838).
9. 'Social costs are not minor exceptions to the rule but are typical phenomena' (Kapp, 1969, p. 334).
10. The possibility of identifying a precise cause allows, at least in theory, responsibility for 'externalities' to be attributed. It is thus an essential premise for any tool, whether Coasian or Pigouvian, proposed by traditional economics.
11. Consistent with his institutionalist approach, he believed that needs have to be contextualised with respect to the social framework.

12. Note that the term 'substantive rationality' is not used in H. Simon's meaning. The adjective 'substantive' refers to the need to lend content to the neutral notion of economic efficiency to arrive at a 'concept of substantive rationality which would take account of actual human requirements' (Kapp, 1976a, p. 94). It is also worth noting, in relation to the production of luxury goods and arms, the close proximity to Georgescu Roegen's 'bioeconomic programme', whose writings are cited by Kapp.
13. The centrality of the stakeholders is today widely acknowledged, as testified by the emphasis on participatory processes. However, as we have seen, Kapp's position involves more than participation. An approach that highly reflects Kapp's ideas is Social Multi-Criteria Evaluation (Munda, 2004).
14. Kapp is aware of Georgescu Roegen's contributions: he cites the famous 'Energy and Economic Myths' of the *Southern Economic Journal* of 1975 and stresses the entropic nature of the economic process (Kapp, 1977b, p. 540).
15. Kapp, for example, states: 'the heterogeneous character of the disrupting flows of damages and the complex interdependencies to which we have referred above preclude any measurement and evaluation in terms of a common denominator' (Kapp, 1970, p. 846)
16. Kapp notes, 'it is inevitable that in a market economy dominated by the desire to minimize entrepreneurial costs and to maximize net entrepreneurial returns, social costs and environmental damage tend to be "externalized" as far as possible within the existing institutional and legal framework, while appropriable monetary benefits (profits) will be internalized. Even if an individual firm wanted, and would be financially able, to consider the negative environmental effects of its products and its residuals in its allocation decisions, it could do so only at the price of reducing its own relative competitive position and its earning capacity' (Kapp, 1977b, p. 532).
17. 'Indeed, the fact that part of the costs of production can be shifted to third persons or to society as a whole is merely another way of saying that costs and hence profits depend at least to some extent on the power of the individual firm to do so' (Kapp, 1969, p. 335).
18. It should be considered that this leads to a 'secondary redistribution of real income primarily (but not exclusively) to economically weaker members of society as well as to future generations' (Kapp, 1976a, p. 99).
19. 'The elaboration and acceptance of environmental goals call for a collective or social choice with direct participation and expression of preferences by all members of society, even those outside the market and without reference to effective demand' (Kapp, 1963, p. 317). 'The so-called free-market economy, in which exchanges and prices have long ceased to be free and have in fact been transformed into prices administered by oligopolists, may be compelled to transform itself under the pressure of the exigencies of the environmental crisis and the deterioration of living conditions into an economy which increasingly will have to take into consideration the social use values or the quality of life. ... The author has no illusions about the fact that such a transformation will come about by itself and without struggle. It calls for a genuine democratisation of the state (that is to say, of the centre of political power) and of the economy at all levels, i.e. at the micro level of the firm, the regional and the central level of policy-making' (Kapp, 1974b, p. 138).
20. The theme of environmental indicators is fairly dear to Kapp who considers them 'indicators of social use value' (Kapp, 1974c).
21. It is rather common to look for such synthetic indexes. Well-known examples are H. Daly's *Index of Sustainable Economic Welfare* (ISEW), the *Genuine Progress Indicator* (GPI), Wackernagel and Rees's *Ecological Footprint*.

REFERENCES

Ackoff, R.L. (1960), 'Systems, Organizations and Interdisciplinary Research', in L. von Bertalanffy and A. Rapoport (eds), *General Systems: Yearbook of the Society for General Systems Research*, Ann Arbor: Mental Health Institute, pp. 1–8.

Angresano, J. (1997), *The Political Economy of Gunnar Myrdal: An Institutional Basis for the Transformation Problem*, Cheltenham, UK and Lyme, USA: Edward Elgar.

Argyrous, G. and R. Sethi (1996), 'The Theory of Evolution and the Evolution of Theory: Veblen's Methodology in Contemporary Perspective', *Cambridge Journal of Economics*, **20**(4), 475–95.

Atkinson, A.B. (2003), 'Income Inequality in OECD Countries: Data and Explanations', *CESifo Working Paper Series 881*.

Berger, S. and W. Elsner (2007), 'European Contributions to Evolutionary Institutional Economics: The Cases of "Cumulative Circular Causation" (CCC) and "Open Systems Approach" (OSA). Some Methodological and Policy Implications', *Journal of Economic Issues*, **41**(2), 527–37.

Fujita, N. (2006), 'Myrdal's Theory of Cumulative Causation', *Evolutionary and Institutional Economics Review*, **3**(2), 275–83.

Giampietro, M. (2003), *Multi-Scale Integrated Analysis of Agroecosystems*, London: CRC Press.

Heidenreich, R. (1998), 'Economics and Institutions: The Socioeconomic Approach of K. William Kapp', *Journal of Economic Issues*, **32**(4), 965–84.

Hodgson, G. (1994), *Economics and Evolution. Bringing Life Back into Economics*, Cambridge: Polity Press.

Kapp, K.W. (1950), *The Social Cost of Private Enterprise*, Cambridge, MA: Harvard University Press.

Kapp, K.W. (1961), *Toward a Science of Man in Society. A Positive Approach to the Integration of Social Knowledge*, The Hague: Martinus Nijhoff.

Kapp, K.W. (1963), *The Social Costs of Business Enterprise*, reprinted in 1978, Nottingham: Spokesman Books.

Kapp, K.W. (1965), 'Economic Development in a New Perspective: Existential Minima and Substantive Rationality', *Kyklos*, **17**(1), 49–79.

Kapp, K.W. (1968), 'In Defense of Institutional Economics', *The Swedish Journal of Economics*, **70**(1), 1–18.

Kapp, K.W. (1969), 'On the Nature and Significance of Social Costs', *Kyklos*, **22**(2), 334–47.

Kapp, K.W. (1970), 'Environmental Disruption and Social Costs: a Challenge to Economics', *Kyklos*, **23**(4), 833–48.

Kapp, K.W. (1974a), 'Environmental Policies and Development Planning in Contemporary China', in Kapp 1974d, pp. 9–56.

Kapp, K.W. (1974b), 'The implementation of Environmental Policies', in Kapp 1974d, pp. 101–26.

Kapp, K.W. (1974c), 'Environmental Indicators as Indicators of Social Use Value', in Kapp 1974d, pp. 127–38.

Kapp, K.W. (1974d), *Environmental Policies and Development Planning in Contemporary China and Other Essays*, Paris/The Hague: Mouton.

Kapp, K.W. (1976a), 'The Open System Character of the Economy and its Implications', in K. Dopfer (ed.), *Economics in the Future: Towards a New Paradigm*, London: Macmillan, pp. 90–105.

Kapp, K.W. (1976b), 'The Nature and Significance of Institutional Economics', *Kyklos*, **29**(2), 209–32. Reprinted in W.J. Samuels (ed.) (1988), *Institutional Economics*, Aldershot, UK and Brookfield, US: Edward Elgar.

Kapp, K.W. (1977a), 'Development and Environment: Towards a New Approach to Socioeconomic and Environmental Development', in R. Steppacher, B. Zogg-Waltz and H. Hatzfeldt (eds), *Economics in Institutional Perspective, Memorial Essays in Honor of K. William Kapp*, Lexington, MA: Lexington Books, pp. 205–18.

Kapp, K.W. (1977b), 'Environment and Technology: New Frontiers for the Social and Natural Sciences', *Journal of Economic Issues*, **11**(3), 527–40.

Kapp, K.W. and L. Kapp (1963)[2], *A History of Economic Thought*, New York: Barnes and Noble. The first edition was published in 1949 under the title *Reading in Economics*.

Mayhew, A. (2001), 'Human Agency, Cumulative Causation, and the State', *Journal of Economic Issues*, **35**(2), 239–50.

Martinez Alier, J. (2002), *The Environmentalism of the Poor*, Cheltenham, UK and Northampton, MA, USA: Edward Elgar.

Mill, J.S. (1843), *System of Logic*, London: John W. Parker and New York: Harper & Brothers. Also available at http://www.la.utexas.edu/vmill/sol/index.html.

Munda, G. (2004), 'Social Multi-Criteria Evaluation: Methodological Foundations and Operational Consequences', *European Journal of Operational Research,* **158**(3), 662–77.

Myrdal, G. (1957), *Economic Theory and Under-Developed Regions*, London: Duckworth, Published in US under the title *Rich Lands and Poor*, Harper & Row.

Myrdal, G. (1978), 'Institutional Economics', *Journal of Economic Issues*, **12**(4), 771–83.

Panico, C. and M.O. Rizzo (2008), 'Myrdal, Growth Processes and Equilibrium Theory', in N. Salvadori, P. Commendatore and M. Tamberi (eds), *Geography and Structural Change in Development: Theory and Empirics*, Cheltenham, UK and Northampton, MA, USA: Edward Elgar, pp. 181–200.

Samuels, W.J. (1995), 'The Present State of Institutional Economics', *Cambridge Journal of Economics*, **19**(4), 569–90.

Steppacher, R. (1994), 'Kapp, K. William', in *The Elgar Companion to Institutional and Evolutionary Economics*, Aldershot, UK and Brookfield, US: Edward Elgar, pp. 435–41.

Swaney, J. and M. Evers (1989), 'Social Cost Concepts of K. William Kapp and Karl Polanyi', *Journal of Economic Issues*, **23**(1), 7–33.

Veblen, T. (1898), 'Why Is Economics Not an Evolutionary Science', *Quarterly Journal of Economics*, **12**(4), 373–97. Reprinted in T. Veblen, *The Place of Science in Modern Civilization*, New York: Viking Press, 1990.

von Bertalanffy, L. (1968), *General System Theory*, New York: George Braziller.

15. Participatory planning of economic development: the co-evolution of economic theory and policy

Martina Pignatti Morano

15.1. INTRODUCTION

Most professional economists and moral philosophers have claimed in recent centuries that economic allocation can be carried out either by markets or by central planning, since human nature and modern technology rule out egalitarian and participatory options. The concept of 'participation' appeared in development studies in the late 1960s as a 'rallying cry for a dissenting vision of development' (Francis, 2002, p. 400), but it has been partly absorbed now by the mainstream discourse. Starting from the radical philosophy of 'conscientization' (Freire, 1968), widespread in Latin America, which encouraged communities to rethink collectively the causes of their poverty and oppression, the participatory approach finally entered the declaration of 117 heads of state at the 1995 World Summit for Social Development: it was recognized that: 'empowering people … is a main objective of development and its principal resource. Empowerment requires the full participation of people in the formulation, implementation and evaluation of decisions determining the functioning and well being of our societies' (UNDP, 1995, par. 26, quoted in Francis, 2002, p. 401).

The present survey attempts an evaluation of the trajectories followed during the 20th century by economic policy and economic thought regarding participatory approaches to economic allocation of resources, with specific focus on economic planning in developing countries. Despite the generally negative evaluation given by conventional economic theory on the pursuit of public participation in development processes, recent economic analysis of social capital and social preferences highlights the feasibility and desirability of participatory mechanisms of economic governance in a wide variety of situations. Case studies and experimental evidence gathered through participatory research methods show that groups of people tend to switch from individual to collective rationality if institutions and incentives are properly set. Participation of local communities entails many possible benefits such as the improved effectiveness, efficiency and sustainability of development outcomes, both in single economic projects and in general planning processes. On the other hand, it may be difficult to implement it due to a lack of human resources to organize the process, social conflict, strong and opportunistic local elites, lack of accountability of local government officials, and hostility by central government and market forces.

Those who use cost–benefit analysis to assess the net value of participation have often concluded that participatory methods are more time-consuming or expensive than conventional procedures, but it is easier to give quantitative evidence of costs than benefits, since benefits are largely of a qualitative nature. While participation can be seen as an end in itself, since it creates more equitable institutional and political arrangements, more research is necessary to evaluate the potential of participatory planning micro-institutions as engines for growth, especially in rural areas of developing countries where capital is insufficient to produce local public goods and infrastructure (e.g. roads). As the experience of industrial districts has shown, social cohesion in a geographical space can be transformed into economic efficiency and higher productivity, constituting the moral and ethical background to the market which Adam Smith deemed necessary. In developing countries, institutions are necessary to identify where social cohesion lies and how cooperation can be enforced to enhance development processes, avoiding capture of public budgets by local elites and allowing economic and political emancipation of the downtrodden masses.

The present survey starts with an overview of how participation of beneficiaries has been introduced into 'democratic planning' schemes by Asian governments since the 1950s, and into development projects being managed by multilateral agencies inspired by liberalist economic thought, experiencing analogous limitations and disillusionment. The third section goes through the generally negative evaluation given by conventional economic theory on public participation, since the economic discipline failed for decades to take into account the alternative microfoundation that participatory planning could suggest for its models. Section 15.4 shows that Collective Action studies have recently focused on successful management of common pool resources by local communities, while different schools of 'participation specialists' designed group-based methods to extract local knowledge directly from beneficiaries of development programmes, and produced action-research that concretely contributed to the improvement of participatory planning processes in African countries. Section 15.5 describes through experimental evidence how groups tend to switch from individual to collective rationality when they are given the possibility to take collective decisions through deliberation. Hence it argues for the need for Deliberative

Institutional Economics to investigate institutional rules which favour these processes. Finally, we draw some concluding remarks and prospects for future research in this field.

15.2. PEOPLE'S PARTICIPATION IN DEVELOPMENT PROGRAMS

When development economics started being recognized as an autonomous discipline in the 1940s and 1950s, the common view was that industrializing countries needed a strong central state to supply the crucial factor for development: physical capital. Democracy was then a 'luxury' that poor states could not afford (Ruttan, 1997, p. 217) but in some South Asian states a planning ideology committed to egalitarianism favoured the establishment of forms of decentralized or 'democratic' planning. In India, President Nehru believed in a process of governance that would organically link people from the Gram Sabha (village assembly) to the Lok Sabha (National Parliament), giving a key role to Panchayats (local village councils).[1] In 1952 the Government launched the Community Development Programme (CD) as an integral part of the First Five Year Plan (see Ministry of Information and Broadcasting, Government of India, 1953, pp. 102–6). The Programme aimed at motivating rural people to take a community-based approach to improve their economic and social condition, strengthening self-reliance and co-operation by 'aided self-help'. Even a special ministry for Community Development was created in 1956, but bureaucracy took over. Despite all the efforts to bring about coordination between government agencies at the block (group of 100 villages) level, in most cases the Block Development Officer and the Tax Collector would take all decisions themselves. Conflict started between the minister for CD and ministers responsible for their subjects: agriculture, irrigation, education etc. since they all wanted to launch their own programmes with subject-wise allocations.[2] By the mid-1960s Panchayats had emerged in over 96 per cent of the rural inhabited villages, but all development programmes were coming from the Government, not from the people, which induced an attitude of eternal passivity.[3]

While in the socialist world worker's participation was sometimes encouraged only for self-management of their own firm or productive unity, people's participation was included in development programmes sponsored by the United States of America for the alleged target of democratization. In the first decade after World War II aid for development from the USA was supposed to foster community development, building grassroots democratic institutions and enhancing the welfare of rural people 'without revolutionary changes in the existing political and economic order' (Holdcraft, 1978, p. 14;

quoted in Ruttan, 1997, p. 221). Community development aimed at involving people in solving their common problems with democratic processes, and was applied by 1960 in more than 60 nations in Asia, Africa and Latin America. However, by the end of the 1960s support for these projects had declined because the programmes were failing both to change the local non-democratic power structures and to increase the economic well-being of people. Another problem, 'seldom stated explicitly, was that when programs were successful they set in motion political forces that were not easy controlled by central authorities' (Ruttan, 1997, p. 222).

Multilateral institutions did not lag behind. By the early 1970s a major symposium on agricultural institutions was convened in Rome by the FAO to discuss the integrated rural development approach, which became the new focus of multilateral agencies. A new emphasis on local participation came from the perception that: (a) rapid growth of income did not ensure availability of necessary services to rural people; (b) institutional design had to integrate the large number of complementary sectoral components in each project; (c) bureaucratic approaches to rural development were an instrument of control. Pioneer programmes were successful, but assistance agencies failed to transfer the good practices in the general model, since they applied decentralized administration ('locating the administrative offices of central ministries at the provincial or district level') but not decentralized governance. Hence they did not succeed in 'strengthening the fiscal and administrative capacity of local people' (Ruttan, 1997, p. 224).

In 1973 the US Congress instructed the US Agency for International Development to focus on meeting the basic needs of the poorest people in developing countries, and in 1974 the UN World Food Conference adopted a declaration for the eradication of hunger. A specific programme was designed following the new *basic needs* approach, where growth objectives were replaced by consumption and health targets. Although the World Bank mobilized many more forces in the delivery of social services, popular mobilization was frequently replaced by bureaucratic approaches to program delivery. In any case the conviction remained that the capacity of a society to resolve the conflict between efficiency in program design and local mobilization of resources is one of the important indicators of political development (Ruttan, 1997, p. 226). International financial institutions of liberalist economic settings and socialist governments were facing very similar constraints when seeking to go down participatory development paths.

In 1980s participation was still advocated to reach the poor in the UN International Drinking Water Supply and Sanitation Decade, but individual case studies 'did not offer convincing evidence that people's participation makes a difference in project performance and, hence, is worth financial investment' (Narayan, 1997, p. 201). In such studies participation is defined as a voluntary process by which people influence or control the decisions that affect them, but it is viewed as 'a means to define ends' (p. 202) which coincide with the project objectives. Since participation is not an end in itself, and since it 'imposes transaction costs on beneficiaries and agencies', it will 'naturally decline over time as goals are met' (p. 203). This instrumental view of popular mobilization is still the rule nowadays in most cases, but the World Bank has devoted increasing attention to the topic in the last decade since a Bankwide Learning Group on Participatory Development was launched in 1991 and produced recommendations to increase participation in WB work (Picciotto, 1995, p. 12). In fact, after recognition by OECD Aid Ministers in December 1989, participation became 'an article of faith for the entire development community' (p. 6) and entered the mainstream discourse of development in the 1990s. Recent signs of it can be detected in the huge World Bank project called *The Voices of the Poor* (2000) which was intended to represent the views of 60,000 poor from 60 countries, in order to prepare the *World Development Report 2000/1: Attacking Poverty*. The IBRD in 1996 also produced *The World Bank Participation Sourcebook* (World Bank, 1996), still an important systematization of project-based experience on stakeholders' involvement in decisions that affect them. Notwithstanding, some still argue that these exercises are not really empowering the poor, but – as Rahnema (1997) argues – just using a language of emancipation to serve a mainstream vision of economics and de-politicize international development.

15.3. ECONOMIC THEORY EVALUATING PARTICIPATION

While development programmes experienced participation, theoretical streams in Economics failed for decades to take into account the alternative microfoundation that participatory planning could suggest for their models. General Equilibrium Theory and, in particular, the two Welfare Theorems demonstrated that under certain assumptions an efficient equilibrium would be reached in an economy through the interactions of self-interested agents. With its focus on the role of individuals, this theorization provides a strong argument for decentralized participation in economic activity, but it also suggests the least costly, simplest institution to organize interaction: the market. Since this theory does not incorporate market failure, it maintains that, for example, the best way to understand which of various potential education projects will be most valuable for beneficiaries is to ask them how much they would be willing to pay to participate in each of them. Every individual should assign a monetary value to the feasible alternatives without dialogue and mediation with the other beneficiaries, and the sum of all virtual contributions for each project would give its estimated value. Later, Mechanism Design Theory (starting with the work of Hurwicz, 1960) conceived more complex non-cooperative institutions that determine the outcome of an interaction between all private information received, but such mechanisms are improperly termed *communication systems.* Indeed, this approach still neglects the possibility of a change in the interest component of preferences through deliberation, for solidarity or equity reasons, or for the recognition of negative and positive externalities of the project and other information that could emerge in the deliberation process.

In the neoclassical framework there was anyway the clear recognition that for the case of non-excludable goods agents had no incentive to reveal their authentic preferences and willingness to pay, hence there would be a problem of under-provision of public goods. Paul Samuelson derived the impossibility of decentralized spontaneous solutions for optimal provision of what he called 'collective consumption goods' (Samuelson, 1954, p. 387), and the need for a central authority that takes that decision based on preferences of a median voter and social acceptance of taxation. Samuelson seemed to consider other decision-making mechanisms when he argued that 'utopian voting and signalling schemes' could be imagined but he confined their value to conditions of 'symmetry' between individuals, since he mentioned examples such as the 'Scandinavian consensus' or 'Kant's categorical imperative' (p. 389). No greater adherence to reality was shown in the following years by those economists who sought market solutions for the provision of public goods. Tiebout (1956) depicted an economy where each local administration would offer a particular mix of services and taxation, and individuals would move to the jurisdiction that better suited their preferences. But where 'spatial mobility provides the local public-goods counterpart to the private market's shopping trip' people tend to move into homogeneous communities, segregated among them (typically, the poor segregated by the rich), with very dubious results in terms of aggregate welfare. Other solutions than Tiebout jurisdictions and clubs are necessary to evaluate how individuals could provide public goods in a heterogeneous society, without delegating all decision-making power to a central authority.

Other streams of literature analysed the aggregation aspect of this problem. Social Choice Theory studied how conflicting preferences can be reconciled and aggregated into a single Social Welfare Function. Arrow (1951), Gibbard (1973) and McKelvey (1976) derived three practical conclusions: there is no mechanism to aggregate the views of all beneficiaries into a social choice that does not violate Arrow's conditions (independence of irrelevant alternatives, Pareto optimality, unrestricted domain and non-dictatorship); there is no reason to believe that actors would not lie about their preferences to affect the final decision; the final choice could be distorted by the order in which the available alternatives were presented to the beneficiaries. This perspective does not support the implementation of voluntary participatory schemes since they are incompatible with economic efficiency. In any case, Amartya Sen showed that this pessimism is justified only if people are endowed with a poor information base: if people could make interpersonal comparisons, for example, Arrow's theorem would be vacuous (Sen, 1970). Dryzek and List (2003) more recently argued that deliberation between agents could, moreover, reduce the 'unrestricted domain' of admissible preferences, promoting the structuring of single-peaked preferences that would allow for a social choice that respects Arrow's conditions.

Completing a brief list of theories that failed to depict the complex microeconomics of participation, we consider the Economics of Collective Action of Mancur Olson, who studied the behaviour of people within a community that shares a common goal. Common sense would suggest that taking collective decisions in this case is easy, but economic theory still identifies the 'free-rider' problem: if all members of the group share the same interest, any action that furthers that interest benefits each member, whether or not he/she bears any of the cost of the action. Hence there is no incentive for such individual action. In large groups each person bears the cost of their action but will not perceive the marginal effect of their action over the aggregate result; hence individuals do not have incentives to participate in collective action. The greater the number of people who have homogeneous views in a society, the less likely they are to organize themselves to reach their goal; therefore local voluntary organizations are likely to represent the extremes of public opinion and not be representative of the whole community. In this case economic theory suggests that greater reliance on participation can have the perverse effect of allowing small interest groups to put their own interests ahead of those of the majority. According to Olson this problem could be avoided only in two cases: when the group is small enough such that each member can appreciate the impact of his/her actions on the likelihood of success; and when 'selective incentives' can reward those who participate or punish those who do not (Olson, 1965). The implications for Political Economy are that voters are unlikely to pay the cost of becoming well-informed when they know that the likely effect of their vote on their own welfare is trivial. A participatory process with voters who have no information whatsoever or biased information about most issues will be in the interests of coercive governments or elites that have influence over public opinion.

All the theories mentioned above have influenced to a varied extent economists working in governmental and multilateral agencies, inducing scepticism on participatory policies. While working in the African Department of the International Monetary Fund, Gerson derived from these streams of economic theory two kinds of predictions for the success of participation in development projects (Gerson, 1993, pp. 5–6). The first concerns how and when participation will be effective, and regards problems of project design: market mechanisms involving the ultimate beneficiaries could be more 'informationally' efficient than consultations with public officials or town meetings; if individuals do not have access to credit they could be asked for contributions in labour or time. Hence those who place a lower value on their time – 'who also tend to be the poor' (ibid., p. 5) – will be selected for the benefits of the project; moreover, participation is more likely to be successful when the benefits of a project can be restricted to a particular group. The second group of predictions concerns problems of revealing preference: potential beneficiaries may misrepresent their true preferences, and local voluntary organizations are likely to hold more extreme positions than the general public or push for measures whose benefit would go to a small fraction of society. The conclusions reached by Gerson confirm the simple instrumental value often assigned by International Financial Institutions to participation, which 'is itself a scarce and sometimes costly commodity' and 'may not always yield benefits sufficient to justify its costs' (p. 5).

15.4. INSTITUTIONS FOR COLLECTIVE ACTION AND PARTICIPATORY RESEARCH

A new approach was accepted in economic analysis only in the 1990s, with the path breaking studies of Elinor Ostrom (1990) on the evolution of Institutions for Collective Action. Through the joint work of interdisciplinary research groups and the use of participatory research methodologies, Ostrom studied the problem of collective management of 'common pool resources': natural resources used by many individuals in common, such as fisheries, groundwater basins, and irrigation systems. To avoid overexploitation and misuse by individuals acting in their own best interests, many communities have designed durable cooperative institutions that are organized and governed by the resource users themselves, without relying on centralized governmental regulation or privatization of the resource. Several design principles of institutions have historically allowed communities in very different circumstances to obtain continuing joint benefits. Ostrom argued that the three dominant economic models – the tragedy of the commons, the prisoner's dilemma, and the logic of collective action – are all inadequate to analyse problems in real terms, since the conditions under which they hold are very particular. They apply only when the individuals involved have high discount rates and little mutual trust, no capacity to communicate or to enter into binding agreements, and when they do not arrange for monitoring and enforcing mechanisms to avoid underinvestment and overuse.

As Elinor Ostrom's research team proved, there is an institutional economic history forgotten or denied by academic studies during the last century. This reach information about the variety of social contracts emerged when some research centres started investigating the practical measures which could help them involving local people in research projects about their own territory. In the late 1970s three factors gave birth to these studies: dissatisfaction with the biases or 'rural development tourism – the phenomenon of brief rural visits by the urban-based professionals' (Chambers, 1994, p. 956), hiding the worst aspects of poverty and deprivation; the disillusion about the utility of questionnaire surveys, the normal instruments of inquiry which were uselessly tedious and often produced unreliable data; the search for cost-effective and timely methods to extract indigenous technical knowledge (ITK) (Institute of Development Studies, 1979), since it was increasingly recognized that rural people had deeper knowledge than outsiders on many subjects touching their lives. From workshops and publications of the Institute of Development Studies (IDS, University of Sussex) and the International Institute for Environment and Development (IIED, London)[4] new interactive methodologies spread between researchers and aid agency officials to gain information and insights from local people and about local conditions. This approach, named Rapid Rural Appraisal (RRA), still focused on an extractive activity carried out by outsiders.

Major changes took place in the 1980s in the fields of applied anthropology, agroecosystem analysis and field research on farming systems, which gave new instruments and motivations to appreciate the validity of rural peoples' knowledge and 'to distinguish the etic – the outsiders' mental frame, categories and world view, and the emic – those of the insider' (Chambers, 1994, p. 955). Participatory research was carried out by social movements all over the world who used dialogue and public meetings to enhance people's awareness and confidence, and to empower their action. These experiences showed that poor people are creative and capable: they can and should do much of their own investigation, analysis and planning, hence outsiders should behave as simple catalysts and facilitators. This is how in the 1990s Participatory Rural Appraisal (PRA) became popular, as 'a family of approaches and methods to enable rural people to share, enhance, and analyze their knowledge of life and conditions, to plan and to act'. The menu of PRA methods is very wide, can be shared and owned by local people, and often uses visual representations of the results: mapping and modelling on the ground or paper; estimating, scoring and ranking with seeds, stones, sticks or shapes; transect walks through an area; Venn diagramming and linkage diagramming; free listing and card sorting; presentations made by local people in front of community assemblies for check and validation, etc. (for a synthetic analysis of these instruments see Chambers, 1994, pp. 959–61). All these methods have found practical applications to investigate many topics (natural resource management, agriculture, poverty, health and food security) and carry out participatory implementation, monitoring and evaluation of development programs.

These studies produced 'action research' for a political venture that started in the last two decades in many developing countries: the construction of new relationships between citizens and the institutions which affect their lives through economic policies. Legal enabling environments for citizen participation were created in the 1990s in many countries of Asia, Africa and South America, driving direct forms of participation throughout the whole planning cycle: needs assessment, planning, implementation, monitoring and evaluation. There is widespread evidence that this process has improved the supply of 'universal services' such as education and health care, but less success was seen in the programmes targeted for the poorest people.[5] An explanation that has been provided is that democratic decentralization simply delivers more power to local elites, who are no more benevolent than those at higher levels. But good synergy between the state and society in local governance has partly disproved these claims in programmes like those of Kerala (India), Porto Alegre (Brazil) and South African township (Heller, 2001). Generally, three enabling conditions of participatory governance have been identified: strong central state capacity, a well developed civil society and an organized political force (such as a party) with strong social movement characteristics. Beyond the social process at the bottom, efficient and accountable vertical links must exist to transmit local decisions upwards as far as national governments and structure an entirely new planning procedure.

An example of action research is represented by issue 49 (April 2004) of the review *Participatory Learning and Action Notes*, with articles by agriculturalists, anthropologists and economists working on practical implementation of community-based planning (CBP): 'planning by communities, for their communities, which links into the local and national government planning systems'. The issue draws mainly on the four-country CBP project: South Africa, Uganda, Ghana and Zimbabwe. Goldman et al. (2004) report the results of their action-research project built in partnership with the key national organization involved in decentralized planning, a local government and a development facilitator. Their research highlighted the major gap between the micro and meso levels: most communities in Africa do not receive sufficient services from government, and depend rather on community-based services such as traditional healers, advice from other farmers, local markets and various forms of reciprocity. The project addressed how community involvement in planning and management can link to decentralized delivery systems of public goods and services. In the first year of piloting, about two million people were covered by the methodology (through a variety of PLA tools, combined into a three- to five-day strategic planning process in six local governments in the four countries, at the ward/parish level). In South Africa and Uganda this was integrated immediately into the local government's real plan, while manuals and training programmes have been developed and are being rolled out between community facilitators in Zimbabwe and South Africa. An important spin-off has also been the development of a positive relationship between participating NGOs and the state, with a recognition by government of NGO knowledge of participatory methods.

15.5. FROM PRACTICE TO THEORY: EXPERIMENTS AND MODELS FOR COLLECTIVE RATIONALITY

Case studies like most of those mentioned in *PLANotes* where researchers dealt directly with the challenges of the planning exercise, the elicitation and aggregation of conflicting interests and preferences in communities, suggest that informed participation – even by disadvantaged groups – can be achieved by proper facilitation methods. Moreover, adequate institutional mechanisms may facilitate a switch from individual to collective rationality by participants in the planning process, granting the achievement of socially desirable outcomes. Despite the fact that positive results have been widely generated and recorded in case studies, their systematization has not yet supported a major change in the microfoundation of economic models that study the allocation of responsibilities to the public, private and voluntary/community sectors. Behavioural economics has expanded the study of social preferences like interpersonal altruism, fairness, reciprocity and inequality aversion, and maintains that fundamental issues in economics cannot be understood on the basis of the self-interest model (Fehr and Fishbacher, 2002). In the last two decades experimental economists have gathered overwhelming evidence (for a survey of experimental evidence see Fehr and Schmidt, 2000) suggesting that a substantial fraction of the people exhibit social preferences. Hence deviations from self-interest have a fundamental impact on economic outcomes. While it is widely debated whether groups are more or less consistent and egoistical than individuals when playing against other actors,[6] it is indisputable that through a process of deliberation people have the opportunity to evaluate externalities produced by their conduct on the welfare of other community members, and have more complete information to apply their social preferences. The more people exchange information on the utility they derive from a public choice, the greater the possibility to apply their social preferences whilst taking into account everybody else's utility. Since reciprocal fairness seems to be the most widely observed social preference, deliberative participation in planning exercises should strongly facilitate groups in overcoming coordination failures.

The importance of the decision-making mechanism in defining which individuals will determine group outcomes, has already been investigated in laboratory experiments. Fehr and Schmidt (1999) showed that in groups with heterogeneous preferences, and a minority of inequality-averse individuals, the mechanism available to negotiate the provision of a public good will determine whether the fair types or the selfish types will dominate economic behaviour: the possibility to punish non-cooperators is generally sufficient to consolidate cooperative behaviour. Even more interesting is the experimental investigation of decision-making and coordination mechanisms in field experiments, performed by social scientists in the context and with the agents that relate directly to the economic problem analyzed. Ostrom et al. (1994) collected a wide series of experimental studies on the management of Common Pool Resources, evaluating how various contribution mechanisms, constituent games, options to interact with other players through communication and sanctions, would significantly change the outcome of the experiment. Face-to-face communication in particular tends to positively affect the cooperation level in both laboratory and field experiments (for a survey of experimental evidence see Cardenas et al., 2003), and suggests once again that deliberative participation in the planning exercise could increase collective action for the provision of public goods.

Such a hypothesis has been confirmed by Pignatti Morano (2007) in framed economic experiments reproducing Public Good Games in rural India, with individuals who usually participate in village meetings where they take decisions regarding individual contribution (through taxation or voluntary work) to provision of local public goods. Experiments were carried out in two villages to evaluate the potential of Gram Sabahas (village meetings) to build trust and enforce collective action in heterogeneous communities. The results show that individuals tend to free ride when asked to take an independent decision and make individual payments for the public good, while they reach binding agreements to pay more when they have the possibility to speak to each other in an open meeting. People tend to stick to the collective agreement even if, after the meeting, they go back to their seats and make individual and anonymous payments. Such an improvement in social efficiency due to communication (with respect to the zero-payment Nash equilibrium of the individual-maximizer) is even more significant for heterogeneous groups, in which people of different castes or wealth quartiles are merged. The major factors favouring the switch from individual to collective rationality are the existence of transparent and accountable institutions and the possibility for people to communicate with each other, giving reasons for their behaviour or their vote, building mutual trust and solidarity. These results are in line with the empirical literature produced through field experiments of economists and anthropologists on Common-Pool Resources management in developing countries (Carpenter et al., 2005).

An attempt to incorporate such empirical evidence in economic theory has been proposed by Anne Van Aaken, who argues for the need to produce a synthesis between the *homo oeconomicus* of Institutional Economics and the *homo communicans* of Discourse Theory. The first behavioural model optimizes given preferences by negotiating and interacting with others and seeking to influence them with the 'carrot and stick' (external incentives), while the second kind 'makes a claim of substantive rightness by presenting arguments in public, and seeks dialogue with partners whose preferences he hopes to alter by offering better reasons. Positions of power or coercion must not be used, and the discourse is subject to rules designed to make it legitimate' (van Aaken, 2004, p. 19). Since people normally use both strategies, it is necessary to think of a *homo rationalis communicans*, whose behaviour would be studied within the field of Deliberative Institutional Economics. Behavioural and evolutionary studies recognized that each economic institution and mechanism design, by shaping the structure of social interactions, may motivate adherence to specific behavioural rules which proved successful in that context (Bowles and Gintis, 2000). Moreover, Bowles and Gintis (2002) assert that community governance – the set of small group social interactions that, with market and state, determine economic outcomes – will probably increase in importance in the future. There is scope in this context for in-depth research on the implications of deliberation for analytical model-building in economics.

Institutional rules that imply deliberation may change the interest component of preferences, and if rules require people to explain reasons for their behaviour they cannot easily present selfish views; hence this may change their position, restricting their strategic or opportunistic behaviour (Benhabib, 1994). In a process of deliberation, moreover, people become more aware of their own interests or purposes, namely their meta-preferences (defined by economist Bruno Frey as the preferred views of an individual on what his/her actual preferences should be). This is due to the cognitive process that occurs during communication, and to the collective emergence of a richer set of pros and cons which would have been costly for an individual alone to search for. When analysing a problem of collective action, where each individual has the private incentive to free ride but the participation of all people produces the socially optimum results, institutions are needed to create space for public communication between stakeholders and potential participants. Taking into account the diversity of psychological types (generous, egoistical, reciprocator etc.) and the typical behaviour codes in each cultural and socio-political setting, institutions can help people visualize the gains from cooperation and gain positive utility from simple participation in the process (procedural utility). As Ostrom highlighted in her studies, successful 'design principles' for managing the commons foster contingent self-commitment among the members (e.g. by selecting monitors who are either resource users or accountable to them), and mechanisms dominated by the users themselves to resolve conflicts and to alter the rules. The rules governing the deliberation process are crucial for planning exercises to succeed in communities where social cohesion is not necessarily strong, and where quotas and reservations might be necessary to take into account interests and arguments of disempowered groups.

In such an inquiry, realism and context-specific knowledge is required to produce models that can make practical contributions to economic policy. Gunnar Myrdal was one of the first economists who analysed forms of 'democratic' and decentralized planning which became popular in South Asia from the 1950s onwards. He analysed with an intended 'undiplomatic' attitude this quest for mass participation in planning, stating that:

> Behind this approach must be the faith that once the masses become aware of their miserable conditions and are shown how to improve them through state policies, they will respond positively by supporting the adoption of these policies and participating in their fulfillment [but] the masses, imprisoned by poverty and tradition, may not be ready to understand or accept the rationalist ideals of planning for development (and still less, the demand for greater equality generally implied) (Myrdal, 1977, pp. 139–40).

The ideological formula that self-government and cooperation should not be applied from above but spring from the wishes of the people is, according to Myrdal, 'largely a self-deception; indulging in it is hardly likely to make the planning of rural uplift rational and effective' (Myrdal, 1977, p. 145). The core problem lies in the failure of past efforts to create a machinery for self-government without changing the basic social and economic structures by some degree of coercion. Such a coercion might lie in the imposition on politicians and administrators to take a precise set of decisions on management of public budgets through deliberative and participatory processes, without bypassing the equality issue. The recipe suggested by

Myrdal is an increase in social discipline in all strata of society, to be enforced by strategies defined by central governments. Evidently, being obliged to give reasons for behaviour in public meetings is an effective and democratic exercise of social discipline.

15.6. CONCLUDING REMARKS

In the last few decades participatory options to foster economic development have acquired growing importance and recognition both in economic theory and in policy practice. Referring initially to participation in projects, this concept is now increasingly related to citizenship rights, governance arrangements and political struggles: there has been a shift from concern for 'beneficiaries' or 'the excluded' to a concern for broad forms of engagement by citizens in policy formulation. Development studies until recently were based on research carried out by professional outsiders who visited local communities with pre-structured beliefs about the abilities of the poor that were self-validating: 'treated as incapable, poor people behaved as incapable, reflecting the beliefs of the powerful, and hiding their capabilities from themselves'.[7] These modes reflected the instrumentalist approach of many economists and international agencies who valued – and still often do – participation as a means to achieve efficiency/efficacy in development projects, depending on the nature of the goods to be supplied. It took a greater confidence and professionalism in rural NGOs and favourable political processes in developing countries to start shifting to a new approach.

We have seen how the main currents of economic theory during the past century and the neo-liberalist approach to economic policy tended to undermine various aspects of participation and highlight its shortcomings rather than its potential as a policy practice. More can be done within the Institutionalist, Evolutionary and Behavioural fields, through interdisciplinary research and field experiments, to show that participatory planning is much more than an exercise in aggregating individual preference rankings into a single group ranking or a single social choice function. Not *aggregation* but *transformation* of individual preferences lies at the core of democracy, and public deliberation in open meetings can change the interest component of preferences. Proper institutions can prevent participants in planning meetings from cutting the cake of local resources in too many small pieces, and might easily allow them to enlarge the cake before deciding how to cut it. As political scientists and law scholars have proposed, a new field of Deliberative Institutional Economics should be established to investigate mechanism design for participatory institutions, that pursue efficiency of social choice but facilitate a switch from individual to collective rationality by participants.

The challenge is that of establishing more democratic strategies for economic development without giving up public planning as a strategy. Chakravarty argued that it is right to discuss the cost and benefits of all conceivable strategies for economic planning, but one does not have to believe in 'elasticity pessimism' or 'structural rigidity' to recognize the need for planning as a strategy in countries with low private savings and insufficient 'social overhead capital', environmental degradation and highly unequal income distribution (Chakravarty, 1991, p. 8). What the critiques to planning reveal, rather than its inadvisability, is something more significant: 'that the "quality" of planning is much more important than the "quantity" of planning' (Chakravarty, 1991, p. 10). Political and social movements from the peripheries of the world tell us that planning is action with a socio-economic purpose and require a more egalitarian plan of social order, the political economy of a participatory society (Albert and Hahnel, 1991). The role of social scientists lies now in giving dignity to these policy reforms and building vertical links between local, regional, national and international institutions, since efficient participatory forms of governance should be based on the least-inefficient mechanism to aggregate social choices and facilitate the bargaining process at a large scale. But economists should take extreme care with the use they make of optimization and equilibrium concepts since, as Tony Killick stated, development planning opens a 'paradigm crisis' for the economic profession, 'in which the returns from our "investment in calculus" are dependent on a level of abstraction from the real world, and … a disciplinary specialization, which threatens the social usefulness of our profession' (Killick, 1976, p.181).

NOTES

1. For an account of private discussions between Nehru and Dey on Panchayati Raj Institutions, see De Ruijter (1998, p. 97). Nehru had changing moods and was often depressed by political attempts to demolish local governance.
2. Outside the purview of PRIs, the Intensive Agricultural District Programme, the Small Farmers Development Agency, the Drought Prone Areas Programme and the Intensive Tribal Development Programme were introduced in the early 1960s (see Mathew, 2000, p. 7).
3. After Nehru's death, in 1964, the CD lost its staunch defender and in 1966–67 the Ministry of CD was reduced to a department, until 1971 when it changed its very title to 'Rural Development'.
4. The IIED publishes for field practitioners the journal *PLA Notes* (Participatory Learning and Action), back issues available at http://www.iied.org/NR/agbioliv/pla_notes/backissues.html

5. Results of a study on democratic local governance in six countries by Blair (2000).
6. See Bone et al. (1999), but also Bornstein et al. (2004) for a contrasting result.
7. And there follows: 'The ignorance and inabilities of rural people were then not just an illusion; they were an artifact of outsiders' behaviour and attitudes, of their arrogant and ignorant manner of interacting with local people' (Chambers, 1994, p. 963).

REFERENCES

Albert, M. and R. Hahnel (1991), *The Political Economy of Participatory Economics.* Princeton, NJ: Princeton University Press.

Arrow, K. (1951), *Social Choice and Individual Values*, New York: Wiley.

Benhabib, S. (1994), 'Deliberative Rationality and Models of Democratic Legitimacy', *Constellations: An International Journal of Critical and Democratic Theory*, **1**(1), 25–53.

Blair, H. (2000), 'Participation and Accountability at the Periphery: Democratic Local Governance at the Periphery', *World Development*, **28**(1), 21–39.

Bone, J., J. Hey and J. Suckling (1999), 'Are Groups More (or Less) Consistent than Individuals?', *Journal of Risk and Uncertainty*, **18**(1), 63–81.

Bornstein, G., T. Kugler, and A. Ziegelmeyer (2004), 'Individual and Group Decisions in the Centipede Game: Are Groups More "Rational" Players?', *Journal of Experimental Social Psychology*, 40, 599–605.

Bowles, S. and H. Gintis (2000), 'Walrasian Economics in Retrospect', *Quarterly Journal of Economics*, **115**(4), 1411–39.

Bowles, S. and H. Gintis (2002), 'Social Capital and Community Governance', *The Economic Journal*, **112**(1), F419–F436.

Carpenter, J., G.W. Harrison and J.A. List (eds) (2005), *Field Experiments in Economics*, Amsterdam: Elsevier.

Chakravarty, S. (1991), 'Development Planning: A Reappraisal', *Cambridge Journal of Economics*, **15**(1), 5–20.

Chambers, R. (1994), 'The Origins and Practice of Participatory Rural Appraisal', *World Development*, **22**(7), 953–69.

De Ruijter, A. (1998), *The Purse and the Power. Aspects of Centre–State Relations in India*, Delhi: B.R. Publishing Corporation.

Dryzek, J.S. and C. List (2003), 'Social Choice Theory and Deliberative Democracy', *British Journal of Political Science*, **33**(1), 1–28.

Fehr, E. and U. Fischbacher (2002), 'Why Social Preferences Matter. The Impact of Non-Selfish Motives on Competition, Cooperation and Incentives', *The Economic Journal*, **112**, C1–C33.

Fehr, E. and K.M. Schmidt (1999), 'A Theory of Fairness, Competition and Co-Operation', *Quarterly Journal of Economics*, **114**(3), 817–68.

Fehr, E. and K.M. Schmidt (2000), 'Theories of Fairness and Reciprocity. Evidence and Economic Applications', in M. Dewatripont, L.P. Hansen and S. Turnovsky (eds), *Advances in Economic Theory*, Eighth World Congress of the Econometric Society, Cambridge: Cambridge University Press.

Francis, P. (2002), 'Community Participation and Decision Making', in C. Kirkpatrick, R. Clarke and C. Polidano (eds), *Handbook on Development Policy and Management*, Cheltenham, UK and Northampton, MA, USA: Edward Elgar.

Freire, P. (1968), *Pedagogy of the Oppressed*, New York: The Seabury Press.

Gerson, P.R. (1993), 'Popular Participation in Economic Theory and Practice', *HRO Working Papers*. no. 18, Washington, DC: World Bank.

Gibbard, A. (1973), 'Manipulation of Voting Schemes: A General Result', *Econometrica*, **41**(4), 587–603.

Goldman, I., J. Carnegie and J. Abbot (2004), 'Linking the Community to Local Government: Action Research in Four African Countries', *PLA Notes*, **49**(April), 16–21.

Heller, P. (2001), 'Moving the State: The Politics of Democratic Decentralisation in Kerala, South Africa, and Porto Alegre', *Politics and Society*, **29**(1), 131–63.

Holdcraft, L.E. (1978), 'The Rise and Fall of Community Development in Developing Countries, 1950-65: A Critical Analysis and an Annotated Bibliography', *Rural Development Paper 2*, East Lansing: Michigan State University.

Hurwicz, L. (1960), 'Optimality and Informational Efficiency in Resource Allocation Processes', in K.J. Arrow, S. Karlin and P. Suppes (eds), *Mathematical Methods in the Social Sciences*, Stanford: Stanford University Press.

Institute of Development Studies (IDS) (1979), 'Whose Knowledge Counts?', *IDS Bulletin*, **10**(2).

Killick, T. (1976), 'The Possibilities of Development Planning', *Oxford Economic Papers*, **28**(2), 161–84.

Mathew, G. (2000), 'Panchayati Raj in India – An Overview', *Status of Panchayati Raj in the States and Union Territories of India 2000*, Institute of Social Sciences, New Delhi: Concept Publishing Company.

McKelvey, R.D. (1976), 'Intransitivities in Multidimensional Voting Models and Some Implications for Agenda Control', *Journal of Economic Theory*, **12**, 472–82.

Ministry of Information and Broadcasting, Government of India (1953), *First Five Year Plan*, New Delhi: Publications Division.

Myrdal, G. (1977), *Asian Drama. An Inquiry into the Poverty of Nations* (An abridgement of the Twentieth Century Fund Study by Seth King), London: Penguin Books.

Narayan, D. (1997), 'Focus on People's Participation: Evidence from 121 Rural Water Projects', in C. Clague (ed.), *Institutions and Economic Development*, Baltimore, USA: John Hopkins University Press.

Olson, M. (1965), *The Logic of Collective Action*, Cambridge, MA: Harvard University Press.

Ostrom, E. (1990), *Governing the Commons. The Evolution of Institutions for Collective Action*, Cambridge, UK: Cambridge University Press.

Ostrom, E., R. Gardner and J. Walker (1994), *Rules, Games and Common-Pool Resources*, Ann Arbor: The University of Michigan Press.

Picciotto, R. (1995), 'Putting Institutional Economics to Work: from Participation to Governance', *World Bank Discussion Paper*, no. 304, Washington, DC.

Pignatti Morano, M. (2007), 'Participatory Planning and Provision of Public Goods in Rural India: An Experimental Investigation', mimeo.

Rahnema, M. (1997), 'Participation', in W. Sachs (ed.), *The Development Dictionary: a Guide to Knowledge as Power*, Hyderabad: Orient Longman.

Ruttan, V. (1997), 'Participation and Development', in C. Clague (ed.), *Institutions and Economic Development*, Baltimore, USA: John Hopkins University Press.

Samuelson, P.A. (1954), 'The Pure Theory of Public Expenditure', *The Review of Economics and Statistics*, **36**(4), 387–9.

Sen, A. (1970), *Collective Choice and Social Welfare*, Cambridge, UK: Holden Day Inc.

Tiebout, C.M. (1956), 'A Pure Theory of Local Expenditures', *Journal of Political Economy*, **64**(5), 416–24.

United Nations Development Programme (UNDP) (1995), *World Summit for Social Development: Copenhagen Declaration and Programme of Action*, New York: UNDP.

van Aaken, A. (2004), 'Deliberative Institutional Economics, or Does Homo Oeconomicus Argue? A proposal for Combining New Institutional Economics with Discourse Theory', in A. van Aaken, C. List and C. Luetge (eds), *Deliberation and Decision*, Aldershot: Ashgate Publishing Company.

World Bank (1996), *The World Bank Participation Sourcebook*, Washington, DC: World Bank.

World Bank (2000), *Voices of the Poor*, Washington, DC: World Bank.

World Bank (2001), *The World Development Report 2000/1: Attacking Poverty*, Washington, DC: World Bank.

16. Political and economic interaction: income distribution and economic growth

Francesco Purificato

16.1. INTRODUCTION

The political system and the economic system continuously interact over time. While economic interests emerge to acquire political influence in the policymaker's decisional process, political decisions influence the economy and the balance of forces among economic interests. The interaction process can be defined as circular: the economic system influences the political one by originating interests able to exert pressure, and the political system affects the economic one by bringing about economic change (see Dixit, 1996).

Since the seminal contribution by Buchanan and Tullock (1962), a wide strand of literature has focused on interest groups and their pressure as the institutional manifestation of economic interests in the political system. The interest group is a collective agent exerting pressure to promote an interest; pressure is political influence, which depends on resources used to support specific policies or particular candidates, and manage the exchange of strategic information (see Olson, 1965; Mitchell and Munger, 1991; and van Winden, 1999, 2003).

In the interaction process between the political and economic system, the role of economic interests connected with single industrial sectors has been broadly analysed. An interesting issue is the relationship between pressure for promoting an economic interest and economic growth. This issue has been amply discussed since the seminal work by Olson (1982), where pressure slows down growth by promoting particular interests against general interests, that is, by promoting restricted markets against competitive markets. Within endogenous growth models, Olson's view has been elaborated by Pecorino (1992), Rama (1993), Tornell and Lane (1999), and Rodrìguez (2004), who have underlined that pressure, aimed at obtaining restrictive market regulations or fiscal transfers, can reduce the growth rate due to an inefficient resource allocation; the same conclusion has been respectively found in Murphy et al. (1993) and Grossman and Kim (1996) with regard to the competition among particular interests and predatory activity.

Other contributions have reached the opposite conclusion, whereby interest groups can enhance growth. For instance, Mork (1993) and Sturzenegger and Tommasi (1994) have shown that interest group pressure can positively affect the growth rate by obtaining more competitive markets or fiscal transfers reducing capital costs.

On balance, from a theoretical point of view, the relationship between pressure and growth is uncertain. Accordingly, the empirical evidence has shown little support for Olson's view (Knack, 2003). Moreover, the two perspectives are not mutually exclusive; within an endogenous growth model focusing on economic policy externalities as in Barro (1990), the contribution by Mohtadi and Roe (1998) has shown that interest group pressure can internalize some externalities of public goods by promoting their supply. Therefore, the search for a public expenditure optimal level is replaced by the search for a pressure optimal level, and a non-monotonic relationship between pressure and growth is obtained.

Hence the previous literature has overlooked some elements. Although it has explained the non-monotonic relationship in terms of supply variations following changes in public good supply, it has omitted to explore how pressure can affect growth by causing demand variations. Moreover, although Przeworski and Wallerstein (1988) suggested analysing the role of income distribution between profits and wages in affecting the interaction process between the political and economic system, the literature has on the whole devoted scant attention to this issue.

This chapter represents a first step in trying to fill these lacunae. It studies how economic interests connected with income distribution can influence political decisions and how, in turn, such decisions can affect the economy. In order to focus on the relationship between pressure for promoting the capitalists' interest or the workers' interest and economic growth, the chapter is structured as follows. Section 16.2 describes the influence of income distribution on political decisions through the 'influence function approach' and the 'interest function approach'. The first approach (see van Winden, 1983; van Velthoven, 1989; Mazza and van Winden, 1996; and Sadiraj et al., 2005), which focuses on the behaviour of interest groups, is used to model their choice regarding the pressure to exert in order to promote the capitalists' and workers' interests; the second approach (see Becker, 1983, 1985; Austen-Smith, 1997; and Ando, 2003), which focuses on political decisions, is used to model the policymakers' decisional process as a mediation between the capitalists' interests and the workers' interests. In Section 16.3, the neo-Kaleckian approach (see Rowthorn, 1982; Dutt, 1984;

Lavoie, 1992; Blecker, 2002; and Commendatore et al., 2003) is used to model the operation of the economy. Neo-Kaleckian models share with the post-Keynesian tradition (see Lavoie, 1992; Setterfield, 2002; and Dutt, 2003) the principle of effective demand: they describe how income distribution leads to economic changes by affecting demand. Moreover, their analytic framework also allows some results of endogenous growth models to be shown (Barro and Xala-i-Martin, 1995). Section 16.4 analyses the relationship between pressure to promote capitalists' or workers' interests and economic growth: it explores how the time change of the balance of forces between the capitalists' interest group and the workers' interest group affects changes over time in the economy. Some conclusions are drawn in Section 16.5.

16.2. THE POLITICAL SYSTEM

In order to analyse the role of income distribution, it is assumed that only the economic interests connected with the income distribution between profits and wages are able to affect the policymakers' decisional process: the first interest is the capitalists' interest, that is, the level of the after-tax profit share; the second interest is the workers' interest, that is, the level of the after-tax wage share. The capitalists' interest group and the workers' interest group promote their interests in the policymakers' decisional process by exerting pressure.[1]

16.2.1. Behaviour of the Interest Groups

The behaviour of the interest groups can be modelled by the 'influence function approach' in a simple and general way (Austen-Smith, 1997). This approach analyses the decisional process of the interest groups in terms of available resources and efficiency in exerting pressure.

With regard to the available resources at time *t* for the interest groups, it is assumed that they are influenced by the income shares, the income tax rate, and the endowments of resources:

$$\begin{aligned} W_{\pi,t} &= (1-\tau_{\pi,t-1})\pi_q E \\ W_{\omega,t} &= (1-\tau_{\omega,t-1})\omega_q E \end{aligned} ; \qquad (16.1)$$

where

π refers to the capitalists' interest group;

ω refers to the workers' interest group;

π_q is the income share of profits;

ω_q is the income share of wages;
E is the endowment of resources for the interest groups;
W are the available resources for the interest groups;
τ_π is the rate of profits tax;
τ_ω is the rate of wages tax.

Since it is not important for the issue in question, it is assumed that the endowment of resources E is the same for both the interest groups. The assumption that the available resources W are positively related to income shares, π_q and ω_q, represents the impact of the economy on the balance of political forces between the interest groups. The assumption that the available resources (W) are negatively related to the income tax rate, τ_π and τ_ω, represents a reduced form for describing the impact of political decisions on the economy and thus on the balance of political forces.

With regard to the interest group efficiency at exerting pressure, the influence function describes the relationship between pressure and resources allocated for political influence:[2]

$$q_{i,t} = z_{i,t}^{\gamma_i}; \tag{16.2}$$

where
$i \neq j = \omega, \pi$;
q is the pressure;
z are the resources allocated for political influence;
$\gamma < 1$ is the ability to exert pressure.

The variable q is the interest group pressure, and can consist of acts of corruption, the buying of votes and strategic information. However, the choice of the variable used to denote pressure is an empirical problem rather than a theoretical one. Parameter γ represents the interest group's ability to exert pressure. The assumption that it is less than one implies decreasing returns for the resources allocated in carrying out political influence; parameter (γ) is also affected by the ideological affinity between policymakers and interest groups and by the strength of the social classes.

The utility function for an interest group describes its preferences regarding pressure, that is, the trade off between its propensity to promote an economic interest and the utility of resources allocated for political influence:[3]

$$U_{i,t} = \alpha \ln q_{i,t}(z_{i,t}) + (1-\alpha)\ln\left(W_t - z_{i,t}\right); \tag{16.3}$$

where $0 < \alpha < 1$ is the preference for pressure.

In the 'influence function approach', the objective function of an interest group is usually identified with its income level, this assumption implying a strategic interaction between the interest groups. However, the empirical evidence does not strongly support this result (Ando, 2003). On the contrary, in this chapter the objective function of the interest group has been identified with its absolute pressure level subject to the constraint of the utility of the resources allocated for political influence. This assumption results in the selection of a strategy for the interest groups that does not entail interaction between them. Indeed, this chapter does not intend to tackle the issue of strategic interaction between the interest groups; its focus is on the impact of the time change of the balance of forces between interest groups on the change over time of the economy.[4]

Parameter α denotes the interest group's propensity to exert pressure, that is, the interest group's propensity to use the available resources to exert political influence. Since it is not relevant to the issues in question, it is assumed that the interest groups do not differ regarding this parameter. An interest group maximizes its utility by choosing the amount of resources to allocate for pressure; the optimization problem of an interest group is:

$$\max_{z_{i,t}} U_{i,t} = \alpha \ln z_{i,t}^{\gamma_i} + (1-\alpha)\ln\left(W_{i,t} - z_{i,t}\right). \tag{16.4}$$

First and second order conditions are:

$$\frac{\partial U_{i,t}}{\partial z_{i,t}} = \frac{\alpha\gamma_i}{z_{i,t}} - \frac{(1-\alpha)}{W_{i,t} - z_{i,t}} = 0\ ; \tag{16.5}$$

$$\frac{\partial U_{i,t}}{\partial z_{i,t}\partial z_{i,t}} = -\left[\frac{\alpha\gamma_i}{z_{i,t}^2} + \frac{(1-\alpha)}{\left(W_{i,t} - z_{i,t}\right)^2}\right] < 0\ ; \tag{16.6}$$

The optimal level of the resources allocated to pressure is:

$$z_{i,t} = \frac{\alpha\gamma_i W_{i,t}}{1+\alpha(\gamma_i - 1)}. \tag{16.7}$$

Equation (16.7) describes the interest group's optimal choice about the resources allocated to political influence. These resources are positively related to the available resources (W), the interest group's ability (γ), and the preference for pressure (α).

16.2.2. The Policymakers' Decisional Process

The 'interest function approach' is used to model the policymakers' decisional process. This approach defines the decisional process as a mediation among economic interests, that is, between the capitalists' interest and the workers' interest.

The interest function is the policymakers' objective function: it allows its decisional process to be represented as the maximization of a weighted combination of economic interests:[5]

$$If_t = q_{\pi,t} \ln(1-\tau_{\pi,t})\pi_q + q_{\omega,t} \ln(1-\tau_{\omega,t})\omega_q ; \tag{16.8}$$

where G is the public expenditure.

Mainly for pragmatic reasons, in the 'interest function approach' it is usually assumed that an economic weight in the policymakers' decisional process is proportional to the people who share that interest. Nevertheless, some contributions have underlined the potential role of other elements, such as ideology and pressure, in affecting interest function weights (van Winden, 1999 and 2003). Thus, the lack of a behavioural model for explaining weights is a major limitation to the 'interest function approach'. This chapter seeks to fill this lacuna by assuming that the economic interest weight is equal to the interest group pressure (q) and using the 'influence function approach' to determine the pressure (q) as a function of interest groups behaviour.

It is assumed a balanced budget for the public sector: tax revenues, coming out from the profit tax rate and the wage tax rate equal the public expenditure. Tax revenues and public expenditure are expressed in terms of income:

$$G = \tau_\pi \pi_q + \tau_\omega \omega_q . \tag{16.9}$$

Policymakers maximize their objective function by promoting economic interests in accordance with interest group pressure at time t (equation (16.8)) and subject to the constraint of the balanced budget (equation (16.9)).[6] By substituting the budget constraint in the objective function, it is possible to obtain the first and second order conditions only with respect to the profit tax rate (τ_π):

$$\frac{\partial U_{s,t}}{\partial \tau_{\pi,t}} = -\frac{q_{\pi,t}}{(1-\tau_{\pi,t})} + \frac{q_{\omega,t}\pi_q}{(\omega_q - G + \pi_q \tau_{\pi,t})} = 0 \tag{16.10}$$

$$\frac{\partial U_{s,t}}{\partial\partial \tau_{\pi,t}} = -\frac{q_{\pi,t}}{(1-\tau_{\pi,t})^2} - \frac{q_{\omega,t}\pi_q^2}{(\omega_q - G + \pi_q \tau_{\pi,t})^2} < 0 . \tag{16.11}$$

On the basis of the first order condition and the budget constraint, the optimal solutions for the income tax rate are:

$$\tau_{\pi,t} = 1 - \frac{(1-G)}{\pi_q} \tilde{q}_t ; \tag{16.12}$$

$$\tau_{\omega,t} = 1 - \frac{(1-G)}{\omega_q} (1-\tilde{q}_t) ; \tag{16.13}$$

where $\tilde{q}_t$ is the power share.

In equations (16.12) and (16.13) the income tax rates (τ_π and τ_ω) depend on the power share of capitalists $\tilde{q}_t$, $0 \leq \tilde{q}_t \leq 1$. The power share is defined by the ratio between pressure of the capitalists' interest group and pressure of all interest groups; it is an index of the policymakers' propensity to promote more or less one or the other interest:[7]

$$\tilde{q}_t = \frac{q_{\pi,t}}{q_{\pi,t} + q_{\omega,t}} . \tag{16.14}$$

Fiscal policy decisions, that is, income tax rates, are the optimal mediation between capitalists' and workers' interests. The profit tax rate (τ_π) and wage tax rate (τ_ω) oscillate between zero and a negative value implying a subsidy; they are positively related to the income shares and the level of public expenditure, while they are negatively related to the pressure to promote their own interest (equations (16.12)–(16.13)). Note that a divergence between the balance of political forces, summarized by the power share (($\tilde{q}_t$) and ($1-\tilde{q}_t$)), and the balance of economic forces, summarized by the income share ((π_q) and (ω_q)), is the necessary condition for bringing about a different income distribution with respect to that affected only by economic forces.

16.3. OPERATION OF THE ECONOMY

In the literature it is possible to identify at least two views about the operation of the economy concerning growth processes: the first includes both neoclassic and endogenous growth models, the second lies within the post-Keynesian tradition. In the first, savings lead growth and investment decisions adapt to saving decisions; in the second, investments lead growth and saving decisions adapt to investment decisions through variations in income or its distribution. Thus, in the analysis of economic policy effects on growth, the choice of theoretical approach used to describe the economy has to take into account these differences (Panico, 2003).

The neo-Kaleckian approach is chosen to describe the economy because it shares with the post-Keynesian tradition the principle of effective demand

and its analytic framework also allows us to show some results of endogenous growth models. A neo-Kaleckian model obtains explicit expressions for the income shares of profits and wages as well as for the equilibrium growth rate.

The basic principle behind the neo-Kaleckian approach is that firms' investment decisions are autonomous with respect to households' saving decisions, the so-called principle of effective demand. The short-run equilibrium condition, where savings equal investment, is guaranteed by production variations; the key hypothesis is that oligopolistic firms, operating with overcapacity, deal with unexpected demand changes by varying output levels and not price levels.

The simplest neo-Kaleckian framework has the following characteristics. The economy is closed and produces a homogeneous good, which is used both for consumption and production. Only two factors are used in production: labour and physical capital. Technology involves fixed coefficients; therefore, in neo-Kaleckian models the labour–capital ratio does not change as factor prices vary. Constant returns to scale and no capital depreciation are assumed; moreover, wages are a variable production cost. The following expressions describe the technology:

$$y^{*}=\min\left\{\frac{L_f}{x_l},\frac{K}{x_k}\right\} \text{ with } \frac{K}{x_k}<\frac{L_f}{x_l}; \tag{16.15}$$

where

Y^{*} is the full capacity output level;

L_f is the existing workforce;

K is the existing physical capital stock;

x_l is the inverse of the average labour productivity;

x_k is the ratio of physical capital to full capacity output.

According to expression (16.15) capital is the only productive factor limiting production; capital and labour are used in fixed proportions.

Within the economy there are two social classes: workers, whose only income source is wages, and capitalists, whose only income source is profits; for simplification, it is assumed that only capitalists save:

$$g_{s,t}=s(1-\tau_{\pi,t})r; \tag{16.16}$$

where

$g_s = S/pK$ is the savings growth rate;

p is the price level;

S represents savings;

s is the average and marginal propensity to save;

r is the profit rate.

Three factors affect firms' accumulation decisions: the entrepreneurs' 'animal spirits', that is, their long-run expectations about the demand growth rate; the after-tax profit rate, which represents an incentive and also an internal source of financing; and the degree of capacity utilization, which is a measure of the demand level:

$$g_{i,t} = \eta + \eta_r (1 - \tau_{\pi,t}) r + \eta_u u \, ; \tag{16.17}$$

where

$g_i = I/K$ is the capital growth rate;
I represents investments;
$0 < \eta$ denotes 'animal spirits';
$0 < \eta_r$ is investment decision sensitivity with respect to the profit rate;
$0 < \eta_u$ is investment decision sensitivity with respect to the degree of capacity utilization;
$u = Y / Y^*$ is the degree of capacity utilization.

All firms are identical; in an oligopolistic market they fix the price level by applying a mark-up to the variable unitary costs of production, that is, the labour cost per unit of output. The mark-up level is influenced by economic factors such as industrial sector concentration degree, demand elasticity with respect to price, firm growth objectives, and workers' bargaining power.

$$p = (1+m) w_n x_l \, ; \tag{16.18}$$

where

m is the mark-up level.
w_n is the nominal wage level;

Expressions for the profit and wage shares are the following:

$$\pi_q = \frac{rpK}{pY} = r \cdot \frac{x_k}{u} \, ; \tag{16.19}$$

$$\omega_q = \frac{w_n L}{pY} = w x_l \, ; \tag{16.20}$$

where w is the real wage rate.

In equilibrium capitalists' saving decisions are always enough to finance firms' investment decisions; that is, the saving growth rate must equal the capital growth rate. Under this equilibrium condition and on the basis of equations (16.16)–(16.20), it is possible to obtain the equilibrium solutions for the income shares, the degree of capacity utilization, and the growth rate:

$$\pi_q = \frac{m}{(1+m)};\qquad (16.21)$$

$$\omega_q = \frac{1}{(1+m)}\qquad (16.22)$$

$$u_t = \frac{\eta \bar{x}_k}{(s-\eta_r)(1-\tau_{\pi,t})\pi_q - \eta_u \bar{x}_k};\qquad (16.23)$$

$$g_t = \frac{\eta \pi_q s(1-\tau_{\pi,t})}{(s-\eta_r)(1-\tau_{\pi,t})\pi_q - \eta_u \bar{x}_k} \quad for \quad u<1;\qquad (16.24)$$

$$g_t = s(1-\tau_{\pi,t})\frac{\pi_q}{\bar{x}_k} \quad for \quad u=1.\qquad (16.25)$$

Within the neo-Kaleckian approach the income distribution is constant over time because it is only affected by the mark-up level,[8] that is, by market concentration degree, demand elasticity, firm growth objectives, and workers' bargaining power (equations (16.21) and (16.22)). Thus, the mark-up (m) summarizes the balance of economic forces between capitalists and workers.

When the degree of capacity utilization is less than one (equation (16.23)), the productive capacity is not fully utilized; equations (16.23) and (16.24) describe a 'neo-Kaleckian' economy where investments lead growth: each change increasing the demand level also increases the degree of capacity utilisation and the growth rate. In particular, according to the so-called paradox of costs, an increase in the ratio of capital to full capacity output level (x_k) raises the degree of capacity utilization and the growth rate because greater production costs mean a greater demand level and hence a greater production level. Moreover, according to the so-called paradox of savings, an income redistribution in favour of economic agents with a higher propensity to consume (i.e. a decrease in m) transferring purchasing power from capitalists to workers or a decrease in the agents' propensity to save (i.e. a decrease in s raising capitalists' propensity to consume) enhances growth by increasing the demand level.

When the degree of capacity utilization is equal to one (equation (16.23)), there is no overcapacity; equation (16.25) describes a 'neoclassical' economy where savings lead growth. Note that according to equation (16.25) the growth rate is equal to savings per unit of capital, as occurs in the AK model with constant marginal productivity of capital. In this context, an increase in production costs (i.e. an increase in x_k) reduces the growth rate because greater production costs mean lower savings per capital unit. Income redistribution in favour of economic agents with a higher propensity to save (i.e. an increase in m) or an increase in the agents' propensity to save (i.e. an increase in s) enhances growth by increasing savings per unit of capital.

In conclusion, the neo-Kaleckian economy (where the degree of capacity utilization is lower than one) and the neoclassical economy (where the degree of capacity utilization is equal to one) work quite differently: in the former growth is demand-driven, whereas in the latter it is supply-driven. Thus, it will be worth analysing the relationship between pressure and economic growth under different assumptions concerning the degree of capacity utilisation.

16.4. POLITICAL AND ECONOMIC CHANGES

In this section the focus is on the impact of the balance of political forces between capitalists' interests and workers' interests on economic growth. The profit power share ($\tilde{q}_t$) (equation (16.14)) denotes the policymakers' propensity to promote the capitalists' interests and it affects the growth rate (equations (16.24) and (16.25)) by influencing the profit tax rate (equation (16.12)). Thus it is worth analysing the time change of power share.

The power share at time t depends on the pressure at time t (equations (16.14) and (16.2)); the pressure at time t is affected by the available resources at time t (equations (16.2) and (14.7)), which depend on the fiscal policy at time $t-1$ (equations (16.7) and (16.1)); the fiscal policy at time $t-1$ is affected by the power share at time $t-1$ (equations (16.1), (16.12) and (16.13)). Thus, replacing equations (16.1), (16.2), (16.7) and (16.12) and (16.13) in equation (16.14), the following difference equation for the power share is obtained:

$$\tilde{q}_t = \frac{\left[\frac{\alpha\gamma_\pi(1-G)E\tilde{q}_{t-1}}{1+\alpha(\gamma_\pi-1)}\right]^{\gamma_\pi}}{\left[\frac{\alpha\gamma_\pi(1-G)E\tilde{q}_{t-1}}{1+\alpha(\gamma_\pi-1)}\right]^{\gamma_\pi}+\left[\frac{\alpha\gamma_\omega(1-G)E(1-\tilde{q}_{t-1})}{1+\alpha(\gamma_\omega-1)}\right]^{\gamma_\omega}}. \qquad (16.26)$$

Equation (16.26) shows the time change of the power share ($\tilde{q}_t$) in accordance with the interest group's ability to exert pressure (γ), the preference for pressure (α), the endowment of resources (E), and public expenditure (G). Note that the overall effect of mark-up on the power share is nil. While the income share positively influences the available resources for interest groups (equation (16.1)), it negatively influences the available resources by increasing the income tax rates (equations (16.1), (16.12) and (16.13)).

An equilibrium state for the political system (EPS) is defined as a position of rest of the power share, such that it does not change from one period to the other; an equilibrium state is asymptotically stable (or unstable) according to whether sufficiently small deviations from it generate (or do not generate) a time path of the power share which leads back to such a state.

In Figure 16.1, intersections between the 45° line and the graph of difference equation (16.26) identify three equilibrium states: the stable equilibrium at point e, where the phase line slope is less than one; the unstable equilibria at one and zero, where the phase line slope is more than one. The power share time path denoting the convergence process to the stable equilibrium at point e implies an increase or a decrease in the power share according to the initial state for the political system (IPS), that is, the initial condition of the power share. The time path is connected with an increase in the power share if the initial state is to the left of the equilibrium state at point e, while it is connected with a decrease if the initial state is to the right.

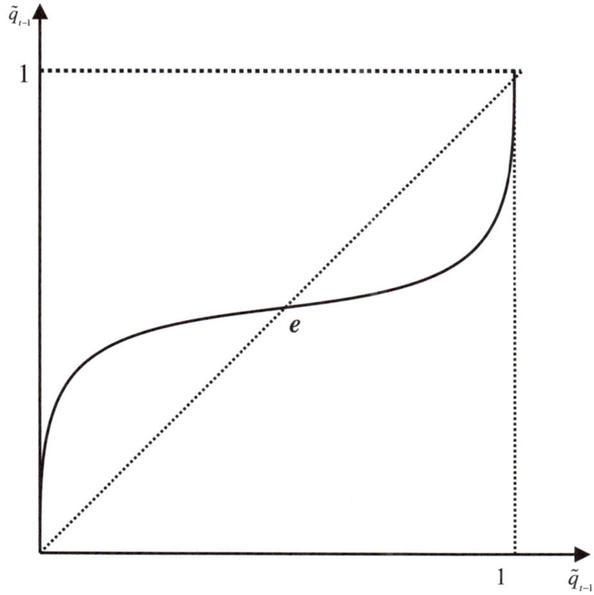

Figure 16.1. The equilibrium state for the political system (EPS)

Figure 16.2 depicts the impact of variations in the interest group's ability to exert pressure (γ). An increase in the ability of one interest group modifies the concavity and convexity of the phase line by shifting the stable equilibrium in favour of the interest group which has become more skilful. The intensity of this change is positively related to the resources allocated to pressure. In other words, it rises with an increase in the preference for pressure (α) and the endowment of resources (E) or with a decrease in public expenditure (G). Note that these parameters do not affect the equilibrium state if the interest groups are also identical in their ability to exert pressure (γ).[9]

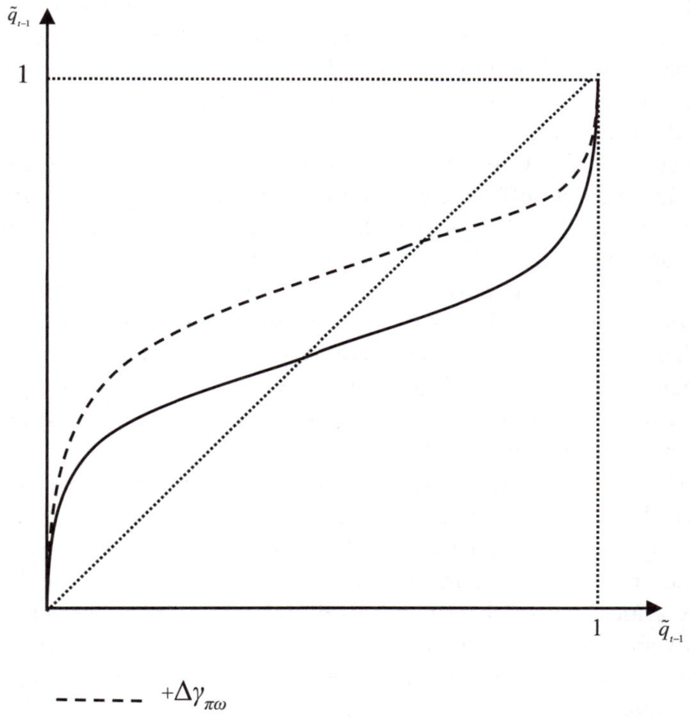

Figure 16.2. An increase in the ability of the capitalists' interest group

In general, policymakers take proper account of the capitalists' interests and the workers' interests only if there is enough equality between the interest groups in terms of efficiency. When this condition is not satisfied, the fiscal policy strongly aims to promote only one interest, that of capitalists or of workers.

16.4.1. Economic Changes

In order to analyse the relationship between time change of the power share and economic growth, it is useful to define the critical state for the political system (CPS) as the power share entailing the full utilisation of productive capacity. By substituting equation (16.12) into equation (16.23) and setting the degree of capacity utilisation at one, the following expression is obtained:

$$\tilde{q}_t^c = \frac{(\eta_u + \eta)\bar{x}_k}{(s - \eta_r)(1 - G)}. \qquad (16.27)$$

Equation (16.27) identifies the power share prevailing in a critical state. For this power share the profit tax rate guarantees the full utilization of productive capacity. The profit tax rate has two effects on the economy: it increases demand by influencing saving decisions via an income redistribution from capitalists, whose propensity to save is positive, to the public sector, whose propensity to save is nil (equation (16.16)); yet it also reduces demand by influencing investment decisions (equation (16.17)). However, the former effect always dominates the latter and the degree of capacity utilization is positively related to the profit tax rate (equation (16.23)). Thus, when the power share is less than its critical level, there is full utilization of productive capacity because demand level is sufficiently high; otherwise, when the power share exceeds its critical level, there is overcapacity because demand is too low. Note that variations in the wage tax rate do not affect the critical state because workers and the public sector have the same propensity to save.

The critical state is affected by parameters such as the public expenditure level (G), the capitalists' propensity to save (s), the firms' propensity to invest (η, η_r, η_u), and production cost level (x_k). These elements synthesize the overall propensity of the public and private sector to sustain the demand level; the critical power share is positively related to this propensity. Note that the overall effect of mark-up on the critical state is nil; on the one hand, it negatively influences demand by redistributing income from workers to capitalists (equation (16.23)); but, on the other hand, it positively influences demand by increasing the profit tax rate and redistributing income from capitalists to the public sector (equations (16.23) and (16.12)).

The relationship between time change of the power share and time change of the growth rate depends on how the equilibrium state, the critical state, and the initial state for the political system are placed in political space; this space is identified by the set of power share.

In Figure 16.3 the equilibrium state and the initial state are respectively represented by the y-axis and x-axis. Therefore, the Cartesian axis and the more external lines parallel to them include all combinations of equilibrium and initial states. In Figure (16.1), the power share time path is monotonic and convergent towards the equilibrium because the phase diagram describes a monotonically increasing function. Therefore, in Figure (16.3) the power share time path is represented by point successions along the dotted arrows ending on the 45° line where the equilibrium state is reached.

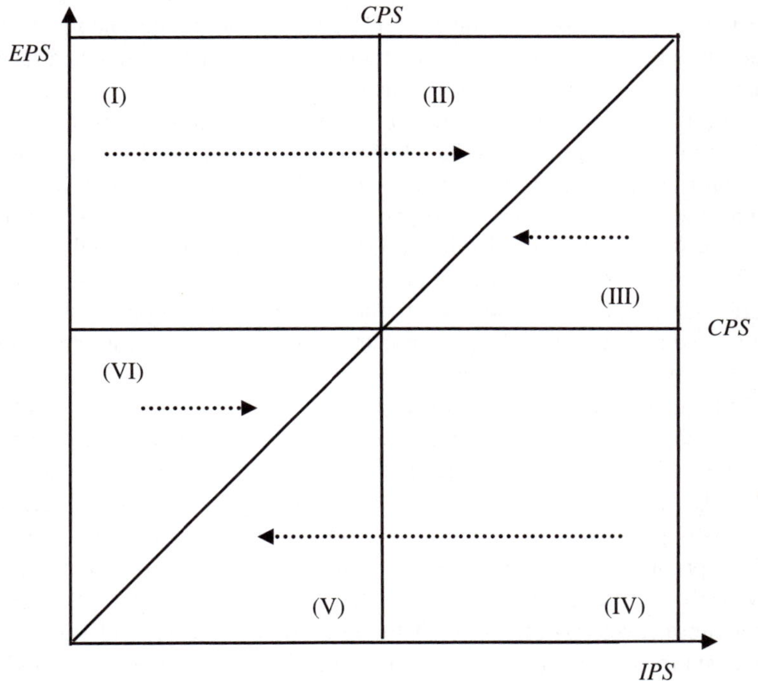

Figure 16.3. Interaction between political and economic dynamics

The more internal lines parallel to the Cartesian axis denote the critical state for the political system: when a combination of equilibrium and initial state is on the right of the line parallel to the *y*-axis, the power share time path starts in the neo-Kaleckian region where there is overcapacity and investments drive growth (equation (16.24)); when the combination of equilibrium and initial state is on the left, the time path starts in the neoclassical region where there is full utilization of the productive capacity and savings drive growth (equation (16.25)). In the same way, when the combination lies above the line parallel to the x-axis, the time path ends in the neo-Kaleckian region, while when it lies below the time path it ends in the neoclassical region. Obviously, an increase in the overall propensity of the public and private sector to sustain the demand level shifts the lines representing the critical state outwards and it extends the neoclassical region. The opposite occurs with a decrease in the overall propensity.

In Figure 16.3 each region identifies a specific relationship between the power share and the growth rate. In region (I) ($EPS>CPS>IPS$), the power share time path implies a decreases in the profit tax rate because the power share increases; in the neoclassical region the growth rate is positively affected by this process (equation (16.25)), while in the neo-Kaleckian region it is negatively affected (equation (16.24)); when the demand level is exactly equal to the productive capacity, the growth rate is maximum because the saving effect of the profit tax rate dominates its investment effect. In region (IV) ($IPS>CPS>EPS$), the time path implies an increase in the profit tax rate because the power share decreases; in the neo-Kaleckian region the growth rate is positively affected by this process (equation (16.24)), while in the neoclassical region it is negatively affected (equation (16.25)). In the other regions, the power share time path is entirely contained in the neo-Kaleckian region or in the neoclassical region, such that an increase or a decrease in the power share is only connected with an increase or a decrease in the growth rate.

With regard to the impact of variations in the parameters, the interest group's ability (γ), the preference for pressure (α) and the endowment of resources (E) directly affect the power share equilibrium state, and they indirectly affect the growth rate by modifying the power share. The capitalists' propensity to save (s), the firm's propensity to invest (η, η_r, η_u), and the production costs (x_k) only affect the power share critical state, that is, they only influence the growth rate. More interestingly, the public expenditure level (G) affects both the equilibrium and critical state of the power share, so that its variations influence both the power share and the growth rate.

In general, in regions (I) and (IV) the power share time path implies a non-monotonic relationship between the power share and the growth rate, while in the other regions this relationship is monotonic. Variations in the parameters modify the equilibrium and/or critical state of the power share, such that a new political convergence process or only economic changes can occur. The intensity of political and economic changes depends on the difference between equilibrium and initial states of the power share. A fairly balanced fiscal policy promoting capitalists' interests and workers' interests is a key element for also producing a balanced change in the economy over time. When there is low inequality between the interest groups in terms of efficiency in exerting pressure and policymakers take proper account of both economic interests, the difference between demand level and productive capacity, which depends on the profit tax rate, is likely to be low, whereby smoother economic changes occur in the economy. On the contrary, when this condition is not satisfied, it is likely that the difference between the demand level and productive capacity becomes large, whereby the economy can experience extreme economic situations such as inflation or stagnation.

16.5. CONCLUSION

This chapter studied how economic interests connected with the income distribution between profits and wages can influence political decisions and how, in turn, such decisions can influence the change over time of the economy. The analysis showed that the fiscal policy has to take proper account of both the capitalists' interest and the workers' interest if it aims to favour a balanced change of the economy over time, that is, a balanced change over time of the demand level and of productive capacity. Thus, policymakers have to resolve the conflict between the capitalists' interests and the workers' interests by avoiding polarization of the fiscal policy. The model also explained the non-monotonic relationship between pressure for promoting the capitalists' interests or workers' interests and economic growth in terms of demand variations depending on changes in the profit tax rate.

In future research the assumption of a balanced budget for the public sector could be dropped and the effect of pressure in promoting the capitalists' interests and the workers' interests on the public debt could be explored. In this context, it could also be worth analysing the role of monetary policy. Another issue that could be explored is the role of mark-up when its effect on the resources of the interest group and the demand level do not balance each other out. In conclusion, it is hoped that this chapter has contributed to understanding reality by exploring issues concerned with the interplay between the political and economic system.

MATHEMATICAL APPENDIX

With regard to the difference equation for the power share (equation (16.27)), the function sign is studied by comparing the numerator and denominator signs; along the x-axis from zero to one, the function is always positive.

The first derivative is:

$$\frac{\partial \tilde{q}_t}{\partial \tilde{q}_{t-1}} = \frac{\left[\frac{\alpha\gamma_\pi (1-G)E\tilde{q}_{t-1}}{1+\alpha(\gamma_\pi -1)}\right]^{\gamma_\pi} \left[\frac{\alpha\gamma_\omega (1-G)E(1-\tilde{q}_{t-1})}{1+\alpha(\gamma_\omega -1)}\right]^{\gamma_\omega} \left[\gamma_\pi \tilde{q}_{t-1}^{-1} + \gamma_\omega (1-\tilde{q}_{t-1})^{-1}\right]}{\left\{\left[\frac{\alpha\gamma_\pi (1-G)E\tilde{q}_{t-1}}{1+\alpha(\gamma_\pi -1)}\right]^{\gamma_\pi} + \left[\frac{\alpha\gamma_\omega (1-G)E(1-\tilde{q}_{t-1})}{1+\alpha(\gamma_\omega -1)}\right]^{\gamma_\omega}\right\}^2} > 0\,; \tag{16A.1}$$

It is greater than zero because the numerator is always greater than zero.

The second derivative is:

$$\frac{\partial \tilde{q}_t}{\partial\partial \tilde{q}_{t-1}} = \frac{\frac{1}{\tilde{q}_{t-1}^2 (1-\tilde{q}_{t-1})^2} \left\{(\bar{\gamma}_\pi \tilde{q}_{t-1})^{\gamma_\pi} \left[(\gamma_\omega - \gamma_\pi)(1+\gamma_\pi - \gamma_\omega)\tilde{q}_{t-1}^2 + 2\gamma_\pi (1+\gamma_\pi - \gamma_\omega)\tilde{q}_{t-1} - \gamma_\pi (1+\gamma_\pi)\right]\right\}}{\left\{(\bar{\gamma}_\pi \tilde{q}_{t-1})^{\gamma_\pi} + \left[\bar{\gamma}_\omega (1-\tilde{q}_{t-1})\right]^{\gamma_\omega}\right\}^4} +$$
$$+ \frac{\frac{1}{\tilde{q}_{t-1}^2 (1-\tilde{q}_{t-1})^2} \left\{\left[\bar{\gamma}_\omega (1-\tilde{q}_{t-1})\right]^{\gamma_\omega} \left[(\gamma_\omega - \gamma_\pi)(1+\gamma_\omega - \gamma_\pi)\tilde{q}_{t-1}^2 + 2\gamma_\pi (1+\gamma_\omega - \gamma_\pi)\tilde{q}_{t-1} + \gamma_\pi (\gamma_\pi - 1)\right]\right\}}{\left\{(\bar{\gamma}_\pi \tilde{q}_{t-1})^{\gamma_\pi} + \left[\bar{\gamma}_\omega (1-\tilde{q}_{t-1})\right]^{\gamma_\omega}\right\}^4} \lessgtr 0 \tag{16A.2}$$

with

$$\bar{\gamma}_\pi = \frac{\alpha\gamma_\pi (1-G)E}{1+\alpha(\gamma_\pi -1)} \text{ and } \bar{\gamma}_\omega = \frac{\alpha\gamma_\omega (1-G)E}{1+\alpha(\gamma_\omega -1)}.$$

Inequality (16A.2) is less or more than zero in accordance with the sign of the numerator; therefore, along the x-axis from zero to one, the function is first concave and then convex.

The following critical points are useful to describe the function shape:

$$\lim_{\tilde{q}_{t-1} \to 1} \tilde{q}_t (\tilde{q}_{t-1}) = 1\,; \tag{16A.3}$$

$$\lim_{\tilde{q}_{t-1} \to 0} \tilde{q}_t (\tilde{q}_{t-1}) = 0\,. \tag{16A.4}$$

NOTES

1. Note that it is assumed that both interest groups have a formal or informal organization to avoid free-riding behaviour by their own members.
2. This functional form is a standard production function for political influence.
3. This functional form allows us to obtain more simple analytical expressions (see Mazza and van Winden, 1996).
4. Purificato (2008) analyses the strategic interaction among interest groups. In comparison with the results obtained in this chapter, there is no major difference in the time change of the balance of forces between interest groups if their available resources are enough to implement the optimal decision on the resources allocated to pressure.
5. This functional form is used by Mazza and van Winden (1996).
6. In Grossman and Kim (1996), and Sadiraj et al. (2005) dynamic optimization is not assumed for agents; it is useful to proceed in the same way in order to obtain a behavioural model consistent with the typical neo-Kaleckian hypotheses about decisional processes (Lavoie 1992; Dutt 2003).
7. Since the chapter does not take into account the role of political institutions, it is not appropriate to distinguish between '*de jure* political power' and '*de facto* political power' as in Acemoglu et al. (2005).
8. The result holds until labour costs are only variable costs of production (Lavoie, 1992).
9. See the Mathematical Appendix for analytical details.

REFERENCES

Acemoglu, A., S. Johnson and J.A. Robinson (2005), 'Institutions as a Fundamental Cause of Development', in P. Aghion and S. Durlauf (eds), *Handbook of Economic Growth*, Amsterdam: North-Holland.

Ando, A.W. (2003), 'Do Interest Groups Compete? An Application to Endangered Species', *Public Choice*, **114**(1–2), 137–59.

Austen-Smith, D. (1997), 'Money, Information, and Influence', in D.C. Mueller (ed.), *Perspectives on Public Choice*, Cambridge: Cambridge University Press, pp. 296–321.

Barro, R, (1990), 'Government Spending in a Simple Model of Endogenous Growth', *Journal of Political Economy*, **98**(5), 103–25.

Barro, R. and X. Sala-i-Martin (1995), *Economic Growth*, New York: McGraw-Hill.

Becker, G. (1985), 'Public Policies, Interest Groups, and Dead Weight Costs', *Journal of Public Economics*, **28**(3), 329–47.

Becker, G. (1983), 'A Theory of Competition Among Interest Groups for Political Influence', *Quarterly Journal of Economics*, **98**(3), 371–400.

Blecker, R, (2002), 'Distribution, Demand and Growth in Neo-Kaleckian Macro-Models', in M. Setterfield (ed.), *The Economics of Demand-Led Growth*, Cheltenham UK and Northampton, MA, USA: Edward Elgar, pp. 129–52.

Buchanan, J.M. and G. Tullock (1962), *The Calculus of Consent. Logical Foundations of Constitutional Democracy*, Ann Arbor: The University of Michigan Press.

Commendatore, P., S. D'Acunto, C. Panico and N. Pinto (2003), 'Keynesian Theories of Growth', in N. Salvadori (ed.), *The Theory of Economic Growth*, Cheltenham UK and Northampton, MA, USA: Edward Elgar, pp. 103–39.

Dixit, A. (1996), *The Making of Economic Policy: A Transaction-Cost Politics Perspective*, Cambridge, MA: MIT Press.

Dutt, A. (1984), 'Stagnation, Income Distribution and Monopoly Power', *Cambridge Journal of Economics*, **8**(1), 25–40.

Dutt, A. (2003), 'New Growth Theories, Effective Demand, and Post-Keynesian Dynamics', in N. Salvadori (ed.), *Old and New Growth Theories*, Cheltenham UK and Northampton, MA, USA: Edward Elgar, pp. 67–100.

Grossman, H.I and M. Kim (1996), 'Predation and Accumulation', *Journal of Economic Growth*, **1**(3), 333–51.

Knack, S, (2003), 'Groups, Growth and Trust: Cross-Country Evidence on the Olson and Putnam Hypotheses', *Public Choice*, **117**(3–4), 341–55.

Lavoie, M. (1992), *Foundations of Post-Keynesian Analysis*, Aldershot, UK and Brookfield, US: Edward Elgar.

Mazza, I. and F. van Winden (1996), 'A Political Economic Analysis of Labor Migration and Income Redistribution', *Public Choice*, **88**(3–4), 333–63

Mitchell, W.C. and M. Munger (1991), 'Economic Models of Interest Groups: An Introductory Survey', *American Journal of Political Science*, **35**(2), 512–46.

Mohtadi, H. and T. Roe (1998), 'Growth, Lobbying and Public Goods', *European Journal of Political Economy*, **14**(3), 453–73.

Mork, K. (1993), 'Living with Lobbying: A Growth Policy Co-Opted by Lobbyists can be Better than No Growth Policy at All', *Scandinavian Journal of Economics*, **95**(4), 597–605.

Murphy, K.M, A. Shleifer and R.W. Vishny (1993), 'Why Is Rent-Seeking So Costly to Growth?', *American Economic Review*, **83**(2), 409–14.

Olson, M, (1965), *The Logic of Collective Action. Public Goods and the Theory of Groups*, Cambridge, MA: Harvard University Press.

Olson, M, (1982), *The Rise and the Decline of Nations. Economic Growth, Stagflation and Social Rigidities*, New Haven: Yale University Press.

Panico, C. (2003), 'Old and New Growth Theories: What Role for Aggregate Demand?', in N. Salvadori (ed.), *Old and New Growth Theories*, Cheltenham, UK and Northampton, MA, USA: Edward Elgar, pp. 53–66.

Pecorino, P, (1992), 'Rent Seeking and Growth: The Case of Growth Through Human Capital Accumulation', *Canadian Journal of Economics*, **25**(4), 944–56.

Przeworski, A. and M. Wallerstein (1988), 'Structural Dependence of the State on Capital', *The American Political Science Review*, **82**(1), 11–29.

Purificato, F. (2008), 'Political and Economic Interaction: A New Framework of Analysis. The Role of Income Distribution', *Working Paper Series Economic Growth: Institutional and Social Dynamics*, no. 36, May.

Rama, M. (1993), 'Rent Seeking and Economic Growth', *Journal of Development Economics*, **42**(1), 35–50.

Rodrìguez, F. (2004), 'Inequality, Redistribution, and Rent-Seeking', *Economics & Politics*, **16**(3), 287–320.

Rowthorn, R, (1982), 'Demand, Real Wages, and Economic Growth', *Studi Economici*, **18**, 3–53.

Sadiraj, V., J. Tuinstra and F. van Winden (2005), 'Interest Group Size Dynamics and Policymaking', *Public Choice*, **125**(3–4), 271–303.

Setterfield, M. (2002), 'Introduction: A Dissenter's View of the Development of Growth Theory and the Importance of Demand-Led Growth', in M. Setterfield (ed.), *The Economics of Demand-Led Growth*, Cheltenham, UK and Northampton, MA, USA: Edward Elgar, pp. 1–16.

Sturzenegger, F. and M. Tommasi (1994), 'The Distribution of Political Power, the Costs of Rent-Seeking, and Economic Growth', *Economic Inquiry*, **32**(2), 236–48.

Tornell, A. and P.R. Lane (1999), 'The Voracity Effect', *American Economic Review*, **89**(1), 22–46.

van Velthoven, B.C.J. (1989), *The Endogenization of Government Behaviour in Macroeconomic Models*, Berlin Heidelberg; Springer-Verlag.

van Winden, F. (1983), *On the Interaction Between State and Private Sector*, Amsterdam: North-Holland Publishing Company.

van Winden, F. (1999), 'On the Economic Theory of Interest Groups: Towards a Group Frame of Reference in Political Economics', *Public Choice*, **100**(1–2), 1–29.

van Winden, F, (2003), 'Interest Group Behaviour and Influence', in C.K. Rowley and F. Schneider (eds), *Encyclopedia of Public Choice*, Boston: Kluwer Academic Publishers.

Index